'In this inspiring and highly accessible book. Leyman take the reader on a journey that inte science of playfulness, illustrating how it has coaching practice. The book is ground-breaking in its integration of concepts and practical applications, which are illustrated through beautiful examples of playfulness in action. This book is an important contribution that will appeal to novice and experienced coaches alike, as well as many mental health professionals'.

Matthew Pugh, *Clinical Psychologist, CBT Therapist, Schema Therapist, and Chairwork practitioner*

'As a playful person, I'm delighted to see this book in print! It is a credible, engaging, and immediately applicable text that reminds us of the value and importance of finding joy in what we do. I particularly appreciate the balance of theory and practice, the numerous anecdotes, and the perspectives of experts. Bravo!'

Christian van Nieuwerburgh, *Professor of Coaching and Positive Psychology, RCSI University of Medicine and Health Sciences, Ireland*

'Play is an essential part of what it is to be human. This new text provides an insight into how coaches can use multiple play-based approaches to facilitate coaching conversations to deepen self and systemic perspectives and create innovative and fun sessions with their clients'.

Jonathan Passmore, *Senior VP, CoachHub; Professor, Henley Business School*

'You won the Golden Ticket! Stephanie Wheeler and Teresa Leyman are the Willy Wonka's of coaching. They will guide you through a marvellous tour of playfulness in effective coaching. Remember, don't eat the chocolate!'

Richard Boyatzis, *PhD, Distinguished University Professor, Case Western Reserve University; Co-author of the new Helping People Change*

'Coaching is too important to be taken seriously. In this evidence-based, thought-provoking book, Stephanie Wheeler and Teresa Layman offer an infinity of scenarios and perspectives to explore playfulness in coaching. An inspiring text with many great lessons and a roadmap to reconsider some of our coaching practices'.

Andrea Giraldez-Hayes, *CPsychol, ESIA & MP (EMCC), PCC (ICF), Director, Wellbeing and Psychological Services Centre; Programme Director, MAPP-CP, School of Psychology, University of East London*

Playfulness in Coaching

What do we mean by playfulness? Playfulness and play are no longer seen as only of benefit to children's learning and development but are being used increasingly for coaching adults in the context of serious challenges and issues. Benefits include better communication, understanding, self-awareness, relationship-building, creativity, ideation, and innovation in a business environment. This book is the first to introduce and expand on the idea of playfulness as an approach in coaching.

Playfulness in Coaching fully explains the serious role of playfulness and provides the *why* and the *how* both for new and experienced coaches. Using case studies throughout, the book takes a broad and evidence-led look at the relevant areas of playfulness in coaching: contracting, developing insights, forming direct communications, how to prime the coach and the client for playfulness, identifying and overcoming barriers, assessing risks, and closing a session. It is packed with theory, research, stories from practice, ideas, and inspiration for understanding and applying playfulness in life and work.

This will be an invaluable resource for coaches, particularly those with experience who are moving towards intermediate and mastery level. The book has been written with coaches working with corporate clients in mind, particularly in the context of challenges in a VUCA environment. It will also be relevant to HR and Learning and Development managers who source coaches for organisations and oversee internal coaches, as well as managers-as-coaches, life coaches and mental health professionals.

Stephanie Wheeler and **Teresa Leyman** are accredited individual and systemic team coaches passionate about supporting the flourishing of individuals, teams, and organisations. Stephanie is a LEGO® Serious Play® facilitator, writes for *The LSP Magazine* and has written peer-reviewed research articles. Teresa is an agile coach and supervisor with experience of leading hi-tech, complex change.

Playfulness in Coaching

Exploring Our Untapped Potential
Through Playfulness, Creativity
and Imagination

Stephanie Wheeler
and Teresa Leyman

Routledge
Taylor & Francis Group

LONDON AND NEW YORK

Designed cover image: © Getty Images / calvindexter

First published 2024
by Routledge
4 Park Square, Milton Park, Abingdon, Oxon OX14 4RN

and by Routledge
605 Third Avenue, New York, NY 10158

Routledge is an imprint of the Taylor & Francis Group, an informa business

British Library Cataloguing-in-Publication Data
A catalogue record for this book is available from the British Library

Library of Congress Cataloging-in-Publication Data
Names: Wheeler, Stephanie (Personal coach), author. | Leyman, Teresa, author.
Title: Playfulness in coaching : exploring our untapped potential through playfulness, creativity and imagination / Stephanie Wheeler and Teresa Leyman.
Description: Abingdon, Oxon ; New York, NY : Routledge, 2023. |
Includes bibliographical references and index. |
Identifiers: LCCN 2022058054 (print) | LCCN 2022058055 (ebook) |
ISBN 9780367544171 (hardback) | ISBN 9780367548483 (paperback) |
ISBN 9781003090847 (ebook)
Subjects: LCSH: Personal coaching. | Executive coaching. |
Employees–Coaching of. | Play.
Classification: LCC BF637.P36 W495 2023 (print) |
LCC BF637.P36 (ebook) | DDC 158.3–dc23/eng/20230415
LC record available at https://lccn.loc.gov/2022058054
LC ebook record available at https://lccn.loc.gov/2022058055

ISBN: 978-0-367-54417-1 (hbk)
ISBN: 978-0-367-54848-3 (pbk)
ISBN: 978-1-003-09084-7 (ebk)

DOI: 10.4324/9781003090847

Typeset in Goudy
by Newgen Publishing UK

With gratitude and love to our families, friends and colleagues who have encouraged us in our explorations and adventures and to all who might tap more into playfulness as a result.

Contents

Part I What Is Playfulness in Coaching?   1

1 Welcome   5

2 Why Playfulness?   27

3 What Do We Mean by Playfulness in Coaching?   39

4 The Benefits of Playfulness in Coaching   55

5 The Be Playful Onion Model   70

6 Our Neurobiology and Playfulness in Coaching   90

7 Adding Emotions into the Mix   114

8 What's so Funny?: A Closer Look at Humour   143

9 Risks: Part and Parcel of Exploring   169

Part II Stepping into Playfulness: From Theory to Practice   193

10 Tending the Seedlings of Playfulness   197

11 Practical Ways to Dial Up (More) Playfulness   225

12 Things to Consider in Practice   254

13 The Playfulness Scrapbook: A Collection of Stories,
     Ideas, and Tools   268
     Barometer of Playfulness   323
     Playfulness Mixing Deck   326
     Take a Playful Moment   328
     Playful Experiments for Life and Work   333

14 The Next Chapter   339

    About the Authors   342
    Index   343

Part I
What Is Playfulness in Coaching?

DOI: 10.4324/9781003090847-1

Welcome to the Sweet Shop

Welcome to the Sweet Shop. There is something for everybody here, or perhaps not. Accustom your eyes as you enter and what do you see? All manner of jars and boxes filled with sweets of different textures, different colours, sweet or sour, large, small, and everything in between, fancy, plain, eye-catching, and understated. What we are doing is selecting almost at random generous handfuls and offering them to you.

We invite you to see the sweets as metaphors for different manifestations of play and playfulness in coaching.

With this handful of sweets, we're extending an invitation to you to broaden your understanding and your perspective of playfulness in coaching and also to sharpen your curiosity, to maybe look at the tools, approaches, and philosophies of coaching which you're drawn to and see what they have to say about playfulness. If they don't have anything to say, then perhaps be curious as to why. Is there space for playfulness? If not, is that a good thing or can it potentially cause problems, miss opportunities? Maybe look at your and your clients' habits; do you always reach for the same sweets? Do they perhaps remind you of past successes, rewards; give you security? See our extended hands as an invitation to try something a little different perhaps, a little out of your comfort zone, possibly beyond what you are used to. Delight in the unexpected. Agree or disagree with us, take ideas, and also challenge what follows.

Go on, try one! Try a few! You might be pleasantly surprised. Even if not, you might learn something. You might create a few new ones of your own. The possibilities for exploration are endless.

1
Welcome

1.1 Introduction

Welcome to *Playfulness in Coaching*. This book is packed with theory, research, stories from practice, ideas, and inspiration for your playfulness in coaching experiments. As you'd expect from two coaches, we have filled the coming pages with generous sprinklings of questions. We offer these to you to support your work with clients, your own reflections, as well as those with peers and in supervision. This book isn't a coach's playfulness manual with a list of universal tools. As you will see, authenticity and discernment are key and instead of presenting you with a list of tools (though we do offer you The Playfulness Scrapbook brimming with inspiration), we invite you to dive a little deeper into understanding and applying playfulness in your life and work. We have written this book specifically with coaches in mind as this is our domain. We do, however, hope that therapists, mental health professionals, leaders, managers, or anyone interested in how to incorporate more playfulness into their life and work, will also find much to support their development and work.

You can, of course, read this book cover to cover. In case you like to dip in and out, we've aimed to make the chapters and their contents relatively stand-alone and easy to find, so you can start with those that call to you the most loudly. Nevertheless, we suggest that you read Chapters 5 and 6. If, for what you're drawn to, it would be useful to refer to previous chapters, we've flagged that up so that you can follow the trail. To make sure that you don't feel that you're missing out, most chapters start with a summary of the key points. Broadly speaking, this book is in two parts: Part I is more focused on the theory and research side of adult playfulness together with stories of playfulness in coaching and introduces our Be Playful Onion Model to build a foundation for practice. Part II moves into accessing more playfulness in yourself and with clients as well as offering you The Playfulness Scrapbook full of stories, inspiration, and ideas for practice.

DOI: 10.4324/9781003090847-2

The chapters are also peppered with boxes that contain more detailed stories from our Storytellers whom you'll meet soon as well as fireside chats with a range of experts who have taken a deep dive into playfulness and its potential. You'll also find easy-to-locate reflection questions and at various points we'll invite you to dip into Playful Moments which are found in The Playfulness Scrapbook. We've included other bits and bobs which we hope will be helpful to ignite and/or support your reflection and action including Playful Experiments and your very own Barometer of Playfulness (short and long versions). In addition, we've left areas blank for your notes and reflections from time to time and we won't be offended if you use a pen to underline, make notes and generally doodle on the pages which follow. In fact, we'd be delighted if you did. Again, you will find these all in The Playfulness Scrapbook and we encourage you to use them freely. At the end of this chapter, we also invite you to get started with a few of them, to take a moment to check in and reconnect with your playfulness.

As you'll read if you dive into Chapter 3, research into adult playfulness and even more so in the coaching context is at an early stage. As a result, we've drawn on a wide range of sources and we thought it would be not only very interesting but also inspiring to include experiences and reflections of a selection of coaches from a variety of coaching backgrounds, philosophies, approaches, and cultures, as well as reflections from a clinical psychologist and therapist so that we widen the lens beyond our own experiences and perspectives. We are very grateful to the 15 practitioners who gave us their time and shared stories of playfulness. Some of their names and work will no doubt be very familiar to you, others you will probably come across for the first time. Each shared insightful and inspiring stories and thoughts about playfulness in their coaching practice, many of which have been included in this book. We've collectively called them our Storytellers and you'll meet them in a moment. Their thoughts and stories which we gathered during our conversations are woven together with our own throughout the book.

Despite the early stages of research (which does appear to be gaining some momentum and traction), we have aspired to include sufficient information in the coming pages to not only help you to better understand playfulness in coaching and in particular *your* coaching, but also to give you the confidence, should you need it, to communicate its potential benefits and impact to your current or potential clients. For those who wish to follow the literature trail, we've placed the references at the end of each chapter.

Thank you for picking up this book. Do you know the Japanese word 'tsundoku'? It means the practice of buying many books and letting them pile up with the intention of reading them and also is the name for the pile itself. We're guessing that like us, you have a tsundoku of coaching and self-development books awaiting their turn for your attention and we're honoured that our book was not only included in your tsundoku but has graduated to being read. We wish you much learning, exploration, connection, and fun, with your explorations into playfulness. Before we start, so you know who you're talking to, we'd like to tell you a little about us and our own explorations so far.

1.2 Once Upon a Me-search (Stephanie)

The seeds of this book were planted through curiosity and in common with a considerable amount of academic research, its origin lies in 'me-search'.[1] Like many of us, as I went through childhood, I learned to separate play from work. Add a good portion of adolescent angst and prolonged challenging circumstances and it makes me a little sad to now realise that by the time I was a lawyer in my early twenties, I had formed a belief that playfulness would be a distraction from the serious business of living. Don't get me wrong, I wasn't Severus Snape.[2] Well, I probably was a lot of the time. Although of course I laughed and had fun and made friends for whom I was and remain very grateful. I also met my husband (hard to believe that it was nearly thirty years ago). It is no accident that as well as falling for him because of his good looks, kindness, and intelligence (he will after all be reading this), the icing on the cake was that he invited me to join him in silliness and fun.

Still, looking back now to when I was working in teams in international law firms mostly on multi-million and sometimes multi-billion pound projects, I can see that when the clock was ticking, decisions had to be made, my thinking narrowed as my adrenaline kicked in and I became less collaborative and to some degree focused on survival. At the time, I associated this feeling, thinking and behaviour with the professional I aspired to be. I can now see that in those moments, focusing on how to do an excellent job in light of the latest challenge (hands up, I was a perfectionist and to me, it felt like the stakes were high), I lost or at least restricted my ability to broaden my thinking, be creative, imaginative, and playful with possibilities. This approach spilled over to the rest of my life. It became a habit for me to approach difficult things in this same way. After all, it had worked. What's more, with one or two notable exceptions, it's what I saw the successful professionals around me doing, though now I wonder whether that was just my perception through the lens of confirmation bias.

Fast forward some years, I had taken a break from my legal career to focus on family as by now, we had two brilliant, playful young children. For several reasons there followed a number of challenging years for us as a family and I became increasingly aware that fun and joy was in danger of being drowned out by uncertainty and worry. Once again, I was retreating into seriousness. I was habitually and without awareness coping by pushing out play and fun lest it lessened my ability to do the serious and important 'stuff'. At least this time, I was starting to become aware of my ingrained habits which kicked in under stress. At some point, I realised that this was an opportunity to approach things differently. One of my first steps in this direction was thinking of ways to foster joy and laughter in our house. By serendipity I came across Martin Seligman's book *Flourish*,[3] started learning about positive psychology and happened across laughter yoga on the internet. Not finding a group/class nearby, I went off to train as a laughter yoga leader to find a way to bring more joy to our home.

In case your reaction was 'Wait, what?' being a laughter yoga leader essentially involves facilitating one or more others to laugh for no reason. Proper belly laughing, so much that you can't breathe, your stomach hurts and tears roll, hopefully as you used to when you were a child. In our day to day lives, the worry didn't go away (at the risk of blowing my own trumpet, I was very good at worrying – a medal contender), however, there was a greater sense of balance and joy. I also began exploring positive psychology more, facilitating community courses for Action for Happiness.[4]

Some years later, when it came to deciding on a research topic for my MSc in Coaching for Behavioural Change at Henley Business School, I reflected on my various experiences and wondered if there were any threads that merited further exploration. I started to be curious about whether and how, as a coach, particularly when dealing with difficult situations or challenges (and perhaps especially when I felt internal pressure to be of service to my clients and my ego and insecurities were elbowing their way in), I could avoid falling back into that old 'serious' thinking habit and access a more playful, curious, and lighter approach with a wider sense of perspective. I was also curious about how I might stop myself from being sucked into an unplayful dynamic with clients grappling with serious issues and how we might together access a different way of thinking, feeling, and doing by tapping into playfulness. Beyond tools and techniques, could I develop my way of being within the coaching relationship so that I could access this stance with ease as and when it was useful for the client? What about the impact on the client? If they were leaders, what impact would this have on others in their organisation? In other words, how and with what consequences could I, we, foster playfulness of the mind, and imaginative and creative thinking, dealing with the serious matters faced by individuals, leaders, and organisations (not to mention communities and societies although I wasn't thinking quite that big). Clearly, the me-search had to expand to actual research, so I settled on a qualitative study exploring playfulness in coaching which later morphed into an article published in the *International Coaching Psychology Review*, a peer-reviewed academic journal.[5] Shortly after, I went on to co-author another peer-reviewed research article, this time on LEGO® Serious Play® and its impact on team cohesion, collaboration and psychological safety in organizational settings using a coaching approach.[6]

Looking back, my early focus on the intellectual aspect of playfulness was to do with my fear of lacking credibility as a 'serious' coach if I focused on playfulness more generally, perhaps mirroring many people's attitude to play (wonderful in your free time but not terribly relevant for the serious business of adult life). In fact, as part of my original research, many of the experienced coaches I interviewed didn't call themselves playful coaches in case they were pigeonholed or it put off new clients, even though playfulness infused their work. Only once their relationship and reputation with the client had been established, did they openly emphasise or promote the playfulness of their work.

It's been a journey, as they say, for me to realise both the potential for playfulness, imagination, and creativity in coaching and how they might be used in the service of clients, and this area is much richer than I conceived when I was starting out. I was incredibly happy and grateful when Teresa joined me on this journey. This book is so much richer and playful because of our co-creation and, of course, we had a lot of fun in the process and kept each other playful during the challenging times.

1.3 My Playfulness Story So Far... (Teresa)

Thank you, Stephanie, for bringing this topic more to the fore. I am heartened to see it gaining more attention, having instinctively incorporated playfulness into my own coaching and business practice over the years. While I have seen the benefits, thanks to our work and research for this book I am now more secure in the knowledge that there is a growing awareness, credibility, and professionalism around this topic. My hope is that through this book and our ongoing work, more coaches will be able to discover and develop a variety of playful, experimental approaches within their practice and realise the true value that playfulness can bring not only in service of their clients but also for them personally.

Let me share a little bit about my own background both to give you some idea of what brought me here and perhaps more importantly, to get you thinking about your own story of playfulness so far. Looking back, I can see different themes that have helped to develop my playful practice. Personally, I wouldn't say that I'm an overtly playful person although I do like to play. Being a mother of two wonderful daughters gave me a good excuse (as if any was needed!) and I love to play in the park with them and miss it now that they have grown. My husband and I have been married for over thirty years and he has a great sense of humour and is very playful which has helped me develop this side of myself more as we've grown older. I still rarely tell jokes as I never remember the punch line and the funniest part of my attempts at joke-telling is me getting the punchline wrong. That said, I do have a ready sense of humour and tap into the funny side of life, even in the more challenging situations. I put this down to growing up in a family of engineers, nurses, and military where life and death can be close companions and perhaps because of that, in very serious and tense situations humour and levity were often used to diffuse tension and move things forward. Over the years I have witnessed and experienced this combination of objectivity and levity in many good working partnerships and team dynamics and often wondered why more isn't done to explore and support this way of collaboration and leadership. My influences also helped me realise the importance of being able to hold a sense of perspective with some levity and compassion. In a storm this can give you the balance needed to steer the ship, as well as bringing some relief during even the most emotional and stressful challenges. Something that has helped me a lot over the years.

From my current vantage point, I can see how my career helped to develop the foundations of playful practice through experience of working with large hi-tech global companies. I started off as part of a software team creating new technical products and later went on to lead large global multicultural teams driving multi-million pound change projects. Quite quickly, in these fast-paced and sometimes stressful VUCA environments, I learned that the effective leaders took more of a servant leader and less command and control approach. Informed by Stephen Covey's[7] work (which I still recommend), my intention was to lead in such a way that the overall climate and team dynamics supported collaboration. Even in high stress and challenging times, there was still some levity, openness and the capability to adapt and respond to whatever was being thrown at us. This coaching-style approach and building/supporting a climate of trust and safety can give the team an ability to collaborate and play with ideas and build and bounce solutions more ably with less egos getting in the way or concern about being hung out to dry if mistakes are made. At this time, I learned much about ways to support creative collaboration using a range of in-the-room materials as well as software, but the most important factor was having a group dynamic that supported the sharing of ideas without concern or fear of failure. These teams were early agile teams and quite ahead of their time. Once I left this industry it took me many years working in a variety of industries and cultures to be able to create the conditions for this again. This elusive ingredient of co-creation and collaboration within teams is what eventually drew me to coaching. I had worked with a coach myself and was fascinated by finding a way to help others to access this way of working together. When I was looking for a research topic in my final year of the MSc in Coaching for Behavioural Change at Henley Business School, I drew on my own experiences and settled on seeking to identify the main ingredients for thriving high performing agile teams. Looking back over my career to date, it seems to me that one of the biggest challenges we collectively face remains the same: how do we play together well enough to create new ideas, new solutions and change?

About mid-way through my career, well-being and stress management took on a whole new level of importance to me as I witnessed a senior director burnout. Unfortunately, he was sectioned (hospitalised under the Mental Health Act) for a week due to stress because of the demands of his role, working in a low trust environment and an authoritarian boss. This was quite a contrast to the climate of my earlier career. It instilled in me that we should always remember that while what we do is important, as leaders we have a duty of care to ourselves and those we lead. This is first and foremost because it's the right thing to do but also from the business point of view, it doesn't make sense to have staff off sick due to stress. After witnessing what happened to this hardworking and dedicated person and hearing of other colleagues struggling, I started to explore new ways to deal with managing my own stress. As well as fitness, I started meditating which back then wasn't so common in the West. In my private life, this then led me onto learning about other complementary health practices.

My increasing interest in this area helped not only me, but those around me, including one of my employers achieving an Excellence in Wellbeing award.

Steph and I met during our studies at Henley Business School and when we were discussing our research projects in our final year, I began to realise how playful my practice was. Before then, it had simply not been on my radar, and it hadn't occurred to me that it might be a credible or professional aspect to mention or advocate. Now that's changed!

1.4 Our Coaching Approaches

We work independently and together as team co-coaches, mostly with leaders and their teams and as we write, have just finished taking part in a 10-month practitioner course on complex adaptive systemic team coaching led by David Clutterbuck, and Stephanie is moving into her second year of Relational Mindfulness training taught by Dr. Emma Donaldson-Feilder (we do love to learn). Stephanie is also a LEGO® Serious Play® facilitator trained by the Association of Master Trainers and is contributing editor of the coaching section of The LSP Magazine. We don't offer playfulness for its own sake; it doesn't always arise but it is available to us (and our clients) when it serves our work together. We also coach and run workshops for coaches and non-coaches around playfulness. Our collaboration and co-creation brings us joy and enables us to draw on our combined strengths, compensate for each other's weaknesses (or shall we say, 'areas for development'?) and enables us to produce work which we would not manage by ourselves alone.

We should perhaps mention that we are influenced by a variety of philosophies and approaches in our coaching, including positive psychology, Gestalt coaching, Relational Mindfulness, ACT coaching, non-violent communication, Nancy Kline's *Time to Think* (we were lucky to be taught by her and other wonderful teachers at Henley) to name but a few. The MSc in Coaching for Behavioural Change at Henley Business School teaches a person-centered eclectic approach and we have used this as a springboard to pursue and deepen our various interests. Our suggestion is not that playfulness is intended to replace any of these (for us or you, whatever coaching approach you take), but it does affect our way of being in the process of coaching (and in our lives generally) and it affects how we might apply different coaching approaches in our work.

We are continually experimenting with our own playfulness and in various forms it is woven throughout our practice. The topics our clients bring to our work together range from personal, business, developmental to emotional. Much of our coaching practice involves intrinsic playfulness in the context of 'difficult' coaching topics and it's not unusual for there to be tears and laughter in the same sessions – almost at the same moment even! We believe that working with playfulness not only supports more expansive thinking but also, when partnered with authenticity, compassion and non-judgment, supports the creation of what Donald Winnicott referred to as the 'holding environment' facilitating greater self-awareness, compassion, joy and even challenge.

This book is a milestone in our continuous exploration and experimentation with playfulness in coaching and we would be disappointed if we didn't change our thoughts and practice as time goes by. We still frequently find ourselves in that place of 'sweet discomfort' (much more on this concept later) including when trying out new or challenging ways of bringing more playfulness into our coaching. When we say 'find ourselves', it's not exactly what we mean. Actually, we make a point of placing ourselves in that place on a regular basis lest we get complacent and too comfortable. We can safely say that writing this book and releasing it into the big wide world has been a walloping example of that.

As we include contact details for our Storytellers shortly, we should probably tell you where you can find us too. We'd love to hear from you:

playfulnessincoaching.com; stephaniewheeler.co.uk; linkedin.com/in/stephanie-wheeler-leadership-coach/; teresaleyman.com; linkedin.com/in/teresaleyman

1.5 Our Storytellers

Our hope in writing this book is to invite a much more nuanced and multi-faceted understanding of playfulness in coaching, with an appreciation of its potential and importance and to nudge the conversation within our profession forward. It seemed to us that while we have stories to tell, it would be so much more interesting to also listen to stories and reflections of playfulness in coaching from a whole range of coaches and a clinical psychologist and ther-apist. For ease of reference, we're referring to them as our 'Storytellers' in the pages that follow.

Several of the practitioners with whom we spoke are influenced by Gestalt (some heavily, some less so), recognising that some of the philosophical and practical elements of Gestalt-like experimentation and the use of self as instru-ment[8] naturally lend themselves to more playful practice. A few specialise in or have experience of improv which builds the ability to be spontaneous, flexible, and resourceful in the moment as well as building a capacity to be comfortable with uncertainty and not knowing. A fair few have a knowledge of positive psychology, others are Ubuntu coaches and there are a range of other phil-osophies and approaches which influence our individual Storytellers. Some, particularly if working with teams and groups, might include playfulness in the planned structure and content of sessions though they adapt the level of playfulness depending on how they read the room. Ultimately all agreed that whatever their approach, being authentic is key, as people will sense when you are not being authentic and then rapport can be damaged. Acknowledging the importance of authentic playfulness is a driver behind why this book isn't a one-size-fits-all manual on how to be playful. We hope to give you enough ideas, questions and resources to access your own unique playfulness (even more).

We were delighted with and grateful for the openness, generosity and enthu-siasm which greeted our inquiries when we set out to find other coaches to share their experiences of playfulness. We are thrilled to introduce them to you below (in alphabetical order). You'll understand that we couldn't include all their stories and reflections, but you will find a generous sprinkling throughout the chapters. We hope that you enjoy reading about the different perspectives, approaches, and experiences. Now, without further ado, let us introduce you.

1.5.1 Kirsten Barske

Kirsten is a systemic team coach working in Austria and internationally, mostly in the great outdoors. She is passionate about the power of discovery through play. In her team and leadership coaching programs she creates spaces for teams, even executive board members, to play in nature. Not as 'team building' as such but as a powerful means of enabling people to gain a fresh perspective on their individual behaviours, other's behaviours, and collective behaviors, the first and most important step for development.

natventure.net

1.5.2 Steve Chapman

Steve is an artist, writer, speaker, coach, and consultant interested in creativity and the human condition. He has spoken around the world on the subject of creativity and works with individuals and organisations to help liberate creative freedom. He is a visiting faculty member on a number of well-regarded MSc programs in coaching and organizational culture. He is at his best when he is not quite sure what he is doing.

canscorpionssmoke.com; @stevexoh

1.5.3 David Clutterbuck

David is a visiting professor at four universities, including Henley Business School. He is author or co-author of more than 75 books. He was one of the two original founders of the European Mentoring and Coaching Council. He is co-dean of the Global Team Coaching Institute and practice lead at Coaching and Mentoring International.

davidclutterbuckpartnership.com

1.5.4 Julie Flower

Julie is a leadership and team development facilitator and coach, and an external tutor at Henley Business School. She is also an improviser with a research and practitioner interest in integrating improv and coaching.

linkedin.com/in/julie-flower-4589874/

1.5.5 Nankhonde Kasonde-van den Broek

Nankhonde is an award-winning executive coach, thought leader and entrepreneur. She is the lead consultant at Nankhonde Kasonde Consultancy and founder of ZANGA African Metrics. She is an accomplished professional with a wealth of African, international, and multicultural experience in designing and leading large-scale organizational change across multiple sectors.

linkedin.com/in/nankhondevandenbroek; zangametrics.com

1.5.6 Graham Lee

Graham is a leadership coach, coach supervisor and individual and couple psychotherapist. He works with senior managers and their teams in a range of settings, where the emphasis is on emotional regulation and relational awareness as the foundations for creativity and productivity. His approach is a synthesis that includes psychodynamics, mindfulness, neuroscience, leadership theory and Attachment Theory. In addition to working with individuals and teams, he has pioneered paired coaching, as featured in his book: *Breakthrough Conversations*.

theawarenesspartnership.com

1.5.7 Auriel Majumdar

Auriel is a creative coach and supervisor, specialising in professional and personal development in the creative, public and third sectors. Her practice has an emphasis on the use of creative techniques to challenge individuals and teams to reflect on their experiences so that they can continuously learn and develop.

aurielmajumdar.com

1.5.8 Nobantu Mpotulo

Nobantu is a human connector, an Ubuntu coach using mindfulness and heartfulness with holistic presence, and is sought out internationally as a facilitator and speaker. Her coaching mantra is 'See, Hear, Love, Illuminate, Be More and Do Less'.

nobantucoaching.co.za; nobantu@xsinet.co.za

1.5.9 Neil Mullarkey

Neil has performed in Whose Line Is It Anyway, I'm Sorry I Haven't a Clue, QI, two Austin Powers movies and The Pentaverate on Netflix, created by Mike Myers, with whom Neil did a double-act in London and created London's Comedy Store Players. He still performs with them every Sunday. Neil now brings the skills of theatre and especially improv to public and private sector organisations large and small, across the world. His book, *Seven Steps to Improve Your People Skills* was published in 2017.

NeilMullarkey.com; @neilmullarkey

1.5.10 Jonathan Passmore

Jonathan is Senior VP at CoachHub, the digital coaching platform, and Professor of Coaching at Henley Business School. He is a chartered psychologist, holds five degrees and three professional qualifications. He has published widely over the past 20 years including 30 books on coaching, change management, mindfulness, and I/O psychology and over 100 scientific papers. His work has been widely recognised with multiple awards from the AC, BPS, EMCC and ABP.

jonathanpassmore.com

15.11 Matthew Pugh

Matthew is a clinical psychologist, CBT Therapist, Schema therapist, and Chairwork practitioner. He is a co-director of Chairwork, teaching fellow at University College London, and a visiting tutor at Henley Business School.

chairwork.co.uk; drmatthewpugh.co.uk

1.5.12 Heather Simpkin

Heather is an eclectic mix of theatre director, playwright, acting and business coach. Inevitably, the influence of 'playacting' has brought much insight and influence to her playful approach when coaching and directing.

bearintheairproductions.com; @SimpkinHeather

1.5.13 Emma Skitt

Emma loves to play 'How do humans work?'. Following manufacturing and HR leadership roles in Unilever, she has coached in large corporations for over 20 years, believing 'people perform better when they feel good about themselves'.

coachingandchange.com; linkedin.com/in/emmaskitt

1.5.14 Robert Stephenson

With a background in physical theatre, Robert's journey to coaching has taken him along a path of varied experience and learning. His coaching focuses on the narrative/story we inhabit and its relation to our bodies/physical states.

linkedin.com/in/robert-stephenson-2491a21

1.5.15 Christian van Nieuwerburgh

Christian is Professor of Coaching and Positive Psychology at the Royal College of Surgeons in Ireland, Global Director of Growth Coaching International and Principal Honorary Fellow at the Centre for Wellbeing Science of the University of Melbourne.

Twitter: @christianvn; Instagram: coachonamotorcycle

1.6 How We Wrote this Book Playfully: From Intent to Reality

Photo of Poppy, Steph's dog, taken by Laura Poole 2022.

When this book was still a seedling, we thought how lovely it would be to include a story of how playfully we had developed and written it. Sitting here two years later, nearly at the point of sending the manuscript to our publishers and having experienced a global pandemic in the meantime, we're struck by how we didn't write this in a way which we originally thought of as playful and how our understanding of playfulness has evolved.

Starting this journey in February 2020, we were so excited, energised, and proud to have been commissioned to write a book (our first and by now with our families hoping that it's our last!) about this under-represented topic. We got together at Stephanie's house to make a plan of action. Full of gusto and good intent we thought that, given the topic, it was important to do this of all things playfully and intended to include a section on our experiences of a playful process. Our session was high energy, involved lots of paper and coloured pens, thinking 'that's playful, right?'. As we settled down, we reflected on what playfully writing a book would look like. Our eyes and thoughts were drawn to tools: coloured pens and a collection of arts and crafts items that were now collecting on the kitchen table. We noted we were missing coloured post-its; an essential we thought, the brighter the better! We thought about what other materials we could use including LEGO® and started planning a growing playful resources kit bag. We imagined that playfulness would show up when we'd get together, in the form of creative materials, creative coaching tools such as drawing and using constellations, mapping out systems, and the like. We thought about creating an environment that would stimulate and inspire us. We didn't get into the substance but felt it was a good start as we began to turn our attention to other *serious* matters concerning our writing project.

A few weeks later, the pandemic arrived in the UK and the world suddenly looked a very different place. From a practical point of view, we weren't able to meet and use all our lovely materials or create the environment in the way that we had envisaged. Swiftly we learned how to collaborate virtually, but we were in a more conversational than actively playful space. We started to reach out and have conversations with our Storytellers, who you've just met, at the same time as pivoting our coaching practice online. We don't need to tell you that it was a tough time of uncertainty, change and isolation for many and we started to give deliberate thought as to how we showed up in our virtual conversations. Steph's daughter Amy, at home with online schooling, spent time changing the dull backdrop behind Steph's desk, rearranging the books in rainbow colours, and placing fun and colourful objects on the book shelves. We added to the vibrant and quirky pictures hanging on the walls. Teresa used a beautiful photograph of a nearby wood as her virtual backdrop. Everyone we spoke to commented upon the impact of these new backdrops on the 'feel' of our meetings. We began to build a sense that materials, objects, and environment were part of the playfulness landscape, yet only a part.

We spoke regularly and while our collaboration was still mostly based around conversations, they always included levity and laughter as well as serious thought. Those conversations were at times like bright balloons during the challenges of helping to keep the wheels on family life as Covid impacted our kids and we balanced our families, working, researching, and writing. We finally got together in person nearly a year later when the restrictions had eased, and our diaries matched. 'Now is the time to incorporate some of that play stuff!' we thought. Stephanie's husband had the idea that we take the day to walk through the countryside to a pub garden, about a 10 mile round walk to walk and talk. We meandered along the Thames on a beautiful sunny day and through fields to a picturesque village which marked our half-way mark. For us, it was a valuable experience giving us many insights and resources which helped shape the content and structure of the book. It reminded us that it's not the activity, but the intent, which needs to be playful. We could have walked like soldiers out on drill practice, but instead, we tapped into the surrounding environment to inspire us, make connections, and stimulate our thinking and creativity. Moving and being in different surroundings helped our thinking, being outside put us in a positive, at times exuberant, and at times reflective mood, and gave us different ideas and perspectives.

We joked that this walking, talking, collaboration experience should be part of our 'playfulness log' but both of us felt a dose of imposter syndrome. Were we playful enough to dare to write a book on playfulness in coaching? It felt playful but didn't sound particularly playful. Fast forward and after all our research and conversations, we have a much broader and more nuanced take on what playfulness is, looks like, and feels like. Importantly, we recognise that it is far more multifaceted and nuanced than we first thought and wide enough to accommodate all personalities and approaches. What's more, being playful is as much about intent, tone and *being* open to opportunities for playfulness than just the activity which one might be *doing*.

To try to explain our evolving understanding of playfulness in coaching, we developed the Be Playful Onion Model. For us, the different forms of playfulness (even at times, during periods of real challenge) all sprung from our relationship. It has a high level of trust and safety, with an abundant mix of authenticity, vulnerability and acceptance and support of each other during our joys and struggles while taking a stance of holding the serious with some levity and together 'laughing at our humanness' (a phrase from our conversation with one of our wonderful storytellers, Auriel Majumdar). We laugh like drains, do serious work together, share pain and joy and feelings of overwhelm and celebration. Our experience has reinforced our belief about the relational aspect of play both with yourself and others. You may notice how in some relationships playfulness seems more accessible and different than in others.

We've also come to appreciate that you can be open to opportunities for playfulness, encourage and nurture it, setting the right conditions, but it can't be forced and sometimes, the timing just isn't right. A playful environment or tools/materials can be helpful but at its heart, playfulness is a way of being, a stance, an attitude, giving the subtle signal and permission that play is ok. As Graham Lee writes, when there is enough trust and safety then play will emerge.[9] On the flipside, if you are expecting or demanding play, the effect is often different.

On reflection, while playfulness (and seriousness to name a few) infused our writing process, it wasn't in such a tangible way as we had expected, or which lends itself to setting out here. We wrote this book on playfulness in coaching during a pandemic (a whole new level of challenge from a practical, cognitive, and emotional point of view) based on our research, our own experiences, reflections, and the conversations with our Storytellers who you've met with laughter and some despair at times (quite often in parallel). As you read on and engage with the book, we hope that you share our own realisations that playfulness has more to offer than you might currently think and may well show up in ways which you will not expect once you are open to it. There is so much more under the umbrella of playfulness than associations with fun and amusement. It is a valuable resource for addressing complex and serious challenges, accessing creativity, and supporting innovation. Playfulness can support work on cognitive as well as emotional complex challenges and be a considerable resource in our practice whether to facilitate change, enable seeing different perspectives, hold the space for respite and solace, or have fun and experience joy. Why would you not want to have this available to you? With this broader perspective, we could also ask ourselves questions such as 'What does serious play look like?', 'What does playful work look like?', 'What does challenging play look like?' and 'How would we experience these and what new benefits could come from this space?'. We hope that this book will help you think about playfulness more and step more into play. We look forward to your insights, wisdom and play as we invite you to join the exploration and adventure for your own benefit, the benefit of your practice, the benefit of your clients, and for the benefit of the wider system.

1.7 Getting Started with Your Playfulness

As we mentioned earlier, we have dotted reflections, Playful Moments and Playful Experiments throughout this book and these are represented by the icons below. You'll find the reflection questions in the relevant chapters and when you see the icons for the others, please turn to The Playfulness Scrapbook where you'll find them set out alongside the Barometer of Playfulness (and shorter version in Chapter 10) .

We'll introduce you to them shortly, so you'll know what to look out for. You might be wondering what the little character in the icons is. It's an onion. Bear with us, all will become clear in Chapter 5.

The reflective onion will appear throughout the book to invite you to pause to reflect on questions which relate to the section which you've just read. As an example to help us to get started, why not take a reflective moment now and consider:

- What drew you to opening this book?
- What are you curious to know?
- What are you hoping will be different as a result?

The Barometer of Playfulness is designed to help you connect with your play-fulness. There's a short (Chapter 10) and long (The Playfulness Scrapbook) version. You can either use it as a quick check-in (for example, before a coaching session) or take a deeper dive and land on areas to develop to support your playfulness further. We invite you to jump to this now and to check it out so that you can return to it whenever you like.

A Playful Moment can be very short or longer, it's up to you. It's a moment or more for you to be playful in whatever way you enjoy and which feels right for you to experience and rekindle your playfulness. We invite you to jump to the Playful Moments in The Playfulness Scrapbook now so you know where they are. It may feel a little odd at first if you're not used to being playful, but give it a go, you are reading this book after all, so a part of you must be looking for more playfulness.

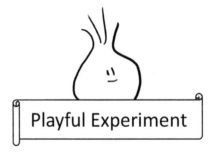

A Playful Experiment is more than a Playful Moment. It is more intentional and reflective, designed with the view to priming yourself as a coach or

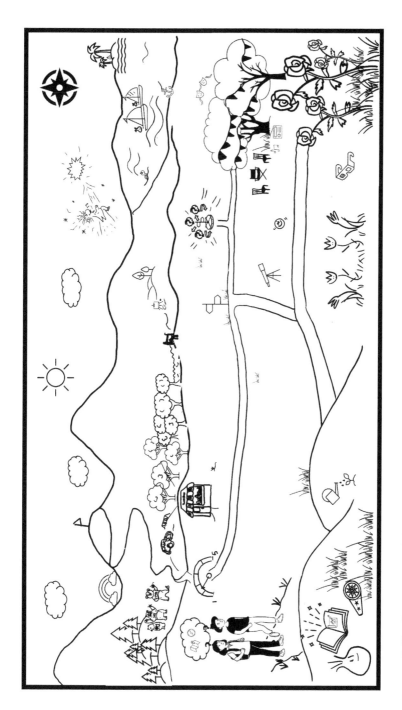

Image 1.7 The Treasure Map of Playfulness

incorporating playfulness into your work with clients. Playful Experiments are also found in The Playfulness Scrapbook.

Finally, as we are nearly ready to start the next chapter, we come to The Treasure Map of Playfulness which contains many stories and images from this book. You could look at it as an alternative table of contents. As you make your way through the book, why not come back to the map to colour it in as you read about the various points on the map (or just for fun), doodle, find an area of interest on the map and look for it in the book. You might also like to add your own imagery or words or draw your own Treasure Map of Playfulness.

Notes

1 Leyman, T., & Wheeler, S. (2022). *The big book of anecdotal facts*. 'Me-search' – a phrase we heard Prof Katy Milkman use in an interview about her book *How to Change* (2021) and Bessel van der Kolk writes about in his book *The Body Keeps the Scord (2014)*.
2 A character from Harry Potter. As an aside, I found this list which rates the most and least playful characters openpsychometrics.org/tests/characters/stats/1/; It might be fun to read through and see who and what resonates with you.
3 Seligman, M. (2013). *Flourish*. Simon and Schuster.
4 //actionforhappiness.org/
5 Wheeler, S. (2020). An exploration of playfulness in coaching. *International Coaching Psychology Review, 15*(1), p45.
6 Wheeler, S., Passmore, J., & Gold, R. (2020). All to play for: LEGO® SERIOUS PLAY® and its impact on team cohesion, collaboration and psychological safety in organisational settings using a coaching approach. *Journal of Work-Applied Management, 12*(20), 141–157.
7 Covey, S. (1989). *The seven habits of highly effective people*. Simon and Schuster.
8 Bluckert, P. (2014). The Gestalt approach to coaching. *The complete handbook of coaching*. Sage, 80–93.
9 Lee, G. (2021). *Breakthrough Conversations for Coaches, Consultants and Leaders*. Routledge.

2
Why Playfulness?

In this chapter, we:

* Discuss why adult playfulness merits attention
* Consider why we focus on playfulness in coaching
* Distinguish between childish and childlike approaches
* Look at the postmodern approach to coaching and why through its lens playfulness is a way of being as well as doing
* Give a nod to barriers and risks
* Share the approach of this book, inviting curiosity and experimentation
* Offer an invitation to be curious about the role of playfulness, imagination, and creativity to find solutions to complex problems on an individual and collective level

Reactions to our news that we were embarking on writing a book about playfulness in coaching broadly fell into two camps: enthusiasm that we were shining a light on this under-explored topic in one corner and scepticism or dismissal of its importance in the other. The latter seemed to be based on an interpretation of playfulness as something frivolous, a bit of fun, a mood-lightener or perhaps team-builder or something that's more relevant for children than adults, especially given the serious work that so often underpins coaching. Luckily, we love a challenge, so we didn't shy away from the scepticism. In fact, we welcomed it. Healthy scepticism brings with it challenge and different perspectives which we hope enabled us to consider frames of reference different from our own and that our resulting reflections have enriched this book. We're also grateful to the well-meaning sceptics as they've made us aware that at times, we were taking things for granted which needed to be addressed expressly. Needless to say, our gratitude extends to the cheerleaders whose enthusiasm buoyed us during times of tiredness or doubt and when our inner critics were particularly vocal.

DOI: 10.4324/9781003090847-3

In the pages that follow, our starting assumption is that as a coach, you are excellent at being rational, logical, figuring out whatever puzzles presents themselves to you in the course of your practice and that you are adept at convergent thinking and working with your clients to develop ideas into practical actions. We also presume that you are skilled at or are building your skills of providing a safe space for your clients as well as building rapport and being culturally aware (to be fair, in our view you never stop learning and refining these or any other coaching skills). These are core coaching skills and we want to clarify that we are *not* proposing playfulness as a substitute for your coaching philosophy, approach or skills or indeed coaching competencies. We *are* proposing that at the very least, it is worth considering what potential benefits to coaching effectiveness could be gained from playfulness in support of your coaching at the right time, in the right context and in service of your clients. We are inviting you to consider what you could support or ignite through playful language and behaviour or more fundamentally, the potential impact of developing or enhancing your ability to adopt a playful way of being or stance in your coaching and to be able to nurture this in your clients. Some readers might find this a relief, permission to suspend their scepticism and accept this book as an invitation to consider what *additional* means might be at their disposal to enrich their coaching and increase its effectiveness. Perhaps think of it as some new and exciting dishes on the buffet table of coaching skills, competencies, approaches, and possibilities. Did we really just say 'buffet table of coaching skills'? Perhaps we should offer a metaphor health-warning. Moving right along ... .

If scepticism is still running high (in which case thank you for not putting this book down), we offer you this thought:

> Whatever the intellectual is too certain of, if he is healthily playful, he begins to find unsatisfactory. The meaning of his intellectual life lies not in the possession of truth but in the quest for new uncertainties.
>
> *Richard Hofstadter*[1]

First though, let us take a step back and consider why we think playfulness is worthy of attention in the coaching context, not to mention the years which we've already spent exploring it.

2.1 Why Playfulness?

Montagu argued over forty years ago, that particularly in a Volatile, Uncertain, Complex, Ambiguous (VUCA) environment (surely, compared to then,

VUCA in the 2020s is on steroids), it is more important than ever that we as adults live up to our full potential by retaining our childhood qualities of:

> Open-mindedness, receptivity to new ideas, malleability, questing, striving, questioning, seeking, critical testing and weighing of new ideas as well as old ones: wide-eyed curiosity and excitement in the enjoyment of new experiences, the willingness to work hard, together with a sense of humor and laughter.[2]

Many of these characteristics are intrinsically related to playfulness, creativity, and imagination. In fact, it's easy to find examples of individuals who have made outstanding contributions to their fields, particularly in the sciences and the arts, who attribute their breakthroughs to bringing a creative, playful, and imaginative mindset to their serious work. Albert Einstein of course springs immediately to mind. It's thought that when he developed the theory of relativity, he began with playful thoughts: 'What if I could sit on a beam of light? What would I see? How about others?'.[3] (Great coaching questions, by the way).

There are countless other examples, including Horton Conway, the 'playful mathematician' whose 'childlike curiosity was perfectly complemented by his scientific originality and the depth of his thinking'[4], and many Nobel prize winners. While this book centres on playfulness, we will also dip our toes into the related and overlapping waters of creativity and imagination. Charlie Chaplin recognised that playfulness does not have to be exclusively related to having fun: 'to truly laugh, you must be able to take your pain and play with it'

and while we'll look at related concepts of positive emotions, fun and humour that are often thought to be synonymous with playfulness, you'll see that we see playfulness as considerably broader.

> Logic will take you from A to B. Imagination will take you everywhere.
> *Albert Einstein*[5]

At societal, organisational, and individual levels, our perception is that there's a general association (with notable exceptions of course) of seriousness with intellect/responsibility/work and playfulness with childishness/free time. What if this is in fact deeply flawed? What if we are missing a crucial distinction between childishness and being able to tap into a childlike attitude? What if we are doing ourselves a disservice by not accessing that part of us in our serious work? When you think about it, doesn't it take a certain amount of gravitas and confidence to allow ourselves to be playful in serious contexts? We wonder too whether our cultural focus on excluding creativity, playfulness and imagination from whole arenas where logic and reason rule has something to do with both the rigidity of Cartesian Dualism (essentially stating that mind and body are separate) which still has an influence particularly on how we feel, think and behave, as well as the messages and norms around work and what it means to be an adult, over the decades. We have been heartened and excited to see an increase in the offer and acceptance of playful approaches to serious solutions in recent years, although to be fair, that may be down to our confirmation bias. Our hope is that playfulness in its broadest sense will be increasingly nurtured and encouraged in adults and children alike.

2.2 Why Focus on Playfulness in Coaching?

Let us get a little deep for a moment (but don't worry, not too deep, we don't want to get lost down a rabbit hole of philosophical discussion even if we could keep up). There are currently broadly two dominant systems of thought in cultural and intellectual inquiry and they have contrasting philosophical underpinnings: the modernist and the postmodernist approaches.[6]

At one end, we have modernism. The American Psychological Association (APA) dictionary explains that:

> Traditional psychology can be seen to be the product of modernism to the extent that it is characterized by faith in scientific method, pursuit of control and prediction of behavior, explanation in terms of laws and principles, and the assumption that human behaviour is ultimately rational as opposed to irrational.[7]

Team that up with a positivist approach which broadly means that you are relying on quantifiable observations that lead to statistical analysis and you start getting a flavour of the approach taken by modernists. Sincere apologies for the oversimplification if you enjoy nothing more than spending an evening having philosophical discussions with friends perhaps over a bottle or two of wine. Delving a bit more deeply into this area has made us relate to our inner Winnie the Pooh: 'For I am a Bear of Very Little Brain and long words Bother me'.[8]

Back to the deep dive at hand: at the other end, a later contender, we have postmodernism which started making itself felt in psychology in the 1980s, though 'Academic mainstream psychology has not yet fully considered "postmodernism"' according to Frontiers.[9] Again, from the APA Dictionary:

> More specifically, they see the ideal of objective truth that has been a guiding principle in the sciences and most other disciplines since the 17th century as basically flawed: There can be no such truth, only a plurality of 'narratives' and 'perspectives'. Postmodernism emphasizes the construction of knowledge and truth through discourse and lived experience, the similar construction of the self, and relativism in all questions of value. It is therefore a form of radical scepticism.[10]

Bear with us. The positivist methodologies (remember those?) of modernism search for certainty and predictability and therefore a sense of control. But postmodernism moves away from this idea of an objective, empirically measurable truth. Instead, we have subjective experience, different perspectives, and no absolute truths or absolute values.

Maybe you can see where we're going with this (and forgive us if you've been tapping your foot impatiently waiting for us to get there). If we look at coaching through the lens of postmodernism which, for example, Professor Tatiana Bachkirova[11] encourages us to do, we see the self of the coach as the main instrument for coaching and also integral to coaching development. Seeing coaching this way means acknowledging that the quality of the coaching is dependent on many and varied influences including the characteristics of the coach and client, the many nuances of the coaching relationship, and the significant role of contextual factors.[12] Just to complicate matters further, the selves of the coach and client are not fixed; they are constantly fluctuating in the process of interacting and are also subject to wider influences.[13]

Goodness, it all feels a long way from a straightforward application of the GROW model! Intrinsic to the postmodernist approach is that the coaching relationship and how the coach turns up is a key ingredient in coaching outcomes rather than any specific coaching tool, intervention, or upon the models used.[14] If we think about coaching from this point of view, we start to think about what factors contribute to effective coaching that are beyond tools and techniques but are more relevant to the capacity of the coach. What we mean by this, as Hawkins and Smith put it, is 'a human quality such as flexibility, warmth, engagement, imagination, etc, rather than a skill. It has more to do with how you are rather than what you do'.[15] There's also something here about the flexibility of the coach. Can you as a coach be challenging and logical one moment and playful and experimental in the next?

Now we see an opening for considering the role and impact of playfulness, imagination, and creativity in coaching and not just the act of play but the ability of the coach and coachee to step into a playful way of being. We will see in Chapter 6 how both humans and animals are wired for play to learn and develop by finding new ways to explore and experiment. Storytelling which has a core of playfulness has been used for centuries as a way of relaying ideas and learnings. What if we include in our contemplations of how we as coaches could show in the coaching relationship an invitation to make space for play and playfulness? At the very least, we would argue that as reflective coaches, seeking to hone our craft, we should be noticing those times when we are and are not playful and reflecting on what impact that had on the relationships, the coaching process, and the outcome. Similarly, by being aware ourselves, we can raise awareness of our client's playfulness at points in the coaching where it's helpful and perhaps invite further exploration around this awareness. It can at times seem like excessive introspection or navel gazing (although to be fair, as coaches, we love a good helping of reflection), but there are calls[16] for a movement towards postmodernism in the assessment of coaches which would conceivably include qualities of playfulness when a greater understanding of its role and effect in coaching has been developed.

2.3 What Can Go Wrong?

Let's pause for a moment here, take a deep breath and focus on the words 'playfulness, creativity and imagination' and a sense of resourcefulness, curiosity, abundance, possibility, freedom, and joy can be tapped into. Yet at some level, most of us also associate a sense of barriers and risks with them: 'yes, but', 'they have their time and place' (in other words, not in professional contexts), 'I'm no good at that', 'some things are too serious for that', you get the picture. They can also evoke a sense of risk of falling short and being judged and shamed. No-one wants to be thought of as David Brent from The Office. Through this lens, it can feel safer and more appropriate to approach life and coaching challenges and opportunities solely through our rational and logical lenses. 'Isn't that fine?' you might ask. 'Isn't that just part of growing up?' 'Aren't some things just too serious/important?'. To quieten these concerns, be reassured that we'll be paying attention to potential barriers and risks as well.

In relation to barriers, making space for childlike (as opposed to childish) approaches, for most of us will involve moving beyond our comfort zones. We know from learning theory, it is in this space of 'sweet discomfort',[17] that we learn new ways of thinking, doing and being. Of course, everyone's zones of comfort, sweet discomfort and overwhelm are different and we'll address possible barriers to playfulness with ideas of how you might start to deconstruct them.

As far as risks are concerned, you will hear us emphasising the need for authenticity in playfulness. If you are trying too hard, you will probably misfire. Poor David Brent, trying so hard that his, at times, desperate playfulness is truly cringe-worthy. As we've explained in Chapter 1, this is why we don't offer you a playfulness by numbers guide. Playfulness in coaching is much more nuanced and needs to be applied with consideration and care. For some this will be instinctive and you might wonder what the point is in conducting a detailed examination (in which case, please do feel free to hop around the book to alight on sections which get you thinking and doing). Even if that's the case, we found that both for Stephanie's original MSc research and for this book, our conversations with our Storytellers were for the vast majority the first time that they had specifically reflected on playfulness in their coaching and its potential implications and we hope that you will find plenty of food for thought here. Whether or not you choose to access playfulness at a particular moment is then up to you, but at least it's a decision which you are consciously taking, a choice-point if you like of which you are aware and deliberate, rather than staying in your comfort zone or riding the wave of habit, assumptions and, stories we tell ourselves. That is after all often what we are trying to help clients to do.

2.4 Approach of This Book

At the heart of this book is curiosity: what rich seams can we cultivate and tap into that will augment our logical, rational coaching approaches? What can we add? What can we hold back on? What could we do differently? How could we be different? What approaches and perspectives divergent from our own can we learn about and bring to our coaching? What different ways of being and doing things might be available to us to support us and our clients with the complex challenges we face? How would we go about experimenting with these? What might the risks and barriers be?

Research into adult playfulness is at a relatively early stage and there is some way to go before there is universal agreement on the basics such as: What is it? How can we measure it? Is it a trait and can you learn it? How can we disentangle it from related constructs such as humour, creativity, and imagination? Nevertheless, there is a growing body of research in the field of psychology which teases apart and examines play and playfulness in adults. The different perspectives on the role and potential of adult playfulness brought by different areas of psychology (such as humour, learning and play therapy, for example) as well as other fields such as anthropology enrich the conversation. While it is a developing field, our collective understanding is continually evolving, and researchers and practitioners are increasingly attracted to this subject which promises potential bountiful contributions to coaching.

Part of the challenge of having conversations about playfulness in coaching is the overly narrow definition we tend to give to play and in particular playfulness in everyday language. We think that contributing to this is the perception that creativity and imagination are more mature and desirable attributes and we hope to challenge this and give playfulness its rightful place. In the following chapters, we will invite you to consider and adopt a much wider definition of play and playfulness in the coaching context. It is likely that you will identify elements of your current coaching practice that find a home within this broader definition of playfulness in coaching. We hope that by helping you to build on that awareness and by bringing together research which supports the potential benefits of playfulness as well as ideas to incorporate into your practice, we will give you a springboard for reflection and experimentation and exploration.

As we've mentioned, the pages that follow don't contain a step-by-step recipe promising you guaranteed access to playfulness in yourself, your coaching practice, and clients. Sorry! Instead, this book very much mirrors our own journey: it's an invitation to listen to stories and learn about relevant research, challenge your preconceptions, take stock of the current level of playfulness in your coaching, what might strengthen it, be holding you back, what risks playfulness in coaching might entail, and to find inspiration. Essentially, this is our invitation to you to increase your self-awareness around playfulness and join in with the exploration and experimentation which is implicit in playfulness, creativity and imagination and see how you can enrich your coaching practice (and maybe even your life …).

2.5 Our Hope

We referred earlier to the benefits of accessing playful, creative, and imaginative thinking in VUCA environments. In the spring of 2020, almost overnight, old norms, held tightly for decades around how best to lead, how teams operate and work best, home and remote working, to mention but a few were turned on their head. By necessity, we were asked to change our behaviour and thinking both as individuals in private and work capacity and as leaders and team members almost overnight. It truly felt like a handbrake turn. Dealing with turbo-charged change, nurturing our resilience, addressing isolation and disconnection, making sense of things, and taking short- and long-term decisions in times of huge uncertainty and stress, challenged many of us.

The idea that within crisis lies opportunity is one that echoes through time. The word crisis comes from the Greek 'to separate, to sift' which means to pass judgement, to keep only what is worthwhile. There are plenty of notable quotes which convey this idea: 'In the midst of chaos, there is opportunity' (Sun Tzu from 'The Art of War'); 'In the midst of every crisis lies great opportunity' (Albert Einstein); 'Every crisis has both its dangers and its opportunities. Each can spell either salvation or doom'(Martin Luther King). You get the gist.

Perhaps already a cliché, which risks softening its impact, but given the challenges we face at organisational, societal and global levels, we can't afford to do things the way that we've always done them. We're not telling you anything new by saying that we'll just get more of the same and that's not currently getting us the solutions that we and future generations need. We believe that creative, imaginative, even playful solutions to incredibly complex, fast changing problems have an important role to play in that evolution. Of course, evidence of the evolution of coaching to meet these challenges is all around and there is now a wealth of different approaches to coaching compared to even a relatively short time ago. Many of these incorporate creativity and others explicitly acknowledge the value of play and playfulness. To borrow Barbara Fredrickson's words (whose work we'll look at in Chapter 7), can we use playfulness, creativity and imagination to broaden our thinking and build our social relationships, both of which are sorely needed at this time. A meta-analysis of the use and effectiveness of playfulness across coaching approaches would certainly be very interesting but is not something which we've attempted to do here. Even so, we will explore some of these coaching approaches more in subsequent chapters with the intention of equipping you to set off or deepen your own explorations.

For now, the idea that play is for children and children aren't serious is still very evident in business and coaching. Yet the more we (Stephanie and Teresa) learn and experience, the more we believe that we are short-changing ourselves and others by limiting ourselves with this thinking. It feels as if we (collectively) are at the beginning of a cultural shift too as employee well-being at work, and for example, servant and compassionate leadership and authentic leadership approaches are gaining more traction,[18] We will see later how the qualities required and fostered by playfulness support this shift. Not least, there appears to be an increasing acceptance in coaching and leadership that we need space for uncertainty, ambiguity, and the whole person (a movement towards post-modernism). We believe that particularly in this context, we need to be able to supplement our rational and logical thought with playfulness.

In our small way, we hope that this book will encourage more coaches to be curious, explore and experiment how they can bring more of this 'magic sauce' into their practice, and in doing so, will open up more opportunities for their clients to experience this way of doing and being. If enough of us engage in this fruitful exploration, perhaps we will effect some change in the systems in which we operate so that this becomes something that feels more access-ible and ultimately which is embraced. Our experience has been (though we are conscious of the potential effects of confirmation bias), that there are an increasing number of coaches, facilitators and clients who see the potential of tapping into this different approach.

> Play allows us to express our joy and connect most deeply with the best in ourselves, and in others. If your life has become barren, play brings it to life again. Yes, as Freud said, life is about love and work. Yet play transcends these, infuses them with liveliness and stills time's arrow. Play is the purest expression of love.
>
> *Dr Stuart Brown (2009)*[19]

Indeed, we wonder whether as coaches, by not opening the door to play, playfulness, imagination and creativity, we are missing an opportunity to help our clients to create something different from that which they are experiencing now and to examine and perhaps change the lenses through which they are seeing their experience, as well as the goals they aspire to. Isn't that partly our job, to help them remove the layers of habit, past experience, perceptions, and work with them to see differently and perhaps to facilitate lasting transformational change? We will look at how we can enrich our coaching by accessing the childlike rather than the childish part of ourselves and helping our clients to do the same.

We offer this book to you then as a conduit for us as coaches to build on each other's ideas and experiences, learning, and developing this area together. In fact, we very much see this as an ongoing conversation rather than our attempt to package up and present to you the definitive version of playfulness in coaching. As you'd expect and hope, although this book captures our current thoughts, as our own personal and professional development journey continues, we mature as coaches, continue to have conversations, and challenge ourselves and, as research into this area grows our own thinking is constantly evolving. You'll see, for example, at the end of Chapter 5, that this book can do no more than mark a line in the sand, though we do hope that it will be a very useful line. We are very keen to hear the questions which we haven't asked; the perspectives which we haven't explored. Our hope is that you will join the conversation, bringing openness, curiosity, your perspective and, of course, challenge so that together we can continue to move the conversation forward within the coaching profession. We believe that it's a serious resource that the world is crying out for both in the context of urgent, complex, and challenging problems and the increasing polarisation seen in many cultures, not to mention the joy and connection it can bring.

Notes

1   Hofstadter, R. (2012). *Anti-Intellectualism in American Life*, 17th edn. Vintage Books.
2   Montagu, A. (1981). *Growing Young*. McGraw-Hill, p53.
3   Piispanen, M., & Meriläinen, M. (2015). Play as Part of Learning – Learning as Part of Play. In C. Shoniregun, & G. Akmayeva (Eds.) Proceedings of IICE 2015, *Ireland International Conference on Education, Dublin*, Ireland, April 20–22, 2015 (pp229–234).
4   princeton.edu/news/2020/04/14/mathematician-john-horton-conway-magical-genius-known-inventing-game-life-dies-age

5 Often attributed, unclear reference, possibly 1970. Einstein, A. (1970). Autobiographical Notes. *In:* Schilpp, P. (translator and ed.) *Albert Einstein: Philosopher-Scientist* (3rd ed). Open Court Publishing Company.

6 Bachkirova, T. (2016). The Self of the Coach: Conceptualization, Issues and Opportunities for Practitioner Development. *Consulting Psychology Journal: Practice and Research*, 68(2),143–156.

7 dictionary.apa.org/modernism

8 A. A. Milne (1926) *Winnie-the-Pooh*. Methuen.

9 frontiersin.org/research-topics/11572/from-modern-to-postmodern-psychology-is-there-a-way-past#overview

10 dictionary.apa.org/modernism

11 *Ibid*, Bachkirova (2016).

12 Cox, E. (2003). The Contextual Imperative: Implications for coaching and mentoring. *International Journal of Evidence-Based Coaching*, 1(1), 9–22. Cox, E., Bachkirova, T., & Clutterbuck, D. (2014). Theoretical traditions and coaching genres: Mapping the territory. *Advances in Developing Human Resources*, 16(2), 127–138

13 Bachkirova, T., & Smith, C. L. (2015). From competencies to capabilities in the assessment and accreditation of coaches. *International Journal of Evidence Based Coaching and Mentoring*, 13(2), 123–140.

14 De Haan, E. (2008). Relational coaching: journeys towards mastering one-to-one learning. Wiley. Hall, L. (2013). Mindful Coaching: How Mindfulness can Transform Coaching Practice. Kogan Page.

15 Hawkins, P., & Smith, N. (2013). Coaching, Mentoring and Organizational Consultancy: Supervision, Skills & Development (2nd ed.). Open University Press, p151.

16 *Ibid*, Bachkirova & Smith (2015).

17 A phrase used by Miki Kashtan in her work with baynvc.org on Nonviolent Communication

18 For example, in October 2021, Carol Kauffman PhD (Harvard Faculty member) was asked to present to 500 CEOs on Compassion and Leadership at a gathering of the Association of CEOs.

19 Brown, S. (2009). *Play: How it shapes the brain, opens up the imagination, and invigorates the soul*. Penguin Books, p218.

3
What Do We Mean by Playfulness in Coaching?

In this chapter, we take:

- A quick canter through why humans play
- A trot through what we mean by play
- A brisk walk-through as to what play, and playfulness might look like in coaching

We also:

- Share a fireside chat with Prof David Clutterbuck
- Consider how playfulness might manifest in a coaching session
- Acknowledge the serious work you can do with playfulness
- Look at the qualities which underpin playfulness in coaching

If you've read Chapter 1, you will have an idea of what drew us to explore playfulness in coaching. There, we referred to the nebulousness of adult playfulness. When rolling up your sleeves and taking a deep dive into the research and theory, it can at times feel like water running through your fingers. Christian Metz, France's leading film theorist in his lifetime, mused that a film is difficult to explain because it is so easy to understand and while it's in a different context, his words still resonate with our exploration. Like love, it can be easy to recognise playfulness when you see it in practice or experience it yourself, yet it's more difficult to explain it and even more so to apply scientific rigour to it. Research into adult playfulness is still at a comparatively early stage and has not yet reached the point where there is universal agreement on its conceptualisation, definition, measurement, and specificity (in other words, where does, for example, creativity or flow or humour end and playfulness begin and vice versa).[1] This makes the job of critical analysis of this already nebulous concept even more difficult as different researchers are possibly using different definitions, measurements and so on, especially if there is

DOI: 10.4324/9781003090847-4

a significant time gap or cultural difference between their research projects. Another limitation is that the research has concentrated in a relatively small number of countries and participants generally come from similar contexts (for example university students), so we need to resist the temptation to see findings as universally applicable. To add to the challenge, there is a sparsity of research specifically on playfulness in coaching. This is the context then, in which we've endeavoured to give you an overview of available research and theory on adult playfulness and to explore how these may be relevant in the coaching context.

3.1 First, a Little Note

It's important for context to know that research into playfulness in children predates that of adult playfulness by some decades, with playfulness, especially in the earlier research, closely linked or defined as the behaviour of play. As our focus is on playfulness in the context of adults, when we refer to 'playfulness' take it to mean playfulness in adults and we will flag it when we're talking about research or otherwise concerning playfulness in children.

3.2 Why Do Humans Play?

While the research into adult playfulness is still at a relatively early stage, playfulness in children, mostly connected to play (the verb), has for many years been the focus of research, including attempts to scientifically identify and measure it.[2] What has emerged is a complex construct and increasing knowledge about it has had major implications including for educational planning and childrearing practices.[3] Although she was later criticised for lacking sufficient grounding in previous theories,[4] Lieberman (1965; 1977),[5] in her studies of child play, initiated a paradigm shift by moving the focus from discrete play behaviours to playfulness as a behavioural disposition. Even though Huizinga (more on his work below) and Groos (1976)[6] for example, had been defining play as an activity performed for pleasure, for many it was much more than that; playfulness was starting to be seen as a particular way of perceiving, evaluating, and approaching situations.[7] Barnett (2007)[8] cemented the move to see playfulness as a predisposition to frame or reframe a situation so as to engage in playful activities and interactions and her definition was adopted in much subsequent research.[9] If you are interested in exploring the theory and research into the role of play in human development, take a look at Anthony Pellegrini's book of the same name.[10]

Give a moment's thought and bring to mind the image of young animals and children at play and it's intuitive to appreciate that play and playfulness lets them try things out, learn, change their perception, and develop social relationships and skills in a relatively low risk context. Think of a kitten chasing a piece of string and thereby developing the cognitive and physical skills which will come in handy when it comes to unlucky mice later on or a child building manual dexterity, vocabulary, and social skills such as sharing and turn-taking when making mud pies. We can see children using play to take on different roles. The quiet ones can find a voice, the loud ones can find some stillness, and tricky situations can be mapped out by projecting the roles and circumstances onto toys. These are all possibilities tapped into during play therapy.

> Play permits the child to resolve in symbolic form unsolved problems of the past and to cope directly or symbolically with present concerns. It is also his most significant tool for preparing himself for the future and its tasks.
> *Bruno Bettelheim*[11]

It's not a big leap to see the potential for adult play through this lens in a coaching context. Even without a detailed dive into the theory and research here, there's a clear case for the value of play in learning and development, not to mention well-being, on an individual and group level. Panning out to take a more long-term and broader view of humanity, there's also a strong case to be made that play has a greater role and significance beyond well-being, learning and development. It plays a role in both our evolutionary development and in the development of our cultures and their transmission within our societies, moving us beyond surviving to thriving.

Perhaps it is no surprise then, that playfulness is a universally recognizable phenomenon[12] and its importance has long been understood. Friedrich Schiller (1759–1805), a leading German philosopher, dramatist, poet, and literary theorist with an immense influence on German literature observed: 'Man only plays when in the full meaning of the word he is a man, and he is only completely a man when he plays'.[13] Whilst we'd phrase that in a more inclusive way now, we do appreciate his sentiment.

Huizinga (1872–1945), the Dutch historian and cultural theorist introduced the concept of homo ludens (roughly translated as 'playing human'), arguing that we are an inherently playful species, where play is primary to and necessary for the generation of culture. Donald Winnicott saw play as the basis for creative living and culture: play helps a person develop their 'true self', the self which is capable of creativity. Manfred F.R. Kets de Vries, management scholar, psychoanalyst and coach who has written a wealth of books and articles on leadership and organisational development, observes in his book *Mindful Leadership Coaching* that:

> In play, connections between the individual and the environment unfold or emerge, helping the individual to develop effective learning strategies. Play accentuates our biological tendency to symbolize and create meaning in order to understand the world around us. ... from an evolutionary perspective, it can even be argued....that our brain is actually best suited to a more playful style of living. Play, artistic expression, creativity and evolutionary human development are closely allied.[14]

The greater the shame then that many of us are brought up to see play and playfulness as something to leave behind in adulthood. Those adults not towing this line are in danger of being described as 'childish' by others, usually not as a term of endearment or approval. You'll see that we frequently make the distinction in our work between 'childish' and 'childlike'. The latter implies access to emotional intelligence and maturity alongside the ability to tap into childlike joy, spontaneity, curiosity, and other characteristics of playfulness. We'll look at how to access this part of ourselves more and help our clients to do so too in Part II of this book.

This idea of maintaining the ability to be childlike leads us to the term 'neoteny'. We'd like to introduce you it if you haven't met it already. Neoteny describes a slowing of the rate of development thereby extending childhood traits or features through adulthood.[15] Many evolutionary biologists believe that neoteny allows us to retain the playfulness of childhood. Following this argument, a lack of playfulness in adults is not a sign of maturity but of 'psychosclerosis', a hardening of the psyche, while retaining a flexible psyche and playful qualities represent healthy development[16] and a state of optimal functioning.[17] Neoteny is responsible for the brain's lifelong synaptic plasticity[18] allowing us to change our 'set points and behavioural grooves' simply by repeating experiences.[19] Play is known to produce neurotrophins which are molecules that support neuron development, survival, and neuroplasticity.[20] The rather exciting and encouraging implication is that it may be that engaging in play increases capacity for playfulness[21] and on a more fundamental level, play is the bedrock of neuroplasticity which, as you'll appreciate, supports lifelong learning and development.

> We don't stop playing because we grow old; we grow old because we stop playing.
>
> *George Bernhard Shaw*

As Manfred F.R. Kets de Vries notes, people who use the word 'childish' as a derogatory term don't realise that play retains its importance, irrespective of age:

> 'Play can function as a protective mechanism against the high demands that work makes of us – for example, a well-timed joke can alleviate a stressful situation. Articulating the fundamental absurdity of all forms of human endeavour ... can help even the most committed workaholic get things into perspective and liberate some mental space'.[22]

As we will see below, there is as yet no universal agreement as to what exactly playfulness is and where it ends and other constructs such as humour, spontaneity, creativity, and flow begin. There is a lot of fuzzy common space between these, precisely because they are potentially so related and interdependent and have so much to add to well-being, decision-making, exploration, and adaptation, particularly in our VUCA world. While distinguishing between these is important for developing the relevant theory and research, in practice, this is perhaps less important where they can weave in and out of and support each other. For this reason, we've included a chapter on humour and also sections on creativity and imagination in the next chapter. For the rest of this book, particularly the practical sections, we'll hold these distinctions lightly as we are predominantly interested in practical applications in coaching.

3.3 Play and Playfulness in Coaching

Benjamin Haydon (1786–1846) was a British painter and critic who specialised in grand historical paintings. His paintings are admittedly not our cup of tea, though it's easy to appreciate the interesting times in which he lived and the company he kept. He told of a dinner where the guests included Keats and Wordsworth (as you do). During the evening, Keats made the toast: 'confusion to the memory of Newton'. When Wordsworth asked him for an explanation before he drank the toast, Keats answered 'because he destroyed the rainbow by reducing it to a prism'. Later, in 1819, Keats wrote the poem *Lamia* which includes the lines:

> ... Do not all charms fly
> At the mere touch of cold philosophy?
> There was an awful rainbow once in heaven:
> We know her woof, her texture; she is given
> In the dull catalogue of common things.
> Philosophy will clip an Angel's wings,

Conquer all mysteries by rule and line,
Empty the haunted air, and gnomed mine –
Unweave a rainbow, as it erewhile made
The tender-person'd Lamia melt into a shade.

Approximately 200 years later, when writing about coaching mastery, David Clutterbuck, and David Megginson[23] observed that writing and thinking about coaching sometimes seems like Keats' rainbow; the more we try to define, classify, and demystify it, the more we diminish it and lose its essence. While the benefit of research and the development of an evidence-led coaching field is clear, this observation has resonated with us frequently over the last few years as we were researching playfulness in coaching. How do we define it, understand it better, find ways of deconstructing it in a bid to learn how to 'do' it without losing the essence of what is an individual coach's playfulness, their way of being rather than doing? How do we understand it better so that we can apply it with awareness and intent without reducing it to a tick-box mechanical exercise which lacks authenticity?

It turns out that we are in very good company. For example, Di Gammage in her wonderful book *Playful Awakening*[24] considers this challenge and quotes Stephen Nachmanovitch, an improvisational violinist, author, computer artist and educator who teaches and writes about improvisation, creativity, and systems approaches.[25] His view is that 'play cannot be defined'.[26] In a similar vein, Stuart Brown, the founder of the National Institute for Play in California observed that analyzing it takes all the joy out of it. On the one hand, there is the challenge of arriving at any definition of playfulness which fully catches its nuances and individuality and appreciates its magic, yet on the other hand, the question of how can we not only distinguishing between play and playfulness but also analyse different aspects of playfulness generally and in the specific context of coaching without first having agreed its conceptualisation, definition, specificity, and measurement?

While 'play' and 'playfulness' are commonly used words, they are also examined in depth in a range of different specialisms (for example psychology, education, anthropology, and ethology – we had to look that last one up, it means 'the study of animal behaviour' in case you didn't know either). Each of these bring with them their own ethical and theoretical assumptions which occasionally are not aligned or contradict each other. This goes some way to explaining the difficulty of arriving at a universally agreed definition of play. This is true even within some of the disciplines, for example, research psychology[27] where, as we noted above, there is yet no universal agreement as to the conceptualisation, definition, measurement, and specificity of adult playfulness. For our purposes, it helps we think, to think of play and playfulness as a 'moving hologram of a jigsaw' as Di Gammage evocatively describes it and to resist the urge to make the subjective objective.[28]

Particularly in the context of coaching rather than, for example, research psychology, it can feel contrived and over-academic to engage in teasing apart the strands of playfulness into its individual threads, trying to describe their colours, textures and weight while at the same time not losing sight of the rich and varied tapestry that is playfulness in coaching. Stretching this metaphor perhaps to its limits, we had a quick look at how you might describe and investigate the physical characteristics of threads which vary depending on the type of fibre and construction. They include tenacity, loop strength, linear strength, elongation, elastic recovery, loop formation, twist construction, ply security, shrinkage, stitch appearance, colour-fastness, resistance to abrasion, chemicals, heat, and light.[29] If we concentrated on these qualities while admiring a tapestry, it would be easy to lose sight of (in this case literally) the bigger picture as well as any nuances and surprises and an appreciation of the artistry.

Similarly, we can break down the component parts of play and playfulness in coaching to increase our understanding, awareness and the range which is accessible to us as coaches. We do want to acknowledge the importance though, of stepping back from the detail, as fascinating as it can be, to keep the tapestry itself in mind. One of the ways in which we do this is by including insights and stories also of our diverse Storytellers and considering how the theory translates into practice in Part II.

You might be relieved to know that we're leaving this overworked tapestry metaphor here. Let's also leave aside for now a debate about reductionism (our inner Winnie the Pooh who you met in Chapter 2 is objecting again). Suffice it to say that we have at times struggled with whether it is possible or in fact desirable to try to dissect and understand playfulness in coaching. While, as Huizinga (who we met earlier) noted long ago, play is universal,[30] our view is that play and playfulness is very dependent on the context, the individuals and the coaching relationship and our concern is that reductionism might lead to a formulaic approach to playfulness in coaching which doesn't sufficiently take account of the relational and systemic nature of coaching.

3.3.1 Fireside Chat with Prof David Clutterbuck

What does 'playfulness in coaching' conjure up for you?

Playfulness is the art of holding things lightly. It allows us to step outside of rigid thinking and unhelpful emotions by taking events less seriously. It allows us then to address those issues in ways that take greater account of context, develop more creative approaches, and empathise with perspectives different from our own.

Why do you think playfulness is important in coaching?

It's very easy to get caught up in the client's narrative. If we are to help them reframe their narrative, we need to first disentangle both ourselves and the client from it. Playfulness presses the pause button. It is also important in experimentation – people are more likely to engage in an experiment, if they think it will be enjoyable.

What would you say to potential clients or coaches sceptical of the role of playfulness in coaching?

What is the impact you want to have on the people and the environment around you? I point out that we learn most effectively and are most creative when we dip in and out of seriousness and playfulness. I introduce the concept of playfulness with a purpose.

Are you always inherently playful or do you intentionally access playful when you think it will be of service to the client?

It's important to join the client where they are. Then invite them into a different space. I sometimes open a session by asking them what's the most ridiculous thing that has happened to them in the past week. That sets the mind up for a more playful conversation. People often come to coaching or supervision with a deeply emotional or traumatic experience, such as a loved one with a serious illness. They have to feel the depth of our compassion before we can help them 'play' with the issue. Often, the outcome is that they discover some lightness that they are able to bring into their conversations with others. Simply focusing on times when the client and his or her partner have laughed together shifts them away from the sense of tragedy.

Can anyone access playfulness? What might support this?

There's a perception that being an adult means giving up playfulness. That's simply denying a key part of what makes us human. For leaders, having an internal 'pomposity meter' can be helpful in making them more authentic, credible, and approachable.

Do you see a need for addressing and developing playfulness in coach training and even perhaps accreditation?

Absolutely! Improv training is a great asset to any coach. It's not just that it allows you to have a variation in tone and colour of conversation (deep to shallow, light to dark). It trains your unconscious mind to be creative and more aware of the incongruous and the unconsidered possible.

What's your personal favourite expression of playfulness?

What's the most ridiculous, out-of-the-question solution you can imagine to this issue? What elements of that solution are worth exploring?

Prof David Clutterbuck is also one of our Storytellers and his biography can be found in Chapter 1.

3.4 What Do Coaches Mean by Playfulness?

It has taken us a significant amount of time to have a clear understanding of what we mean by playfulness in coaching. Stephanie admits with a sprinkling of embarrassment that a year after starting to explore the concept for her MSc research dissertation, she was still struggling to articulate what exactly she meant by playfulness in coaching. Inner Winnie the Pooh aside, precisely because playfulness is so nuanced, individual, contextual and rich in potential, an understanding which lends itself to articulation has taken time to evolve. We'll introduce you to the model which we've cultivated from our explorations in Chapter 5.

From our own experience, Stephanie's research, and the research which we've undertaken for this book, it seems to us that there are two main reference points when talking about playfulness in coaching. These are how playfulness manifests in the coaching session, and the qualities which underpin playfulness in coaching.

3.4.1 How Playfulness Manifests in the Coaching Session

Again and again, it became clear that playfulness is far richer than certain playful activities. As Julie Flower reflected, 'playfulness' in day-to-day language might be understood in an extreme way; maybe in coaching, you might visualise a high-energy activity with lots of movement and laughter. This was one of the main reasons for Stephanie's early focus on intellectual playfulness in coaching. Yet rather than being limited to such extremes, playfulness in coaching can be very nuanced and show up in lots of different ways. Jonathan Passmore reflected how playfulness can mean different things in different contexts, for example, in a high-tech company, playfulness might be evident in the environment and behaviour such as ping pong tables or ball pools whereas in a steel work company, playfulness might be expressed in joshing, and humour. Rather than being limited by the initial preconceptions which might pop to mind, playfulness in coaching can be far more nuanced and expressed through activities of course, but also the choice of words, stories, metaphors to name but a few (see The Playfulness Scrapbook in Part II for more examples and inspiration).

Peel back the layers further and the theme which kept coming up in conversations and represented what we were trying to capture was that playfulness is a state. We'll look at Emma Skitt's inner rag doll metaphor more in Chapter 10 where she describes a loose, flexible, at ease, playful feeling. In the same chapter during our fireside chat with Graham Lee, he described it as a fluidity of movement (of mind and body, internally rather than physical) between different emotions and ideas. Steve Chapman reflected that to examine our own playfulness as coaches, we need to take a look inside and turn the light of our self-awareness onto considering the epistemological and ontological bases of our coaching practice and indeed how we make sense of life. Steve, for example, doesn't follow particular models; like a master playfulness virtuoso, his plans and improvisations are fundamentally navigated by his bedrock of Zen philosophy and Gestalt coaching. His ability to laugh at his foibles, tap into experiencing everything in the present and believe that the only way to change is to deepen our awareness all emerge as a playful way of being in his coaching. We repeatedly heard our Storytellers express something which mirrored our own experiences: playfulness turns up as a welcome guest rather than as a predetermined intention. As Auriel Majumdar said, playfulness in coaching can be super generative and while tools and techniques can get playfulness going, ultimately, it's more about stance and way of being rather than doing. Furthermore, if we can embody playfulness in our state or way of being, as Robert Stephenson noted, as part of our DNA, then by just being in the coaching space, rather than by you being playful, there is playfulness in that space. As Auriel reflected, playfulness might be expressed through what we do, for example, being exploratory, drawing a picture, imagining something, but more than anything it's in the invitation; the way you speak, the tone, the serious intent and lightness in tone, sharing vulnerability and so on. Honouring the human experience by showing up authentically and creating a space for our clients to join us, often in a fun way. In this space we can do serious, transformational work by being and creating in this playful space. One of the preconceptions we've come across more generally is that playfulness is at odds with holding the seriousness of the work, particularly if the playfulness is expressed through fun, yet our experience (which is also reflected in conversations with our Storytellers) is that it is precisely in this playful space that we can create the conditions for serious work. The idea of holding the space for serious work while also accessing playfulness within that space sits nicely alongside Prof Proyer's concept of serious playfulness[31] which we'll look at in Chapter 5.

Another key characteristic of playfulness in coaching seems to be that its essence is an invitation to explore. It is not something being done to the client as such, but an invitation to enter into a space (whether that's through language, action, or whatever other form) of exploration and co-creation. Neither the coach nor the coachee know what is going to emerge and the attention isn't on the predetermined end goal. Sure, you might have agreed on a number of coaching goals and milestones in advance, but in the moment of the session, these are not the drivers. You know that something will emerge, whether it's, for example, a new insight or perspective, but neither of you know in advance what shape that will take or its impact on the overall goals. This space of not knowing can be a scary one for coaches, especially those cutting their teeth. Nevertheless, this willingness to sit with not knowing appears to be paramount to the space being created for effectiveness of playfulness in coaching. As Steve Chapman reflected, while you can have some idea and preparation of how you will navigate the session, you need to trust that you will know what to do in the moment and be increasingly familiar with the discomfort of not knowing (much more on this later). The coach being comfortable in this space will then support the client stepping into the unknown and the two of them together genuinely enter into a space of exploration and experimentation which is being held by the coach in such a way that there is enough discomfort for learning but not so much as to cause overwhelm.

Playfulness in coaching can also bring value as a disruptor, for instance by managing the energy in the room. Nankhonde Kasonde-van den Broek considered how playfulness, for example through humour, can help lighten the atmosphere if there is tension in the room or it might help to change the energy levels depending on what is needed by the group. In Chapter 8, we will look in a little more detail at how humour can be both a facilitator and a disruptor. Kirsten Barske, working experientially in nature, incorporates the unfamiliar and often awe-inspiring surroundings and playful activities into her work to disrupt patterns of behaviour and stories which participants hold about themselves and others which participants carry with them in their usual work environments (be that in person or virtual). Playfulness can disrupt in another sense too, Steve Chapman shared with us how dyslexia is a form of super power as his brain can go off at different tangents which shows up in different experiments which he curates/initiates which help his clients to see things from different perspectives and help deepen his work.

To recap then, on the theme of how playfulness manifests in coaching sessions:

- Playfulness through tools or materials
- Playfulness as a state or way of 'being' rather than 'doing'
- Holding seriousness of intent with lightness of tone
- Invitation to explore/experiment
- Focus on process rather than prejudged outcome
- Fluidity of movement of thought, emotion, and state
- Facilitation, for example, different perspectives, collaboration, or creativity
- Disruption, for example, of energy, thought patterns, or group dynamics

3.4.2 The Qualities Which Underpin Playfulness in Coaching

For us, these are key and we were incredibly heartened when they came up again and again in conversations with our Storytellers. Effective playfulness (and we will look at risks in a later chapter) has underlying qualities of kindness, respect, and compassion, even when it is challenging or provocative. The coach brings a curiosity and wonder and genuine interest in understanding the coachee and while approaches differ, try to foster this same compassionate curiosity in the coachee. This has overlaps with some schools of meditation, encouraging an attitude of non-judgmental awareness. In a recent session, Stephanie and her client were talking about moving towards cultivating an awareness of difficult emotions which arise rather than trying to push them away. Stephanie shifted her energy, childlike (again – not childish) and asked her client with a playful tone: 'What would it be like if you were to sit in that moment and truly wonder 'oh, this seems like stress … I can feel pressure in my chest … look, my hands are tightening … gosh look, this old story has come up in my thoughts, I wonder what that is … and so on'. Her client smiled and he reflected that the next time he's aware of these feelings arising in him, it would be a learning opportunity to bring out the explorer's magnifying glass and have a good nose-around to see what's happening (applying a mix of non-judgment and self-compassion as required to what's discovered).

We'll look at some of the benefits of playfulness in coaching in the next chapter, and one of these is the psychological distance which playfulness can create in our clients as they reflect on the topic at hand. Through playfulness, the client can step out of their shoes and change perspectives and frames of reference and the space and lightness this can bring can help them sit as authentic selves with their vulnerability within the container of the coaching session. The authenticity and vulnerability which is facilitated can hold true for the coach too. If I am to offer playfulness lightly, as an invitation to enter into experimentation and exploration, where we focus on the present moment and what emerges without following a predetermined path and neither of us know where this is going to take us, then I as a coach also need to be prepared to be authentic and vulnerable. We are deeply drawn to the idea that playfulness allows us to be with and communicate with each other as human to human, bringing, as Nankhonde Kasonde-van den Broek reflected, humour (the ability to be lighthearted in the moment), curiosity (willing to see what will emerge without attachment to fixed expectations) and self-acceptance (by taking the moment lightly and distancing yourself from the situation and taking yourself a little less seriously, accepting yourself) facilitating growth.

To recap, the second theme is the qualities underpinning playfulness (in no particular order and non-exhaustive and with the degree depending on the type of playfulness):

- Intent (in service of the client)
- Kindness
- Respect
- Compassion
- Genuine interest, non-judgment
- Psychological distance (not hooked on our own thoughts/preconceptions)
- Childlike wonder and curiosity
- Spaciousness and willingness to be in uncertainty
- A degree of levity
- Fluidity
- Authenticity
- Vulnerability

Now might be a good time to consider what playfulness means to you and your practice. Check out the Barometer of Playfulness in The Playfulness Scrapbook to get a gauge personal to you.

3.5 Final Thoughts

Despite all of the above considerations, clearly, we still need to be able to attempt to put into words what this book is about. More importantly, if we as coaches and supervisors are going to communicate about this topic, we need to have some understanding of what we each mean. While acknowledging the complexity, what more specifically do we mean then, when we talk about playfulness and play in coaching? Before we go on to that, let's take a small detour to look at why this is worth spending our time on: what are the benefits of playfulness in coaching?

Notes

1   Proyer, R. & Wagner, L. (2015). Playfulness in Adults Revisited: The Signal Theory in German Speakers. *American Journal of Play*, 7(2), 201–227.
2   Barnett, L. (1990). Playfulness: Definition, design, and measurement. *Play & Culture*, 3(4), 319–33.

3 Lieberman, J. (1977). *Playfulness: Its relationship to imagination and creativity.* Academic Press.

4 Reifel, S. (Ed.) (1999). *Play Contexts Revisited.* Ablex Publishing Corporation.

5 Lieberman, J. (1965). Playfulness and divergent thinking: An investigation of their relationship at the kindergarten level. *Journal of Genetic Psychology, 107,* 219–224. Lieberman, J. (1977). *Playfulness: Its relationship to imagination and creativity.* Academic Press.

6 Huizinga, J. (1955). *Homo Ludens; A Study of the Play-Element in Culture.* Beacon Press. Groos, K. (1976). The play of man: Teasing and love-play. In: J. Brunner, J., Jolly, A. & Sylva, K. (Eds.) *Play, development and evolution.* Penguin Books, pp62–83.

7 Guitard, P., Ferland, F. & Dutil, É. (2005). Toward a Better Understanding of Playfulness in Adults. *OTJR: Occupation, Participation and Health, 25*(1), 9–22.

8 Barnett, L. (2007). The nature of playfulness in young adults. *Personality and Individual Differences, 43*(4), 949–958.

9 E.g., Magnuson, C. & Barnett, L. (2013). The Playful Advantage: How Playfulness Enhances Coping with Stress. *Leisure Sciences, 35*(2), 129–144.

10 Pellegrini, A.D. (2009). *The Role of Play in Human Development.* Oxford University Press, Inc.

11 Bettelheim, B. (1976). *The uses of enchantment: The meaning and importance of fairy tales.* Random House.

12 *Ibid,* Huizinga (1955).

13 Schiller, F. (1794). *Letters Upon the Aesthetic Education of Man, Letter XV.*

14 Kets de Vries, M. F. R. (2014). *Mindful Leadership Coaching: Journeys into the Interior.* Palgrave Macmillan, pp156–157.

15 Gould, S. (1977). *Ontogeny and Phylogeny.* Belknap Press. Montagu, A. (1981). *Growing Young.* McGraw-Hill.

16 Montagu, A. (1981). *Growing Young.* New York: McGraw-Hill.

17 Gordon, G. (2014). Well Played: The Origins and Future of Playfulness. *American Journal of Play, 6*(2), 234–266.

18 Hebb, D. O. (1961). Distinctive Features of Learning in the Higher Animal. In Delafresnay, J. (Ed.). *Brain Mechanisms and Learning,* pp37–46.

19 *Ibid,* Gordon (2014).

20 Lauder, J. (1993). Neurotransmitters as Growth Regulatory Signals: Role of Receptors and Second Messengers. *Trends in Neurosciences, 16,* 233–40. Poo, M. (2001). Neurotrophins as Synaptic Modulators. *Nature Reviews Neuroscience, 2,* 24–32. Hua, J. & Smith, S. (2004). Neural Activity and the Dynamics of Central Nervous System Development. *Nature Neuroscience, 7,* 327–32.

21 *Ibid,* Gordon (2014).

22 *Ibid,* Kets de Vries, M. (2014, p169).

23 Clutterbuck, D. & Megginson, D. (2011). Coach maturity: An emerging concept. In Wildflower, L. (Ed.), *The Handbook of knowledge-based coaching: from theory to practice.* John Wiley and Sons, pp299–314.

24 Gammage, D. (2017). *Playful Awakening: Releasing the Gift of Play in Your Life.* Jessica Kingsley Publishers.

25 Nachmanovitch, S. (1990). *Free play: Improvisation in life and art*. Jeremy P. Tarcher/ Putnam.
26 *Ibid*, Gammage (2017, p44).
27 *Ibid*, Proyer & Wagner (2015).
28 *Ibid*, Gammage (2017, p54).
29 amefird.com/technical-tools/thread-education/thread-science/#:~:text= Physical%20characteristics%20that%20vary%20from,chemicals%2C%20 heat%2C%20and%20light
30 *Ibid*, Huizinga (1955).
31 *Ibid*, Proyer & Wagner (2015).

4
The Benefits of Playfulness in Coaching

In this chapter we bring together a selection of 12 key benefits of playfulness in coaching and:

- Consider how accessing different perspectives we open up different possibilities
- Muse on how playfulness can help create space for exploration
- Ponder how playfulness can help us access the state in which we can learn, connect, co-create, and expand
- Bring to mind the interrelatedness of playfulness and creativity, flow, and imagination
- See how playfulness can help us find balance, increase our capacity to deal with change, complexity, and the 'hard' stuff
- Ponder how playfulness can help us go beyond the mind, deepening connection to heart and body
- Think about how playfulness can help us deepen relationships and give rise to positive emotions
- Honour the relationship between playfulness and well-being

As you read this book, you will see that there are a multitude of benefits to playfulness in coaching. Rather than set them all out here and risk repeating ourselves later on, we've put together a collection of the headliners so to speak. We thought it would be remiss of us not to gather an assortment in one place for you to access easily, especially as you might wish to reassure yourself or others from time to time why playfulness in coaching deserves to be taken very seriously. The list, of twelve, below isn't exhaustive and we've given many resources throughout the book for you to explore further should you wish.

> It is play that is the universal, and that belongs to health: playing facilitates growth and therefore health; playing leads into group relationships; playing can be a form of communication in psychotherapy; and, lastly,

DOI: 10.4324/9781003090847-5

psychoanalysis has been developed as a highly specialized form of playing in the service of communication with oneself and with others.

Winnicott[1]

4.1 Through Accessing Different Perspectives, Opening Up Different Possibilities

We'll see in Chapter 6, we are hard-wired for play and in fact it is the basis for neuroplasticity. Children and young animals learn through play by experimenting and learning from experiences. Through play, as we explore and experiment and draw conclusions in an endless cycle, we are changing our brains through neuroplasticity, enabling us to get better at performing many activities and in the process, we develop a picture of ourselves and our relationship to ourselves and others. As we mature, through play and playfulness, we step into imagining different possibilities, perspectives different from our own. We also build our capacity in so many different ways as we explore, experiment, connect and experience positive emotions with others. Thankfully, neuroplasticity doesn't stop with the onset of adulthood and this also means that everyone can engage in play and grow neural circuits that allow for the incredible power of play and through play grow new neural circuits which enable our learning and development more broadly (we look at ways of reconnecting or dialling up playfulness in Part II).

✿ A TODDLER'S RULES OF POSSESION

1. If I like it, it's MINE.
2. If it's in my hand, it's MINE.
3. If I can take it from you, it's MINE.
4. If I had it a while ago, it's MINE.
5. If it's MINE, it must never appear to be yours in any way.
6. If I'm doing or building something, all the pieces are MINE.
7. If it looks like mine, it's MINE.
8. If I saw it first, it's MINE.
9. If you are playing with something, and you put it down, it automatically becomes MINE.
10. If it's broke, it's yours.

It's through play that we (well, most of us) learn to move past the toddler's rules of possession lens of seeing the world and new possibilities of how we can interact with our environment open up, new ways of doing, new ways of relating to others and ourselves. As Stuart Brown argues, 'The genius of play is that, in playing, we create imaginative new cognitive combinations. And in creating those novel combinations, we find what works'.[2]

As Dr Andrew Huberman, professor in the Dept of Neurobiology at the Stanford University School of Medicine outlines,[3] assuming different identities during play is immensely powerful to improve creative thinking, leadership capability, studying and much more. He explains play as essentially contingency testing in low stakes environments (in other words, we have the freedom to explore without risk of adverse consequences). We love this lens on play as it moves beyond the idea of play purely for the purposes of fun (not to denigrate that; fun and other positive emotions are incredibly important and powerful as we'll see). Through play and the inherent exploration and experiment which it entails and opens up to us, we can change how we see ourselves, others, and the world at large, building the capacity for showing up and behaving differently. You can see why this might get coaches excited. Playfulness is such a powerful potential resource beyond childhood and while we think (and hope!) the tide is turning, it has not been taken seriously enough. Let's change that together.

4.2 Creating Space for Exploration

Playfulness creates space for exploration by creating openness and flexibility. Sutton-Smith[4] sees playfulness as a vehicle for disruption and raising awareness of new and unusual possibilities (qualities which Langer[5] suggests are similar to mindfulness). There is a connection between playfulness and novelty and allowing detachment from givens and the taking of different perspectives. There's also a strong link between playfulness and ambiguity tolerance[6] and with preference for complexity.[7] Both of these contribute to coping skills found in individuals with high levels of playfulness.[8] Space for exploration and deliberate choice (rather than habitual reaction) is also created by curiosity as well as a sense of detachment, as supported by Ibarra & Petriglieri's (2010)[9] research on identity change. A core driver of exploration is curiosity and Kashdan et al. (2013)[10] found a link between curiosity and playfulness:

> A curious personality was linked to a wide range of adaptive behaviors including tolerance of anxiety and uncertainty, positive emotional expressiveness, initiation of humor and playfulness, unconventional thinking, and a non-defensive, non-critical attitude.

We'll see later, particularly in Part II, that playfulness and curiosity are best friends. We have found in practice that playfulness supports curiosity and curiosity supports playfulness, together supporting exploration of different perspectives and possibilities.

4.3 Accessing the State in Which We Can Learn, Connect, Co-create and Expand

As we explore in Chapter 6, to access playfulness, our Parasympathetic Nervous System (PNS) needs to be activated. It is in this state that we can access the higher brain functions which allow for more complex thinking, creativity, and long-term memory retrieval; the state which we and our clients need to be in while we're in the coaching space. In a reinforcing loop, while our PNS needs to be activated for us to be playful, we can activate the PNS through play. Play is a powerful stress emollient which is in itself a significant benefit and it can support not just well-being but also transformation and openness to ideas, to others, and to change, learning and growth.

4.4 Flow

Mihalyi Csikszentmihalyi[11] the father of the concept of 'flow' argued that activities can be rewarding in themselves, irrespective of goals or outcomes. Flow is a very enjoyable state of being, when you're so immersed in something that you are fully present, you step out of yourself and become unaware as to what's going on around you. It is found when you have just the right mix of challenge level and skill level (broadly speaking, too hard you give up or struggle, too easy and it's boring). The connection of playfulness and flow is something which has been of interest to researchers particularly in the context of video and virtual reality games.

Finding flow helps us to be more creative, productive, and happy. Flow became of great interest to positive psychologists researching areas including emotions and creativity as well as intrinsic motivation. Martin Seligman[12] considers it to be a huge part of improving our human experience, for its role in living a meaningful life. If you'd like to explore this concept more, a great place to start is an article by Steven Kotler, the co-founder of the Flow Genome Project in the Harvard Business Review which explains the concept in more detail as well as its effect on for example learning, productivity, innovation, and creativity in the workplace.[13]

We heard a story on the grapevine that when Csikszentmihalyi was researching flow in the early days, he referred to it as 'play'. He was told though that it would be very difficult to get research funding and that he'd have more success if he came up with a different name – hence 'flow'. It makes sense to us given some of the preconceptions around play and, in the moment of playfulness, you are in flow.

4.5 Creativity

> Creativity is intelligence having fun.
>
> *Albert Einstein*

The film director Taika Waititi describes creativity as 'looking at the world through the eyes of a child ... and having fun ... with an innocent view point'. He points to the painter Rousseau who was told he couldn't paint, but really just couldn't paint in the style of others in his time and developed his own, wonderful style. Di Gammage[14] describes play as 'fundamentally a way of creatively engaging with the world'. The similarities of creativity and playfulness include that there's no right or wrong; it's all data and mistakes drive learning. Experimentation is at the heart of both. We are prepared not to know the outcome before we start and we focus on the process (being present in the moment) rather than a predetermined outcome. For both, safety is required, for example, improv's 'yes, and' approach, as fear of criticism and judgement will close down creativity and playfulness.

> It is in playing and only in playing that the individual child or adult is able to be creative and to use the whole personality, and it is only in being creative that the individual discovers the self.
>
> *Winnicott*[15]

Playfulness and creativity are closely related (imagine a Venn diagram which includes humour, playfulness, and creativity). Mihalyi Csikszentmihalyi[16] identified ten Paradoxical Traits of highly creative individuals including that they combine playfulness with discipline, responsibility with irresponsibility and alternate between imagination and reality, noting that one word to describe the difference in their personalities is 'complexity'. You'll see in Chapter 5 that Proyer's definition of playfulness includes a preference for complexity.[17] Proyer has found that overall, playfulness relates to higher self-estimates of ingenuity particularly for creative but also expressive and spontaneous variants of playfulness.[18] There is evidence supporting a positive relation between playfulness and divergent thinking[19] and a long tradition of research relating playfulness to creativity[20] though little work yet on the underlying mechanism.[21] West et al.'s (2017) pioneering study empirically testing the effect of team playfulness on creative performance found a positive correlation.[22] This is particularly noteworthy as creativity is often a collaborative co-creating process[23] as coaching can be.[24] In relation to humour, which has overlaps with playfulness, there have been a few studies showing a causal link between engaging in humour and creative outcomes and a humour-creativity link in organisations, though there's still much to learn and discover in this area.[25]

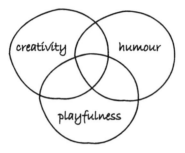

4.6 Imagination

Like adult playfulness, research into imagination and particularly its potential in the context of coaching is at a relatively early stage and there is much left to discover. It's surprising perhaps given how frequently we tap into imagination during the coaching process, whether, for example, we're imagining our ideal self, conjuring up metaphors, giving voice and shape to our inner dialogue or creating psychological distance through imagining what a superhero would do (all of which you'll encounter in later pages). The links and overlaps of imagination and playfulness in coaching are self-evident; the exploration of possibilities and perspectives, being able to create some order in systemic complexity, the connection within teams, and the coaching relationship through shared experiences and the potential for experiencing positive emotions and the knock-on effect which this has (see Chapter 7) to name a few. Imagination, creativity, and playfulness are distinct yet interwoven and through playfulness we can fuel our imagination, a potent resource in challenging, complex times.[26]

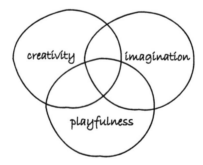

4.7 Capacity to Deal with Change

The flexibility associated with playfulness means that we cultivate our capacity to see what is around us and respond with 'I wonder what might happen if I tried this'. As Michael Rosen[27] reflects, play is a state of mind that can cope with the unexpected, knows that we can change the rules, that play can create new order (by which he means structure, organisation, patterns, a classification; the opposite of chaos). He concludes that play gives us both adaptability and order, 'Through play, we may discover that an object, an activity, a relationship, a situation or a social circumstance can be changed, reorganised, and reordered'.

> Nothing is fixed, and everything is full of potential.
>
> *Michael Rosen*

4.8 Finding Balance

One of the aims and benefits of a sustained mindfulness practice is to find a place of balance with our emotions. We notice them, feel them but don't get activated by them or at least less so, learning to honour them from a place of discernment. Many of the meditation teachers whom we follow[28] reflect on the huge role of playfulness and humour (linked with self-compassion) to their practice and achieving this balance. As Ram Dass jokes in *Be Here Now*,[29] it's not that his neurosis disappeared after years of practice, but that he became a connoisseur of his neurosis. With deep-seated 'neurosis' (in the non-clinical sense), we can still help our clients to find that balance (remembering the therapy/coaching boundaries), through creating psychological distance through humour and playfulness, for example inviting a client to imagine an emotion as a character in a way that invites them to take this emotion less seriously (see The Playfulness Scrapbook for practical ideas). Oren Jay Sofer in a course on the Ten Percent meditation app referred to another meditation teacher who had said to him that at some point in your practice, you realise that your mind is completely insane, going down a hill on a cart with no brakes and it's actually progress in our practice if we can laugh at ourselves and recognise this. We'll come to the idea of balance again when we consider *Well-being* below.

4.9 Capacity to Deal with the 'Hard' Stuff

As well as the above ways in which play can help us reflect on and take action regarding the 'hard' stuff (for example, difficult relationships or conversations, limiting belief, negative self-talk), it can also help us create psychological distance. Ethan Kross' research[30] shows that by creating this distance, we can have a much more productive relationship with our inner 'chatter'. ACT (Acceptance Commitment Therapy) based coaching relies heavily on building the ability to step into the Observing Self to create sufficient distance from our perception of our lived experience to create the space for values-led action. Many of the ways in which playfulness can support coaching have the effect of allowing access to this Observing Self. It can extend not just to having a more objective stance towards our own thoughts, feelings, actions and situations, but to more complex systemic issues. For example, in LEGO® Serious Play®, the Real Time Strategy for the Organisation workshop allows a team to build complex adaptive systems representing the organisation and its various stakeholders and the wider systemic context which they can then explore by taking different perspectives and through role play. By building representations of the various complex adaptive systems, play can create a sense of space and objectivity, giving rise to different perspectives, possibilities and options.

Let's take a sideways leap and look at some research into how humorous public health messaging (sun lotion to prevent skin cancer and condoms to prevent STDs) was found to be more effective for certain groups. Conway & Dube (2002)[31] found that people scoring high on the trait of masculinity (irrespective of gender, it's to do with being dominant, forceful, and independent with an orientation towards being assertive and instrumental) responded better to humorous health messaging. Conway and Dube contend that this was because the high-masculinity participants were more persuaded by the humorous messages as it was consistent with their distress-avoidant response to threat and allowed them to engage in peripheral (heuristic) processing of the message rather than central (elaborative) processing. In case you're wondering, the low-masculinity trait participants responded equally to the humorous and non-humorous messages. Admittedly, it's a leap to make the connection, but it's also consistent with our experience. For those people who tend to avoid feelings of distress or difficult emotions, perhaps humorous playfulness is a way to engage in these topics in coaching in a more accessible way. This might then have a knock-on effect of helping them to stay in a state where their Parasympathetic Nervous Systems stays activated with all the resultant benefits for the coaching process (see Chapter 6 for more on this).

4.10 Beyond the Mind: Deepening Connection to Heart and Body

> You can discover more about a person in an hour of play than in a year of conversation.
>
> *Plato*[32]

Some forms of play allow you to disengage the mind, to leave your inner monitor and critic aside, be in the present moment, be prepared to stay in the not-knowing exploratory space, involved in the process rather than being goal oriented. To do this, we need more than our brains, but to engage our hearts and often our bodies. Actors understand this; to embody a character they need to move beyond the intellectual and understand how the character's body 'works' and for their body both to be and to move in a way that is authentic to the character and to feel the emotions of the character. Various degrees of this might show up in playful coaching, for example, trying to embody an imagined dialogue partner in Chairwork. More broadly, this space beyond filters might be accessed without involving the body, for example, through art (in the loosest sense, mark-making rather than anything with artistic merit), where we feel safe enough to be honest, spontaneous, vulnerable, and open to be surprised by what might happen. The resulting spontaneity and honesty might lead to new insights, new perspectives, and our capacities for being in this space can be cultivated through playfulness (for example through improv exercises).

Let's look at this in the context of serious play for a moment. Roos et al. (2004)[33] define serious play as activity that 'draws on the imagination, integrates cognitive, social, and emotional dimensions of experience, and intentionally brings the emergent benefits of play to bear on organizational challenges'. During serious play, participants are invited to 'think with the hands through creating a model'.[34] For example, you'll hear that LEGO® Serious Play® facilitators frequently invite participants to think with their hands. The underlying assumption of serious play is Polanyi's (1969)[35] tacit integration, namely that the participants hold the ideas and answers to challenging questions without being aware of them. Modelling or creating, for example, building LEGO® models, allows participants to represent metaphors which offer a way of creating awareness of participants' own understanding[36] as well as understanding others' metaphorical frames enabling 'knowing through objects'[37] which supports meaning-making and relationship building.[38]

Kets de Vries describes how for prehistoric humans, 'problem solving, and decision making were spontaneous and opportunistic, and these behavioural necessities would have created a foundation for intuition, improvisation, exploration and adaptation'.[39] By returning to play, we strengthen these capacities which are so valuable in the complex adaptive systems in which we find ourselves.

4.11 Deepening Relationships and Positive Emotions

Playfulness can bring fun into our coaching relationships and practice and in doing so help build rapport, trust, and to benefit from experiencing positive emotions. These positive emotions are vital for our well-being and also have a 'broaden-and-build' effect (which we'll look at in Chapter 7). For teams, playing together can also reduce stress and help the individuals see each other in a kinder, more fun, and relaxed light, sometimes seeing each other for the first time as the humans that they are rather than through the two-dimensional assumptions that might come with job roles or titles. The result may well be that trust, collaboration, cohesion, and well-being are supported and can be built on to support psychological safety.

Playfulness can also be a vehicle for deeper compassion, empathy, unconditional positive regard and at its core, love (if this sounds puzzling or even controversial, we look at this more in Chapter 7). This, we believe, is one of the reasons why when we are coaching, we can navigate emotional or (for the client) difficult terrain with varying levels of playfulness, sometimes with a softer, light touch, compassionate approach and sometimes with a more challenging approach. Coachees can walk side by side with us through these challenging experiences because they feel and know our intent, compassion, and respect which allows us both/all to be playful.

In the right context, for the right reasons and with sensitivity (and we'll look at some for the risks in Chapter 9), playfulness supports the coaching relationship. In our experiences and reflected in the conversations which we've had with others, there is a progression of the type of playfulness emerging as the coaching relationship develops. The implicit and explicit communication of safety/non-judgement which is needed for playfulness also deepens rapport. This seems to be supported by the research of Panksepp (2009),[40] Fredrickson (2009)[41] and Porges (2011).[42] The space created by playfulness can support vulnerability of both coach and client, perhaps linked to Boyatzis & McKee's (2005)[43] assertion that emotional intelligence may be used to build shared playfulness, hope, compassion, and mindfulness in relationships. This relational aspect of playfulness is significant given that in therapy, the therapeutic relationship is the one factor that is common to successful outcomes across all therapeutic modalities and theoretical perspectives[44] and it is believed that the same applies to coaching.[45]

4.12 Well-being

Kets de Vries[46] notes that play, artistic expression, creativity and evolutionary human development are closely allied, and he wonders whether our brains have had time to catch up with progress or whether the lack of play in many of our lives today is an invitation to stress disorders and mental health problems.[47] The links between play and playfulness and adult well-being is supported by research, for example, recently during the COVID pandemic.[48] Intuitively, you know it makes sense.

More specifically in a coaching context, the lightness which can be created through playfulness has a number of supportive effects. One is resilience of the coach. There is analogous support for this in the literature where humour has been found to support therapists' resilience.[49] We can bolster our resilience by holding the process and our responsibility seriously but lightly, possibly with gentle irreverence and perhaps reflecting Magnuson & Barnett's (2013)[50] argument that coping styles and playfulness are similar in their cognitive-emotional attributes. Our resilience and that of our clients can also be supported by playfulness through shifting in perspective and relief during difficult conversations. Also, playfulness can give rise to and heighten positive emotions in the coaching process including joy but also relief or catharsis. The lightness which playfulness can bring can bring balance to difficult conversations and help us from getting caught up in our clients' seriousness/heaviness, helping us keep a sense of perspective (and perhaps infuse our part in the process with this) even in the midst of deep work. For both coach and client, playfulness might just be the difference between surviving and thriving.

Playful Moment

Before we move on to the end of the chapter, perhaps take a Playful Moment and think about these potential benefits again and how they resonate with you now.

4.13 Conclusion

We hope that this has given you a taste of the many and varied potential benefits of playfulness in coaching. We'll see in Chapter 7 why playfulness is so much more than fun, though even infusing our coaching with fun when and if it's appropriate can have substantial impact and benefits, to our clients as well as ourselves (more on positive emotions later). Increasing our capacity to bring playfulness into our practice has the potential to widen the depth and breadth of our work for the benefit of our clients and ourselves. As we continue, we will look at many of these benefits in more detail including through stories of practice.

Taking a step back to a more systemic view beyond coaching, it seems to us that the world needs us to be more playful. From here, we can be more open to not knowing, flexible, bring a 'yes, and' mindset which requires us to listen and connect. Playfulness opens up a degree of irreverence towards the 'givens', it can help us change the narrative and give us imaginative, creative ways to act and respond[51] as well as helping us make sense of complexity. For us (Teresa and Stephanie), playfulness brings with it compassion and greater connection. Given the huge complex challenges we collectively face, we think that we need that lightness, willingness to take different perspectives and to experiment, to make the most of potential and address challenges imaginatively and creatively. As coaches, in our small way, we can work with our clients at times playfully causing ripple effects as they gain experience, capacity and willingness to approach things in this way.

Coming back to the coaching space, the time has come to get more specific and take a closer look at what we mean when we talk about playfulness in coaching.

Notes

1 Winnicott, D. (1971). *Playing and Reality*. Routledge, p56.
2 Brown, S. (2009). *Play: How it shapes the brain, opens up the imagination, and invigorates the soul*. Penguin Books, p37.
3 In his podcast hubermanlab.com/using-play-to-rewire-and-improve-your-brain/
4 Sutton-Smith, B. (1997). *The Ambiguity of Play*. Harvard Business School Press.
5 Langer, E. (1989). *Mindfulness*. Addison-Wesley. Langer, E. (1997). *The power of mindful thinking*. Addison-Wesley.
6 Tegano, D. (1990). Relationship of tolerance of ambiguity and playfulness to creativity. *Psychological Reports*, 66, 1047–1056.
7 *Ibid*, Proyer (2017).
8 Magnuson, C. & Barnett, L. (2013). The Playful Advantage: How Playfulness Enhances Coping with Stress. *Leisure Sciences*, 35(2), 129–144.
9 Ibarra, H. & Petriglieri, J. (2010). Identity work and play. *Journal of Organizational Change Management*, 23(1), 10–25.
10 Kashdan, T. Sherman, R., Yarbro, J. & Funder, D. (2013). How are Curious People Viewed and How Do they Behave in Social Situations? From the Perspectives of Self, Friends, Parents, and Unacquainted Observers. *Journal of Personality*, 81(2), 142–154.
11 Csikszentmihalyi, M. (1990). *Flow: The Psychology of Optimal Experience*. Harper and Row.

12 Seligman, M. (2002). *Authentic Happiness*. The Free Press, p249.
13 *Create a Work Environment that Fosters Flow*. Harvard Business Review, 6 May 2014 hbr.org/2014/05/create-a-work-environment-that-fosters-flow Accessed on 22 March 2023.
14 Gammage, D. (2017). *Playful Awakening: Releasing the Gift of Play in Your Life*. Jessica Kingsley Publisher, p54.
15 *Ibid*, Winnicott (1971, p54).
16 Csikszentmihalyi, M. (2013). *Creativity: The Psychology of Discovery and Invention* (3rd ed.). HarperCollins, p55.
17 Proyer, R. (2017). A new structural model for the study of adult playfulness: Assessment and exploration of an understudied individual differences variable. *Personality and Individual Differences*, 108, 103–122.
18 Proyer, R. (2012). Examining playfulness in adults: Testing its correlates with personality, positive psychological functioning, goal aspirations, and multi-methodically assessed ingenuity. *Psychological Test and Assessment Modeling*, 54(2), 103–127.
19 e.g. Barnett, L. & Kleiber, D. (1982). Concomitants of playfulness in early childhood: Cognitive abilities and gender. *The Journal of Genetic Psychology*, 141(1), 115–127. Truhon, S. (1983). Playfulness, play, and creativity: A path analytic model. *The Journal of Genetic Psychology*, 143(1), 19–28.
20 e.g. Barnett, L. & Kleiber, D. (1982). Concomitants of playfulness in early childhood: Cognitive abilities and gender. *The Journal of Genetic Psychology*, 141(1), 115–127. Barnett, L. & Kleiber, D. (1984). Playfulness and the early play environment. *The Journal of Genetic Psychology*, 144(2), 153–164. Glynn, M. & Webster, J. (1992). The Adult Playfulness Scale: An initial assessment. *Psychological Reports*, 71(1), 83. Glynn, M. & Webster, J. (1993). Refining the Nomological Net of the Adult Playfulness Scale: Personality, Motivational, and Attitudinal Correlates for Highly Intelligent Adults, *Psychological Reports*, 72(3), 1023–1026. Barnett, L. (2007). The nature of playfulness in young adults. *Personality and Individual Differences*, 43(4), 949–958. *Ibid*, Proyer (2012). Proyer, R. (2012). A Psycholinguistic Study on Adult Playfulness: Its Hierarchical Structure and Theoretical Considerations. *Journal of Adult Development*, 19(3), 141–149. Proyer, R. (2012). Development and initial assessment of a short measure for adult playfulness: The SMAP. *Personality and Individual Differences*, 53(8), 989–994. Proyer, R. & Brauer, K. (2018). Exploring adult Playfulness: Examining the accuracy of personality judgments at zero-acquaintance and an LIWC analysis of textual information. *Journal of Research in Personality*, 73, 12–20.
21 Sutton-Smith, B. (2009). *The Ambiguity of Play*. Harvard University Press.
22 West, S., Hoff, E. & Carlsson, I. (2017). Enhancing team creativity with playful improvisation theater: a controlled intervention field study. *International Journal of Play*, 6(3), 283–293.
23 Sawyer, R. & DeZutter, S. (2009). Distributed creativity: How collective creations emerge from collaboration. *Psychology of Aesthetics, Creativity, and the Arts*, 3(2), 81–92.
24 O'Broin, A. & Palmer, S. (2010). Exploring key aspects in the formation of coaching relationships: Initial indicators from the perspective of the coachee and the coach.

Coaching: An International Journal of Theory, Research and Practice, 3(2), 124–143.
Kempster, S. & Iszatt-White, M. (2013). Towards co-constructed coaching: Exploring the integration of coaching and co-constructed autoethnography in leadership development. *Management Learning, 44*(4), 319–336.

25 Robert, C. (Ed.) (2017). *The psychology of humor at work.* Routledge.

26 If you're looking for more resources on imagination, visit the Imagination Institute (www.imagination-institute.org/}

27 Rosen, M. (2020). *Book of Play!* Wellcome Collection, p20.

28 For example Oren Jay Sofer, Joseph Goldstein and Jeff Warren.

29 Ram Dass (1971). *Bere Here Now.* The Crown Publishing Group.

30 Kross, E. (2021). *Chatter: The Voice in Our Head, Why It Matters, and How to Harness It.* Crown.

31 Conway, M. & Dube, L. (2002). Humor in persuasion on threatening topics: Effectiveness is a function of audience sex role orientation. *Personality & Social Psychology Bulletin.* 28(7), 863–873.

32 It's not clear that this quote did actually originate from Plato, but it's often attributed to him and seemed too good to leave out!

33 Roos, J., Victor, B. & Statler, M. (2004). Playing seriously with strategy. *Long Range Planning, 37*(6), 549–568.

34 Roos, J. & Victor, B. (1999). Towards a new model of strategy-making as serious play. *European Management Journal, 17,* 348–55.

35 Polanyi, M. (1969). *Knowing and Being.* Routledge.

36 Schulz, K.-P., Geithner, S., Woelfel, C. & Krzywinski, J. (2015). Toolkit-based modelling and serious play as means to foster creativity in innovation processes. *Creativity and Innovation Management, 24*(2), 323–340.

37 McCusker, S. (2019). Everybody's monkey is important: LEGO® Serious Play® as a methodology for enabling equality of voice within diverse groups. *International Journal of Research and Method in Education,* 1–17.

38 Lee, C. & Amjadi, M. (2014). The role of materiality: knowing through objects in work practice. *European Management Journal, 32*(5), 723–734.

39 Kets de Vries, M. F. R. (2014). *Mindful Leadership Coaching: Journeys into the interior.* Palgrave Macmillan, p157.

40 Panksepp, J. (2009). Brain emotional systems and qualities of mental life: From animal models of affect to implications for psychotherapeutics. In: Fosha, D., Siegel, D. and Solomon, M. (Eds.) *The healing power of emotion: Affective neuroscience, development, and clinical practice.* Norton, pp1–26.

41 Fredrickson, B. (2009). *Positivity: Top-notch research reveals the upward spiral that will change your life.* Three Rivers Press.

42 Porges, S. (2011). *The polyvagal theory: Neurophysiological foundations of emotions, attachment, communication, and self-regulation.* Norton.

43 Boyatzis R. & McKee, A. (2005). *Resonant leadership: renewing yourself and connecting with others through mindfulness, hope and compassion.* Harvard Business School Press.

44 Crenshaw, D. & Kenney-Noziska, S. (2014). Therapeutic presence in play therapy. *International Journal of Play Therapy, 23,* 31–43. Kestly, T. (2016). Presence and Play: Why Mindfulness Matters. *Journal of Play Therapy, 25*(1), 14–23.

45 De Haan, E. (2008). *Relational coaching: journeys towards mastering one-to-one learning*. Wiley.
46 *Ibid*, Kets de Vries (2014, p157).
47 See also *Ibid*, Magnuson Barnett (2013).
48 Clifford, C., Paulk, E., Lin, Q., Cadwallader, J., Lubbers, K. & Frazier, L. (2022). Relationships among adult playfulness, stress, and coping during the COVID-19 pandemic. *Current Psychology*, 1–10.
49 Franzini, L. (2001). Humor in therapy: The case for training therapists in its uses and risks. *The Journal of General Psychology*, *128*(2), 170–93.
50 *Ibid*, Magnuson & Barnett (2013).
51 Just one example – meeting hate with clowning: www.nytimes.com/2017/08/17/opinion/how-to-make-fun-of-nazis.html and   www.opendemocracy.net/en/transformation/why-are-nazis-so-afraid-of-clowns/ and   www.colorlines.com/articles/clowns-attack-kkk-rally-charlotte-nc-humor

5
The Be Playful Onion Model

In this chapter we:

- Introduce you to the shiny new Be Playful Onion Model
- Explore how this may help navigate the realm of playfulness
- Integrate the OLIW model of playfulness
- Examine the idea of serious playfulness
- Share a fireside chat with Professor Proyer, leading adult playfulness researcher
- See that playfulness is so much more than fun
- Look at Graham Lee's Character Compass Model and start to experiment with integrating this model with the Be Playful Onion Model

Albert Einstein threw down a gauntlet that if you can't explain something simply, you don't understand it enough and 'everything should be made as simple as possible, but no simpler'. With the caveat that much brighter minds than ours are engaged in full-time research on deconstructing and understanding adult playfulness, we'd like to introduce you to our brand new, shiny Be Playful Onion Model of playfulness in coaching. We offer it lightly as a framework to support practice, conversations, reflections, and supervision. The key to remember is that as much as we've tried to rise to Albert Einstein's challenge (stretch goals are good they say), with playfulness in coaching, there isn't a one-size-fits-all because it is, in our view, so context and relationship dependent.

5.1 The Onion

Before we share our Be Playful Onion Model with you, let's just give a nod to the British statistician George E. P. Box, to whom the quote 'All models are wrong, but some are useful' is often attributed.

DOI: 10.4324/9781003090847-6

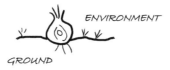

Provisos aside, in essence, we've come to see play and playfulness like the layers of an onion still growing in the ground (in other words, it's not fixed but changing, developing, and growing, and also grounded, see further below). Here then is our Be Playful Onion Model (ta-dah!):

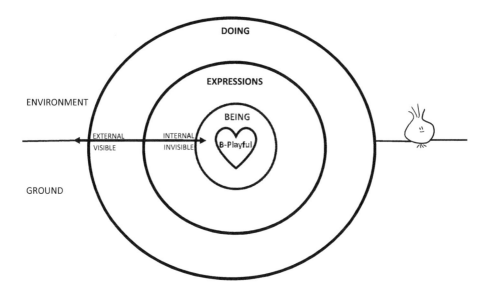

Figure 5.1 Be Playful Onion Model

5.2 The Outer Layer – 'Doing' Play

Let's start from the outside layer of the Onion as 'play' is perhaps easiest to observe. What do you think of as soon as you hear the word 'play'? We're guessing it's children at play; physical behaviour which you can see and which is often the expression of joy and fun. Though perhaps not always so obviously, when our kids were young, we spent many hours at the make-shift teddy bear hospital where they were administering first aid with suitably serious demeanours to unhappy injured teddies. Now, watching them as teenagers and young adults sometimes engrossed in gaming, to the observer, more obvious emotions appear to be tension, concentration, and determination, with not a smile in sight.

For ease of reference, as most people we've spoken to associate 'play' in the coaching context as something which is observable, for our purposes, let's see 'play' as the verb, the physical manifestation of playfulness. This approach, though not perfect and all-encompassing, is sufficient for our purposes and takes into account that 'play' is a process, not a thing, for the most part focussing on the experience rather than accomplishing goals (as distinct from playing sports where often the objective is to win or perfect your technique).

Just as there are layers to the Onion, there is range and nuance within each layer as it gets closer to the next layer down. If the outside of the exterior 'play' layer is a physical manifestation of play which is readily observable, then as we move inwards, within this outer level of 'play' also sits the notion of imaginary or imaginative play which is observable to greater and lesser degrees depending on what form it takes. For example, you might see a team engaged in an improv exercise where you can see their physical play behaviour and at the same time, participants (and the observer) are drawing heavily on their imagination. Go a little deeper still in this layer and 'play' might look like an invitation to your client to play out a scenario in their mind (rather than with tangible materials such as for art or LEGO®) or to play with an idea and there might be no verbal interactions during those moments between coach and client and no physical evidence of play, though the client's mind might be deeply immersed in play. So, play can be visible to the observer in terms of physical behaviour, or it can be invisible and take place purely internally.

In their book *Psychology of Humour, An Integrative Approach*, Rod Martin and Thomas Ford point to the absence of universal agreement as to what play is but that most play researchers would agree that:

> It is an enjoyable, spontaneous activity that is carried out for its own sake with no obvious immediate biological purpose (Berlyne, 1969). Michael Apter (1982) suggested that play is best viewed as a state of mind, rather than a specific characteristic of certain types of activities. Thus, one can engage in almost any activity in a playful way, as long as one has a nonserious, activity-oriented (rather than goal-oriented) mindset.[1]

We think that this is an important point in the coaching context too and part of the reason we haven't presented you with a 'playfulness in coaching user manual'. It's possible to offer inherently playful approaches/tools in an unplayful way, just as it's possible to engage in inherently unplayful tools/approaches in a playful way. Equally, the emphasis on the process rather than the goal is an important one we'll come back to again and again.

With a cheery wave to Dilts and his Logical Levels (we like Alison Hardingham's description of them as 'psychological levels'[2]), if we see 'play' as a verb, a coach incorporating play might therefore consider any changes that may need to be made to the coaching environment to facilitate play and what materials she/he might need to provide to enable the exterior or interior play behaviour. As a coach finding play in ourselves and facilitating it in our clients, we can ask:

- How suitable is our environment for play?
- Are there any resources which we need?
- What skills do we have?
- What is working and not working with individual clients and contexts?
- What do we need to learn?
- What do we need to unlearn?

5.3 The Middle Layer – Expressions of Playfulness

Moving into the middle layer of the Onion, 'playfulness' in coaching becomes harder to define as we're moving closer towards mindset and heartset. In other words, what we are thinking, the assumptions we make and the beliefs we hold (mindset) as well as the emotions which we are feeling and which filter our perceptions, shape our beliefs, and influence our actions (heartset). As an aside, our mind – and heartsets don't exist in isolation but in the context of relationships and systems (we are affected by and affect others' by our own) which we'll explore more in Chapter 6. Arguably, another paradigm shift in how we see playfulness is underway, this time led by Professor Proyer of Martin-Luther University Halle-Wittenberg in Germany. He has been researching adult playfulness for some years and is at the forefront of psychology research on this topic. He identified facets of playfulness which exist independently from positive and closer to serious mood[3] with such 'serious playfulness' possibly associated with creative thinking, problem-solving or specific task/goal focus. In this light, he proposes the following global definition of playfulness:

> Playfulness is an individual differences variable that allows people to frame or reframe everyday situations in a way such that they experience them as entertaining, and/or intellectually stimulating, and/or personally interesting. Those on the high end of this dimension seek and establish situations in which they can interact playfully with others (e.g., playful teasing, shared play activities) and they are capable of using their play-fulness even under difficult situations to resolve tension (e.g., in social interactions, or in work type settings). Playfulness is also associated with a preference for complexity rather than simplicity and a preference for – and liking of – unusual activities, objects and topics, or individuals.[4]

While there are a number of models of playfulness, most are based on the propensity to play and/or have links to fun and enjoyment (for example, the Adult Playfulness Trait Scale[5]). We think that Proyer's model together with the above definition is the most useful for a coaching context. This model is the OLIW (pronounced 'olive') model of playfulness.[6] We're stuffing an olive into the middle layer of the Onion so to speak (sorry, we couldn't resist). The OLIW model is a four faceted model, uniquely not a universal measure and therefore more nuanced than other models.[7] The OLIW model is composed of[8]:

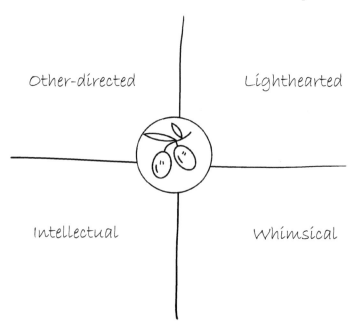

Figure 5.2 The OLIW Model

Other-directed	Playful behaviours in social situations to ease tense situations and cheer others up. An enjoyment of engaging in playful interactions with others and horsing around with friends.
Lighthearted	Spontaneous, carefree view of life. Not too occupied with possible consequences of one's behaviour but a preference for and enjoyment of improvising as opposed to elaborate preparation.
Intellectual	Enjoyment of playing with ideas, puzzling over problems, and coming up with new, creative solutions for problems.
Whimsical	Preference for breaking ranks, and for extraordinary people and things and amused by oddities. Others often regard them as extravagant.

One of the reasons the OLIW Model is so useful is that it represents the distinct characteristics of playfulness while uniquely avoiding significant overlaps with broader personality traits[9] or incorporating related but distinct constructs such as humour.[10] The intention of the OLIW model of playfulness is to isolate playfulness and its potential consequences to avoid previous possible misinterpretations[11] such as focusing on potential associations with fun and entertainment.[12]

In her own earlier research, Stephanie was particularly interested in looking at the *Intellectual* component of the OLIW playfulness model in the coaching context. The idea of *Intellectual* playfulness as characterised by the enjoyment of playing with ideas, puzzling over problems, and coming up with new, creative solutions seemed to resonate strongly with the coaching process. For many, this is perhaps initially the easiest way to access playfulness in coaching (or may help them realise that in many respects, their coaching already includes playful elements).

Staying with this idea a little longer Huizinga, who we met in Chapter 3, introduced the concept of homo ludens (roughly translated as 'playing human'). Meanwhile, the German theologian Hugo Rahner[13] (1900–1968, German Jesuit theologian and ecclesiastical historian and – fun fact – older brother of Karl, one of the. most influential Roman Catholic theologians of the 20th century) introduced the idea of *Ernstheiterkeit*, a German neologism consisting of *Ernst* meaning serious/seriousness and *Heiterkeit* meaning cheerfulness/mirth, as distinct from joy. Directly translated, it means 'serious cheerfulness' and represents holding joy with perspective and sadness/worries with lightness, contradicting commonly held perceptions of playfulness having as its ultimate goal cheerfulness/joy. The cheerfulness of the homo ludens is founded on his solemnity and only from this solid foundation may profound cheerfulness arise. To us, this seems similar in some respects to the Buddhist concept of equanimity which we'll look at briefly in the context of playfulness in Chapter 7. Both concepts bring to mind the Dalai Lama's or the late Archbishop Desmond Tutu's way of being and ability to hold profoundly serious issues with openness, curiosity, and playfulness. If we play with this idea a little, we can see the idea of 'serious playfulness' emerge.

Perhaps on first thought, playfulness and seriousness seem on opposite sides of a spectrum, and this approach is reflected by some researchers.[14] However, *serious playfulness* suggests that you can be both serious and playful simultaneously. In their research, Proyer & Rodden (2013)[15] found that participants who scored high in seriousness and cheerfulness were amongst the ones scoring highest for playfulness. This apparent paradox is certainly very evident in our work where moments of playfulness often emerge in the midst of seriousness in our coaching; laughter and tears co-existing effectively.

We find it fascinating then, that Professor Proyer considers that this idea of serious playfulness will be very important for shaping the future understanding of playfulness. For example, further research may determine whether specific beneficial effects of playfulness might be more prevalent in those who can access serious playfulness.[16] The complexity allowed for by this concept together with the *Intellectual* facet of playfulness strengthens its potential in a coaching context. The move away from seeing playfulness as propensity to play requires further development of our understanding of what play, especially for/ by adults, can be at different levels (both the different layers of the Onion and within each layer), for example *Intellectual* playfulness as a propensity to play with ideas. We hope that our humble Be Playful Onion Model goes even a little towards this.

Coming back to psychological levels, looking at OLIW and the idea of serious playfulness, we could ask ourselves the same questions about our environment, behaviour, and skills/capabilities as we had asked for the outer layer of the Onion. We might also ask ourselves:

- *What are our values?*
- *What are our beliefs especially around playfulness and coaching conversations?*
- *How recently have we considered these?*
- *Are they facilitating or obstructing our ability to find a playful mindset and heartset?*

5.3.1 Fireside Chat with Professor René Proyer

What sparked your interest in embarking on research into playfulness?

I was interested in humour and laughter. My starting point was studying the overlap among, for example, humour and playfulness. After seeing that there wasn't much literature available on playfulness in adults, I decided to carry out research myself where I could see gaps, starting with the measurement of playfulness and learning more about its distinctiveness from related traits.

What are your key insights into playfulness based on your research?

Fun and entertainment are important characteristics of being playful. However, there is more to playfulness; for example, there is intellectual playfulness or adults use playfulness to manage social relationships. Hence, playfulness probably requires a differentiated perspective.

Do you see playfulness as something which we can learn (or perhaps re-learn)?

I think we can learn to be more playful (for example, using playfulness in certain situations) or to be more aware of playfulness in our lives. Whether this makes us more playful or not is probably only of secondary importance. However, there are many areas in our lives in which we can capitalise on playfulness. One might think of examples such as making learning more interesting and/or engaging, or as a leadership skill when working with teams.

Do you have any advice on developing our own playfulness and enabling others to be more playful?

Allowing for playfulness in one's daily life (sounds easy and trivial, but I think it's neither easy nor trivial), we found that people experienced themselves as being more playful after they observed for one week how many playful incidents they experienced during each day (irrespective of whether they were playful themselves, observed something playful in others, had a playful idea, and so forth). They were asked to reflect about their day and write down that day's number of playful incidents each evening. As a result of the study, we suggest that this makes people more aware of how much playfulness and opportunities to be playful they experience and potentially this also helps them to engage more with play-fulness. A further point that I'd like to mention (in particular in the con-text of coaching) is authenticity. There are many types of playfulness. Don't forget that your clients can also be playful internally. Having a playful thought or idea that might or might not be shared with others is as much playful as engaging in wordplay with another person. Exploring individual paths to playfulness and its many expressions is important. More authentic expressions may be more beneficial to your client.

Where do you think future research into playfulness might be headed?

From a research perspective, we still know comparatively little about playfulness in adults and there are many areas for future research. My lab will work on a model for playfulness in work settings over the next few years. We want to see whether the facets of the OLIW model suffice in the work context, or whether others are probably more important, and what outcomes this might lead to. I also think that more research is needed on potential negative outcomes of playfulness. For example, we found that *Light-hearted and Whimsical* playfulness are not in all cases posi-tive predictors of relationship satisfaction. Doing more research in this field will help with a better understanding of playfulness. Finally, further research in the field of personality development and how playfulness can help people cope (for example, when thinking about imposter syndrome or work-related stress) is needed.

What's your personal favourite expression of playfulness?

Intellectual playfulness. I also like Hugo Rahner's notion of Ernstheiterkeit (serious cheerfulness) as a core characteristic of the homo ludens.

René Proyer is a professor of Psychological Assessment and Differential Psychology at the Martin-Luther-University Halle-Wittenberg (MLU), Germany. He completed his master's thesis at the University of Vienna in Austria and his PhD and habilitation thesis at the University of Zurich, Switzerland. He is particularly interested in the study of individual differences variables such as playfulness in terms of their basic structure, measurement, and potential malleability. He currently serves as president of the European Association of Psychological Assessment (EAPA) and is Vice Dean of the Philosophical Faculty I at MLU.

Also within this middle layer of the model is the place where the 'doing' and 'being' merge in the expression of playfulness. We listed some of the qualities underpinning playfulness in coaching in Chapter 3. It is in this space that we are expressing these qualities through our body, heart, mind in our presence and the questions we ask or tools/activities we offer and hold the space for. Here then, some of the ways we are expressing playfulness in this middle layer are by:

- 'Doing' intent (in service of the client)
- 'Doing' kindness
- 'Doing' respect
- 'Doing' compassion
- 'Doing' childlike wonder and curiosity
- 'Doing' spaciousness and willingness to be in uncertainty
- 'Doing' groundedness
- 'Doing' curiosity
- 'Doing' genuine interest, non-judgment
- 'Doing' a degree of levity
- 'Doing' exploration
- 'Doing' fluidity
- 'Doing' authenticity
- 'Doing' vulnerability.

5.4 The Heart of the Onion – Playful Way of Being

We are now moving towards the inner core of the Onion and a playful way of being. You may find it helpful to bring to mind again the Dalai Lama and the late Archbishop Desmond Tutu (or other examples you relate to). We are acutely aware that we are in part trying to explain one nebulous concept 'playfulness' by relying on another, 'way of being'. Bear with us, as we try to bring some granularity to this idea of 'way of being'. Let's turn for a moment to Abraham Maslow's work on self-actualisation (in a nutshell, becoming the best version of yourself) in which he defined transcendence as:

> The very highest and most inclusive or holistic levels of human conscious-ness, behaving and relating, as ends rather than means, to oneself, to sig-nificant others, to human beings in general, to other species, to nature and to the cosmos.[17]

As an aside, Scott Barry Kaufman in his book *Transcend*[18] picks up Maslow's unfinished theory and integrates Maslow's ideas with the latest research on building blocks of a life well lived including creativity, purpose, connection, attachment, and love.

According to Maslow, one of the marks of the self-actualized individual is a higher frequency of peak experiences[19] of which associated qualities include playfulness. In his work, he made the distinction between 'doing' and 'being' so for example, in the context of love, he made the distinction between 'D-love' ('deficiency love', representing 'needing love') and 'B-love' ('love for the being of another person' representing 'unneeding love').[20] Although, unfortunately, Maslow does not seem to have considered the idea of playfulness in depth, in *Toward a Psychology of Being*,[21] he does describe B-playfulness. He wrote:

> It is very hard to describe this B-playfulness since the English language falls far short here (as in general it is unable to describe the 'higher' subjective experiences). It has a cosmic or a godlike, good-humored quality, certainly transcending hostility of any kind. It could as easily be called happy joy, or gay exuberance or delight. It has a quality of spilling over as of richness or surplus (not D-motivated). It is existential in the sense that it is an amusement or delight with both the smallness (weakness) and the largeness (strength) of the human being, transcending the dominance-subordinance polarity. It has a certain quality of triumph in it, sometimes perhaps also of relief. It is simultaneously mature and childlike.

Here again, we have this idea of playfulness being simultaneously mature and childlike. It is the embodiment of this playful outlook on life and the world around us, the 'state of mind, an attitude, a spirit' as Di Gammage puts it[22] and we'd add a quality of lightness (with groundedness), spaciousness, authenticity and presence in the moment, a certain quality of mindset and heartset which we are trying to describe by a 'way of being'. It involves working on rejecting the deep-seated messaging that many of us have absorbed since early childhood, that there is a time and place for play and it is not within the serious world of work or adulthood for the most part. It also involves examining our underlying philosophy with questions such as:

- *How do we make sense of life?*
- *How do we hold existentialism? Or do we? If not, what else?*
- *What's our view on human potential?*
- *What is our belief system and how does it affect how we show up and 'are' in the world and in our work?*

Indeed, the pioneering play researcher Brian Sutton-Smith suggested that '*the opposite of play ... is not a present reality or work, it is vacillation, or worse, it is depression*' because play involves '*the willful belief in acting out one's own capacity for the future'.*[23] Dr Stuart Brown explains how play shapes the brain, opens the imagination and invigorates the soul.[24]

Why is this relevant to coaching? As we considered in Chapter 2, coaching, seen through the lens of postmodernism, such as Bachkirova's complex adaptive system perspective.[25] sees the self of the coach as the main instrument for coaching and the good use of self as an instrument as integral to coaching development. Seen in this way, the quality of coaching is dependent on diverse influences including the characteristics of the coach and client, the many nuances of the coaching relationship and the significant role of contextual factors.[26] The selves of the coach and the client are not fixed; they are constantly fluctuating in the process of interactions and subject to wider influences[27] with relationship a key ingredient in coaching outcomes rather than any specific coaching tool, intervention or models used.[28] Christian van Nieuwerburgh in his book *An Introduction to Coaching Skills*[29] also makes this distinction between applying coaching tools and your way of being as a coach. If we take the postmodernist view that the self of the coach is the main instrument for coaching, we believe that being able to access playfulness and doing so with awareness and reflection deepens the offering which we can make to our clients' development (as well as our own). It's quite an ephemeral concept and we'll try to capture practical examples throughout the book.

To reflect on how much space our way of being creates for playfulness, these are some of the questions we might ask ourselves:

- *Who am I?*
- *How do I define myself?*
- *How do others define me?*
- *How do I see myself?*
- *How do others see me?*
- *What is my outlook on life?*
- *Does this have openings for playfulness?*
- *What are the underpinning beliefs of my coaching philosophy?*
- *Can I make space for playfulness in these?*
- *What possibilities of playfulness can I nurture in my chosen coaching approach/ tools?*

Playful Moment

This might be a good time to take a break for a Playful Moment. Also, you might want to quickly check out your Barometer of Playfulness levels before and after.

5.5 Reflections on the Be Playful Onion Model

As a result of her MSc research and as a precursor to our Be Playful Onion model, Stephanie proposed a working definition of playfulness in coaching in her *International Coaching Psychology Review* article as:

> a quality of thought and interaction unlimited by associations with fun which emerges from and deepens the coaching relationship, is rooted in authenticity and mindful presence and encompasses a cognitive attitude towards exploration, supporting shifts in perspective.[30]

One way of looking at the Onion is that as we move through the outer to the inner layers, it can represent the spectrum of what the words 'play' and 'playfulness' attempt to capture – moving from 'doing' (the act of play) represented by the outer layer and gradually moving to 'being' (a playful stance, way of being in the world, both mindset and heartset) represented by the inner layer or core. Bridging these two are expressions of playfulness and as we move closer to the core, the qualities required include curiosity and humility embodied by a growth mindset and comfort with 'quality fails' (more of these later in Part II).

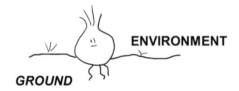

GROUND   ENVIRONMENT

Let's go back for a moment to why our Onion is still growing in the ground. Its roots represent our groundedness, presence, steadiness, and confidence (which also enable us to hold silence, discomfort – ours and our clients, and be in a place of not knowing). This groundedness keeps us and our client (and if we are working with groups/teams, our clients), from getting carried away with playfulness, for example getting untethered or letting the dark side of humour come out (more of which in Chapters 8 and 9). If we zoom out, we can see the landscape within which our Onion grows; the environmental conditions which are necessary for playfulness to arise and flourish within coaching. Here, we mean conditions such as the strength of the coach-client relationship and the level of trust and safety (in teams/groups, this will include psychological safety), authenticity, and mindful presence, the mindset and heartset of the coach and client and the agreed 'rules of play'. As the Onion grows in the right conditions, so does the capacity for playfulness and the myriad of ways in which it manifests.

Silence is better than unmeaning words.

Pythagoras (c. 570 BC – c. 496 BC)

With awareness, the coach can assess and possibly adjust the landscape and move along the different layers of the Onion, deciding what is appropriate with particular clients in particular moments in particular contexts. An unoriginal but helpful metaphor is the jazz musician, who, having mastered the fundamentals through experimentation and practice, learns the ability, in time, to co-create original work in the moment. This idea is embodied by Shuhari, a Japanese martial arts concept which describes the three stages of learning; roughly translated as 'first learn, then detach, and finally transcend'.

It's important to note that you can be operating on all three levels simultaneously. The *Bob and the Daffodils* story in The Playfulness Scrapbook is a lovely illustration of this. Equally, you can be playful on just one or two levels of the Onion during a coaching session. If you are coaching solely in the outer layer 'play', for effective playfulness in coaching, it still needs to be offered authentically. While you can offer it as an experiment and hold it lightly if it fails, you still need to have sufficient confidence in that offer to retain the client's trust and your credibility. In our fireside chat, Professor Proyer advocated acknowledging and working with the playfulness preference of individuals. In the coaching context, that involves a sensitivity to how and in what way playfulness can best support our work together. What playfulness is more authentic for our clients and us, being flexible around that rather than just assuming that our preference is necessarily the same as our clients. It doesn't mean that we are necessarily stuck on a level; we have noticed that our own playfulness can fluctuate depending on the relational context. With some people, we easily slip into certain kinds of playfulness while with others, we can have trouble accessing playfulness at all, or if we do, it might be on a different level in the Be Playful Onion Model. The next chapter gives some clues as to why this might be.

Right, the Onion has done enough heavy lifting for now, let's leave it for a while.

5.6 What's Fun Got to Do With It?

You'll have noticed that in the original working definition which Stephanie proffered above, in line with the idea of serious playfulness, playfulness in coaching was suggested as not necessarily being tied to having fun. However, ask someone about playfulness or play and, in our experience, more often than not it is associated with fun. While we do think that there can be a strong link, and indeed Catherine Price in her book *The Power of Fun*[31] lists the three components of fun as playfulness, connection, and flow, we don't think that playfulness must always be or lead to fun and this is supported by Proyer's concept of serious playfulness. As we've seen, the OLIW model was a big step towards seeing playfulness as a multi-faceted concept and, together with Professor Proyer's and others' further research aims to drill down into the specificity of playfulness (in other words, untangling it from fun, humour, flow, and creativity to name a few). There is still much to discover and fuzzy and overlapping spaces (like a big, colourful Venn diagram) remain. Again, as coaches, while we are fascinated by the theory, in practice, we'd suggest it's not as important to be granular and specific as it is to have an expansive awareness.

What's more, we certainly appreciate the value of having fun whether in a 1:1 context or in groups for a myriad of reasons, not least to experience positive emotions, support well-being as well as to help us connect with others and deepen relationships (both of which of course have knock-on effects for our thriving and effectiveness at work). We are writing this nearly two years into a global pandemic and are both aware of a longing for fun in the broader systems – be it home, work or socially. Both for this reason and because of the fuzzy spaces, we'll look at positive emotions, humour, laughter, and fun in subsequent chapters.

5.7 Conclusion

In their article about coaching maturity which referred to Keats' rainbow.[32] David Clutterbuck and David Megginson suggest that the most liberating mindset for a mature coach is the systemic eclectic mindset. Such coaches, they write, have a very wide array of ways of working and a toolkit amassed from many sources, both within coaching and from very different worlds. They have integrated this into a self-aware, personalised way of being with the client. They exhibit an intelligent, sensitive ability to select a broad approach, and within that approach, appropriate tools and techniques, which meet the particular needs of a particular client at a particular time, relating to what Webb[33] calls coaching for wisdom. Within this context, we see the ability to access playfulness and to enable the client(s) to do so too as a rich source of enriching the systemic eclectic coaching mindset.

What we've found both in Stephanie's original research and in research for this book is that unsurprisingly, the lack of consensus in the literature as to what playfulness is is reflected by the growing number of coaches we've spoken to. Nevertheless, or perhaps because of this, we offer our Be Playful Onion Model as a useful framework for reflection. *Lighthearted*, *Whimsical* or *Other-directed* playfulness (from the OLIW model), reflect the layperson's understanding and predominant emphasis in the relatively small body of available literature on playfulness more generally and in coaching. Our Onion idea developed after we had spoken to many of our Storytellers, so we didn't offer it to them for reflection and consideration. However, our experience of speaking with not just our Storytellers but coaches more generally about playfulness and introducing the multiple facets and types of playfulness including *Intellectual* and serious playfulness, is that the result for those who didn't already see their work as containing playfulness was a widening of their reflection with many appreciating how much playfulness was in fact part of their coaching approach, with some struggling to differentiate it from their coaching itself. Reflection and self-awareness alongside supervision are keys to coach development and effective coaching. If we are missing or overlooking something by being unaware of playfulness in its many guises or the part it plays in our coaching or haven't specifically reflected on that aspect of our practice and the implications, then we feel we are missing an opportunity to learn and develop and enrich our coaching tapestry. We hope our little Onion helps.

Perhaps it struck you in the conversation with Professor Proyer above that he said the future holds more research into whether the OLIW model suffices in the work context or whether there are other facets which are equally or more important and he was curious as to what outcomes this might lead to. Such research has the potential to have considerable implications for playfulness in coaching (and we raise our hands with humility and suggest that the relational element of playfulness deserves further exploration too).

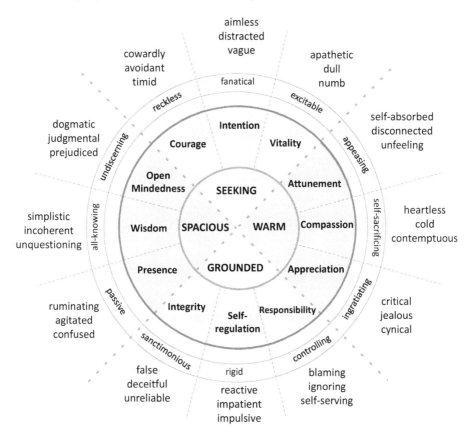

Figure 5.3 Character Compass Model

In our conversation with Graham Lee, he started to bounce around some thoughts about how playfulness might show up in relation to his Character Compass Model which is explained in his book *Breakthrough Conversations*. In brief, the model is designed as a practical basis 'for exploring how conversations can be used to cultivate character habits of being one's best self; to provide a basis for identifying strengths and gaps in character habits and for prioritising specific habits that clients wish to develop in conversational contexts'.[34] Given that Graham puts playfulness right at the top of his ladder of capabilities for facilitating change[35] ('converting insights and ideas into practical achievable outcomes'), we thought it would be fun and thought-provoking to start to think about what might emerge if we played around with integrating the Be Playful Onion and Character Compass Models.

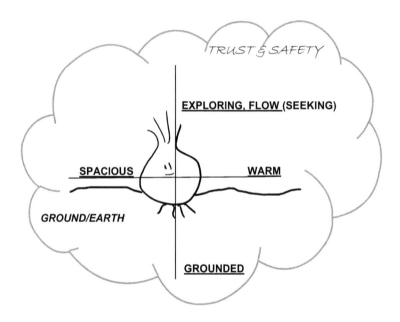

Figure 5.4 The Onion and the Compass

Graham explained to us that since finishing his book, he has adapted the model slightly. As you can see above, it has four cardinal directions of character: Spacious and Warm, Grounded and Seeking. He has since thought of replacing 'Seeking' with 'Exploring' and during our conversation he reflected that perhaps 'Flow' would be even more apt and perhaps playfulness sits somewhere in this mix between Flow and Exploring. In all of us, whether in leadership, coaching or life, there's a part of us which needs to explore, seek, look outwards, find energy, have the courage to try out things, take risks, all of which can be seen as inherently playful. However, we also need, at the same time, to be grounded in qualities like integrity, self-regulation, and responsibility. Graham reflected a paradox that all three of us experience in practice:

> I think that's true about coaching actually in that, as we play with play, there's a bit of us that's saying 'Oh, hang on, am I serving my client? Is this indulgent for me or in this am I holding in mind what they really wanted to get out of this particular session? And am I tuned in to what their emotional energy is as I play?

In our Be Playful Onion Model, the Onion is still growing in the ground, representing groundedness, presence, steadiness and confidence and the environment in which the Onion is growing contains trust and safety, which are both necessary for (adaptive) playfulness. We love the added complexity of seeing this in light of the Character Compass Model where Grounded and Flow (Exploring or Seeking in the original model) and Warmth and Spaciousness hold the system in which playfulness (itself multi-faceted and multi-layered) is floating. We told Graham that we have started playing with the two models and he noted that the key thing about the Character Compass is that it is intended to capture the range of qualities we need to be at our best in life. Linking this to play, he suggests we could say:

- *Being Grounded ensures that the play in coaching is respectful and relevant to the work of development (namely, not a diversion to avoid something uncomfortable)*
- *Being Seeking ensures that the play is inviting the client to step towards their developmental frontier with courage, energy, and purpose*
- *Being Spacious ensures that the play is expansive, invitational, and open and so ripe with possibility*
- *Being Warm ensures that the play is emotionally sensitive, appreciative, and self-compassionate.*

We had our conversation with Graham when this book was already quite advanced (and we've come back to this chapter to add this in), so we haven't explored the inter-relationship of the two models in the pages which follow. For now, we are letting these models percolate in our minds (and hearts and bodies) to see what will evolve and what can be applied to reflection and practice as a result. We hope this little post-script might also give you food for thought and we've included a Character Compass with Playfulness Experiment in The Playfulness Scrapbook.

Notes

1 Martin, R. & Ford, T. (2018). *The psychology of humor: an integrative approach.* Academic Press, p220.
2 Hardingham, A. (2004) *The Coach's Coach.* CIPD.
3 Proyer, R. (2014). A Psycho-Linguistic Approach For Studying Adult Playfulness: A Replication and Extension Toward Relations With Humor. *The Journal of Psychology,* 148(6), 717–735.
4 Proyer, R. T. (2017). A new structural model for the study of adult playfulness: Assessment and exploration of an understudied individual differences variable. *Personality and Individual Differences,* 108, 113–122. Copyright ScienceDirect, Elsevier (2017).
5 Shen, X., Chick, G. & Zinn, H. (2014). Validating the Adult Playfulness Trait Scale (APTS): An Examination of Personality, Behavior, Attitude, and Perception in the Nomological Network of Playfulness. *American Journal of Play,* 6(3), 345–369.
6 *Ibid,* Proyer, R. (2017).
7 cf. Proyer, R. (2012). Development and initial assessment of a short measure for adult playfulness: The SMAP. *Personality and Individual Differences,* 53(8), 989–994.
8 Brauer, K., Proyer, R. & Chick, G. (2021). Adult playfulness: An update on an understudied individual differences variable and its role in romantic life. *Social and Personality Psychology Compass,* 15(4), p.e12589.
9 Proyer, R. & Jehle, N. (2013). The basic components of adult playfulness and their relation with personality: The hierarchical factor structure of seventeen instruments. *Personality and Individual Differences,* 55(7), 811–816.
10 *Ibid,* Proyer, R. (2017).
11 Proyer, R. & Brauer, K. (2018). Exploring adult Playfulness: Examining the accuracy of personality judgments at zero-acquaintance and an LIWC analysis of textual information. *Journal of Research in Personality,* 73, 12–20.
12 cf. Proyer & Ruch (2011); *Ibid,* Proyer & Jehle (2013).
13 Rahner, H. (2008). *Der spielende Mensch* [Person at play] (11th ed.). Johannes. (orig. published 1948).
14 O'Connell, K., Gerkovich, M., Bott, M., Cook, M. & Schiffman, S. (2000). Playfulness, arousal-seeking and rebelliousness during smoking cessation. *Personality and Individual Differences,* 29(4), 671–683.
15 Proyer, R. & Rodden, F. (2013). Is the Homo Ludens Cheerful and Serious at the Same Time? An Empirical Study of Hugo Rahner's Notion of Ernstheiterkeit. *Archive for the Psychology of Religion,* 35(2), 213–231.
16 *Ibid,* Proyer & Rodden (2013).
17 Maslow, A. (1971). *Farther Reaches of Human Nature.* Viking Press, p269.
18 Kaufman, S.B. (2020). *Transcend: The New Science of Self-Actualization.* TarcherPerigee.
19 Maslow, A. (1968). *Toward a Psychology of Being* (2nd ed.). D. Van Nostrand Company.
20 *Ibid,* Maslow (1968, p47).
21 *Ibid,* Maslow (1968, p123).

22 Gammage, D. (2017). *Playful Awakening: Releasing the Gift of Play in Your Life.* Jessica Kingsley Publishers, p45.

23 Sutton-Smith, B. (1997) *The Ambiguity of Play. Harvard Business School Press*, p198.

24 Brown, S. (2009). *Play: How it shapes the brain, opens up the imagination, and invigorates the soul.* Penguin Books.

25 Bachkirova, T. (2016). The Self of the Coach: Conceptualization, Issues and Opportunities for Practitioner Development. *Consulting Psychology Journal: Practice and Research*, 68(2), p143.

26 Cox, E. (2003). The Contextual Imperative: Implications for coaching and mentoring. *International Journal of Evidence-Based Coaching*, 1(1), 9–22. Cox, E., Bachkirova, T. & Clutterbuck, D. (2014). Theoretical traditions and coaching genres: Mapping the territory. *Advances in Developing Human Resources*, 16(2), 127–138.

27 Bachkirova, T. & Smith, C.L. (2015). From competencies to capabilities in the assessment and accreditation of coaches. *International Journal of Evidence Based Coaching and Mentoring*, 13(2), 123–140.

28 De Haan, E. (2008). *Relational coaching: journeys towards mastering one-to-one learning.* Wiley. Hall, L. (2013). *Mindful Coaching: How Mindfulness can Transform Coaching Practice.* Kogan Page.

29 Van Nieuwerburgh, C. (2014). *An Introduction to Coaching Skills: A Practical Guide.* Sage.

30 Wheeler, S. (2020). An exploration of playfulness in coaching. *International Coaching Psychology Review*, 15(1), 45.

31 Price, C. (2022). *The Power of Fun.* Penguin Random House.

32 Clutterbuck, D. & Megginson, D. (2011). Coach maturity: An emerging concept. In: Wildflower, L. (ed.), *The Handbook of knowledge-based coaching: from theory to practice.* John Wiley and Sons, 299–314.

33 Webb, P. (2008). Coaching for Wisdom: Enabling Wise Decisions. In Drake DB, Brennan, D & Gørtz, K (Eds). *The philosophy and practice of coaching.* Wiley.

34 Lee, G. (2021). *Breakthrough Conversations for Coaches, Consultants and Leaders.* Routledge, p106.

35 *Ibid*, Lee (2021, p16).

6
Our Neurobiology and Playfulness in Coaching

In this chapter we:

- Tell you some stories which we will come back to during this and the next couple of chapters
- Invite you to embrace both complexity and simplicity
- Learn about the turtle and its relevance to Porges' *Polyvagal Theory*
- Consider the implications for coaching
- Explore two theories about how our state impacts our creativity and thinking
- Consider Intentional Change Theory
- Examine how all of the above interplay and their relevance to playfulness in coaching
- Refer to Graham Lee's work on body-brain state awareness
- Give our view of the implications for practice from the perspective of the coach and the client
- End with reflective questions to help take the theory into your development and practice

6.1 Once Upon a Time ...

We have mentioned our nervous systems, emotions and humour a few times and we're going to look at the role they play in playfulness in coaching in more detail soon. Before we go any further, let's pause for a few stories. We will come back to these in the next few chapters.

Once upon a time, Mary, although an experienced and accomplished professional, is relatively new to coaching. She's learned the theory at an excellent coach training provider and has embarked on coaching professionally. She understands the power and potential of coaching and passed her coach training

DOI: 10.4324/9781003090847-7

with flying colours and yet still … before every session she feels nervous, worrying whether she will add value to the conversation. She's uncomfortable with the not-knowing of what will emerge in a session so prefers to plan ahead, have several tools to hand which she will use, and her focus is mainly on the coaching process. In another room in another place at another time, Simon, a very experienced coach is about to work with a new leadership team for the first time. They have a reputation as not suffering fools lightly and a good result with this client is likely to lead to lots more work for Simon. He feels nervous and hopes that his deodorant is working …

Once upon another time, Monday morning and the weekly team meeting. Your to-do list seems to have grown exponentially since Friday evening and your heart sinks. For now, another two hours in a meeting which you think you can ill-afford just add to your feelings of being on the back foot. The meetings would be generally seen by most of the team as pleasant enough, if their diaries weren't full to bursting, but not productive and this causes stress given the unrelenting workload. Although John, the team leader, enjoys these meetings as a time to chat and fill the team in, the others get increasingly uncomfortable. Part of the problem is that John doesn't see that he's alone in seeing these long meetings as valuable and the team does not feel they can raise this with him. As time goes on, frustration grows, and team members start seeing the meetings as indicative of a wider feeling of not being listened to …

Once upon yet another time, the senior leadership team has come together with their co-coaches to discuss the imminent merger of their company and how best to lead the organisation through this period of uncertainty. They are all very worried, though trying hard not to show it, for their own futures, the people whom they are responsible for, and about what lies in store for the organisation they have worked so hard for. In another place, at another time (you get the picture), a community group is coming together with their coach to discuss how they can address the climate crisis locally. There is a general sense of overwhelm as different aspects of the crisis are being discussed, with passions running high and a sense of fear overshadowing hope …

And finally, once upon a time, a team is nearing the end of a two-year project. With the deadline looming, there's still lots to do, but it is possible within the timeframe (just). Everyone is exhausted but focused on the task at hand. Thinking is very much in the convergent rather than divergent stage with loose ends being tied up and finishing touches being applied. A new member of the team notices something which could improve the project and a time extension is possible. It would be possible to deliver this, but it requires divergent thinking and a fresh bout of energy. Six months earlier this would have been embraced by the rest of the team, but now …

These are a few stories from the many we could have picked by way of example of the sort of situations you might come across. We're going to look at these through the lenses of the impact of body-brain states, emotions, and humour. Of course, it's artificial to think of wearing just one pair of glasses at a time; in reality you'd be wearing all three at once (and probably looking a little silly).

6.2 Honouring Complexity

'I would not give a fig for the simplicity this side of complexity; but I would give my life for the simplicity the other side of complexity'. It seems to be unclear whether the quote came from Oliver Wendell Holmes Jr (former US Supreme Court Justice) or Sr (physician, poet, and polymath) and whether he would give you anything he had; one of his arms or his life for simplicity on the other side of complexity, but let's go with the sentiment.

Play and playfulness is at once incredibly simple; you know it when you see it or experience it but start digging a little deeper and what you encounter is complexity. Our aim is to get to the other side of complexity, to equip those inviting playfulness into their coaching with an understanding of what might be happening and in doing so, through awareness, create more space for deliberate and informed playfulness (alongside, of course, intuitive and spontaneous playfulness) in the service of our clients.

When we say, 'what might be happening', in the next few chapters, we're going to concentrate particularly on our body-brain systems (and what that looks like in a relational space), emotions, and humour. By necessity, we are writing about this in quite a linear way, but remember, we are talking about systems, and we want to pause for a moment to emphasise the complexity and interrelationship of the various things that might be going on internally and externally often simultaneously when we invite playfulness into our work. Don't be put off, though. At times we've felt ourselves being overwhelmed by the complexity of the theory and research and it can stand us in good stead (and by extension our clients) to bear this complexity in mind as we come back to the underlying simplicity. With that in mind, let's start by looking at our neurobiology and playfulness.

6.3 Our Neurobiology and Playfulness

Thinking about the various stories in *Once upon a time*, take a moment to imagine yourself in the different situations. How do you feel? How is that showing up in your body? What about your thinking? Do you feel ready to be playful (thinking of the Be Playful Onion Model)? Do you think the others in the stories are ready to be playful or engage or think playfully, imaginatively, or creatively? The stories describe situations where our characters might be experiencing frustration, nervousness, fear, or overwhelm, to name but a few. Are these states conducive to learning and development and behavioural change, supported by playfulness? Even without looking for explanations on a neurobiological level, your instinct and intuition is pretty likely to respond with a firm 'no'. Intuitively we know that these aren't places from which playfulness emerges easily or which support it. Think of a child experiencing broadly similar reactions. Would they be ready to play?

Understanding why we or others might find it difficult to access playfulness and equally, how we can create environments and relationships which support playfulness, can help support our awareness and inform how we show up and our actions. One of the main reasons why such awareness is so important is that as coaches, our aim surely is to take our ego out of our work so that how we are in the coaching space and what we do is motivated purely by what we perceive to be in the service of our clients rather than any of our own needs. We're going to use this idea of taking our ego out of our work with this very specific meaning for the rest of this chapter. On the road to doing this, as far as possible, we need to come out of autopilot or reactivity and bring awareness to what might support or get in the way of this. There are, of course, many potential barriers, for example, transference or when our insecurities are driving our thoughts, feelings, or actions. In this chapter, we're focusing on a particular potential support or barrier, namely what's going on in our (and our clients') body-brain systems. To help navigate this, we're going to take a whistle-stop tour (we promise we'll leave the journey-related metaphors here) through the different states which our body-brain systems might be in and how they influence us. We'll then consider what implications this might have for playfulness in coaching, both from the point of view of the coach, the clients and the impact which they have on each other.

We use the term 'state' in different ways in this book; for this chapter, when we say 'state', we mean the state which the body-brain system is in, and we'll be exploring what these different states are in the next section.

6.3.1 Understanding the Impact of the State We're in

You will of course be aware of fight and flight responses and we're going to have a look at these, together with the other states. If these concepts are familiar to you, you might wish to skip to the next section. Maybe choose a Playful Moment with the extra time you have just found (you're welcome).

Playful Moment

Let's talk about turtles for a moment. You might be surprised that we have something quite significant in common with turtles. In recognising this in his Polyvagal Theory, Stephen Porges had a significant impact on therapy particularly relating to trauma with important implications for coaching including, we think, in the context of playfulness. His theory is complex and while paying homage to its complexity, as we are concerned specifically about its implications for playfulness in coaching, we're going to offer you a simplified summary in the knowledge that there is a wealth of resources in the literature and online for you to explore should you wish and we'll mention a few resources along the way.

In brief, the Polyvagal Theory explains how our defence systems have evolved since the time of our reptilian ancestor which was similar to the turtle in terms of biology. Rather than the brain ruling the roost and determining all of our actions and even emotions, our nervous system, specifically our Autonomic Nervous System (ANS) has a huge part to play. Porges[1] considers the ANS as percolating information up to the brain stem which then passes information to higher brain structures. Its role, essentially, is the detection of risk.

The ANS is made up of two parts, each with opposite effects. The Sympathetic Nervous System (SNS) is the part which jumps into action when your nervous system is unable to detect safety and you switch into fight or flight mode. Physically you can tell when the SNS is activated as your adrenaline flows, your heart beats faster, you might feel a bit shaky, your breathing quickens and is shallower and your palms and elsewhere might start sweating. More than that, you switch into an excited mental state and when this happens, subtle complex memories may become unavailable (that explains the potentially embarrassing blanking when you're put on the spot). In this state, we're more likely to mis-read other people's cues, so a neutral face is more likely to be interpreted as aggressive and a fearful face as angry. The SNS is designed for our protection; to act when confronted with imminent threat with the cost of this being tem-porary cognitive, physical, perceptual, and emotional impairment.

Balancing this out is the Parasympathetic Nervous System (PSN) which takes over once the perceived threat is dissipated and our bodies return to a state of rest and digestion; a state in which we are then able to engage socially. Trying to have a meaningful conversation while adrenaline is coursing through our veins is very challenging if not near impossible. Outward signs that the PNS is activated include regular breathing, regulated body temperature (no more stress induced sweating) and maybe even a rosy glow. This is partly caused by stimulation of the vagus nerve, also known as the vagal nerves, the longest of the cranial nerves and a major component of the PNS. The vagus nerve triggers the release of hormones including oxytocin and vasopressin. It originates in the brain (cranial nerve 10) and travels down your neck and around the digestive system, liver, spleen, pancreas, heart and lungs. The 'tone' of the vagus nerve is key to activating the PNS; if you would like to explore this further, there has been a significant amount of research on the ventral vagal system and its signifi-cance, for instance in emotional regulation, by Porges[2] and others. Prof Dacher Keltner, co-director of the Greater Good Science Center, for example, has researched and generated a wealth of resources including YouTube videos on vagal tone and its links to emotions including compassion, gratitude, and awe.

> **The Autonomic Nervous System:** *is a control system that acts largely uncon-sciously and regulates bodily functions, such as the heart rate, digestion, respiratory rate, pupillary response, urination, and sexual arousal.*[3]
> **The Sympathetic Nervous System:** = SNS = *fight or flight*
> **The Parasympathetic Nervous System:** = PNS = *rest, digest, and social engagement*

(Tip: if you get confused between SNS and PNS, think of **para**medics coming to give care)

Coming back to the PNS, once it is activated, it allows you to be more open to new ideas, emotions, and people, socially engage, think creatively, and consider possibilities for the future,[4] putting you in a better place for deeper understanding, collaboration, learning, and development. All of which sound like fertile ground for playfulness. This is of course, a gross simplification of the complex, interconnected systems working on many levels which have imme-diate implications and cumulative longer-term implications, including for health. Though, as our inner Winnie the Pooh[5] lets out a quiet sigh of relief, for our purposes, we're going to stay on this higher level.

We have then, three circuits co-existing within us that have adapted with our evolution (calling to mind Goldilocks and the Three Bears):

- The oldest, which we share with turtles, responding to life threat: the freeze response, which includes disassociation (introduced by Polyvagal Theory) which might look like withdrawal or non-engagement; then
- The relatively younger one for dealing with danger and risk: the SNS responsible for fight or flight and task focused thinking ('How do I escape from the sabre-toothed tiger which is hot on my heels?'); and finally
- Relatively the youngest one associated with safety: the PNS, responsible for rest and repair, digestion, social engagement, and a more expansive and collaborative way of thinking ('Now that we've escaped and recovered, what shall we draw on the cave walls this evening and how?').

It's worth pointing out that we're not saying that one state is better or worse than any other; they all serve their purpose although problems might of course arise if we find ourselves predominantly or become stuck in one state. Nevertheless, the state which is probably most helpful for our context is the third, when the PNS is activated. Having said that, some forms of playfulness might involve the SNS, for example, a client taking themselves out of their comfort zone into the zone of discomfort and we'll look at this towards the end of the chapter.

6.3.2 Meanwhile, in the Brain...[6]

We've already mentioned a few times that the state that we're in will have an impact on our thinking. Let's turn our attention then to two neural networks: the Default Mode network (DMN) and the Task Positive network (TPN). They are referred to as networks as they activate different parts of the brain during different behaviours. The type of imaging studies (usually fMRI) which are the basis of research in this area measure relative rather than absolute activity, in other words, seeing which network(s) or brain area(s) is more or less active in a given situation and/or for a given person. It merits saying that relevant studies are only roughly indicative of neuronal activity and there are likely to be key differences between behaviours which are not captured by them at all. It's tempting to seek understanding by creating categories of, for example, behaviours, or feelings, and then try to map them onto brain areas/networks/neurons. While this is a perfectly reasonable thing to do, it's important to remember that these categories might not line up accurately with what the brain has evolved to do (for instance, rather than the category of 'creativity', specific behaviours which we might classify as creative). For instance, thinking of putting meat into fire to change its texture, which supports our survival, will be reinforced, and affect the evolution of our brain. These networks then, are perhaps better understood in terms of the behavioural functions that are associated with them rather than categories into which we sort them after the fact. With these caveats in mind, the association of certain networks with outward-looking and inward-looking states is very robust.

> *Task Positive Network* = TPN
> Executive Attention Network and Salience Network are subsets of the TPN
> *Default Mode Network* = DMN

The TPN consists of the brain areas which light up and correlate when you are doing a task (outward focused) and the Executive Attention network is in essence a subset of the TPN which is specifically associated with the deliberate focus of attention on that task. As an aside, the Salience network is the other major subset of the TPN associated with the processing of sensory input relevant to the task. Broadly speaking the TPN is responsible for focused concentration, working memory, learning language, most maths and abstract reasoning tasks, in other words, analytical tasks, problem solving and evaluating choices in order to make a decision. You'll recognise some coaching tools which rely on these no doubt. The other major brain network, the DMN, scans the environment and because of it, we see and are sensitive to others, participate in social engagement, are open to moral reasoning and emotions. You can see that from a coaching perspective, not to mention a balanced approach in life and work, we need both.

6.3.3 Relevance to Coaching

Let's consider how the states and our neural networks are relevant to coaching before we turn our focus on playfulness. Again, intuitively, we think you'll agree that the activation of the PNS system and the impact on our thinking, feeling and behaviour seems most useful out of the three states in a coaching context. We can probably discount the freeze state as being useful (apart from providing potentially useful information)! We can go beyond intuition though as the impact of our states of mind on our coaching is an area which has received attention, for example in the context of mindful coaching.[7] What's more, the effect of states of mind and the activation of different brain networks on the mental state which we are in and how this is relevant to coaching is the basis of Intentional Change Theory.[8] Developed by Richard Boyatzis, Tony Jack, and colleagues, it proposes that 'coaching with compassion' which builds on getting clarity of the client's ideal self is more effective than coaching using a fact based, purely analytical approach for example, 'fixing' weaknesses termed 'coaching for compliance'. They argue that coaching with compassion engages the DMN (parts of which are associated with the PNS) much more frequently than the TPN and also avoids the activation of the SNS as weaknesses and problems are not given the main focus of attention. Where we get excited is that ways in which to activate the PNS include eliciting compassion, mindfulness, and hope (supported by your imagination, for example by imagining your ideal future self) and playfulness.[9] It is likely that these experiences have unique physiological profiles which are being investigated by, for example, monitoring physiological arousal during coaching conversations using the stress hormone cortisol (Howard, 2009[10]) and measuring autonomic activity (Passarelli, 2014[11]). In coaching, this might look like asking a coachee to reflect and develop a personal vision for their ideal self, and their future life and work. Ideal self-related questions can have a spirit of playfulness (Passarelli, 2015[12]). The activated PNS allows a person to be more open to new ideas, emotions and people and consider possibilities for the future. This means that in a way which is appropriate for our client, we can use playfulness both to support our rapport (which can only help to create safety and therefore support the PNS activation) and also to move ourselves and our clients into the state in which they can move towards change and support their change process. Prof Boyatzis and colleagues are garnering support for this theory with experiments involving brain scans of participants taking part in coaching with compassion (eliciting hopes, ideals, and aspirations) versus coaching for compliance with brain scans showing strong and consistent activation of the DMN in compassionate coaching particularly for more than one coaching session.

Not to get too much into the detail here, though it is fascinating, the 'cooperation theory' of brain networks takes a somewhat different approach and, based on research which is starting to give insights into this question, suggests that creative thought involves dynamic interactions between brain systems, with the most compelling finding being that the DMN and TPN (which can show an antagonistic relationship) actually cooperate during creative cognition and artistic performance.[13] Really interesting, for our purposes, is that this hypothesis of network cooperation has 'implications for understanding how brain networks interact to support complex cognitive processes, particularly those involving goal-directed, self-generated thought'.[14] Following the cooperation hypothesis, it would be possible to tailor coaching interventions to facilitate the connections between different networks, in other words, to support creativity (which as seen in previous chapters has overlaps with playfulness) by starting off with inward looking activities and gradually adding outward focus to the mix, slowly increasing the difficulty. Future research might throw further light on such interventions and other explorations and experimentations.

We find it really interesting to consider underlying neurobiology, though our understanding is: that for now, it's probably best to keep a little distance between the discussions of coaching outcomes and relative effectiveness and neurobiology. At present, there is not enough certainty, as far as we understand, to definitely establish and characterise the association of certain patterns of brain activity to effective coaching outcomes. On the other hand, the association of certain coaching approaches with certain outcomes is probably much better characterised at the moment. So, for us in practice, when we are deciding which coaching approach to use, we would base it in partly on what has been shown to work best in the circumstances, without considering in detail the brain regions/networks involved. Our own approaches are very aligned with coaching for compassion, and Intentional Change Theory argues that coaching with compassion is more effective at achieving a flexible mindset and effective outcomes than coaching for compliance. Coaching for compassion also activates the DMN and PNS more effectively/to a larger extent, suggesting that these brain networks may be important in eliciting playfulness, creativity, imagination, mindfulness, and hope. Research is ongoing and perhaps in the future we will be able to custom-build new techniques based on areas of the brain that they activate, but our understanding is that there is still a way to go before the evidence/data is clear enough.

Aside from the relative merits of theories of whether the main neural networks cooperate or compete so to speak, what matters for coaching is whether we and our clients can be in a receptive body-brain state for the conversations and experiences during the coaching process. What's more, we are not just two (or more in the case of team or group coaching) completely independent beings taking part in the coaching process. Instead, the relationship forming the basis of coaching itself is a system. One theory is that our brains operate on an 'open- loop';[15] brains are hardwired to read the emotions of others and at an eye-watering speed of 8 to 40 milliseconds.[16] So not only are our brains constantly picking up on the emotions of others, but this is largely going on at such a speed that we don't even realise we're doing it. Simultaneously, as we know from Polyvagal Theory, the responses of our nervous system which set us off into one of the three different states are triggered below the level of our consciousness. For us as coaches then, this implies that we would do well to be aware of and manage our own state and be aware of and avoid being affected by the state of our clients if it is not supportive of the coaching process and be mindful of this potential effect on ourselves and others when working with teams. This ties in nicely with our approach of seeing playfulness in coaching as a relational as well as an individual construct.

6.3.4 Implications for Playfulness

Why does it serve us (and more importantly our clients of course) to think about states and their potential effects on us (and again, our clients of course) in the context of playfulness? Panksepp, who we'll meet properly in the next chapter, identified brain circuitry dedicated to play that lies deep in the instinctual action apparatus of the mammalian brain.[17] We will not be able to access our PLAY circuitry if we don't feel safe and our SNS is activated. When we do feel sufficiently safe our PNS is activated and we can access higher cortical functions; the more of these we access, the greater our ability for diversity of action, expression, and social engagement, all of which support playfulness. How's this for a fascinating thought: depending on which of the three states we are in, we have a different neural platform for different behaviours and even emotions and thoughts. The ANS is not peripheral to our brain but is connected with it in a bi-directional way, so our visualisations, thoughts, our listening, what our facial muscles are doing, our cognitions (the mental processes involved in gaining knowledge and comprehension through thought, experiences, and our senses) as well as our reactions to other people can be transmitted from our brain to our body as well as our body to our brain. It's a two-way street so to speak.

This is worth emphasising: it is important to appreciate that our feelings are dependent on which physiological state we are in and our states are determined by our ANS. Not only that, but our physiology also colours our perception of the world. The same stimulus can trigger a very different physiological response with different psychological experiences depending on which state our ANS is in. And this is where it gets truly fascinating. Porges invented the term 'neuroception' to convey that when safety, risk or life-threat is detected, it is done so by our body *outside of the realm of our awareness*. In other words, our internal system scans our environment for clues about whether it is safe, poses a risk, or there is imminent threat to our life, and it does so without us being conscious of it. Depending on which it selects, it will trigger the adaptive neural circuits and put us in the place where we can socially engage (necessary for play), or fight/flight (in which we can engage in only certain types of play) or freeze (not very useful for play except perhaps musical statues). Then, when we react in a certain way, we come up with complex narratives *to retrospectively explain what we just experienced*. The story which we tell ourselves might in fact have nothing to do with what just happened in our body-brain system. Let that sink in for a moment. This brings to mind Prof Lisa Feldman-Barrett's (and others) Theory of Emotions which we'll dip into in the next chapter. Now go back to *Once upon a time*, consider the various states that the characters might be in and consider the impact this will have on their ability to engage playfully and their potential influence on others.

All this needs to be seen in the context that our basic biology including the ANS and the chain of processes with which it is involved has not changed significantly since the time when we needed to be constantly alert to threats and danger to life and be able to rest, digest, and socially engage (remember, we're designed to live in groups). Not only that, but the effect of perceived danger and risk on what goes on inside us is not proportionate to the actual objective danger/risk; a difficult situation such as a confrontational conversation (or we'd suggest, for some, being strong-armed into play in a group situation) will trigger the same physiological and neurological reactions as coming across a sabre-toothed tiger. Quite remarkably, this applies not only to actual events but also to an extent to actively remembering an event, for example replaying the experiences in a coaching conversation. Though it is important to add that the thresholds for switching us into the different states aren't set in stone and it's possible to move to a place where your SNS does not activate as readily (for example, through therapy for trauma or learning to meditate).

6.3.5 Bringing it Together: Implications for Playfulness in Coaching?

Let's round up this jaunt through neurobiology and playfulness by considering the possible implications for play and playfulness in our coaching practice. A few things to bear in mind given what we've just explored:

1   Developing the ability to bring awareness of our own state as coach and using self as instrument as well as being curious about the state(s) of our clients, gives us an additional lens through which to appreciate when there are supports for, or barriers to playfulness in our work. By learning to manage our states and helping clients to manage theirs we can increase our capacity for being authentic and agile generally but also specifically in our playfulness.

2   It is potentially helpful to appreciate that sometimes the supports for, or barriers to playfulness are below the level of our conscious awareness; our nervous system is calling the shots.

3   Our nervous systems don't work in isolation; we have an impact on each other. Awareness of this and learning to manage our states brings agility and authenticity to our playfulness.

4   We can take (and help our clients to take) active steps to manage our states rather than being driven by them, making it easier and more likely for playfulness to emerge and be sustained. What's relevant here is not just the immediate circumstances of the coaching session but what is happening (in terms of states) in the wider context for the relevant person.

6.4 Both Client and Coach

If we are not hostages to our nervous systems, then how do we increase our capacity for autonomy both so that our SNS doesn't activate so readily and if it does, to be able to activate the PNS? If we are regularly or chronically stressed or our SNS is otherwise habitually in the driver's seat, it may well impact our ability to work effectively together in the coaching space or engage playfully during our work as well as translating any insights gained into change after-wards (clients) or reflecting and learning from our experience (coach).

We (clients and coaches) can learn to at least be a co-driver with our body-brain systems and eventually take over the wheel. As with most things coaching, awareness is often the first vital step. There are then a range of practical ways of building our capacity to be the driver. ACT (Acceptance Commitment Therapy) uses the metaphor of dropping the anchor; taking time in the day to check in and see what's going on within us. We can use this to get to know our body-brain system and recognise when we're in different states. On a simple level, we can apply principles of mindfulness to 'be' with whatever state we're in; not trying to change it but to acknowledge it, bringing some curiosity and compassion asking things such as: What is my experience now? How am I feeling that? Where in my body? What does that feel like? You might like to breathe into that place. Useful for activating the PNS, there are a wealth of grounding tools available online such as grounding through the five senses (focus on five things you can see, four things you can hear, three things you can touch, two things you can smell and one thing you can taste right now). Deb Dana writes and speaks about practical ways of learning to be the driver of your nervous system, for example, in her book with Stephen Porges *Polyvagal Exercises for Safety and Connection: 50 Client-Centered Practices*.[18]

Another interesting perspective is that how we interpret the activation of our SNS has a major impact on the effect that it has on us. Kelly McGonigal's research focuses on the mind-body connection and how to cultivate resilience and compassion; see, for example, her TedTalk or book, *The Upside of Stress*.[19] For instance, before a coaching engagement, you notice your SNS is activated and rather than saying to yourself, 'Oh no, I'm stressed/nervous/scared!' you can reframe your experience by saying to yourself, 'I'm excited!'. You are experiencing the same physical effects of SNS activation but learning to make it work for you through reframing what is happening.

We've also seen that the 'tone' of the vagus nerve is key to activating the PNS and getting you to a state in which you are able to socially engage, play, and think creatively. The great news is that you can strengthen your vagal tone including through meditation, singing, yoga and relevant for our context, laughter. How gratifying then that you can use playful approaches to help you and your client strengthen your vagal tone and access positive emotions and PNS activation (more on which in the next chapter) to support your work together.

6.5 The Coach

6.5.1 Activating Our PNS

It is liberating to know that we are not at the mercy of emotional contagion and the whims of our ANS. Developing greater self-awareness lets us know if we are heading towards or are already in a state which is unhelpful and there are steps which we can take to help us to enter the social engagement state. Learning this skill and developing the capacity can help us to move beyond what is going on for us in the coaching space to focus on what's in the service of the client and where appropriate, serving this through, or helped by, playfulness. We can also use our awareness of our emotions to check with our clients whether we are mirroring theirs (using the instrument of self). We can do this with curiosity and a degree of lightness in how we ask whether our experience resonates with that of our client and this might open up fruitful avenues of conversation. Working and building on our state awareness and helping our clients to do so supports more authentic, agile and attuned conversations.[20]

As a reminder, to be able to access our own playfulness and invite our clients to do so, we need to be in and stay in the social connectedness state. In turn this means that we need to cultivate an ability to be aware of our own feelings, emotions, moods, and states, and of how our state might be influencing our clients. A detailed consideration of cultivating state awareness and learning how to support clients to observe and manage their states during conversations to support more authentic, agile, and attuned interactions is the basis of Graham Lee's *Breakthrough Conversations*.[21] Professor Boyatzis challenges us coaches to manage our own stress levels so that we don't negatively affect our clients, particularly if we find the coaching session challenging. More specifically, he suggests that we need to have more renewal moments outside of, and during our work. We've often heard of the term 'stress bucket' and in a way, this is our PNS bucket. We need to regularly fill it with playfulness, relaxation, moments of social connection, activities such as mindfulness or yoga, savouring positive emotions such as love and awe (you will find your own bucket-fillers) in order for us to access our PNS especially when those around us have their SNS activated.

6.5.2 Accessing Playfulness in Coaching

Put yourself into Mary's shoes in the *Once upon a time story*. Even if you are an experienced coach, we bet you can well remember the nervousness before or during your first coaching sessions. Will I ask the right things? What if the client doesn't see any benefit? What value am I adding? We are sure you'll relate. Going back to stepping beyond our ego (in the sense of being driven by what is going on for our body-brain system and how this is driving us), we need to learn to manage our reactions to feelings and thoughts such as Mary is experiencing so that we can influence our states. By implication, this will impact the neural networks which we can access which in turn will enable us to access playfulness. If not, our concerns might well take centre stage or at least a strong supporting role, getting in the way of playfulness rather than fade into the background.

It's not just a point of reflection and development for novice coaches. We have both recently completed a longer complex adaptive systemic team coaching course and an experience in that context made us think about how ego can be a barrier to playfulness. We were assigned to different practice groups and, during a session, were role playing and working through some of the systemic complexity involved in team coaching. Stephanie: I noticed that as I was trying to find a foothold in the material that we were working with, feelings that were coming up for me included confusion, uncertainty, and a fear of being judged by others and coming up short (of course this was my own story as the group was open to learning and very supportive). I noticed that on some level, I was reacting to the perceived 'threat' of the situation and my state reflected this. I noticed a feeling of heaviness, wanting to do the role play 'right' (yes, I know, silly) which also narrowed my thinking. This heaviness was the opposite of the perspective and lightness needed for playfulness. At the beginning of the session, I had updated the group on the progress of this book, so we had spoken about playfulness and our facilitator encouraged us to bring a playful and creative approach to the material we were working with. Later, immersed in the session, I noticed that I wasn't feeling at all playful and the way that I was thinking (logic, problem-solving, task focused and ego-driven) was getting in the way of my capacity for experimentation and learning. In the moment, there was too much going on for me to manage my state as much as I would have liked, which would have freed me up to be more playful. I recognised though, that what was also impacting me was the general level of stress that I was experiencing at that time (diary too full, pending deadlines, the inevitable juggling of family and work, and so on). Through recognising that I was tired and overworked and needed to find more rest and connection, I filled my PNS bucket in the following days through practical steps like getting an early night, and renewal moments to enable me to access playfulness in my work and keep me going until there was an opportunity for much needed proper rest and play.

Let's switch to the story in *Once upon a time* of the team approaching a project deadline. The stress of the impending deadline and exhaustion of most of the team members is likely to have an impact on the readiness of their SNS to be activated or stay activated. As we look at in Part II, we need to tend to the basics if we want playfulness to land and flourish and it will stand us in good stead to be sensitive with regard to the timing of our invitations for playfulness and what is going on for our clients in their wider context so that we can discern whether playfulness in appropriate and be agile as to its form.

Let's jump now to a team coaching engagement in some of the other scenarios in *Once upon a time* and imagine a particularly 'messy' moment (which are inevitable) in a team coaching session. It is likely that in these moments when the co-coaches are sitting with uncertainty and ego-driven fears of judgment and so on, that the team will also either feel the uncertainty which complexity provokes and/or pick up on the coaches state. As coaches, you can see the need, we're sure, to pay attention to our state during coaching, and more generally, and to take practical steps to nurture ourselves so that we can remain in and access PNS activation when it is of service to our clients. This will allow us, in that moment with the team, to have the capacity to step beyond what is happening to us, and our needs, and to bring a gentle lightness and wider perspective to the complexity and opportunities for learning which the team coaching brings. From this place, we can then suggest and explore playful ways in which we can support the team to begin to make sense of the complexity, collaborate, be creative and to move forward.

6.5.3 Different Perceptions of Safety

If, in simple terms, we need to feel sufficiently safe (in the broadest sense including our body-brain system) to engage in playfulness then it's vital to appreciate that of course we all have different perceptions of safety. Imagine you are Simon in the *Once upon a time* story. You might be nervous about working with the new team but once you get into the flow of your work, you are comfortable with the discomfort associated with the not-knowing of inviting playfulness to the work. Each team member will have their own levels of safety within the group, depending on many factors including the level of psychological safety, other team dynamics, their own thoughts, beliefs and experiences around playfulness, and the wider context. Remember too that just recalling a stressful experience when it didn't feel safe to play, will also have an impact. What might feel to Simon like a safe invitation to play might have a different effect on others in the room.

Some of the team may experience a feeling of safety; they are ready to socially engage and access the more developed areas of their brains for collaboration and creativity. Others might experience anxiety, and others might freeze. All are having a psychophysiological (combining psychological and physiological processes) reaction to being in that environment and situation, much of it under their level of awareness. Add to this that they may have had a difficult experience previously, for example, taking part in a team building exercise which left them feeling very much *not* part of the team, so their ANS could react to the 'danger' based on their previous experience. Further additions to the mix are any formative and learning experiences during childhood, young adulthood, work, and different systems. This cocktail leads them to think, feel and behave in a certain way. They then try to construct a narrative for what just happened, so the first person who was calm might think to themselves, 'Great, let me get going', the second, 'Don't ask me to experiment, I am not a playful person, I never have been' and the third 'I can't even think, just leave me alone, this is just not for me'. The likelihood of different levels of safety felt by members of the group/team during different stages of the session adds to the complicated mix. We can look at this with curiosity and as a rich opportunity for learning (ours and our clients') rather than as an overwhelming challenge. We'll explore this further in Chapter 9 and let's take a leaf from Gestalt's book and remember that everything is data. If we can hold whatever is happening with curiosity and a degree of lightness and perspective, the different reactions to our invitation to playfulness (and the reactions to those reactions) might reveal very useful information about, for example, the team dynamics or level of psychological safety.

Armed with awareness of states and their impact on playfulness (and other things of course), Simon can reflect-in-action and the questions he might ask might include: Am I nervous? What do I need to do to tend to myself and my state? What's going on for members of the group? What's going on in terms of neuroception? Do they look comfortable enough to play (remembering that we like a bit of discomfort as that's where learning happens)? Do I need to do anything to help the team feel safe enough to engage in playfulness? If I am feeling nervous or there are other signs that my SNS is activated, would it be helpful to use what I am noticing to reflect back to the team? What behaviours am I seeing? Does it look like people are very task focused? Or are they also collaborating, thinking creatively and expansively? Knowing what I know about states, what does this tell me about what the team might need?

Playful Moment

There is quite a lot to think about here. If you fancy a break before we move onto the client's perspective, why not take a Playful Moment?

6.6 The Client

6.6.1 Creating Safety through Play

Another thing for us to consider is how we can use play to prevent our client's SNS being activated (at least to a level where it gets in the way of our work together) or even activate the PNS in order to facilitate collaborative, creative expansive thinking. For example, in the story of John in *Once upon a time*, imagine a scenario where team coaches are working with the team and one of the areas for development which have been identified is learning to communicate more effectively with one another. The team coaches have found that the team members don't feel listened to by John and his habitual behaviour is to talk more than listen. This dynamic is causing a considerable amount of tension which John is blissfully unaware of. After one or more 1:1 coaching sessions with John, imagine a playful way of supporting John's learning of his new listening behaviour; finding a way with the team to do this in a light, compassionate way, for example, agreeing a total number of times that John is allowed to speak in a team coaching session (after which he can speak but he must ask the team's permission) and keeping score with numbered cards, a sticker chart, or smiley faces. Through humorous playfulness, the potential for John to feel judged or threatened is diluted if not defused and there is an appreciation by the team that he is trying to learn a new way of behaving (and just as for the rest of us, this can take time and effort).

Similarly, we can tackle subjects which might otherwise feel unsafe, whether personal triggers or, for example, situations outlined in the third of the *Once upon a time* stories. By bringing in play sensitively, we can help keep ours and clients' SNS at bay, balancing groundedness and respect for the topic at hand. We are not being flippant or frivolous, but also bringing a quality of lightness, perspective, and essentially hope, which allows us to create a measure of psychological distance and supports positive emotions around topics which might otherwise feel overwhelming or fear inducing and likely to inhibit the activation of the PNS.

6.6.2 Safety as a Base for Play

Let's look at this idea of safety as a base for play a little more closely and from the perspective of the coaching relationship. We've mentioned Graham Lee's *Breakthrough Conversations* earlier in which he considers the states that are necessary for effective coaching and communication. He suggests that there are three body-brain states: RED/reactive, AMBER/habitual and GREEN/reflective, and in his book he helps you (and in turn, you can help your clients) to identify and distinguish your subjective experience of RAG states, giving you (and with your support, your clients) the ability to 'observe and manage potentially disruptive RED or AMBER states' to stay in a GREEN state. In essence, breakthrough conversations occur in the GREEN state which is characterised by trust and safety and where:

The key capability at this stage is playfulness, which consists of three elements: the creativity arising from examining different viewpoints and sustaining uncertainty, the collaboration to sustain a balance of listening and speaking, owning potential triggers, and moving between different perspectives and the pragmatism to translate ideas into tangible plans and actions.[22]

We can use the safety of the coaching relationship to create and hold the space for playfulness to help our clients consider potentially challenging topics for example, those in some of the stories in *Once upon a time*. Porges' (2011) argues that play blends the social engagement system (neuroception of safety) and the SNS. In the context of play therapy, we came across an interesting paper[23] proposing a model which integrates the emotional brain system of play (Panksepp 2009), Polyvagal Theory (Porges, 2011), and resonant therapeutic relationships (Fredrickson, 2009) to support the benefits of play relationships, the core of play therapy when therapists are mindfully present in relational play. While it is more directly related to play (physical behaviour), in therapy, we think it has relevance in particular to serious and intellectual playfulness (remember the Be Playful Onion Model) in a coaching relationship.

This integrated model allows the therapist and client to rely on their social engagement system as 'home base' so that they can venture into the SNS (in the absence of danger) to explore and play out different scenarios. To use the language that we've used in other chapters, especially in Part II, the safety of the relationship and the space created allows the client to venture into the zone of discomfort that might otherwise have led to overwhelm. You can see the parallels with coaching, and it supports the idea that playfulness can be used not only to generate positive emotions but to explore and resolve difficult issues. Within what Winnicott called 'holding'[24] and Bion 'containing'[25] (and all the consequences that flow from this safety), the coach and client venture into areas that will arouse the SNS by exploring and playing out different scenarios but in the absence of actual danger, thus providing that safe space for exploration, curiosity and learning. We think that this is relevant not just for play therapy but also for engaging in playfulness during coaching. In Part II especially, we look at the need for a willingness to come to accept that the uncertainty and resultant discomfort that playfulness often entails is fertile ground for learning for both the coach and their clients. That uncertainty may well arouse the SNS but in the container of the coaching space can be the route to enabling awareness and change.

This greatly resonates with our experience of playfulness in coaching. Both of us love to laugh and we both also have the stance that there are no 'bad' or 'good' emotions; everything is welcome in our sessions. Particularly in our

1 : 1 work, it's not uncommon for a client to cry and laugh in the same session. We're mindful that we're not therapists and we stay within the ethical boundaries which that entails. Equally, for the most part, we have no set expectations or structure for 1 : 1 sessions (depending on the engagement, team coaching might require more structure, but much of the work is still co-created with the teams and emergent). When we work with difficult topics with clients, playfulness will be somewhere in the system, even if it's 'just' by our tapping into a playful way of being. We've found that this creates a space in which clients can touch difficult topics, acknowledge and release emotions while exploring them with a degree of lightness, perspective, and compassion which can be transformational for them.

Our clients' SNS arousal might be also intentional in some forms of playfulness in coaching. Take, for example, some of Kirsen Barske's work with client teams in nature where they might encounter challenging physical circumstances which will get their adrenaline surging. Such experiences will create collective and individual memories and the positive emotions associated with conquering fears or overcoming challenges collectively or individually.

6.7 Conclusion

The theories which we've sneaked a peak at in this chapter give us interesting perspectives from which to try to understand what might be going on for us and our clients and in the relational system which we form to understand how this might impact playfulness in our work together. There are psychophysiological processes at play, often below our level of awareness which can impact positively and negatively on playfulness in coaching (and coaching more generally). With practice we can build our capacity for greater awareness of our own and our clients' states and not be at their mercy, supporting our coaching and playfulness. Or, we can leverage playfulness to enable the state most conducive to effective creativity, collaboration and coaching. If we can work with our clients to find ways of using playfulness to create a space where we feel safe on a neuro-biological level, we are helping them to be more open to hearing each other's perspectives, collaborating and being creative about possible ways forward. It's not a giant leap of the imagination to consider how impactful this might be in many coaching scenarios including helping to create and support psychological safety or diversity and inclusion or in dealing with challenging or frightening topics such as climate crisis. It's incredibly powerful that through practice and awareness as well as intentional and informed use of playfulness, we can create spaces which can be of greater service to our clients in supporting coaching processes and outcomes.

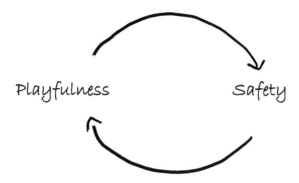

Just like playfulness itself, we'd encourage you to consider these theories not in a dualistic, binary way (for example, playfulness leads to safety leads to playfulness) but as complex systems and a reinforcing loop: playfulness and safety mutually supporting each other in order to arrive at and stay in the appropriate body-brain state and relational dynamics to create insight and change. Also, to keep these in mind as you navigate your exploration and experimentation.

As we come to the end of this chapter, we invite you to engage in a little reflection on what you've read and how it might impact your practice, particularly in the context of playfulness. Questions which you might find useful to ponder on include:

- *What state are you mostly in (at work, in different areas of your life)?*
- *How aware are you of your states?*
- *Do you have control of the wheel or are you a passenger?*
- *What can you do to support your bid for the wheel if you are a passenger?*
- *How many renewal moments do you build into your life and your work?*
- *Do you do this consciously?*
- *What else could you do?*
- *What has this chapter made you reflect on and how might this impact your work?*

Remember too that states are of course just part of the system that is relational playfulness in coaching:

> If we can tend to our state
> And be aware of and supportive of our client's
> While not letting our own needs be in the driving seat
> But instead, be driven by what is in service of our work together,
> All the while respecting boundaries
> And an awareness of what's going on for our client and ourselves;
> Holding all this with curiosity and compassion,
> Then we're ready to play!

Notes

1   Porges, S. (2018). Polyvagal theory: A primer. *Clinical applications of the polyvagal theory: The emergence of polyvagal-informed therapies*, 50, 69.
2   Porges, S. (1991). Vagal tone: An autonomic mediator of affect. In Garber, J. & Dodge, K. (Eds.). *The development of emotion regulation and dysregulation*. Cambridge University Press, pp111–128.
3   Waxenbaum, J., Reddy, V. & Varacallo, M. (2019). *Anatomy, autonomic nervous system*. StatPearls Publishing.
4   Boyatzis, R., Smith, M., Van Oosten, E. & Woolford, L. (2013). Developing resonant leaders through emotional intelligence, vision, and coaching. *Organizational Dynamics*, 42(1), 17–24.
5   If you haven't come across our inner Winnie the Pooh, this will probably sound strange. If you're curious, have a look at Chapter 2.
6   Our heartfelt gratitude to Stephanie's dear friend, Prof Aideen Sullivan who just happens to be Head of the Department of Anatomy and Neuroscience of University College Cork, Ireland, and her colleague Dr Cian McCafferty for helping us make sense of this area (any errors are ours).
7   For example, Chaskalson, M. & McMordie, M. (2017). *Mindfulness for Coaches: an experiential guide*. Taylor and Francis.
8   For example, Boyatzis, R., Rochford, K. & Taylor, S. (2015). The role of the positive emotional attractor in vision and shared vision: Toward effective leadership, relationships, and engagement. *Frontiers in Psychology*, 6, 670.
9   Boyatzis R. and McKee, A. (2005). *Resonant leadership: renewing yourself and connecting with others through mindfulness, hope and compassion*. Boston, MA: Harvard Business School Press.
    Ayan, S. (2009). Laughing matters: seeing the bright side of life may strengthen the psyche, ease pain, and tighten social bonds. *Scientific American Mind*, 20, 24–31.
    Passarelli, A. (2014). *The heart of helping: Psychological and physiological effects of contrasting coaching interactions*. PhD thesis, Case Western Reserve University.

Passarelli, A. (2015). Vision-based coaching: optimizing resources for leader development. *Frontiers in psychology*, 6, 412.

10 Howard, A. (2009). *An Exploratory Examination of Positive and Negative Emotional 72 Attractors' Impact on Coaching Intentional Change*. Ph.D. thesis, Case Western Reserve University, Cleveland, OH.

11 *Ibid*, Passarelli (2014).

12 *Ibid*, Passarelli (2015).

13 Beaty, R., Benedek, M., Silvia, P. & Schacter, D. (2016). Creative Cognition and Brain Network Dynamics. *Trends in cognitive sciences*, 20(2), 87–95.

14 *Ibid*, Beaty et al. (2016).

15 Goleman, D., Boyatzis, R. and McKee, A. (2002). *Primal Leadership: Realizing the Power of Emotional Intelligence*. Boston, Mass.: Harvard Business School Press.

16 See, for example, the work of Joseph LeDoux on emotions and the brain and news. mit.edu/2014/in-the-blink-of-an-eye-0116.

17 Panksepp, J. (2009). Brain emotional systems and qualities of mental life: From animal models of affect to implications for psychotherapeutics. In D. Fosha, D. J. Siegel, & M. F. Solomon (Eds.), *The healing power of emotion: Affective neuroscience, development & clinical practice* (pp1–26). WW Norton & Company.

Panksepp, J. (1998). The periconscious substrates of consciousness: Affective states and the evolutionary origins of the self. *Journal of consciousness studies*, 5(5–6), pp566–582.

18 Dana, D., & Porges, S. W. (2020). *Polyvagal exercises for safety and connection: 50 client-centered practices*. W.W. Norton & Company.

19 McGonigall, K. (Avery Publishing Group)

20 Lee, G. (2021). *Breakthrough Conversations for Coaches, Consultants and Leaders*. Routledge.

21 *Ibid*, Lee (2021).

22 *Ibid*, Lee (2021, p188).

23 Kestly, T. (2016). Presence and Play: Why Mindfulness Matters. *Journal of Play Therapy*, 25(1), 14–23.

24 Winnicott, D. (1960). The theory of the parent-infant relationship. *International Journal of Psycho-Analysis*, 41, 585–595.

25 Bion, W. (1962). *Learning from Experience*. Heinemann.

7
Adding Emotions into the Mix

In this chapter we:

- Share some thoughts on emotions generally including Feldman-Barrett's theory of emotions
- Look at playfulness and positive emotions starting with Panksepp's tickled rats
- Offer an ode to joy
- Ask what's love got to do with it?
- Marvel at the kaleidoscope of positive emotions in playfulness in coaching
- Ask why it matters if playfulness in coaching generates positive emotions
- Explore ideas around playfulness, positive emotions, and behavioural change
- Consider negative emotions and playfulness in coaching
- Leave you with a little musing on equanimity

7.1 Before We Begin

Although it is often positive emotions that are associated with playfulness in coaching, in particular amusement and fun, in this chapter we explore the range of emotions which you and your client might encounter in a playful space and what impact this might have on your work together. Rather than being limited to a small range of positive emotions, our experience is that many emotions may be present in a high trust, safe and playful space, and acknowledging, being, and working with these can be very helpful for your work together.

Most of the chapters in this book are stand-alone with cross-references to other chapters so that you aren't restricted in how you read and use this book and you can do it in any way that tickles your fancy. This chapter is an exception.

DOI: 10.4324/9781003090847-8

Unless it's an area with which you're familiar, it's probably worth reading the previous chapter as we'll be referring to the ideas in it frequently. As a reminder, in case it's helpful:

> PNS = Parasympathetic Nervous System, associated with the
> DFM = Default Mode Network
>
> SNS = Sympathetic Nervous System, associated with the
> TFN = Task Focused Network

For the sake of simplicity in this chapter, when we speak of the state associated with the SNS, we're including the 'freeze' state.

7.2 Adding Emotions into the Mix

Turn back, if you please, to the stories in *Once upon a time* at the beginning of Chapter 6 and imagine that the characters are working through the relevant topics with their coach(es) either individually or in their teams/group. Playing through these scenarios while keeping the previous chapter in mind, imagine that some or all of the clients' SNSs are activated – they are in fight or flight or freeze. What emotions are likely to be present? How will this affect the interactions, thought processes and what emerges in the coaching space and possible outcomes? Now imagine that with explicit or implicit facilitation by the coach(es) supported by playfulness within the wide range envisaged by the Be Playful Onion Model, the clients are in the state associated with PNS activation. What emotions are likely to be present now and what effect is this likely to have on the individuals, their interactions, and the team/group collectively?

Take a moment to reflect upon what emotions are prevalent for you when your SNS and then your PNS is activated (generally and in the context of 1:1 or team work). The presence of positive or negative emotions (together with whether PNS/SNS or DMN/TFN are activated) will have an impact on the group dynamics, psychological safety, creativity, and collaboration, to name but a few, as well as the coaching process and effectiveness. In the previous chapter we looked at the relationship of playfulness in coaching with the different brain-body system states and in this chapter, we are adding emotions into the mix. You might also want to consider this and how it relates to your own Barometer of Playfulness at some point in this chapter

7.3 Thoughts on Emotions in Coaching More Generally

It's probably worth clarifying that we'll be using the labels 'negative' and 'positive' emotions even though we're not fans of the labels in coaching practice as they might imply that some are more welcome than others. From our perspective, as coaches we aim to create spaces where all emotions are welcome and greeted with compassion and curiosity. Whatever arises is information and if you take the time to give voice to emotions and acknowledge them, they often become more manageable. You and your client can then work through the issue at hand with greater awareness and agility, but that's another story. For this chapter, the distinction and labels are useful and necessary in terms of the research and literature, so we'll adopt them.

With a respectful nod to the complexity at play, let's also recognise that there is likely to be a mix of emotions present, some which might be positive and some negative. While we will look at positive and negative emotions separately, we want to acknowledge that this is to some extent artificial in practice. Let's make sure though that we acknowledge and embrace the mix of emotions that are often present in a coaching session, for example, we can experience fear, regret, or anger (seen as negative emotions) and especially within the cradle of playfulness, also experience self-compassion and forgiveness (seen as positive emotions). The 'mix' of emotions can be very intricate rather than there being a clear separateness. Think, for example, of 'bitter-sweet'. What's more, while not experienced in the same precise moment, they come together in the collection of moments that make up a coaching session and our experience is that there will be a range of emotions present if we and our clients are open to making space for them. Just like yin and yang, there is a need for, and a balance in, working with negative and positive emotions, particularly if we are to be person-centred in our approach and working with the whole person rather than isolated topics.

Just as we encouraged you to look through a systemic lens in the previous chapter, here too, we encourage you to think about adding emotions to the mix though a dynamic systemic lens. Not only will there likely be a mixture of positive and negative emotions present during the session (even more so of course in group or team contexts), but at the same time our body-brain systems will quite possibly move in and out of different states and different neural networks will become more or less activated. We also need to see this in the context of the whole person, including their beliefs, values, experiences, and their place within various systems. So, while we're talking in quite a dualistic way of positive and negative emotions, please do bear in mind that they are a part of these broader systems with which we are working.

This seems like a pertinent moment to encourage you to widen your thinking about emotions further and introduce a different way of looking at them. A common lay view of emotions is that they are distinct and recognisable, each with their own physiological 'fingerprint'. Professor Lisa Feldman-Barrett offers a radically different take on emotions: they are not innate and universal, instead they vary from culture to culture, and they are not triggered but created.[1] She points out that research has failed to identify a consistent physical fingerprint for even a single emotion. Feldman-Barrett proposes that emotions are not the universal components of human experience but instead, what we should look at is the changes on the continuums of high and low arousal and pleasantness and unpleasantness. So, for example, if you experience high arousal and high pleasantness, your brain might construct 'ecstasy' and low arousal and low pleasantness might prompt you to create 'misery'. A similar physiological state in a different country, culture or language could therefore be described subtly or completely differently depending on who is interpreting the physiological state in question. In the previous chapter, we came across Porges' concept of 'neuroception' which describes how outside of the realm of our awareness, our body scans our environment for detection of risk. Well, at the same time, also largely below conscious awareness, our brain constantly scans the state of our bodies (with information from our heart rate, breathing, immune system, and hormone levels, to name but a few) in a process known as 'interoception'. This determines 'affect', the feelings of pleasantness/unpleasantness and arousal/non-arousal which in turn feed into our emotions. The end product, if you like, the emotion which we then feel depends on our culture, language, and earlier experiences.

Feldman-Barrett's ideas are not universally accepted and she says herself that she's 'extremely controversial' with her detractors who 'cling onto the idea that emotions are innate'.[2] There is, however, very strong neuroscientific evidence for emotion being innate (measured by facial expressions in humans and many other species), especially fear, disgust, and pleasure. This is, though, quite separate from Feldman-Barrett's explanation of interoception and how our brains interpret physical changes (ANS, somatic, hormones) as being emotionally salient and construct a 'story' based on the context and prior experience, and so on, to explain these bodily sensations and changes. There is a lot of neuroscientific evidence to support this aspect of her theories.

We've included Feldman-Barrett's work here as it's fascinating and encourages us to maintain a degree of playful irreverence in that current knowledge and theories in this area and beyond are very likely to evolve and perhaps change significantly over time. Also, we've included it as an invitation to be culturally sensitive and to hold our own assumptions lightly and with curiosity. What is giving rise to positive emotions for us in the context of our coaching and playfulness might register on a different place on the arousal/non-arousal and pleasant/unpleasant continuums for our clients (and each of them differently in a group/team). Even if they fall on broadly similar points, how they are interpreted and translated into emotions might be very similar or strikingly different. Particularly in the context of multiculturalism, this requires sensitivity, curiosity, and a level of humility on the part of a coach introducing play and playfulness into the coaching process. Consider, for example, the effect on trust and psychological safety if it misfires. If the prospect of potentially misfiring makes you a bit concerned, don't worry, we hope that Chapter 9 will leave you feeling more aware of and equipped for some potential risks of playfulness in coaching.

Having acknowledged the complexity of considering emotions and particularly, for our purposes, in the context of playfulness in coaching, let's come back again to relative simplicity as we turn our attention to playfulness in coaching and positive and negative emotions. Playfulness is more often and readily associated with positive emotions, so we'll spend more time with these. However, it's worth noting that Proyer & Brauer (2018) found, contrary to their hypothesis, that global playfulness and facets of playfulness were unrelated to the use of positive emotion words, arguably supporting the notion of serious playfulness.[3] Our playfulness embraces this complexity!

7.4 Playfulness and Positive Emotions

You've briefly met in the previous chapter, but if you don't know each other already, we'd like to introduce you to Jaak Panksepp (1943–2017). He was a neuroscientist and psychobiologist who coined the term 'affective neuroscience', the study of the neural mechanisms of emotions. Oh, and he tickled rats. Let us explain. Having spent his early career studying attachment and separation anxiety, he felt he had done sufficient work on Melpomene, the tragedy mask of life so to speak and wished to move his focus onto Thalia, the comedy mask. As he put it:

> Play is a brain process that feels good, that allows the animal to engage fully with another animal. And if you understand the joy of play, I think you have the foundation of the nature of joy in general. Part of its benefit is simply taking away the psychological pain of separation. Play is engaging in an attachment-like way with strangers, which you have to do later in life.[4]

In other words, Panksepp[5] was looking for the neuroevolutionary sources of human laughter and joy. He was primarily interested in how emotions arise in the structures, regions, and networks of the brain as well as related substances such as neurotransmitters and hormones, collectively known as neural mechanisms. As it was not possible to map the subcortical brain systems that are shared by all mammals in the required detail in humans without causing damage to the participants (a bit tricky as regards to ethical approval), Panksepp concentrated his research on rats. He became known as the 'rat tickler' with a laboratory of laughing rats.[6] By tickling and observing laughing and playing rats, Panksepp was hoping to find an animal model for studying some of the fundamental properties of laughter circuitry in humans as well as the brain mechanisms that facilitate positive social engagement. In other words, find a theoretical and empirical handle on the sources of social joy in the mammalian brain.

Through his work, he charted seven interwoven and interactive emotional (or affective/motivational) systems: SEEKING, RAGE, FEAR, LUST, CARE,

PAIN/GRIEF and (cue drum roll please) PLAY. He spelled them in capital letters to underline their fundamental importance across different species of mammals including us humans. All are relevant to relationships. The brain circuitry which is dedicated to PLAY lies deep within the instinctual apparatus of the mammalian brain. So Panksepp's research tells us that even in adulthood, we are deep wired for play and laughter and that play supports relationship building and experiencing joy. Both of these are important contributors to coaching effectiveness (we'll come back to joy a little later). Now the concept of 'neoteny' (introduced in Chapter 3) makes more sense. Many evolutionary biologists believe that neoteny allows us to retain the playfulness of childhood even as we mature into adults.[7] If you accept this view, then Montagu[8] argues that the commonly held perception that adults growing out of playfulness as a natural part of the maturation process, is misguided. Being able to retain a flexible psyche and playful qualities are healthy signs of development, while losing these as we enter into adulthood are a sign of 'psychosclerosis', a hardening of the psyche. Gordon[9] takes this argument further, suggesting that retaining our childhood playfulness is necessary for optimal functioning and we saw in Chapter 3 the argument that through play, individually and collectively, we move from surviving to thriving. We would layer on top of that the wider multifaceted definition of playfulness including serious and intellectual playfulness[10] and consider what impact retaining the ability to tap into these aspects of playfulness might have not only in the coaching space but also on our lives and the systems in which we live and work. This in turn evokes the work of playful scientists, mathematicians, and artists, some of whom we met in Chapter 2 who find joy in their work and whose work is fuelled by playfulness.

Being deep-wired for play and the importance of playfulness throughout our lifespan makes sense when you consider these in the context of our psychobiology and the connection of play and our PNS which allows more openness to new ideas, emotions and people and considering possibilities for the future.[11] The obvious question then is, if we are hard-wired to play, what is it that stops most of us playing or being playful particularly in a work context as we grow into adulthood? Is it social conditioning, the messages we hear as we grow up and in the work systems in which we find ourselves as adults? Why do some people not lose this ability? We'll be looking at some barriers and ways of accessing playfulness (more) in Part II. For now, we can be encouraged in that whatever individual barriers we may or may not face, we are all hard-wired for play. Playfulness is a natural and resourceful state during all stages of our lives even those which might involve doing serious work in serious organisations and one we can tap into in coaching.

7.5 Ode to Joy

If we are hard-wired for play and play supports relationship building and experiencing joy, let's look at joy a little more closely, particularly its potential relevance to coaching. As we've mentioned above, it's rare that laughter doesn't make an appearance in our coaching sessions at some stage. We don't go into a session with the intention of making clients laugh (that would feel inauthentic to us and incongruent with being present without expectation and being open to what emerges in each session). We do, however, bring with us a playful way of being and often laughter bubbles up or erupts at a-ha moments or when a lighter perspective is brought to a difficult topic. Also, as we've mentioned before, sometimes the laughter is in close proximity to tears and there can be joy in release and finding new awareness and insight. Through helping our clients create psychological distance (essentially seeing themselves and their internal and external experience with more objectivity) and encouraging compassion (often self-compassion is what is most wanting) the mood invariably lightens with challenges feeling more possible and less daunting. Sometimes laughter helps this to fall into place, sometimes it comes after the a-ha realisation, either way, moments of joy are experienced. This seems to us to unlock something in the clients and help them feel less stuck with their challenge, whether it's internal, external or both, with more options being available to them. This appears to be consistent with Fredrickson & Cohn (2008)[12] who describe joy as a high-activation pleasant emotion which motivates to play and explore the limits, which eventually leads to building social bonds and increasing levels of creativity. This built on Fredrickson's earlier finding that:

> Joy sparks the urge to play, interest sparks the urge to explore, contentment sparks the urge to savour and integrate, and love sparks a recurring cycle of each of these urges within safe, close relationships.[13]

To see what this might look like in practice, have a look back at some of the *Once upon a time* stories (Chapter 6) and imagine the following: during the coaching session, assuming there is enough trust and safety, the client(s) experience joy. This sparks the innate urge to play which allows us (clients and coach) to push limits and be creative. Rather than being bogged down by the topic, the client is freer to consider other perspectives, bring a sense of lightness, let go of restrictions when considering what might be possible to address their challenge, making room for a more creative and collaborative response. This might mean in the Monday morning meeting story that the team and John look at the purposes of the meetings and come up with playful and creative alternatives which fulfil their various needs. In the impending merger story, the senior leadership team might use LEGO® Serious Play® to identify the organisational values, and role play the systemic possible effects of the merger. By doing so, they might experience greater interest in uncovered areas which in turn could spark their urge to explore, to take in more and new information, experiences, and perspectives. In the community group story, during or after playfulness, its members might also experience contentment (perhaps also facilitated by flow and connection with others that they experienced during play) which sparks the urge to savour what they have discovered about themselves and others during play and to integrate the discoveries, realisations, and experiences into how they see themselves, others, and the world, deepening social relationships, and creating a positive reinforcing loop.

We invite you to stop for a reflection. Think back to a time when you experienced working creatively, expansively with curiosity when you were working on your own. Now repeat thinking about a time when you experienced this working with others.

- *What emotions were present?*
- *What impact do you think these had?*

Let's take a moment also to talk about love, one of the positive emotions specifically named above in the recurring cycle of the urges to play, explore, savour, and integrate.

7.6 What's Love Got to Do with It?

Think back to different times when you've experienced playfulness in coaching and elsewhere and the positive emotions which you arose. Does love feature in your list? Our own experience is that we feel love for our clients (at its core, an appreciation of our common humanity and linked to Carl Rogers' unconditional positive regard and not dependent on playfulness). It is worth saying that we felt a bit hesitant to write this. The classic romantic view of love prevalent in Western culture and in particular Hollywood notions of what love is are so ingrained in our sense making and speaking about love in an organisational context is still not the norm. Yet the positive emotion of love which is potentially (dare we go so far as to say 'hopefully'?) present during coaching involves those moments of connection which create recurring cycles of the urge to play, being interested, curious and ready to explore and experiment within the context of safe, close relationships. In her book *Love 2.0*,[14] Fredrickson argues that love, like the other positive emotions, follows the ancestral logic of the broaden-and-build theory of positive emotions (more on which later); those pleasant and fleeting moments of connection which you experience with others and which expand your awareness in ways that accrue to create lasting and beneficial changes. As she sees it, love is found in those moments of warmth, connection, and openness to another person. Perhaps it is helpful, as with playfulness, to go beyond our initial understanding of the word and consider the different types of love which there are. There are many sources which define different kinds of love, and they might include:

Eros: erotic, passionate love
Storge: love of parents for children
Philia: love of friends and equals
Agape: love of mankind

In the context of playfulness in coaching, embracing a wider definition of love, you could say that the coach and clients can and do at times experience love when immersed in playfulness.

7.7 The Kaleidoscope of Positive Emotions

We hope by now to have widened your assumptions of the positive emotions which might be experienced through playfulness in coaching beyond fun and amusement which are typically the main ones to spring to mind. Before we turn to the possible impact of this, let's stay here a little longer to see if we can develop the kaleidoscope of positive emotions associated with playfulness in coaching further.

Fredrickson lists the top ten positive emotions that she has come across (in random order) as: joy, gratitude, serenity, interest, hope, pride, amusement, inspiration, awe, and love. Curiosity can be both a positive and negative emotion, which is perhaps why it's not included here, though decades before positive psychology, pioneering social psychologist Sylvan Tomkins believed that curiosity was of profound evolutionary significance.[15] What's more, it is of course very relevant to playfulness, and we look at it later in Part II.

Perhaps the key to thinking about positive emotions and playfulness in coaching is in appreciating how nuanced we can be when we are looking at the emotions which support and arise from playfulness. For example, from a Nonviolent Communication perspective, emotions are likely to arise when our needs are or are not being met. As a starting point for deepening self-discovery and facilitating greater understanding and connection with others rather than intending to be an exhaustive list, Inbal Kashtan and Miki Kashtan created a feelings/emotions list. It includes 'Playful' as one of the main categories and is further broken-down into:

Energetic
Invigorated
Zestful

Refreshed
Impish
Alive
Lively
Exuberant
Giddy
Adventurous
Mischievous
Jubilant
Goofy
Buoyant
Electrified[16]

This is just a starting point of course and perhaps also have in mind that some of these might be more closely linked to physical play, whereas serious or intellectual playfulness might generate a different list of emotions. The point is we're asking you to be imaginative and creative in thinking about and labelling the different positive emotions that might arise in the context of playfulness in coaching. Why spend time and effort on this? Awareness is key to coaching and if we can be more aware of and nuanced about what is arising (for us and our clients and in the relational space) as a result of and in support of playfulness which is supporting the work with our clients, the more discernment we have at our disposal. Being aware of the emotions arising or at least being curious about them means that we can be agile in our approach. We can also use those emotions as information which we may or may not reflect back to our clients and be aware of their impact on us so as to inform our feeling, thinking and actions.

We invite you again to look at the stories in *Once upon a time* (Chapter 6) and consider a coaching session (team/group or individual) in one of the scenarios which is progressing well and includes elements of playfulness. Think about the positive emotions that might be arising, and which playful emotions might be in the room. If we take the Gestalt approach that everything is data, what insights can you gather from looking at what's happening in the room from this perspective and how might these influence your work with your clients in the moment?

Playful Moment

We're going to invite you to reflect on some questions in a moment. To get into a helpful frame of mind, would you like to have a Playful Moment first?

- *What do you notice about how you are imagining these stories?*
- *What do you notice about how you are thinking and feeling about playfulness in coaching?*
- *Where are you feeling this in your body?*
- *What does it make you think about your own practice and playfulness?*

7.8 Why Does it Matter if Playfulness Generates Positive Emotions?

Beyond awareness and discernment which are already powerful coaching supports, why does the kaleidoscope of positive emotions that might arise through or be supported by playfulness in coaching matter? We've said above that playfulness can, amongst other things, unlock a more collaborative, creative, experimental, curiosity-led approach which is a rich resource in the coaching space. Let's look at some of the research and literature and consider what might happen in practice.

7.8.1 Emotions and How We Think, Feel and Behave

Do you remember in the previous chapter we invited you to see the relationship between playfulness and safety not as linear but as a reinforcing loop? It seems that positive emotions and play also appear to create a positive or reinforcing loop. According to the broaden-and-build theory,[17] during the broadening process positive emotions:

> Create the urge to play, push the limits and be creative, urges evident not only in social and physical behaviour, but also in intellectual and artistic behaviour.[18]

We'd like to propose a super-loop that includes safety, positive emotions, and playfulness. On the one hand, generating positive emotions in the coaching space can facilitate and sustain playfulness and on the other, playfulness can generate positive emotions and the cycle continues (though it can of course be interrupted – again more on this in Chapter 9). Equally, trust and safety is required for playfulness and the experience of playfulness in this container is likely to give rise to some positive emotions (and also possibly some negative emotions depending on the work being done). For example, in the *Once upon a time* stories, the leadership team being coached around the merger, could spend some time sharing their hopes and positive expectations. If necessary, the team coach(es) could spend some time working with the team to increase their levels of trust and feelings of safety. Either or both of these might calm down their SNSs sufficiently to move into a playful way of considering the consequences of the merger or taking stock of aspects of the organisation, for example through LEGO® Serious Play® (LSP). The experience during the building of the LEGO® models individually and collectively and sharing their metaphors and stories in a space where everyone's voice is heard (one of the fundamental principles of LSP) is likely to support trust and safety and give rise to positive emotions. These will further support their ability to bring a degree of levity, curiosity, objectivity, and perspective (all associated with playfulness) to the issues, generating more positive emotions, trust, and safety and so on.

Play   Positive Emotions
Trust

If you remember from the previous chapter, Intentional Change Theory looks at how the state in which our body-brain system is in affects our mental state and how we can think in the coaching space. What we didn't tell you is that there is a third aspect to the theory which is the interrelationship of the body-brain systems and the emotions, explained by concepts, called the Positive and Negative Emotional Attractors (PEA and NEA). Seen as a whole, these are essentially states which have distinct emotional, physiological, and neuro-logical characteristics which in turn affect how we think, feel, and behave.

PEA = Positive Emotional Attractor
NEA = Negative Emotional Attractor

The theory suggests that for the PEA to be activated, a person needs to experi-ence a positive emotion; the arousal of the PNS and the DMN. On the flipside, for the NEA to be activated, you need negative emotion; activated SNS and TMN. Studies have shown that PEA activation leads to increased cognitive and emotional openness and physical vitality. Broadly speaking, there's a growing body of evidence that the PEA plays a growth-oriented role in pre-paring the coachee emotionally, cognitively, and physiologically for enacting change. It either calms or energises (Boyatzis & McKee, 2005; Ayan, 2009) and is associated with the experience of positive emotions, cognitive openness, and a greater influence of the PNS autonomic functioning (Jack et al., 2013). The resultant Intentional Change Process proposes that while sometimes the NEA gives us the prompt for change, change starts predominantly in the PEA, with sustained change also requiring PEA.

7.8.2 Fireside Chat with Prof Richard Boyatzis

Playfulness features quite often in Intentional Change Theory. *How would you describe playfulness in the context of coaching and behavioural change?*

Playfulness and laughter are key human experiences that invoke the Para-sympathetic Nervous System. Regardless of gender, race, or culture, these basic human experiences are two of the few that actually ameliorate the damage caused by stress (cognitive, emotional, and perceptual impairment); even mild, annoying stress experiences. In Intentional Change Theory (ICT), the tipping points to moving ahead with sustained, desired change are moments in the

Positive Emotional Attractor (PEA) versus the Negative Emotional Attractor (NEA). Playfulness and laughter are moments in the PEA, at the neurological, hormonal, and psychological levels. They quite literally open us up to possibilities and neural activation that allows us to learn and change. They also stimulate our immune system and neurogenesis.

You often refer to playfulness as well as compassion, mindfulness, and hope as ways of activating PEAs and the PNS. At first glance, they don't necessarily seem connected. What prompted you to include playfulness?

These are different emotions and experiences that each can invoke the PEA. They may or may not occur in the same experiences or at the same time.

Do you have any advice on developing our own playfulness and enabling others (particularly coaching clients) to be more playful?

It first requires being in a renewal state. But you can use emotional contagion to get there. So, if one person in a group acts playful, others may get infected!

Where do you think future research into playfulness in the context of coaching and behavioural change might be headed?

To further validate how it helps and distinguish playfulness that may cause harm to others versus be helpful. Like playing with firearms will seldom invoke the PEA!

What's your personal favourite expression of playfulness?

Walking with my wife and two Golden Retrievers on the beach, throwing balls in the water, dodging waves, and laughing!

Richard E. Boyatzis is Distinguished University Professor of Case Western Reserve University, Professor in the Departments of Organizational Behavior, Psychology, and Cognitive Science, and HR Horvitz Professor of Family Business. He has a BS in Aeronautics and Astronautics from MIT, a MS, and Ph.D. in Social Psychology from Harvard University. Using his Intentional Change Theory (ICT), he studies sustained, desired change of individuals, teams, organizations, communities, and countries since 1967. He is the author of more than 200 articles and 9 books on leadership, competencies, emotional intelligence, competency development, coaching, neuroscience, and management education, including the international best-seller, Primal Leadership with Daniel Goleman and Annie McKee and the recent Helping People Change with Melvin Smith and Ellen Van Oosten. His Coursera MOOCs, including Inspiring Leadership Through Emotional Intelligence has over 1,400,000 enrolled from 215 countries. He is Fellow of the Association of Psychological Science, the Society of Industrial and Organizational Psychology, and the American Psychological Association

A nod quickly to the complexity of the systems we're talking about as it can be tempting to oversimplify the influence of stressful experiences on decision-making which seems to be much more complex than suggested by the fight or flight model which has been around since the early 1900s. For example, anxiety increases your threat perception which means that your SNS is more easily activated to prepare you for an emergency. It's been found that threat perception increased by anxiety tends to result in self-interested and even potentially unethical behaviour. Another example, recent advances suggest that stress exposure influences basic neural circuits involved in reward processing and learning, while also biassing decisions towards habit and modulating our propensity to engage in risk-taking. Applying these examples in the context of playfulness in coaching, you can see, for example, that while we think that the playfulness we are offering to a team/group is 'safe' (with all the implications that has for the PNS activation and so on of participants), the perception of safety (sometimes below the level of conscious awareness) by the individual participants are likely to all be different for various reasons. These perceptions of safety will influence their reaction to the playfulness invitation, and we know from the previous chapter, are likely to influence each other (again, sometimes below the level of conscious awareness). So, while we're presenting some ideas to you in a linear way by necessity on the written page, we encourage you to see each piece as part of a complex system both for individuals, dyads, and teams. We don't want to put you off though! We are hoping that developing a more sophisticated awareness around playfulness in coaching will equip you to hold a space where you may experience different reactions to your invitation with more agility, compassion, understanding and curiosity, all of course in the service of your clients.

While holding this complexity, let's return to relative simplicity. Approaches such as Cognitive Behavioural Theory are based on the premise that what you think determines how you feel and act. So, if you change your thoughts, you can change how you feel and behave. Apologies to CBT researchers and practitioners for this over-simplification. What if the relationship is the other way around? We've seen in the previous chapter how our nervous system decides on the level of safety which then determines which system is activated which in turn impacts our capacity for different ways of thinking and behaving. Bringing in the PEA/NEA also suggests that our thoughts are the result of our body-brain system states and emotions and other writers such as Raja Selvam argue that cognition, emotion, and behaviour are all embodied in the body, brain, and the environment and whilst they affect each other, emotion is the strongest mediator of cognition and behaviour.[19] Regardless of which comes first, it's fair to say that there's an intricate relationship between our thoughts and emotions. If we can bring in more positive emotions and challenge our clients' thinking through playfulness (with the knock on effects we've been discussing) we can have a substantial impact.

7.8.3 Broaden-and-build Theory

We've previously mentioned the broaden-and-build theory of positive emotions. Let's look at this a little more closely for those who are unfamiliar with it. It resulted from Barbara Fredrickson's curiosity about why positive emotions have survived the evolutionary process and what functions they serve. Her work has made her one of the most cited scholars in psychology. Rather than tying specific positive emotions to specific behaviour, the theory argues that positive emotions increase our 'momentary thought-action repertoires', the 'broaden' element. The result is that instead of a restricted fixed-price lunch menu with limited choice, positive emotions open the door to the extensive à la carte menu of thoughts and action impulses presented to our mind to select from.[20] Access to this menu builds intellectual, physical, and social resources that we need to withstand life's challenges and which in turn can give rise to positive emotions. By the way, the opposite has been borne out by research too: negative emotions present us with the fixed-price menu.

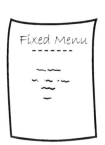 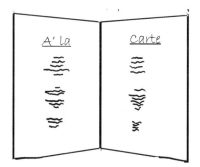

Research cited by Fredrickson to support the 'broaden' aspect of her model includes that on brain development (by, for example, Panksepp who we've already met) and creativity[21] as well as two decades of research by Isen and her colleagues which suggests that positive affect produces a 'broad, flexible cognitive organization, and the ability to integrate diverse material'.[22] Alice Isen (1942–2012) almost single-handedly, initiated the modern scientific study of positive affect, becoming one of the most highly cited business school faculty members in the world. As a psychologist and researcher, she spent decades alongside colleagues researching positive affect and particularly its effect on decision making.

> Affect is the experiential state of feeling. In everyday language, terms like affect, emotion, and mood are often used interchangeably. Affect is the superordinate category; emotions and moods are states belonging to this category [and....] mainly distinguished by their duration, and by whether they are directed at a specific cause.[23]

Isen concluded that positive affect facilitates creativity, successful problem-solving and negotiation as well as thoroughness and efficiency in decision-making.[24] Thought processes in the presence of positive affect are characterised by creativity and flexibility as well as being open to information and being integrative. Not only that, but people also experiencing positive affect also have an increased preference for variety and accept a broader array of behavioural choices. This seems to us to be compatible with one of Proyer's earlier definitions of playfulness:

> Playfulness is also associated with a preference for complexity rather than simplicity and a preference for – and a liking of – unusual activities, objects and topics or individuals.[25]

All of these capacities sound like fertile ground for coaching and we invite you to have a look at the *Once upon a time* stories (Chapter 6) again and see them through the lens of the capacities enabled and supported by positive emotions. Then think again about the value of playfulness in supporting those positive emotions. Perhaps we should reiterate that we don't intentionally set out to use playfulness to 'make' clients feel positive emotions – just like playfulness in coaching, for us, this isn't an end in itself. Knowing the potential benefits of positive emotions does give us discernment in the moment though. If we notice that our client is getting stuck or unable to integrate information or learning, we can playfully experiment together whether encouraging positive emotions might unlock their thinking. Like in Intentional Change Theory, we can exercise awareness and discernment in working with emotions rather than being passive.

The 'build' element of the model explains the purpose of the 'broaden' effect. Negative emotions are useful when immediate behaviour (for example, to fight, run away) is called for. Positive emotions, on the other hand, benefit us in the longer term. Seen through an evolutionary lens, repeatedly experiencing positive emotions means that we accrue resources which help our survival. The types of resources which Fredrickson and her team are researching which might be bolstered include physical (immunity and sleep quality), psychological (resilience and optimism traits), intellectual (creativity and mindfulness) and social (expanded social connection and support). The beauty is that experiencing positive emotions builds up your resources and ability to experience yet further positive emotions.[26] Seen this way, the reason that positive emotions survived evolution is that when we experience them, we have greater cognitive flexibility which supports the building of resources over time. So even though the positive emotions might be fleeting, their lasting impact is in the traits, social bonds, and abilities which they help to establish and support, and they are therefore valuable for growth, development, and flourishing.

You might now be asking; this is all well and good but what has this got to do with play and playfulness in coaching? For individuals, for example, Proyer's research found that playfulness increased a person's positive emotions which in turn increased their thought-action repertoire (the more extensive à la carte menu of thought and behavioural options) and helped to discover new coping strategies.[27] This suggests that if we infuse playfulness into coaching which increases our clients' positive emotions, they will most likely be able to think of more options, possibilities, and ways of behaving. We come back to our super-loop as, interestingly, from our perspective as coaches, there's been research which suggests that positive emotions and interpersonal trust are mutually supportive.[28] Trust is necessary not only for play but also the coaching relationship, which we know to be a key factor for coaching effectiveness. Perhaps there's something in the willingness of the coach to venture into the unknown (which playfulness demands) with the client. When we play, we are more likely to co-create rather than to impose our expertise, and this willingness to be authentic and vulnerable might support our clients' trust which is then mutually supportive of the positive emotions that are experienced through play.

If we are working playfully with teams, which gives rise to positive emotions, the broaden-and-build theory argues that the team members will have a greater range of thought and behavioural options and as a result, they will build enduring team resources, such as a sense of belonging, social support and bonds which build and strengthen connections between team members[29] (even promoting a feeling of closeness and friendship[30]). This seems to be borne out by our and our Storytellers' experiences that playfulness supports the broadening of choices of thoughts and behaviours, sometimes with clients overcoming previous stories which they had told themselves about their limitations (along the lines of 'I can't do that' or 'I'm not the type of person who …') and about other members of their team. Feedback which we've had is that the participants felt like the playful experience was 'human to human'. The experience which the team has had together builds collective memories and sometimes a shared language which can have enduring effects on the team relationships and dynamics. We can use play and playfulness in this context to help team members develop each other's ideas and encourage communication (for example, through LEGO® Serious Play®), supporting team cohesion, collaboration and psychological safety.[31]

7.9 Playfulness, Positive Emotions and Behavioural Change

It seems intuitively logical that if we can learn to associate new behaviour with positive emotions then we are more likely to repeat that behaviour particularly if we can also tie in our values. This area is getting attention with positive affect and emotion becoming major topics in behavioural science.[32] A growing body of research suggests that positive affect and emotions can promote change by acting as rewards linked to the desired behaviour. For example, BJ Fogg, the founder of the Behaviour Design Lab at Stanford University is the creator of *Tiny Habits*.[33] This links intentionally calling up positive emotions through celebrating the success of taking tiny steps (as there was no previous word which captures this emotion, he calls it 'shine') as positive experiences reinforce habits. The method is imbued with playfulness in the approach to identifying the tiny steps, developing curiosity about the experience of the process and in how shine is created. This playfulness helps create positive affect which supports motivation for behavioural change.

Another example is Katy Milkman, co-founder, and co-director of the Behaviour Change for Good Initiative (bcfg.wharton.upenn.edu). In her book *How to Change*,[34] she describes the effect of integrating immediate fun as opposed to the delayed gratification of doing the right thing. A vivid example is the transformation of stairs into a piano keyboard at the Odenplan metro station, which encouraged 66% more users to take the stairs (joyfully, curiously, many energetically). It was part of thefuntheory.com, a campaign by Volkswagen; there are three videos on-line (the piano stairs, the world's deepest bin and the bottle bank arcade) showing how play and fun can encourage healthy and pro-environmental behaviour. Do have a look if you haven't seen them already, they'll make you smile and maybe inspire you. As Milkman argues, fun and enjoyment can provide Mary Poppins' spoonful of sugar to support overcoming short-term obstacles in support of longer-term goals, providing immediate gratification rather than relying on overestimated willpower. We can also be playful in designing and placing behavioural cues, this is something we use ourselves and encourage our clients to use, such as mini, colourful, playful sticker charts or pictures or fun objects next to relevant objects. Milkman also considers the concept of 'gamification'; essentially supporting desired behaviour or behavioural change by making the activity seem more engaging and less monotonous. It's an approach which can be very successful, though as the research which she includes points out, participants have to buy into the process. Like any form of play, it's not something which you can impose on others (we'll look at this in Chapter 9 again).

Finally, Dr. Jud Brewer, psychiatrist and neuroscientist specialising in addiction and habit change, works with rather than against the natural reward-based learning process of our brains. Instead of carrying out our habits on auto-pilot, he encourages us to cultivate curiosity alongside lightness and playfulness (which feel good and create psychological distance) as we build our awareness of what is driving our behaviour supported by mindfulness training. This facilitates the breaking of fear-based reactive addiction/anxiety habit patterns as we become disenchanted by those habits on a visceral level, letting them go and forming newer, healthier habits.

Contrast this to, for example, shame or fear driven behavioural change which in our experience rarely have lasting effect or promote happiness and well-being. Recent research has looked at the role of positive affect and emotions in areas such as healthy diet and exercise, pro-social and pro-environmental behaviours and showed a strong potential by behavioural interventions based on this approach.[35] Perhaps the ways in which we can tap into the power-house of affect and emotion in playful ways is only limited by our imagination and creativity. The researchers concluded that while the extent to which positive affect experience prospectively drives behaviour change (as distinct from rewarding the desired behaviour) is less clear, the different possible indirect pathways involving incidental effects of positive affect and specific positive emotions deserve rigorous future study. Fredrickson's research paper with Casey Brown (2021) suggests that experiencing positive affective states with others has distinctive characteristics from experiencing them by ourselves.[36] This suggests that similar to the systemic approach, what we experience individually is different to what we experience with one or more others. Amongst their findings were that co-experienced positive affect is characteristic of high-quality relationships and cooperative groups and is likely to have important implications for health and well-being. It's an area that needs further research and has exciting potential implications for playfulness in coaching, which as we've proposed has a significant relational element and is likely to support positive affect experiences. Future research exploring such questions could have profound impact on how we approach behavioural change not just through coaching individuals, teams or groups but also on a bigger scale in organisations and wider society. For more information on this, see for example *Play and Playfulness For Public Health and Wellbeing*.[37] Future research might also cast more light on the role of positive affect and emotions in sustaining behavioural change and how playfulness can support this.

Awareness of how playfulness can support behavioural change can enrich your coaching, not only in the divergent stage of thinking when your client is exploring but also particularly at the convergent stage when clients who have identified changes they wish to make are figuring out how to support and sustain that change. We've found that bringing a sense of fun and lightness to this stage of behavioural change has been very effective for our clients and a counterbalance to the negative emotions which invariably crop up on the path to change. Speaking of which …

7.10 Negative Emotions and Playfulness in Coaching

The label 'negative' can bring with it assumptions that these types of emotions are bad, mad, or dangerous to know, to borrow Lady Caroline's words.[38] Ask most people if they associate playfulness in coaching with negative emotions, we're willing to bet they'd say 'no' or mainly in the context of resistance, or if something's 'gone wrong'. Yet if we focused only on positive emotions, we'd be missing a large piece of the moving hologram of a jigsaw that is playfulness (see Chapter 3). Rather than avoiding or fearing negative emotions, through playfulness they can be held in a space which allows them to be understood and managed. They have the potential to be a rich source of learning and motivation. It is, of course, particularly important to acknowledge and respect the coaching/therapy boundaries here. When we are working with negative emotions as coaches, we need to work with our clients to ensure that they decide where and how far they want to go and that we stay within our capability as coaches and coaching ethical guidelines (for more on this, see Chapter 9).

This being human is a guest house.
Every morning a new arrival.

A joy, a depression, a meanness,
some momentary awareness comes
as an unexpected visitor.

Welcome and entertain them all!
Even if they're a crowd of sorrows,

who violently sweep your house
empty of its furniture,
still, treat each guest honorably.
He may be clearing you out
for some new delight......

Be grateful for whoever comes,
because each has been sent
as a guide from beyond.
Rumi (13th Century)[39]

In the beginning of this chapter, we spoke of the need for balance, for appreciating the yin and yang of positive and negative emotions. It's worth noting that negative emotions can also counterbalance too much of a positive emotion, for example, balancing the 'tyrannies of optimism' with pessimism's 'keen sense of reality'.[40] After all, in the coaching space, we are not being (or doing) playfulness for its own sake and after divergent thinking, when we move to convergent thinking, there needs to be a level of pragmatism in order to support the coaching outcomes.

Through playfulness, we can also, for example, leverage negative emotions to strengthen our coping ability. The astronaut Chris Hadfield describes the training programme at NASA where he was deliberately confronted with seemingly endless simulations of imagined difficult or dangerous scenarios. Through this he developed a pessimistic mindset crucially about those factors which were in his control. This strategic pessimism supported his sense of empowerment to cope with whatever might be thrown his way, forging 'the strongest possible armor to defend against fear: hard-won competence'.[41] You can see parallels with this and the LEGO® Serious Play® Real Time Strategy workshops. Here, once models of the team or organisation (depending on the focus of the workshop) and their stakeholders are built and the connections are made (using a mind-boggling array of LEGO® connectors to represent the quality of the connections/relationships), participants play out the impacts of imagined scenarios and how the team/organisation could react as well as the effects that might have on relevant stakeholders and systems. This phase of the workshop can be intense with detailed consideration of challenges and consequences which might give rise to a host of negative emotions yet allows the participants to deepen their awareness and frames of reference to be more empowered to adapt when inevitable challenges and change arise in real life. Of course, using LEGO® Serious Play® is just one example; you can use a variety of resources to create the imagined scenarios and work through them including art, modelling, and visualisation. We'll explore this more in The Playfulness Scrapbook.

In fact, we've seen in the previous chapter that through playfulness in the coaching space, within what Winnicott called 'holding' and Bion called 'containing' (and all the consequences which flow from this safety), the coach and client can venture into areas which will arouse the SNS by exploring and playing out different scenarios but in the absence of actual danger, so providing that safe space for exploration, curiosity, and learning. In Part II, we often refer to the discomfort which can arise for coaches and clients during playfulness as they venture into the unknown. This discomfort is likely to bring with it a measure of negative emotions and yet, it is in this zone of discomfort (but not overwhelm) where discovery and learning occurs.

By extension, in such holding or containing spaces, as we venture into areas where our clients' (and sometimes our) SNS is activated, a different relationship can be formed towards negative emotions and we can also be with these negative emotions in a way which allows space for positive emotions through moments of lightness, perspective and connection. Pertinent in the coaching context, positive emotions can offset the negative effects of negative emotions, a phenomenon called 'undo hypothesis'.[42] This positive emotion resilience effect[43] has been observed in participants using LEGO® bricks to explore their strengths, empowering the participants to face their fears and overcome challenges without ruminating over their negative emotions.[44] This resonates with our experience; seeing moments of joy, connection, love in the midst of a difficult or painful coaching session, yet through playfulness, the negative emotions are somehow held more lightly, enabling more distance and therefore easier to see and overcome, making space for the à la carte menu of attentions and actions again.

In the Nonviolent Communication model, negative emotions tell us that one or more needs are not being fulfilled. Through this lens, we can co-create inquiry into negative emotions, holding a space where we can support our clients to be aware of the negative emotion(s) which is arising for them, be curious about it, see why it is there, and hold it with compassion to themselves and others. Kirsten Neff who, alongside Chris Germer, is the pioneer of research into self-compassion suggests in *Fierce Self-Compassion*[45] that once we can hold our negative emotions with self-compassion, we are then able to discern what action is needed to address the situation which gave rise to that emotion. She uses the metaphor of the Mama Bear who is angry as a result of injury or injustice and discerns what action needs to be taken. This brings to mind Aristotle: 'Anyone can become angry – that is easy, but to be angry with the right person and to the right degree and at the right time and for the right purpose, and in the right way – that is not within everybody's power'.[46] In the *Once upon a time* story of the community group, through playfulness, their difficult emotions can be held and worked through validating, bringing awareness and wisdom to negative emotions, and allowing them to be motivators for values-led action rather than fuelling reactivity or obstructing collaboration or discerning action.

How can we do this? Through playfulness, for example, we can help our clients gain psychological distance (in ACT coaching terms through stepping into the Observing Self) to examine what negative emotions they are holding, to label their internal experience while dialling down as much as possible any criticism, judgment, or evaluation. Steve Biddulph in *Fully Human*[47] writes that there are four basic feelings: joy, anger, sadness, and fear and every 'hue and shadow of human emotion' is mixed from these primary emotions. We can play with this with our clients. There are practical ideas in The Playfulness Scrapbook which can be used in this context. For example, we can invite our clients to don their curiosity glasses and then represent their emotions through LEGO®, art materials, poetry, music, and so on, or we can help our clients to work with their Whole Body and imagine their negative emotions as shapes or colours or characters (see more in Part II). In teams and groups, by creating representations, it may also be easier to communicate and understand each other's negative emotions. They can also examine a team's collective negative emotion and how that impacts its members and also its stakeholders. In a playful way, we can come to a place that has much in common with mindfulness: bringing a non-judgmental curiosity to emotions and holding them with compassion which supports values-led discernment rather than habit or reactivity.

7.11 Conclusion

In this chapter, we've added positive and negative emotions into the mix of playfulness in coaching and hope that we have given you new insights and ideas for practice. While we have separated out positive and negative emotions, we invite you to see them as part of a whole, mixed in with the many other influences on our clients' thoughts and behaviours. We'll leave this chapter with a little musing. Adrianne Lenker, the lead singer of Big Thief, reflected in a radio interview in March 2022 about inspiration for their music and how she thought playfulness and sorrow stem from the same place. In our conversation with Graham Lee, he reminded us of the Buddhist quote that everyone will experience '10,000 joys and 10,000 sorrows' in their lifetime and that rather than seeing play as limited to a space of exuberance, when we are playful, we are actually in a space of equanimity; there is both groundedness and lightness from which we can see life with its opportunities and challenges. This idea is echoed in Rahner's concept of *Ernstheiterkeit* that we came across in Chapter 5.

There often seems to be a playfulness to wise people, as if either their equanimity has as its source this playfulness or the playfulness flows from equanimity; and they can persuade other people who are in a state of agitation to calm down and smile.

Edward Hoagland

Notes

1 Feldman-Barrett, L. (2018). *How Emotions are Made: The Secret Life of the Brain.* MacMillan.
2 'I'm extremely controversial': The psychologist rethinking human emotion. *The Guardian*, 25 September 2020. www.theguardian.com/books/2020/sep/25/im-extremely-controversial-the-psychologist-rethinking-human-emotion
3 Proyer, R. & Brauer, K. (2018). Exploring adult Playfulness: Examining the accuracy of personality judgments at zero-acquaintance and an LIWC analysis of textual information. *Journal of Research in Personality, 73*, 12–20.
4 www.discovermagazine.com/mind/discover-interview-jaak-panksepp-pinned-down-humanitys-7-primal-emotions
5 Panksepp, J. (1998). *Affective neuroscience: The foundations of human and animal emotions.* Oxford University Press. Panksepp, J. (2009). Brain emotional systems and qualities of mental life: From animal models of affect to implications for psychotherapeutics. In: Fosha, D., Siegel, D. & Solomon, M. (Eds.) *The healing power of emotion: Affective neuroscience, development, and clinical practice.* Norton, pp1–26. Panksepp, J. & Biven, L. (2012). *The archaeology of mind: Neuroevolutionary origins of human emotions.* Norton.
6 You can listen and see one of his laughing rats here: www.youtube.com/watch?v=ieP3lpyOHtU
7 Gould, S. (1977). *Ontogeny and Phylogeny.* Belknap Press.
  Montagu, A. (1981). *Growing Young.* McGraw-Hill.
8 *Ibid*, Montagu (1981).
9 Gordon, G. (2014). Well Played: The Origins and Future of Playfulness. American Journal of Play, 6(2), 234–266.
10 Proyer, R. (2017). A new structural model for the study of adult playfulness: Assessment and exploration of an understudied individual differences variable. *Personality and Individual Differences, 108*, 103–122.
11 Zhou, F., Wang, N. & Wu, Y. (2019). Does university playfulness climate matter? A testing of the mediation model of emotional labour. *Innovations in Education and Teaching International, 56*(2), 239–250. Boyatzis, R. Smith, M., Van Oosten, E. & Woolford, L. (2013). Developing resonant leaders through emotional intelligence, vision, and coaching. *Organizational Dynamics, 42*(1), 17–24.
12 Fredrickson, B. & Cohn, M. (2008). Positive emotions. In Lewis, M., Haviland-Jones, J. & Barrett, L. (Eds.) *Handbook of emotions.* Guilford Press, pp777–796.
13 Fredrickson, B. (2004). The broaden-and-build theory of positive emotions. *Philosophical Transactions of the Royal Society B: Biological Sciences, 359*(1449), 1369.

14 Fredrickson, B. (2013). *Love 2.0*. Plume.
15 Tomkins, S. (1962). *Affect imagery consciousness: Volume I: The positive affects.* Springer, p347.
16 Excerpted from list adapted from © 2014 Inbal Kashtan and Miki Kashtan- nvc@baynvc.org – www.baynvc.org
17 Fredrickson, B. (2001). The Role of Positive Emotions in Positive Psychology. *The American Psychologist*, 56(3), 218–226. Fredrickson, B. (2009). *Positivity: Top-notch research reveals the upward spiral that will change your life*. Three Rivers Press. Fredrickson, B. (2013). Updated thinking on positivity ratios. *American Psychologist*, 68, 814– 822.
18 *Ibid*, Fredrickson (2004).
19 Selvan, R. (2022). *The Practice of Embodying Emotions: A Guide for Improving Cognitive, Emotional, and Behavioral Outcomes*. North Atlantic Books.
20 http://peplab.web.unc.edu/research/#broadenandbuild for more information, including on positive leadership.
21 E.g., Sherrod, L. & Singer, J. (1989). The development of make-believe play. *Sports, games, and play*, 1–38.
22 Isen, A. (1990). The influence of positive and negative affect on cognitive organization: Some implications for development. *Psychological and biological approaches to emotion*, pp75–94.
23 From https://link.springer.com/referenceworkentry/10.1007/978-1-4419-1005-9_1088
24 E.g., Isen, A., Daubman, K. & Nowicki, G. (1987). Positive affect facilitates creative problem solving. *Journal of personality and social psychology*, 52(6), 1122–1131.
25 Proyer, R. (2017). A new structural model for the study of adult playfulness: Assessment and exploration of an understudied individual differences variable. *Personality and Individual Differences*, 108, 113–122.
26 E.g., Fredrickson, B., Cohn, M., Coffey, K., Pek, J. & Finkel, S. (2008). Open hearts build lives: positive emotions, induced through loving-kindness meditation, build consequential personal resources. *Journal of personality and social psychology*, 95(5), 1045.
27 Proyer, R. & Ruch, W. (2011). The virtuousness of adult playfulness: the relation of playfulness with strengths of character. *Psychology of Well-Being*, 1(1), 1–12.
28 Burns, A., Brown, J., Sachs-Ericsson, N., Plant, E., Curtis, J., Fredrickson, B. & Joiner, T. (2008). Upward spirals of positive emotion and coping: Replication, extension, and initial exploration of neurochemical substrates. *Personality and individual differences*, 44(2), 360–370.
29 Van Der Schalk, J., Fischer, A., Doosje, B., Wigboldus, D., Hawk, S., Rotteveel, M. & Hess, U. (2011). Convergent and divergent responses to emotional displays of ingroup and outgroup. *Emotion*, 11(2), 286.
30 These group momentary thought-action repertoires build enduring group social resources, such as a sense of membership, social support and bonds, a feeling of closeness and friendship (e.g., Rhee, S., 2007). Shared Positive Emotions and Group Effectiveness: The Role of Broadening-and-Building Interactions. *KAIST College of Business Working Paper Series* (2007–012).

Spoor, J. & Kelly, J. (2004). The evolutionary significance of affect in groups: Communication and group bonding. *Group processes & intergroup relations*, 7(4), 398–412.

31 Wheeler, S., Passmore, J. & Gold, R. (2020). All to play for: LEGO® SERIOUS PLAY® and its impact on team cohesion, collaboration, and psychological safety. *Journal of Work-Applied Management*, 12(2), 141–157.

32 E.g., Shiota, M., Sauter, D., & Desmet, P. (2021). What are 'positive' affect and emotion? *Current Opinion in Behavioral Sciences*, 39, 142–146.

33 Fogg, B.J. (2019). *Tiny habits: The small changes that change everything*. Eamon Dolan Books.

34 Milkman, K. (2021). *How to Change: The Science of Getting from where You are to where You Want to be*. Penguin.

35 Shiota, M., Papies, E., Preston, S. & Sauter, D. (2021). Positive affect and behavior change. *Current Opinion in Behavioral Sciences*, 39, 222–228.

36 Brown, C. & Fredrickson, B. (2021). Characteristics and consequences of co-experienced positive affect: understanding the origins of social skills, social bonds, and caring, healthy communities. *Current Opinion in Behavioral Sciences*, 39, 58–63.

37 Tonkin, A. and Whitaker, J. (Eds.) (2019). *Play and playfulness for public health and wellbeing*. Routledge.

38 Lady Caroline described her lover Lord Byron as 'mad, bad and dangerous to know' (early 19th Century).

39 Rumi, J. (1995). *The Essential Rumi*. (Barks, C. Trans.). Harper, p109.

40 Seligman, M. (1990). *Learned Optimism*. Pocket Books, p292.

41 Hadfield, C. (2013). *An astronaut's guide to life on Earth*. MacMillan, p54. Thanks to Ivatz, I., Lomas, T., Hefferon, K. & Worth, P. (2016). *Second Wave Positive Psychology*. Routledge, p14 for drawing our attention to this and the Rumi poem.

42 Fredrickson, B. & Levenson, R. (1998). Positive emotions speed recovery from the cardiovascular sequelae of negative emotions. *Cognition & emotion*, 12(2), 191–220.

43 Fredrickson, B. (2009). *Positivity: Top-notch research reveals the upward spiral that will change your life*. Three Rivers Press.

44 Harn, P. & Hsiao, C. (2018). Strength-4D career model with LEGO® SERIOUS PLAY® and six bricks. *International Journal of Management and Applied Research*, 5(4), 157–173.

45 Neff, K. (2021). *Fierce Self-Compassion: How Women Can Harness Kindness to Speak Up, Claim Their Power, and Thrive*. Penguin Life.

46 Aristotle (2000/350 BC). *Nicomachean Ethics* (Crisp, R. Ed.). Cambridge University Press.

47 Biddulph, S. *Fully Human: A new way of using your mind*. Bluebird, p86.

8
What's so Funny?:
A Closer Look at Humour

In this chapter we:

- Take you on a whistle stop tour of humour and laughter and how it relates to coaching and playfulness
- See how humour and playfulness are distinct but overlap
- Explore what humour is
- Consider the functions of humour, laughter, and play
- Remember the shadow side of humour
- Turn specifically to humour (closely interlinked with playfulness) in coaching
- Go deeper on what humour can add to coaching conversations
- Get personal and consider individual differences in traits and styles
- Offer you plenty of reflection questions about you and your practice and questions which you can add to your arsenal during your practice, reflection, and supervision

When was the last time you laughed? Really laughed? Pause for a moment to take yourself back there (close your eyes if you like) and reflect on what it felt like, how you felt afterwards, and how you felt about others that you laughed with. In this chapter, we explore humour in the context of playfulness in coaching and how it can be a rich resource for your practice.

DOI: 10.4324/9781003090847-9

Q: *What's round, white and giggles?*

A: A tickled onion!

We invite you to turn to the *Once upon a time* stories at the start of Chapter 6 through positive emotion lenses again and this time focus on how humour and laughter might feature as you play with evolving the different scenarios. As we suggested in the previous chapter, we think that playfulness in coaching goes beyond associations with fun and amusement. Nevertheless, it's fair to say that in our experience, there is often an element of fun and amusement at least to some degree. In addition, the lightness and changes in perspective associated with playfulness in coaching almost invariably give rise to humour and laughter, even when the playfulness is more on the middle or inner levels of the Be Playful Onion Model (the outer level 'doing' play is probably more readily associated with humour and laughter at first glance).

In the early years of our exploration of playfulness, we both questioned whether we were playful as coaches. Reflecting back, our doubts were part of the process of developing the Be Playful Onion Model. As we looked around, we didn't identify our work with more overtly 'doing' play through inherently play-based or playful tools (LEGO® Serious Play® aside for now). We came to realise that much of our playfulness is in the 'being' space often expressed through joy, humour, and laughter, though of course sometimes in small doses if the topic is heavy and sensitivity is called for. Even when we and our clients are engaged in serious or intellectual playfulness (both considered in Chapter 5), we can't think of any sessions which didn't involve at least a little humour and laughter. At times, the lightness and perspective of a humour infused playful approach has helped us to stay within coaching/therapy boundaries.

It was interesting that when we spoke to our Storytellers about their work, some didn't consider themselves particularly playful either until we explored further together and playful stories emerged. Yet, in all of our conversations with the Storytellers, our serious confabulations (what a lovely word) and reflections were infused with lightness, humour, and laughter. Equally, as you'd expect, given what we've just said, our clients share this space of humour and laughter even in the midst of challenging conversations (it would be a bit strange and not very effective if we were laughing only to ourselves!).

> When describing their ideal partner for learning dialogue, people typically talk about someone who stimulates them in a positive, light-hearted manner, who empathises while maintaining a positive sense of detachment, and who is able to use humour to break cycles of negative or over-introspection.
> *David Clutterbuck & David Megginson*[1]

Understanding more about our own and our clients' humour, how it is related to what is going on for us internally and the role it plays in dyad and group dynamics is not only interesting but arguably necessary if we're going to welcome playfulness in our practice. If we take the Gestalt approach that everything is data (or even if you don't but wish to deepen your reflection on your own and/or in supervision), then it stands to reason that humour and laughter in the playfulness in coaching space is potentially a rich source of inquiry, information and insight.

8.1 Playfulness and Humour

Researchers of playfulness in children have observed that laughter and humour develop in children in the context of play.[2] Many view humour as a particular form of mental play and early and very influential writers and researchers on child playfulness included humour as one of the dimensions of play.[3] As we explored in Chapter 5, in the context of adults, there have been moves towards a greater untangling of threads of playfulness and related constructs such as humour. These include the notion of serious playfulness, the OLIW model[4] and the proposal that humour and playfulness are best seen as non-identical but strongly overlapping.[5] People can be playful without being humorous and humorous without being playful.[6]

If we invite playfulness into coaching and humour comes along for at least some of the ride, it can be quite a challenge in practice to untangle the threads. We're not suggesting that such untangling is always necessary or even helpful in practice; during reflection-in-action, we don't consciously ask ourselves 'In this moment, am I offering playfulness or humour?'. However, it's useful to know that they don't necessarily go hand-in-hand and open up different avenues of exploration.

8.1.1 What is Humour?

If playfulness and humour are not the same, then let's take a step back and ask ourselves what we mean by 'humour'. The answer seems rather obvious at first glance, but perhaps surprisingly, as with playfulness, researchers, academics, and laypersons mean different things by humour depending on the context. Martin & Ford (2018) in their comprehensive and rich integrative collection of research and literature *The Psychology of Humor*,[7] observe that there is in fact no universally agreed definition. In this context then, they offer the following definition:

> Humor is a broad, multifaceted term that represents anything that people say or do that others perceive as funny and tends to make them laugh, as well as the mental processes that go into both creating and perceiving such an amusing stimulus, and also the emotional response of mirth involved in the enjoyment of it.[8]

In essence, it can pop up as a behaviour, a reaction to another's behaviour or as a trait[9] and importantly, it's essentially a social phenomenon, a form of social play. Interestingly, although positive psychology has been slow to pay the deserved attention to adult playfulness, it sees humour as a core component of emotional psychological well-being. It was identified by Peterson and Seligman (2004)[10] as a character strength allowing people to see the light side of adversity and which contributes to the virtue of transcendence (the ability to find meaning and purpose in one's life by connecting with the wider world outside the self).

We don't yet have agreed models of the dynamics of humour and its different components which reflect its complexity and help show causal links between humour and its possible effects and implications. Like playfulness, its maladaptive functions are likely to get greater attention from researchers in the future. So, you see, while humour has a head start on playfulness in terms of research, particularly in the context of therapy, in many ways we're still at a relatively early stage of our understanding and there's much left to discover. This is important work. Just as Panksepp discovered PLAY circuitry in mammals including humans (which we explored in the previous chapter), researchers are beginning to identify specialised brain circuits for humour and laughter in humans.[11] As Martin & Ford (2018) suggest, the ability to enjoy humour and express it through laughter seems to be an essential part of what it means to be human.

In that case, why? Let's turn our attention to the functions of humour to enrich our awareness and insight of what's going on for us and our clients whether at an individual level, in dyads or groups when humour is in play.

8.2 Functions of Humour, Laughter and Play

> The best thing about humor is that it shows people that they are not alone.
> *Sid Caesar*

Have another look at the *Once upon a time* stories (Chapter 6) and concentrate on the one which you're drawn to for now. Think about how humour might bubble up in the story and what functions it might serve. For example, in the Monday morning meeting story, the team might be resigned (in the absence of a team coach!) that the meandering Monday morning meetings are going to stay a fixture despite their pressing workloads. They might develop a funny way of referring to the meetings (probably without John's knowledge), inject humour during the meetings to soften their feelings of frustration or anxiety. By finding a humorous way of looking at their predicament they might feel closer as a team, though again probably to the exclusion of John or they may bring humour into the equation in a way which includes the whole team, John too, and which makes the meetings less frustrating and more enjoyable. These examples reflect Martin & Ford's (2018) suggestion that the psychological functions of humour can be broken down into three broad categories: tension relief and coping, emotional and interpersonal benefits of mirth (the positive emotion associated with humour and laughter) and social functions in group contexts. Let's look at these in a little more detail in the context of playfulness in coaching.

8.2.1 Tension Relief and Coping

The first category is pretty self-explanatory and includes supporting our coping ability and resilience to stress which are vital to our well-being. The levity that comes with humour (always laughing *with* rather than *at* our clients) is a powerful way to help shift perspective and for clients to see their situation in a different light, giving them the space for holding their emotions and broadening their options. Auriel Majumdar gave us an example of this when she was working with a client who was very stressed and referred to it as 'going through the fire'. They talked about what that meant for her, how it felt, staying with not knowing and exploring what would happen when she came through it. It was really serious work and yet within a few minutes, they were roaring with laughter as something Auriel's client shared struck them as really absurd. She had mentioned a course she was on and was relatively relaxed about as long as she got the minimum grade that she had set herself. Auriel asked her what that grade was. Her client shared a wildly ambitious grade and in that moment they both laughed. The contrast between the client's continued drive and ambition to excel and her previous reflections on the toll that life was taking on her struck them both as absurd, and spontaneous laughter erupted. The shared laughter felt playful and appropriate; light but not minimizing, and dipping in and out of playfulness even in tough moments built on rapport and knowing her client. The client knew Auriel fully respected her and the laughter was not directed *at* her.

Moving to teams, you might notice ripples of laughter at times which don't appear to be sparked by something proportionately funny, This might signal a release of tension in the team. As coaches, we can notice these ripples and be curious about what they might signify, noticing any patterns or perceived effects. Where it feels appropriate and of service, we can share our observations and curiosity with the team and invite them to join us in exploring further.

8.2.2 Emotional and Interpersonal Benefits

It's pretty obvious that humour can lead to positive affect, and we've seen in the previous chapter that this supports creativity, motivation and much more. In our work, we've found humour invaluable in establishing rapport and trust quickly. Humour usually surfaces very early on in our conversations with clients and is often present, if only in small doses in the midst of topics that are challenging for them. It makes sense then that Sutton-Smith (2003:13) suggests that one of the essential functions of play 'is to make fun of the emotional vulnerabilities of anger, fear, shock, disgust, loneliness, and narcissism'[12] (again, in coaching, laughing *with* rather than *at* our clients of course). You can see how this might play out in coaching. Through humour, we can make sense of difficult emotions or perceptions of our experiences or see them from a different perspective which might feel more manageable or give us more options. Moving from the personal to the interpersonal, criticism or disapproval can be communicated with levity in a way that might create space for dialogue and change rather than defensiveness. We've found that the mixture of compassion (and facilitating self-compassion for our clients) and humour can be a potent one, bringing levity to difficult topics and opening up space for different perspectives and change.

8.2.3 Social Functions

Other people provide the context in which we experience humour, so it is fundamentally a social phenomenon. It's essentially a way for people to initiate and monitor relationships. From a psychological perspective, humour is a form of social play. While it's not an essential component of positive social interactions, it's often a desirable one. Nankhonde Kasonde-van den Broek shared with us how she finds that humour works well in teams when they are at a difficult impasse or in strong polarised positions. When she needs the room to come back together, she often does it with humour without validating one or other individual or group. Humour can unify, strengthen group bonds, smooth over conflict, build a sense of belonging and cohesiveness and contribute to moving towards group goals.

Humour and laughter are related, of course, but also distinct, and there is also much that remains to be understood about specific functions of laughter. In essence, we laugh to communicate positive emotional states to others, signal that we are engaging in play, create and maintain connections with others and communicate within groups. If you haven't seen them already, do watch Prof Sophie Scott's TedTalks on laughter. Laughter and humour act as social lubricants, strengthening bonds and diffusing threats (not just physical but hopefully more relevant in a work context, emotional and psychological such as feedback, complaints, conflict, and so on).

In *The Psychology of Humor at Work*, the authors[13] invite us to notice how humour and laughter patterns are often ingrained in a team's interactions, for example, sharing insider jokes or laughing at something which is only funny to those who have understood the context or took part in shared complex group experiences. This is consistent with the reflections of participants in research on the LEGO® Serious Play® Real Time Strategy for the Team workshop which Stephanie co-authored,[14] some of whom spoke about the experience as helping the team to create a 'shared language' which had meaning and effect long after the workshop. Crowe et al. (2017)[15] argue that humour triggers and emergent patterns in teams should be the focus of future research, something which will be of interest to team coaches.

8.3 The Shadow Side of Humour

If our work is infused with playfulness and humour is present whether with individual clients or in groups/teams we are working with, let's not be naïve and let's be aware of the shadow side of humour. While it is useful to appreciate the positive ways in which humour can support our work and our clients, precisely because there is also a shadow side, it's worth looking a little deeper when humour is present in individuals, dyads, and groups/teams and, in group/team contexts, to be curious as to how it's used and by whom. We'll look at this in more detail in the next chapter in the context of risks. There we'll see, for example, that particularly in group contexts, humour can also divide, isolate, humiliate, manipulate, foster discrimination, establish social boundaries, and build up status at the expense of others. It's worth bearing in mind that whether used in a positive or negative way, humour can evoke laughter and genuine feelings of mirth. Humour can help to identify members of an in-group, reward efforts to cooperate and enhance interpersonal bonding and group cohesion (while the shadow side of humour can serve to achieve the opposite); all potentially of interest to team coaches as well as coaches working 1:1. Once again, our playfulness embraces the complexity!

We'll consider some of the things to look out for in this chapter and come back to the shadow side in Chapter 9. Paying attention as to when, why and how humour is used will help deepen our awareness of what's playing out in the coaching space and enable us to act with more discernment and wisdom. It can give us clues as to what might be of service to the client for us to explore and tap into more, or to address, whether we are working in the moment or being more deliberate in our planning of humour and playfulness in our work.

8.3.1 Humour (Closely Interlinked with Playfulness) in Coaching

Jeff Warren is a meditation teacher whose playful and humorous style Stephanie loves. In one meditation Jeff describes humour as 'irreverent and generous'[16] and this is the energy which we believe can be tapped into in coaching. 'How?', you might ask. We'll meet Louis Franzini in a moment. He suggests that therapeutic humour (and we'd add humour in the coaching space) can take almost any form[17] and we've experienced a range both in our own coaching practice as have most of our Storytellers. Ideas Franzini suggests the inclusion of spontaneous puns, behavioural or verbal parapraxes or spoonerisms (we'll leave you to explore what these are), humorous comments pointing out absurdities or illogical reasoning, exaggerations ('Always?', 'So, when you … ?'), illustrations of universal human frailties or comical observations of current social events and for the brave-hearted (depending on your point of view) formal jokes or riddles or limericks.

More broadly and rather wonderfully, there is an Association for Applied and Therapeutic Humor based in the US which provides a wealth of resources on humour and also playfulness. It offers this definition of therapeutic humour:

> Any intervention that promotes health and wellness by stimulating a playful discovery, expression, or appreciation of the absurdity or incongruity of life's situations. This intervention may enhance health or be used as a complementary treatment of illness to facilitate healing or coping, whether physical, emotional, cognitive, social, or spiritual.[18]

We can use an awareness of humour and laughter to support our coaching interventions and we can also design coaching interventions that draw on humour and laughter in service of our clients. It's time then to look more specifically at what humour can add to our practice.

8.3.2 What Can Humour Add to Coaching?

Just as with playfulness, there appears to be relatively little direct research on humour in coaching. However, conveniently for us, humour in therapy has received research attention particularly in the last 10 years. What's more, humour has been recommended as a useful tool in individual therapy and counselling as well as group therapy by therapists from diverse theoretical approaches, some of which have evolved into coaching approaches. To make sense of how we might play with humour in service of our clients, let's look at it through the lenses of the coaching relationship, working with emotions, working with thoughts, and supporting behavioural change. Once again, we're pretending that these fall into neat categories, but of course they are part of a dynamic system, so do please see them as such and also as part of the bigger context of considerations about you, your client (and the additional layers which come with teams if that's relevant) as well as the relational coaching space between you. Again, by bringing more awareness, we can increase our discernment as to what might be in service to our client in that moment or in any planning we might be doing in advance and particularly for our purposes, what that means for the level of playfulness which we want to include and how.

8.3.2.1 The Coaching Relationship

It sounds obvious, but worth acknowledging that humour can help build rapport. We've mentioned before how one of the functions of humour is to relieve tension and support coping. The research bears out what we would intuitively expect: humour can help put clients at ease and reduce tension. Better yet, it's a social skill that can be honed and developed like any other.[19] What's more, in the context of coaching where we are working as equals collaborating and co-creating with our clients rather than presenting ourselves as the experts with the answers, humour can help us seem more human and relatable. For example, through humorous self-disclosure or self-disparaging stories, we can convey empathetic understanding of our client's story, and this supports rapport. In this context, humour can help the coach and client create a transitional 'play space' with a 'shared reality and rewarding interchange'.[20]

> Laughing together may promote feelings of intimacy and friendliness and facilitate the client's trust in the therapist.
>
> *Martin and Ford (2018:322)*

At the heart of laughter is communication: communicating playfulness, safety, and connection. So perhaps experiencing authentic laughter (beyond a polite chuckle) allows a space to be created where we can communicate in a more authentic, more vulnerable way. In these moments, perhaps sometimes we are creating what Fredrickson writes about in *Love 2.0* as micro-moments of love.[21] the effects of which, particularly in the context of playfulness in coaching, we looked at in the previous chapter.

Can you remember when you last laughed uncontrollably? If you can't and you miss it, we'd encourage you to find your laughter, whether through a book, film, sharing laughs with a friend, laughter yoga class or an improv class or whatever else might tickle you. When you laugh uncontrollably and you feel like you are teetering on the divide between laughing and crying, it is an overwhelmingly somatic experience. You let go of a sense of control and are fully present in your emotions and body. Perhaps in these moments, we can't help but disengage our controlling, judging mind and drop our mask; we have no choice but to be authentically ourselves. Perhaps by laughing together with our clients, they, and we, are present as human-to-human in the space we have created together, deepening our relationship and leaving aside status, assigned roles, releasing some of the 'shoulds' and so much more which can be invaluable for our work together.

In this authentic space, we think that sensitivity is called for, creating a space in which we and our clients can find expressions of humour that allow for individual preferences (we'll look at these more in detail later) just like we described in relation to playfulness with the Be Playful Onion Model in Chapter 5. For some, a subtle and quiet expression of humour might feel most natural and most support the work together (in terms of rapport and other aspects of the work). For others, a more expressive style of humour might work best. A phrase which anchors us when we notice a possible disconnect is: 'It's not about me!'. Whatever form of humour you are using and encouraging in the coaching space, it is hopefully in service of your client. This requires being aware of your own preferred style, how it is coming across and being received, the impact which it is having and whether your ultimate motivation is in service of the client or more to serve you in some way (you might need to dig a little through reflection and/or supervision). The proviso to this is that learning takes place in zones of discomfort – more on this in the next chapter and Part II.

8.3.2.2 Working with Emotions

There is a considerable body of research which supports the view that humour functions as a way of regulating emotions, increasing the experience of positive emotions, and decreasing negative emotions such as depression and anxiety. Through modelling and encouraging a humorous outlook, therapists and coaches can help clients regulate their emotions which in turn can create greater choice points.

> If you have no tragedy, you have no comedy. Crying and laughing are the same emotion. If you laugh too hard, you cry. And vice versa.
> *Sid Caesar, American comic actor and writer*

Come back to the image of teetering on the divide between laughing and crying. We've seen in the previous chapter that sorrow and joy often sit closely together. Why is this relevant to coaching? Perhaps by helping our clients access laughter, they are also getting closer to making space for any sorrow which they hold, allowing them to truly feel and release their difficult feelings. Research into people with a condition called 'forced laughter' (in a nutshell, bursts of involuntary laughter) suggests that some of the brain centres in charge of controlling crying and laughing are found very close to each other. This may indicate a close link between the distressing emotions associated with social separation and the positive emotions of social play.[22] This really resonates with what we've seen in practice. Sometimes the sessions which have been the most emotionally challenging have also involved the most laughter.

Stephanie relates: *I once held a coaching session at home while my husband was in a different part of the house. Afterwards he said bemusedly that it sounded like we were having a party. In fact, we had been talking about a painful and significant decision which my client needed to make. Through humour and playfulness, we created a space in which I introduced non-inherently playful or humorous tools in a way that we could consider the issue with a degree of lightness and perspective (and at times a lot of laughter, as well as my client's tears) which allowed my client to come to a decision. The playful humour in the session also prevented her from being overwhelmed by difficult emotions, whilst still acknowledging them, thus enabling her to reflect and think, as well as notice positive emotions which were also arising. This approach also helped to keep us in a coaching rather than therapeutic space. Really critical again, was that it was very clear from our rapport and trust that I was holding the space with unconditional positive regard[23] and compassion and laughing with and not at my client.*

8.3.2.3 Working with Thoughts

Humour can facilitate finding new ways of thinking. Humour is a way in which coaches can avoid being sucked into the client's story respectfully and with trust and rapport responding with lightness and compassion. We can also model a different way of responding to criticism or complaints. Olson (1994)[24] looked at how by responding with mild self-deprecation or taking a humorous perspective to criticism from the client, the therapist can show how a potentially embarrassing or threatening situation can be dealt with through humour in a way that is hopeful and positive.

With awareness, including awareness of humour styles (more on which later), a coach can mine a client's humour like a detective to help facilitate insights into their perceptions, assumptions, attitudes, and feelings about a particular topic. Martin and Ford[25] (the number of times we're citing their book really is a testament to the rich resource it is) note how therapists can often nudge clients towards such insights by using gentle humour to highlight any absurdity or irrationality of the client's attitude or assumptions and also to help gain a sense of proportion about the challenges being faced. This is inherent in the approach of provocative therapy/coaching too, more on which later. Having supported insight, humour can then help develop alternative perspectives and new ways of thinking. This is how humour often crops up in our coaching. When we've established trust and rapport with our clients, unconscious assumptions and beliefs are brought to the surface and examined, often while we model curiosity and a lightness through compassion. The result is that they often gain a new perspective and then comes the 'aha' moment accompanied by spontaneous laughter. When we then laugh too, that new perspective is reinforced. We then encourage our clients to think of new ways forward with sprinklings of humour either in terms of how they think about options or how to make the options have a playful element (or both of course).

> Can we laugh together at the absurdity of the limiting mindset?
> *Graham Lee (in conversation)*

Stephanie relates: *In a session on a different topic, it emerged that my client was holding on to shame over poor school exam results even though, decades later, he was a successful professional. I decided to respond with humour and joked that he was missing a trick, many successful professionals and especially entrepreneurs almost wear theirs as a badge of honour. We both laughed and played with this idea a little. It seemed a release, a compassionate way to encourage reframing rather than the intellectual reasoning which hadn't worked – he had known for years that there was no need to or benefit from holding on to the shame but was unable to let go. With humour, he was able to see a different perspective and create some psychological distance from the school exam results and the associated shame. Laughing together reinforced this change in perspective. In the context of conversations that we were having around developing self-compassion, the joke and shared laughter enabled a swift shift.*

You'll find more examples in The Playfulness Scrapbook.

As demonstrated by this story, humour can facilitate a new way of thinking by being a disruptor. From a Gestalt perspective, humour (and playfulness of course) can be used in coaching to disrupt thinking patterns and you can see disruption through humour in several other schools of therapy from which coaching approaches have evolved. To give you an idea and direction for further exploration, we've selected three to look at a little more closely: Rational Emotive Behaviour Therapy, Provocative Therapy and Acceptance Commitment Therapy.

Albert Ellis who developed rational emotive behaviour therapy (REBT), the forebearer of cognitive behaviour therapy, saw the use of humour as a powerful way of undermining what he saw as a major cause of emotional disturbance: taking yourself and life too seriously. He advocated the use of humour to build a strong therapeutic alliance and accept clients' limitations and uncertainties of life by challenging unhelpful beliefs and reinforcing emotional and behavioural change. Wood et al. (2019)[26] use the lovely phrase of 'humour and anti-awfulizing'. Such humour can take many forms including songs, jokes, parables, and aphorisms ('a bad penny always turns up'). Listen to this short song 'Whine! Whine! Whine!' which illustrates it perfectly: huzzaz.com/video/283211. For those who like the idea of using songs, there are lots of resources available online based on Albert Ellis' approach including recordings, lyrics, and ideas. In some of these approaches, we find ourselves in the comfort zones of extroverts and perhaps the discomfort zones of introverts. We can't yet see ourselves belting out tunes to clients to help them disrupt their thinking patterns, but that's the beauty of the exploration into playfulness in coaching. We all have different comfort zones, and our sincere hope is that in a few years' time, we'll be working in ways which aren't even on our radars yet, and which at the moment, would be more likely to be in our zones of overwhelm rather than discomfort (again, more on these zones and their relationship to playfulness in coaching in Part II).

Another style of therapy of which humour is an important component is provocative therapy and coaching. Developed by Frank Farrelly in the 1950s,[27] its name comes from the root meaning of 'provocative' which is to 'call out' rather than to aggressively challenge. When we first heard the term some years ago, we had an image of a coach almost aggressively confronting clients and this felt quite alien to us and to be honest, potentially intimidating (for the client). In fact, the style of this calling out is by warm-hearted humour in various forms including irony, exaggeration, self-deprecation, and absurdities. It is done with awareness and deliberateness, a smile playing on your lips, a twinkle in your eye, the warmth you'd extend to your close friend in affectionate banter. What the therapist or coach does is effectively to play devil's advocate, amplifying the negative voice of the client's ambivalence towards the areas they are working on. The therapist may also facetiously agree with the client's negative feelings and expectations, goading them to continue with their self-defeating attitudes and behavioural patterns.[28] Neil Mullarkey told us of the general approach of bouncing something unexpected at someone and they will tell you 'yes, it's like that' or 'no, it's not' and, when they laugh, you know that you have hit on their truth or, it's so absurd that it's not true but helps the coachee realise what the truth is for them.

And finally, Acceptance and Commitment Therapy (ACT) coaching is full of playful, humorous interventions supporting for example acceptance and cognitive defusion. You'll find short ACT videos online which explain these concepts in fun, accessible, and memorable ways, such as the sushi conveyor belt or passengers on a bus both representing the thoughts which we can notice and be discerning about rather than attaching to them. Stephanie has found that the simple but memorable imagery and use of metaphors in ACT coaching to be highly effective with clients particularly when used in a space of compassionate humour.

8.3.2.4 Working with Thoughts (Extra Considerations for Groups)

Let's move our focus for a moment to groups. In this context, humour can be a useful signal of transitional points in conversations. Research conducted by Carmine Consalvo that might have implications for team coaching, found that humour and laughter occur most frequently in transition points in managerial meetings, for example, when the group moves from problem-identification to problem-solving. She concluded that at these transition points, the humour signalled a willingness to collaborate to solve the problem and conveyed an open, accepting and mutually supporting attitude among group members. Crowe et al. (2017) who we met above in the context of the social functions of humour in groups, suggest that research results imply that shared team humour patterns can serve an important function for team problem-solving and creativity processes. For group/team coaches then, humour can also be data which we can gather and consider as we observe what is playing out in front of us as we decide how we dance with the group/team in the moment.

8.3.2.5 Humour Supporting Behavioural Change

In the previous chapter, we looked at how positive emotions are intentionally incorporated in a variety of approaches to support behavioural change and we can of course incorporate humour into these approaches too. Humour can also support behavioural change through using shared laughter to reinforce positive change by finding and supporting more flexible and adaptive ways of coping with situations, for example, laughing together when a client reports back how they have tried out a new way of thinking or behaving since the last session. Research supports the effectiveness of using humour in a sensitive empathetic way in therapy[29] and it doesn't seem unreasonable to assume that the same holds true for coaching.

Mulling over what you've just read, pause for a little to reflect on how this might affect your practice:

- *How does humour and laughter show up in your life and practice?*
- *What is the role which humour currently plays in your life and practice?*
- *How much is your playfulness interwoven with humour?*
- *Do you see a pattern in the functions of humour which you rely on (tension relief and coping, emotional and interpersonal benefits, and social function)?*
- *How alert are you to the shadow side of humour in yourself and others?*
- *What role does humour play in your work through the lenses of:*
  - *the coaching relationship*
  - *working with emotions*
  - *working with thoughts*
  - *supporting behavioural change*
- *Where is there scope for experimentation?*
- *What needs more attention?*
- *What needs to be let go of?*
- *Where is the laughter in the system that is you and your professional practice?* (This last question is one of David Clutterbuck's)

8.4 Let's Get Personal

So far, we've spoken about humour as if it's homogeneous (another lovely word). But of course, we're not all the same, so why should our humour be?

With greater awareness, we can recognise this and bring curiosity to individual differences at play in humour. What does a person's humour style tell you about how they relate to themselves? How do they relate to others? Does their style vary depending on context? Remember that humour is a social phenomenon and noticing the impact of a person's humour style on a group/team individually and collectively means that we can gather more information for us to consider, reflect back, reinforce or challenge.

Before we dive in, let's also acknowledge that some people just don't display much humour (not you of course, you're very funny). Yet just like adult playfulness, humour has serious functions, social impact, and ramifications. It seems an important question to ask therefore whether everyone can find and strengthen their funny bone. William Fry (1924–2014), self-proclaimed as the first gelotologist (we just had to include that word, it means an expert in the science of laughter) argued that humour is a skill that can be learned. This might be worth exploring with a client if their circumstances suggest they might benefit from doing some muscle (of the humour kind) strengthening exercises.[30] Indeed, McGhee (1996, 2010)[31] developed his *Seven Humor Habits Program*, a practical training to sharpen people's sense of humour and humour training has been found to be effective for all ages.[32] On the flip side, we or our clients might have developed a maladaptive form of humour (the shadow side) and here we can invite an exploration of the effect and possible space for development/change.

Turning to individual differences in humour, what might this look like? There appears to be an emerging view in the research, that different personalities (open/closed, conscientious/unconscientious, introverts/extroverts, agreeable/hostile, or neurotic/emotionally stable) and in particular, unique personality traits are expressed through different humour styles and enjoy different comic styles.[33] There's also a temperament-based approach to classifying humour traits (which then influence the humour style).[34] In case this needs clarification, in essence a trait is a personality characteristic that is stable, consistent and varies from person to person and the humour style is how you express that humour. This is further refined by the comic style which you might use (for instance sarcasm). With the temperament-based approach, you see where you sit on the spectrum of three key traits of cheerfulness, mood, and playfulness and the unique combinations relate to different humour styles. To illustrate, you might be described as having the trait of having a 'good sense of humour' and you'd display this pretty consistently in different circumstances, for example, mostly being in a cheerful mood and having a playful (non-serious) attitude to life compared to someone who is more often than not in a hump with a serious attitude. Different styles of humour, for example, caustic and acerbic might be related to different permutations of the three temperament traits. This approach throws up interesting future areas of research, for example, high cheerfulness is associated with resilience to psychosocial stress (which might arise from poor work design, organisation and management[35]) and there might be some interplay between high cheerfulness and the mental and physical health benefits of humour. Like playfulness, there is a lot more complexity than first meets the eye!

We're going to add to the complexity a little further and layer in that different humour styles can be expressed through different comic styles. While we (Teresa and Stephanie) laugh a lot, the idea of either of us telling structured jokes with a killer punchline especially to a big group doesn't make us smile, if fact, quite the opposite. This got us pondering and noticing the different expressions of humour in our work and conversations with our Storytellers. For example, David Clutterbuck told us of working with teams as he and they compose songs, write limericks, tell jokes (sometimes quite provocative). Emma Skitt told us of using humorous metaphors as the basis for work with individuals and teams and an exercise that she calls the 'Ambassador and Gremlin'. Steve Chapman's approach is full of humour and warmth, with the story of Bob and the Daffodils as an example (see the Playfulness Scrapbook in Part II for more on both). Other stories involved more gentle humour, perhaps pointing out ironies/inconsistencies, being the oil of the conversation supporting rapport, bringing some perspective to challenges and laughing at what it is to be human. In a bid to broaden (and deepen) our understanding of humour, Ruch et al. (2018) looked at how different comic styles differentially tap into individual temperament, character and ability and came up with eight comic styles: fun, humour, nonsense, wit, irony, satire, sarcasm, and cynicism.[36] Interesting from a coaching perspective is that the stated ultimate aim of the researchers in identifying a comprehensive list of narrow and specific comic styles is that they can be 'enacted, trained, and modified'.[37] For us, we can add this awareness of differences in comic styles into our toolkit both in our observation of ourselves and our clients and in our assumptions around humour in our playfulness in coaching (for example, what might tickle us might leave another cold).

As fascinating as this foray into detail is, we'll pop back out of the rabbit hole. We thought a quick detour might be worthwhile to give a nod to complexity and how much we still don't know. If you are excited to discover the complexity and would like to explore it further, have fun! If on the other hand, you're not, that's fine too; it can be helpful to simply be aware that there are different humour traits and these are likely to be expressed through different humour and comic styles. Not least, appreciating that there are different humour traits and styles can make it less tempting to think 'I'm just not funny' just as some coaches we've spoken to who find it hard to access playfulness generally or during our workshops have said, 'I'm just not playful'. (You'll have spotted the limiting beliefs and association with identity there and a dash of fixed mindset and are no doubt bubbling with insightful questions.) If you appreciate that there are many ways to access and communicate humour and playfulness, it gives you: more space for developing those capacities in a way that is authentic to you; greater awareness of how you want to be in the coaching space; and enhanced appreciation of and inquiry into the significance and impact of what's playing out in front of you. With that in mind, let's look at how being aware of different humour styles might be helpful in practice.

8.4.1 Humour Styles

As we've said above, humour can give useful clues as to the internal world of our clients. From a well-being perspective, Martin et al. (2003)[38] developed the Humor Styles Questionnaire which looks at the different uses of humour in daily life. They found four types of humour styles, two of which could support well-being (affiliative and self-enhancing) and two of which might be damaging (aggressive and self-defeating). The self-enhancing humour style is a very healthy style which relates most strongly to positive psychological well-being. On the flip side, self-defeating humour is an especially unhealthy style and relates most strongly to lower levels of psychological health and higher levels of psychological distress. While once again, we're mindful of the coaching/therapy boundary, it is useful to be aware of the different styles demonstrated by our clients (and ourselves of course) and where relevant this might help our client to explore further.

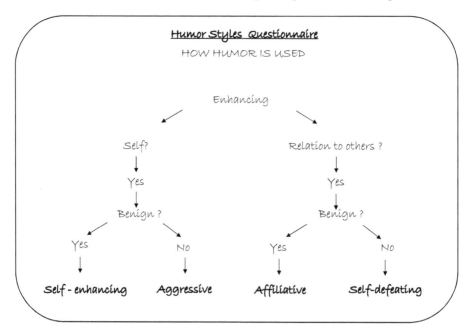

Figure 8.1 The Humor Styles Questionnaire

Turning to the impact of humour styles in social contexts, awareness of these can be useful both in 1:1 coaching and team coaching. In their book *Humour, Seriously*,[39] Bagdonas & Aaker look at two scales to identify humour style: affiliative to aggressive, and expressive to subtle. Depending on where you sit, they suggest that you are demonstrating one of four styles:

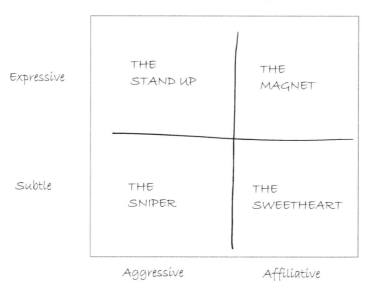

Figure 8.2 The Humour Styles Matrix

> *The Stand-up* (Aggressive-Expressive) happy to stand up in front of a crowd, play pranks, crack jokes and relaxed about being laughed at in turn.
>
> *The Sweetheart* (Affiliative-Subtle) the more understated and planned with their humour, optimistic, honest, and earnest, using humour to bring people together rather than isolate and tease.
>
> *The Magnet* (Affiliative-Expressive) warm, positive, and uplifting, happy to improvise, do impersonations and radiating charisma.
>
> *The Sniper* (Aggressive-Subtle) sarcastic and nuanced, happy to cross lines in pursuit of a laugh, watching from the side-lines in groups before they pitch in with dead-pan one-liners.

If we see these different styles play out either with a team we are working with or in our work with 1:1 clients, we can be curious as to how this is impacting the topic of the coaching session or if it's relevant, more broadly. Helping our clients build their curiosity and awareness of theirs and other people's different humour and comic styles and to consider the possible impact can be the source of rich insight and learning. Turning to ourselves, just as with playfulness, by bringing greater awareness of our own humour trait, styles, strengths and shadows and the potential impact to our work (and life more generally) to our reflections, we can deepen our learning and development and create greater choice points for ourselves in the coaching process.

Playful Moment

We've covered quite a lot of ground so far. Before we invite you to reflect, if you'd like to, please do take up the opportunity to experience a Playful Moment.

Let's pause for a moment for some reflection on how any of this might play out in your practice. We'll focus for now on your clients (with many questions relevant to a team context) and we'll come back to reflections about yourself and your practice towards the end of this chapter.

Remembering, again, that in practice, humour and playfulness are often intertwined and distinctions often held lightly if made at all, some questions to ponder in reflection and during practice include:

- *How aware are you of your clients' humour, how it shows up and the impact it may be having in your work together whether as individuals or in teams/groups?*
- *What beliefs and internal experiences in dyads and groups are underpinning a particular style?*
- *What other impact is this style having on the self and others?*
- *What is the impact on well-being individually and collectively?*
- *What is the impact on performance individually and collectively?*
- *What other style would be useful to develop?*

For leaders with influence over the climate of a team, team of teams or culture and also for team members, looking at the humour styles and observing laughter as a means of communication:

- *What is this humour or laughter telling us?*
- *What team norms are being created or endorsed?*
- *What is the impact on psychological safety?*
- *What is the impact on individuals and the team/group as a whole?*
- *What impact is your status in the group having on what humour style you're adopting and the possible impact?**
- *What is the impact of this on others in the system?*
- *Is what's happening supporting thriving and value-adding by individuals, teams, and the organisation?*
- *What in the system is supporting humour and what is needed more of and less of?*

*There's plenty of interesting reading on this including the already mentioned *The Psychology of Humour*,[40] *The Psychology of Humor at Work*[41]and for a more practical take, *Humor, Seriously*[42] and Bryant et al.'s (2020)[43] article on the different laughter sounds in the context of status. For example, hierarchy might undermine the power of laughter and humour to support group functioning and influence the nature and impact of humour and laughter. There is also a considerable amount of research in social psychology on the role of in-groups and out-groups and how their members are affected by laughter.[44]

These are just a few of the questions you and your clients might consider in this area where humour, laughter, playfulness, and creativity sit. Bringing awareness and intentionality can create conditions for thriving and also address negative, unhelpful, and damaging humour.

8.5 As We Alight From Our Whistle-stop Tour...

If you are embracing playfulness, whatever that means for you and your practice by reference to the Be Playful Onion Model, it is likely that humour and laughter will be present in some form at some time. Often the act of authentically laughing and seeing each other as fellow human beings beyond our roles and preconceptions/misconceptions can strengthen rapport, support our work together and provide us with different perspectives and avenues of exploration. Additionally, in dyads and groups/teams, humour and laughter in coaching can support connection, bonding, collaboration, and the sharing of positive emotions with lasting memories which continue to have an effect after the sessions.

We've skirted along the complexity to give you an idea of the explorations which await you, should you wish, in this area. As we're coming to the end of our whistle stop tour, it may be helpful to take another moment or two to reflect. Just like in our Be Playful Onion Model, where we each have our own favourite spots (which will probably be different in different situations/relationships) and we have the capacity to expand our range, so too, you will have your own humour traits and styles and the capacity to expand your range and increase awareness of its place in your practice in service of your clients.

- *How does humour and laughter show up in your practice?*
- *What is the role which humour currently plays in your practice?*
- *What is your humour and comic style?*
- *Does this change in different contexts? For instance, if you're nervous with a particular client, do you use self-deprecating humour or one of the less helpful humour styles we looked at previously?*
- *How are you with group dynamics and what might certain situations with groups bring up for you? How might this affect your humour? Can you put all your 'stuff' aside so you can observe how a group uses humour and the inter-relationship with group dynamics?*
- *Where and how might you cultivate your humour further?*
- *Where might you reign in your humour or become more sensitive in its use?*

8.6 Conclusion

We hope that you've gained some insight and new perspectives from looking at humour in the context of playfulness in coaching. Before we get too carried away, Franzini reminds us that to benefit the client, therapeutic humour must be relevant to the broader purpose of therapy relating to the client's specific problems, issues, conflicts, or other personal characteristics. In other words, the therapist is not an entertainer and there is purpose to the humour. It is also worth mentioning that research suggests that humour could be helpful as long as therapists and clients enjoy it together[45] but it has thrown up some potential risks and need for caution. We'll look at some of these in the next chapter.

There's much to be said for sharing humour and having a good laugh whether in a 1:1 session or with groups/teams and we've seen in the previous chapter the benefits of experiencing positive emotions both individually and collectively. What you focus on tends to develop (a bit like muscle building), so bringing an awareness to humour and laughter in general terms might already get the ball rolling for you to break out of grooves and habits and introduce or increase humour and laughter in your practice and generally. Sometimes, that's enough and we're not suggesting that you have to overcomplicate things, though it is useful to bear individual differences and preferences as well as humour's shadow side in mind.

As we suggested at the beginning of this little expedition, we can draw on humour and laughter as useful information (about us and our clients) to support our coaching and we can leverage humour and laughter (hand-in-hand with our awareness of emotions which we discussed in Chapter 7) in our work. Many questions remain to be explored, yet Martin & Ford (2018)[46] argue that from a practitioner's perspective, more recent findings suggest that clinicians can use humour and laughter therapy protocols in a sensitive empathetic way in a variety of settings as effective, practical interventions which have positive therapeutic outcomes. They also suggest that more recent studies seem to support that to be effective, humour and laughter need to be integrated into daily life and relationships rather than just the therapy sessions, so we can help our client be more aware of humour in our sessions and if helpful, explore with them what they could do differently in humour terms between sessions. From our own experiences, the playfulness and humour we access with our clients during our coaching sessions often accompanies them into the wider world afterwards. We have, perhaps, found a humorous perspective on something they were grappling with, sometimes holding the space for our clients to decide on an image, sound/music or characters which represents this and gives them easy access to this lighter perspective when they are back in the thick of it. It's wonderful to see the energy and sparkle when clients report back that they took whatever humorous and playful approach we experimented with and applied it with significant impact after our session.

Notes

1   From a speech by David Clutterbuck to the annual conference of the Oxford School of Coaching and Mentoring, 2005 based on Clutterbuck, D. & Megginson, D. (2005). *Making coaching work: Creating a coaching culture*. CIPD.
2   For example, Barnett, L. (1990). Playfulness: Definition, design, and measurement. *Play & Culture*, 3(4), 319–336. Barnett, L. (1991). The playful child: Measurement of a disposition to play. *Play & Culture*, 4(1), 51–74. Bergen D. (1998). Play as a

context for humor development. In Fromberg, D. & Bergen, D. (Eds.). *Play from birth to twelve and beyond: Contexts, perspectives, and meanings.* Garland, pp324–337. Bergen, D. (2002). Finding the humor in children's play. In Roopnarine, J. (Ed.). *Conceptual, social-cognitive, and contextual issues in the fields of play.* Ablex Publishing, pp209–220. McGhee, P. (1979). *Humor: Its origin and development.* W. H. Freeman.

3 For example, Lieberman, J. (1965). Playfulness and divergent thinking: An investigation of their relationship at the kindergarten level. *Journal of Genetic Psychology, 107,* 219–224. Lieberman, J. (1966). Playfulness: an attempt to conceptualize a quality of play and of the player. *Psychological Reports, 19* (3), 1278–1278. Lieberman, J. (1977). *Playfulness: Its relationship to imagination and creativity.* Academic Press. Barnett, L. (1990). Playfulness: Definition, design, and measurement. *Play & Culture, 3*(4), 319–33.

4 See Chapter 5 and also Proyer, R. (2017). A new structural model for the study of adult playfulness: Assessment and exploration of an understudied individual differences variable. Personality and Individual Differences, 108, 103–122.

5 Proyer, R. & Ruch, W. (2011). The virtuousness of adult playfulness: the relation of playfulness with strengths of character. *Psychology of Well-Being, 1*(1), 1–12.

6 Proyer, R. & Wagner, L. (2015). Playfulness in Adults Revisited: The Signal Theory in German Speakers. *American Journal of Play, 7*(2), 201–227.

7 Martin, R. & Ford, T. (2018). *The Psychology of Humor: An integrative approach.* Academic Press.

8 *Ibid,* Martin & Ford (2018, p14).

9 Cooper, C. (2005). Just joking around? Employee humor expression as an ingratiatory behavior. *Academy of Management Review. 30*(4), 765–776.

10 Peterson, C. & Seligman, M. (2004). *Character strengths and virtues: A handbook and classification* (Vol. 1). Oxford University Press.

11 For example, Yamao, Y., Matsumoto, R., Kunieda, T., Shibata, S., Shimotake, A., Kikuchi, T., … & Miyamoto, S. (2015). Neural correlates of mirth and laughter: a direct electrical cortical stimulation study. *Cortex, 66,* 134–140.

12 Sutton-Smith, B. (2009). *The Ambiguity of Play.* Harvard University Press.

13 Crowe, J., Allen, J. & Lehmann-Willenbrock, N. (2017). *Humor in Workgroups and Teams.* In Robert, C. (Ed.) (2017). *The Psychology of Humor at Work.* Routledge, p101.

14 Wheeler, S., Passmore, J. & Gold, R. (2020). All to play for: LEGO® SERIOUS PLAY® and its impact on team cohesion, collaboration and psychological safety in organisational settings using a coaching approach. *Journal of Work-Applied Management, 12*(2), 141–157.

15 Crowe, J., Allen, J. & Lehmann-Willenbrock, N. (2017). Humour in Workgroups and Teams. In Robert, C. (Ed.). *Psychology of Humour at Work.* Routledge, pp96–108.

16 'A ridiculous meditation' with Jeff Warren on Ten Percent Happier Podcast.

17 Franzini, L. (2001). Humor in therapy: The case for training therapists in its uses and risks. *Journal of General Psychology, 128*(2), 170–193.

18 www.aath.org/

19 For example, Franzini, L. (2001). Humor in therapy: The case for training therapists in its uses and risks. *Journal of General Psychology. 128*(2),170–193. Saper, B. (1987). Humor in psychotherapy: Is it good or bad for the client? *Professional Psychology: Research & Practice. 18*(4),360–367.
20 Gelkopf, M. & Kreitler, S. (1996). Is humor only fun, an alternative cure or magic: The cognitive therapeutic potential of humor. *Journal of Cognitive Psychotherapy. 10*(4),235–254.
21 Fredrickson, B. (2013). *Love 2.0*. Plume.
22 Panksepp J. (1998). *Affective neuroscience: The foundations of human and animal emotions*. Oxford University Press.
23 Rogers, C. R. (1959). A theory of therapy, personality, and interpersonal relationships as developed in the client centered framework. In S. Koch (Ed.), Psychology: A study of a science, Formulations of the person and the social context (Vol. 3, pp. 184–256). McGraw-Hill, p208.
24 Olson, H. (1994). The use of humor in psychotherapy. In Strean, H. (Ed.). *The use of humor in psychotherapy*. Jason Aronson, pp195–198.
25 *Ibid* (2018).
26 Wood, A., Turner, M. & Barker, J. (2019). Bolstering psychological health using rational emotive behaviour therapy. In Breslin, G. & Leavey, G. (Eds.). *Mental health and well-being interventions in sport: A case study analysis*, Routledge, pp45–62.
27 Farrelly, F. & Brandsma, J. (1974). *Provocative therapy*. Meta Publications. Farrelly, F. & Lynch, M. (1987). Humor in provocative therapy. In Fry, W. & Salameh, W. (Eds.). *Handbook of humor and psychotherapy: Advances in the clinical use of humor*. Professional Resource Exchange, pp81–106.
28 For more, see for example, www.provocativetherapy.com
29 Ibid, Martin & Ford (2018), Chapter 9 *The Clinical Psychology of Humor*, pp294–229.
30 Fry, W. & Salameh W. (1987). *Handbook of humor and psychotherapy: Advances in the clinical use of humor*. Professional Resource Exchange.
31 McGhee, P. (1996). *Health, healing, and the amuse system: Humor as survival training.* (2nd ed.). Kendall/Hunt. McGhee, P. (2010). *Humor: The lighter path to resilience and health*. AuthorHouse.
32 Goldstein, J. & Ruch, W. (2018). Paul McGhee and humor research. *Humor, 31*(2), 169–181.
33 *Ibid,* Martin and Ford (2018, p136).
34 Ruch W. & Köhler G. A temperament approach to humor. In: Ruch W, ed. (1998) *The sense of humor: Explorations of a personality characteristic*. Walter de Gruyter, pp203–228.
35 For example, osha.europa.eu/en/themes/psychosocial-risks-and-stress
36 Ruch, W., Heintz, S., Platt, T., Wagner, L. & Proyer, R. (2018). Broadening humor: comic styles differentially tap into temperament, character, and ability. *Frontiers in Psychology*, 9, 6.
37 *Ibid*, p17.
38 Martin R., Puhlik-Doris, P., Larsen, G., Gray J. & Weir K. (2003). Individual differences in uses of humor and their relation to psychological well-being:

Development of the humor styles questionnaire. *Journal of Research in Personality.* *37*(1), 48–75.

39 Aaker, J. & Bagdonas, N. (2021). *Humor, Seriously.* Currency.

40 *Ibid*, Martin & Ford (2018).

41 *Ibid*, Robert (Ed) (2017).

42 *Ibid*, Aaker & Bagdonas (2021).

43 *Ibid*, Bryant et al (2020).

44 Platow, M., Haslam, S., Both, A., Chew, I., Cuddon, M., Goharpey, N., … & Grace, D. (2005). It's not funny if they're laughing: Self-categorization, social influence, and responses to canned laughter. *Journal of Experimental Social Psychology, 41*(5), 542–550.

45 For example, Pierce, R. (1994). Use and abuse of laughter in psychotherapy. In Strean, H. (Ed.). *The use of humor in psychotherapy.* Jason Aronson, p105–111.

46 *Ibid*, Martin and Ford (2018, p299).

9
Risks: Part and Parcel of Exploring

In this chapter, we:

- Put potential risks of playfulness into context
- Draw your attention to the shadow side of playfulness and humour
- Invite you to consider your attitude to risk
- Discuss some risks which might arise with individuals and groups
- Share ideas for addressing the risky

At the heart of playfulness in coaching is being prepared to explore and experiment (we will just refer to exploring for now as it'll get repetitive otherwise). By definition, if you are setting out on any exploration, there will be an element of the unknown and that will inevitably come with an element of risk. For the risk-averse among us, even saying that there will be risks might well sound daunting, possibly off-putting, and maybe even frightening. Take heart! Just like an explorer, you can calibrate the degree of risk that you're willing to encounter by deciding the scale and direction of your exploration. You could, if that felt more like your cup of tea, start with mini-expeditions, and leave your sleeping bag at home. As your zone of comfort grows and as you encounter and overcome hiccups, you might decide to challenge yourself further and increase the risk which you're happy to potentially encounter by going on more elaborate expeditions. For the risk tolerant, the first expedition might be a much more ambitious one. However, only the foolhardy would stretch the challenge beyond their competence.

DOI: 10.4324/9781003090847-10

Applying the metaphor to coaching, your boundaries of exploration and experimentation are your competence, coaching ethics, and the contract with your client. Within that, you have the ability to decide how much (broad and deep) playfulness you would like to invite and by making a deliberate choice you are having an influence on the likely level of risk. Our aim with this chapter is to help you make that deliberate choice and also to consider what you might do if you encounter an unexpected hiccup. Of course, it's your choice to extend the playfulness invitation, but it is also your clients' choice not to accept it given their levels of comfort and attitude to risk. If you are both to embark on setting sail into the unknown, then you both need to agree to it and we hope that it will be helpful for you (as coach) to be aware of signs of potentially more choppy waters and what you might do to navigate these.

9.1 A Note on Our Approach in This Chapter

As we have seen in Chapter 8, playfulness and humour are separate and distinct but often intertwined and sometimes hard to tell apart, particularly in practice. We're going to reflect this in what follows and look at both humour and playfulness together as we're concentrating on implications for practice rather than fine research distinctions. What's more for our purposes, in the absence of a bank of research specifically relevant to playfulness in coaching, we rely on our experience, the experiences of our Storytellers, other coaches in our network as well as Stephanie's MSc research and other research which seems relevant by analogy (for example, in the context of therapy). As we are focusing on playfulness in coaching, we'll focus here on relational aspects of the shadow side. If you wish to dive further into the shadow sides of humour and playfulness, we invite you to follow the trail of relevant academic references in this and the previous chapter as well as the three books which we recommended in Chapter 8.[1]

Sometimes in practice, it's difficult to untangle barriers and risks so you will see some of the ideas in this chapter pop up again in Chapter 12. Although you can of course dip in and out of this book, we suggest that you read both chapters.

9.2 The Shadow Side of Playfulness

When we see playfulness as a complex, multi-faceted construct, it opens the door wider to the possibility that it might also have a negative side. Consider, for example, the potential links between playfulness and gambling; not all of its facets are associated with subjective well-being (Proyer, 2012, 2013).[2] We saw in the previous chapter that there is a shadow side to humour that is receiving attention both in theory and practice. As research into adult playfulness (also in the context of coaching and therapy) develops and expands, it is likely that the shadow side of playfulness will get more attention too. Examples of research relating to humour's shadow side include looking at crossing social interaction boundaries such as laughing at instead of with others.[3] For adult playfulness, researchers have examined its relationship to sensation or risk seeking,[4] lower conscientiousness,[5] lower inclinations to self-regulation[6] and less careful behaviour in general.[7]

9.3 Your Attitude to Risk

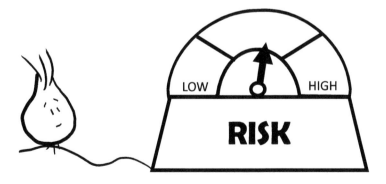

Stephanie relates: *My training and work in the legal profession established a well-honed risk radar and, early on in coach training, my first questions inevitably focused on risk: what if a tool doesn't work, what if it misfires, what if we breach the coaching/*

therapy boundary? I have learned to respect my 'risk glasses' but to not necessarily make them my go-to pair always at the expense of others. Clients come to us seeking to affect change, possibly relating to self-awareness, relationships to their emotions or changing their behaviour; they are seeking to disrupt existing patterns or facilitate processes which lead to change, both of which playful approaches to coaching offer in spades and both give rise to possible risks. Whether playfulness is acting as a disruptor or a facilitator, we need to have a responsible ethical awareness of and attitude to risk. At the same time, we are inviting you to consider whether, like for me at the start of my coach training, there is room for increasing your self-awareness around your attitude to risk.

Using the metaphor of a sword and shield, are you using your approach to risk as a sword to protect your client or a shield to keep you within your own comfort zone or to protect you from something else, a fear perhaps? One fear might be your relationship to uncertainty and the unknown which we address in Part II. Another might be that of denting your credibility by offering playfulness. What's more, as we pointed out at the beginning of this chapter, exploring and experimenting are implicit to playfulness and by definition there's a risk that an exploration or experiment might fail. What sprang to your mind when you just read 'fail'? Doesn't it depend on what you mean by failing in this context? If you are concentrating on the process rather than a predetermined outcome, contracting for and co-creating the playful experiment with your client, you will be curious, flexible, resourceful, and spontaneous (as well as grounded in the orbit of your contract and ethics and checking-in that you are led by your client's needs). Where you go together during the experiment and what the outcome is might surprise you; it might be very different from what you expected might happen. To us, that's not failure, that's success.

Framing the playfulness invitation as an experiment not only allows for things to go wrong but almost implies that things might go wrong and that's ok. Working together in co-creation can be liberating and open up the space for insight and learning. As with any learning journey, mistakes will be made. Again though, question what you mean by 'mistakes'. We look at some examples of mistakes, such as misfiring, a little later and yet from a growth mindset perspective, they are to be welcomed as opportunities for reflection and learning. A different type of mistake from the ones considered below that we've both made is where we contracted with a 1 : 1 client to try a particular tool – and that's the kind of wording we deliberately use: 'try', 'explore', 'experiment', and so forth, as we contract in the moment – only for us to forget the details of the tool or for it to become clear that it was not resonating with the client. Rather than seeing it as a potentially embarrassing mistake, we played with it, let the client know where we were at and invited them to use what we had started as a basis for developing something together which resonated with the client and met their needs in that moment.

ABC (Always Be Contracting) is particularly important in this wider context of 'failures' and 'mistakes' and we look more at this in Part II. Learning to have a different relationship with the fear of 'failure' and 'mistakes' is linked to letting go of being the expert and instead stepping into a space of true collaboration. This is quite a paradox to navigate: on the one hand, we invest years in training, supervision and shiny accreditation and qualification badges to build our expertise, on the other, we are not there to fix our clients or their issues but to walk alongside them and hold our expertise lightly. Heather Simpkin who works very playfully with teams and groups shared with us the importance of believing in the process (and being grounded) without being fixed on a certain way of doing things or imposing an outcome; believing that everyone will find their own way and making space for this. This requires being willing to work in the space of not-knowing and letting go of our expectations. Steve Chapman reflected that the trouble with playfulness and humour is we think it has to be something and we strive for it to be something other than what it actually is. Building the capacity to be in this space without attachment is part of the development journey of working playfully. Steve suggests that we tune into what's there, see everything which is to hand as a resource (the basis of improv) and treat everything as potentially relevant. He shared with us Robert Poynton's triangle for creating the flow which improvisers create regardless of the circumstances (based on practice and discipline): 'Let go, notice more, use everything' and we love the implications of its application in coaching.[8] In practice, this might be as simple as saying to the coachee(s) 'I don't know what to do right now'. This has supported some of Steve's best work with groups (and a similar story was shared with us by David Clutterbuck). Saying this to a group (and when we say 'group' we mean 'teams' too) can be inherently playful and rather than trying to fix or be the expert, it creates awareness and space for the group/team to address what is going on in that moment. It helps to ground everything back into the moment but can be a scary thing to do if we think as a coach we need to be in control and in charge. Clearly your tone and demeanour is important here as well as staying grounded (remembering neuroception which we looked at in Chapter 6) – emitting inquiry rather than nervous ego-fuelled desperation!

Before we start looking at risky things you might encounter as you welcome more playfulness into your coaching, let's take a moment to consider your attitude to risk and how that might affect your evaluation. When you are considering the risks of playfulness in coaching, is your underlying motive one of calibrating risk rather than closing off to playfulness? If it's the latter, is there work you might do here to give you the choice of more playfulness? For clarity, we are not saying all coaching should be playful (ours certainly isn't) but that we and our clients stand to benefit hugely if we are able to access playfulness with awareness and discernment.

- *What is your attitude to risk generally?*
- *What is your attitude to risk in your work?*
- *How much of your thinking does the possible risk of playfulness take up?*
- *How happy are you with your responses to the previous questions?*
- *What is at the heart of your concern?*
- *What is your underlying fear?*
- *Is what is at the heart of your concern something to do with your client, yourself, or a mixture of both (see also Part II)?*

Let's have a look at potential risks then, first in the context of working with individual clients and then additional things to consider at group level. Needless to say, these are not exhaustive. Afterwards, we will share our top tips on how you might respond if you hit choppy waters.

9.4 On the Individual Level

On the individual level, let's start with general risks to bear in mind before we move onto thinking about some specific risks in more detail.

9.4.1 General Things to Look Out For

Once again, psychotherapy literature may well have lessons for coaches. As we saw in the previous chapter, it is fair to say that there has been increasing interest in the positive use of humour and playfulness in therapy. It's not all positive though. Even though it is seen as an extreme view, it's helpful to consider what Kubie (1970) thought about the use of humour in psychotherapy in a frequently cited article:

> Humor has its place in life. Let us keep it there by acknowledging that one place where it has a very limited role, if any, is in psychotherapy.[9]

Helpful because whilst it is quite an extreme view, when you think about it, the underlying concerns are valid. The risks that concerned Kubie were:

- Clients might think that their issues weren't being taken seriously or the therapist's use of humour might make it difficult to express negative feelings or disagreement.
- Clients might think that humour about a particular issue means that it's not to be discussed seriously and therefore avoid it or feel pressure to hide underlying distressing feelings.
- Clients might use humour as an unhealthy defence mechanism, either by avoiding the issue or self-mocking and thereby devaluing their own strengths;
- If clients have a maladaptive humour style, this might be reinforced by the therapist by engaging in humour together.
- A therapist might use humour for their own reason, not the clients, for example, as a defence against anxieties or showing off their humour skills.

We'd also add that we've seen clients minimize a belief or assumption through humour. Depending on the context, it's been fruitful to challenge them on this and invite them to explore it further rather than to dismiss it with a laugh. In fact, while needless to say we celebrate the potential benefits of humour and playfulness in coaching, we think that we can all agree with Thomas Kuhlman (1984)[10] that humour, and we'd add playfulness, has the potential to be used as a diversion from the underlying topic. Pierce (1994) suggested that the use of humour would be inappropriate if the underlying reason was to be defensive and avoid a difficult topic, if it's irrelevant to the process and for the therapist's gratification or indeed, used to belittle, mimic, or laugh at the client.[11] Again, we can see the relevance to playfulness by analogy. Bearing all of these potential risks in mind can be very helpful for increasing our awareness and avoiding or repairing the consequences of potential pitfalls of humour and playfulness in our work.

9.4.2 Damaging Rapport

The cumulative finding of over four decades of research into psychotherapy effectiveness[12] is that the largest portion of outcome variance, regardless of pre-existing client characteristics, individual therapy differences, technique or school of therapy is the relationship between the client and the therapist. Well, that puts this book into perspective! Joking aside, we do need to take the potential risk for damage to the coaching relationship seriously as it is thought that relationship is also a key ingredient in coaching outcomes rather than any specific coaching tool, intervention or models used.[13] Indeed, this is often the first concern for coaches we speak to and for some is linked to fears around playfulness impacting their credibility and, by extension, the coaching relationship. A degree of trepidation around the possibility of damaging that relationship is understandable and responsible. Indeed, if playfulness (or humour) is intended to be, or felt as destructive, or if it causes the client to feel misunderstood, or their feelings or perceptions as being dismissed or denigrated, misfires in such a way as to damage the coach's credibility, or even is used by the coach to mask their own feelings, it could be that playfulness (or humour) damages the relationship as well as working against the objectives of coaching, or it might even do harm.

We've been clear that we are not advocating a one-size-fits-all or tick-box approach to playfulness in coaching; quite the opposite. On the specific point of a rupture in the relationship, available research in psychotherapy suggests that there is more rupture evident when there is rigid adherence on the part of the therapist to a treatment manual and an excessive number of transference interpretations.[14] There are lessons which we can draw from this by analogy in the context of playfulness in coaching.

To address this risk, we stay with lessons which we may learn from research into psychotherapy. John Norcross in the *Heart and Soul of Change, Delivering What Works in Therapy*[15] draws on the findings of a meta-analysis of hundreds of research studies on therapeutic outcomes which resulted in a list of elements of effective therapy relationships. The elements which were definitely important were:

- Empathy
- The alliance
- Cohesion (in group therapy)
- Goal consensus and collaboration.

Probable important elements but with a less compelling body of evidence to support them were:

- Positive regard
- Congruence/genuineness

- Feedback (from the therapist)
- Repair of alliance rupture
- Self-disclosure
- Management of countertransference
- Quality of relational interpretations.

Seen through the lens of a playful approach, a number of things spring to mind. Firstly, we've seen that playfulness can be a powerful vehicle for empathy and compassion, strengthening the relationship and connection (with the coach and in teams/groups). Playfulness, like empathy, promotes exploration and the creation of meaning. It's worth noting that empathy is not a one size fits all construct; whether or not the client perceives a response as empathetic depends on their unique needs.[16] Only the client knows if the coach's intervention has landed empathetically (and we'd add playfully).

Alliance refers to the quality and strength of the collaborative relationship and is typically measured in agreement on therapeutic goals, consensus on treatment tasks, and the relationship bond.[17] Norcross suggests that to support goal consensus and collaboration, the therapist may build a sense of togetherness by using language like 'we' 'us' and 'let's'[18] and as you'll see in Part II, this is built into a playful approach. It seems to us that the co-creation of playful approaches together with frequent checking in whether they are landing (and re-contracting where necessary) is helpful in supporting the alliance. On that note, to make sure that you have an accurate assessment of how things stand with all of the elements above and perhaps particularly while you are experimenting with more playful approaches, we'd suggest that you find a way to request real-time feedback from clients not just on the process but also on your relationship. Similarly, at the end of the coaching sessions and the relationship, we'd suggest that you check in and ask what has been the most helpful. To be fair, we think that this is good practice anyway and not limited to the context of playfulness.

9.4.3 Misfiring

In the context of playfulness (and humour) it seems especially important to be sensitive as to how a client is likely to react.[19] Sultanoff (1994) advises assessment of humour receptiveness[20] and it is, needless to say (but we'll say it anyway), very important that you are laughing with rather than at your client and that this is how your client is experiencing it. Particularly in light of certain barriers to playfulness, for example, gender, culture and language, there is a risk that playfulness might misfire, so sensitivity is important. It may be necessary to go through some calibration and/or scene setting/explanation and/ or contracting/recontracting beforehand. We assume that an experienced or mature coach would at least unconsciously make such an assessment prior to and during playful (and humour) interventions. Our invitation is to consciously turn the spotlight onto these considerations in the context of playfulness and your reflections both in, and on action, as well as in supervision.

Cultural differences in humour perception, usage and implications is receiving more research attention[21] and this is an area ripe for future research in the context of playfulness too. As Martin and Ford (2018) note:

> Humor is a universal human activity that most people experience many times over the course of a typical day and in all sorts of social contexts. At the same time, there are obviously important cultural influences on the way humor is used and the situations that are considered appropriate for laughter.[22]

While of course we need to be sensitive (remember that playfulness is always an offer and not an imposition), perhaps in today's climate, the fear of misfiring might close down our opportunities for playfulness sometimes more than is warranted and block us from being relaxed and authentic. The emphasis is of course rightly on staying within the appropriate boundaries, though within that, there is space for levity and a playful irreverence. As Graham Lee reflected in our conversation, 'If I get it wrong, I hope I'm really attuned to see that I got it wrong and then play with that fact that I got it wrong'. Of course, we need to get the basics right, but creating this space also allows us to coach as our authentic selves, bringing our unique selves to the process rather than rigidly applying tools.

9.4.4 Misreading

This is in a similar ballpark to the risk of misfiring. Especially in 1:1 coaching which can be an intensely authentic space. Playfulness, particularly if it has a physical element, has the potential of being misconstrued and sensitivity to that possibility is required.

9.4.5 Hard to Read

When we are not in the room with our clients (perhaps coaching virtually or by phone), it can be harder to read how invitations to playfulness are landing (for example, does your client think you're mad, bad, or making fun of them?). In The Playfulness Scrapbook, Stephanie tells the story of a telephone coaching session while her client was walking in the countryside. Stephanie asked permission to try a playful experiment, but in that moment, it was difficult to see how it landed; did the silence mean that he would take the invitation and run with it or that it didn't land? Parallel to offering playfulness lightly and being comfortable in the unknown (more on which in Part II), it can be difficult for the coach to keep assessing if they can dial up the playfulness a bit more and it can be easier to misfire in these circumstances. The antidote is that playfulness comes from a solid base of rapport and trust, invitation, and continual contracting or re-contracting.

9.4.6 Hitting Barriers Too Hard

As we've reiterated, play is always by invitation, and we'd hope in the context of the sensitive eye (and ear and heart) of the coach. If discomfort is detected, keep an eye out and if appropriate check-in with your client whether it is a reflection of stretching the comfort zone (and hasn't gone too far into overwhelm) or if there's something else going on. We look at potential barriers in Chapter 12 and the role for playfulness in approaching these barriers with a degree of irreverence which goes hand in hand with awareness of self and other, frequent checking-in and re-contracting, feedback, and debriefing. There is a risk that if this is not done skillfully or sensitively that the barriers might be hit too hard and it's worth checking whether your intent and actions are in the service of the client. As you gain more experience, your intuition will stand you in good stead too. What is your Whole Body (see more in the next chapter) telling you in this moment? What, if anything, needs to be said or done?

9.4.7 For the Coach, Not the Client(s)

At the risk of repeating ourselves, it is important to remind ourselves that playfulness in coaching should be in service of the client. Proyer and Ruch (2011) found potential negatively connoted aspects of playfulness when looking at the relationship of playfulness and character strengths. One of their conclusions was that there was a need for more studies on adult playfulness in general but also to develop 'a classification that also encompasses its darker, more negatively connoted aspects'.[23]

Their findings are consistent with our view and the findings of Stephanie's MSc research[24] which emphasised the need for the coach to be aware of their own motive for playfulness (for example, discomfort, avoidance, or deflection). In the absence of more direct research on coaching and playfulness, we may again find some guidance in the literature on therapy and humour. Here we see that therapists should continually engage in self-monitoring to ensure a particular intervention is used for patient's benefit and not, for example, for self-gratification (Franzini, 2001).[25] Equally, as with all coaching interventions, we need to be aware of our reason for choosing a particular intervention and be cautious of motives of avoidance or deflection,[26] for example, of discomfort, difficult feelings, or not knowing what to do or say next.

The coach-centered motive might also be more subtle; for example, if your place in the family of origin story was the entertainer, you might assume that role in certain group dynamics and take on that mantle if you are team or group coaching. We're not suggesting that there's anything wrong with this, but an awareness of why you are being playful or finding it difficult, can tease out your own story from that of your client(s) and put you in a place of greater clarity in deciding whether or not being playful and how (remembering the Be Playful Onion Model) in that moment it is of service to your client.

9.4.7.1 Check-in Question for Reflection-in-action and Reflection-on-action

- *What is/was at the heart of my drive to be playful in that moment?*
- *Is/was it to do with me or my client?*
- *Is/was it in service of and of benefit to my client?*

9.5 Playfulness Can Lead to Deep Work – What if I Cause Harm?

We started this chapter by reminding you that exploration, experimentation, and not-knowing are implicit to playfulness in coaching. That brings with it great potential for transformation and growth but also a risk of opening up areas more suited to therapy. Play, playfulness and creativity in coaching can be significantly more powerful than traditional cognitive based coaching approaches. Our client might have experienced trauma of which we are not aware and trauma is stored in the body, so doing embodied work can release things. Even in the absence of trauma, care and not wild abandon is called for. Steve Chapman suggests the way to do this is to stay with the client in the sweet spot of discomfort that lies somewhere between their comfort and distress zones, neither of which are conducive to transformation. It's also important to bear in mind that only the individuals we are working with will know if they are in discomfort or veering into overwhelm and that this is reflected in contracting; we can invite them to move towards discomfort if they are too comfortable or to step back if it's too much. As you're recontracting, two very useful questions to pose are: 'How are you doing?' and 'Is this helpful?' Steve, who invites clients on adventures into playfulness, sometimes agrees a 'safe word' in advance for big set-pieces that he has set up when he feels it will add an extra level of control for the client.

We will look at the zone of discomfort in more detail in Part II. Our clients being in this zone requires a basis of trust, respect, and safety in our relationship and regular checking in by us. This is a space which requires sensitivity and an awareness of and adherence to coaching ethics but not paranoia. What space you're willing and/or able to hold will change as you mature as a coach. In Chapter 7, we spoke about developing a comfort with and welcoming difficult or negative emotions into the coaching space and it's helpful to be aware of your own reaction to what is unfolding: is it your 'stuff' or the clients? Even so, we and our Storytellers err on the side of caution rather than taking a maverick approach, if unsure. This is of course where awareness, reflection, and supervision are invaluable.

Playful Moment

Just in case all this talk of risks is getting a bit concerning and possibly off-putting, we invite you to take a Playful Moment to reconnect to play.

9.6 Additional Considerations at Group Level

In the previous chapter where we were looking at humour in the context of playfulness in coaching, we started to explore its shadow side and how that might play out in groups/teams and we'll go into more detail here. As an aside, we're not going to address the work of organisational humour consultants as we're focusing on coaching contexts and there are resources available if you'd like to explore this aspect of humour in organisations further.[27]

9.6.1 Meeting the Group/team Where They're At

It can be tempting to be enthusiastic and energetic about a playful idea and assume that participants are going to engage (in 1 : 1 coaching also, though there it's perhaps easier to notice a disconnect). Julie Flower shared with us a learning story of when she was running a virtual session with a group. A few had their cameras off or were more passive in the beginning. Julie introduced the Morph Ball game (explained in The Playfulness Scrapbook) which usually creates energy and camaraderie but on this occasion felt a bit sluggish and laggard and seemed to be having the opposite effect. Julie took away the learning that if she's noticing low energy/engagement at the beginning, to consider having a conversation around how we show up, what are the first steps we can take to be more present and involved. What falls within our comfort zones is individual. Something that I consider easy and comfortable might be a real stretch for you (generally, or at that particular time, or in that particular circumstance). In this instance, switching cameras on could have been a stretch for some, let alone throwing around an imaginary ball.

9.6.2 The Shadow Side of Humour: Things to Have on Your Radar

While not a given, humour is likely to play a role in playful and creative coaching. It is worth emphasising though that not all humour is positive and research indicates that it is important to understand the types of humour that are already occurring and the social functions they serve[28] particularly in group contexts. In the previous chapter we looked at a model of four main humour styles in social contexts and saw that we want to have these on our radar to notice and address if the maladaptive styles surface either in ourselves or in our clients. More broadly, we started to explore the impact humour may have in terms of damaging psychological safety, inclusion, group dynamics and reinforcing status.

Humour is described by Meyer (2000) as a 'double-edged sword' in social settings.[29] It has long been recognised that just as humour often works on the understanding of paradox or ambiguity, humour too can have two sides. We're drawn to the metaphor used by the sociologist William Martineau (1972) who described humour acting as either a 'lubricant' or an 'abrasive' for inter- and intra-group settings. It:

> Serves as oil pumped from an oil can...to keep the machinery of inter-action operating smoothly and freely.[30]

For example, work colleagues might use humour and playful teasing in a positive way to let each other know their differences in opinion in a light-hearted way, minimizing their differences and avoiding escalation of conflict. However, it can also act as a 'measure of sand' that causes interpersonal friction, attempting to throw a cloak of purported fun and frivolity over prejudice which can injure, discriminate, divide or isolate with the intention that the cloak will shield this from any challenge or opposition which would probably arise if said without humour.[31] I'm sure we've all come across 'I was only joking; where's your sense of humour?' in the context of gender or race-based jokes for example. Indeed, it's no joking matter for it seems that gender harassment in the form of sexist jokes and teasing is the most commonly experienced type of sexual harassment by women in the workplace.[32] Socially sanctioning prejudicial humour can act as a 'releaser' of prejudice[33] and the coach is in a position to be able to step in and call it out when witnessed. Why do we mention this in relation to playful-ness? If participants are relaxed and having fun or perhaps getting carried away or the use of playfulness has brought 'measures of sand' to light, it's an oppor-tunity for us to pause, check-in with participants and explore (if appropriate, in a playful way perhaps) what we've observed.

The shadow sides of humour and playfulness can also emerge in the context of status. How humour is interpreted depends on the status of the person making the joke. For instance, innocent horseplay from a co-worker might be seen as inappropriate from a manager, which can require extra awareness and reflection from leaders to navigate. For us, for example, if we're using improv-based exercises in team/group coaching, one of the rules of play agreed by the group is usually to 'punch up', in other words, don't make jokes or stories at the expense of people who might be perceived as lower status lest social boundaries are reinforced. It's also interesting to note that humour is used in group settings, especially in the early stages of interactions, to establish and maintain status[34] and it might be helpful to be aware of this and per-haps reflect it back to the team/individuals, possibly alongside the its pos-sible impact on the team's psychological safety. In practice, it's important to recognise that humour can serve multiple lubricating and abrasive functions simultaneously.[35]

9.6.3 Damage to Psychological Safety or Group Cohesion

We can help build team psychological safety through playfulness if it is done with awareness and sensitivity. If the psychological safety is low, we need to be especially aware and prepared to be playful ourselves by improvising, being flexible, working with what's in the room rather than imposing a prepared play-fulness agenda on the group. Perhaps this is the mark of a maturing coach: how much can they be in the moment, dip into their resources with flexibility, nuance, creativity, bringing awareness of self and others and offering playfulness lightly without attachment and co-creating at the level of playfulness which is right for the group/team. There is a risk of going too far and causing rupture. On the other hand, fear of coming close to this needs to be balanced with the, at times, benefits of disruption. Disruption of the norms and the stretching of comfort zones might be what's needed. This is a judgment call and of course depending on the circumstances, you can call this out too and agree with the client(s) what's needed. There might be a need for re-contracting whether in the moment or more formally.

An antithesis to psychological safety, 'jeer pressure' refers to ridicule or humour being used to pressure an individual to conform with group norms. The higher the status of the 'jeerer', the more pressure the individual feels to conform[36] and in the extreme can be used to manipulate. While hopefully unlikely, permutations of 'jeer pressure' might arise during team coaching if an indi-vidual finds it difficult to engage with playful methods. If that did occur, while we can draw awareness to the discomfort of learning, it's important yet again to remember that playfulness is an offer which can be freely declined. If it is declined, that *might* be data about the person or the group dynamics which may be useful for us.

The reality for some teams is that they don't have supportive group dynamics and they may not even like each other very much. Kirsten Barske's work with teams is nearly always experiential and leads to greater awareness of self, others, and group dynamics which in turn can lead to insights and real change. It's dif-ficult to keep telling yourself only negative and one-dimensional things about a colleague when you've had an impactful experience together and laughed, or maybe struggled, or seen them struggle and you came through it together. Yet Kirsten is very aware of the power of these experiences and the need for sensitivity. As she says, you don't want to end up in a situation where people care even less for each other afterwards! When the team she's working with does have a lot of friction/dislike, her approach is not to be overtly playful in terms of fun and laughter, but to focus on a task. By doing so, the team members are engaged in serious play and the task focus then opens up opportunities for questions and reflections about the individual behaviours and group dynamics. Kirsten might explore with them how they felt during the task and together create a space where the team members listen to each other's felt experiences. Sometimes the dynamic shifts to the team deciding that they all were frustrated and they might turn that frustration onto Kirsten (she's happy to take it and hold that space where they can experience it collectively and then reflect on it afterwards). Care is needed not to end up in a therapeutic space. Depending on the group dynamics and the intensity of the experience, skill and experience is necessary to navigate this sometimes 'fuzzy space' between coaching and therapy.[37]

9.6.4 Group Dynamics

Just as humour and playfulness can be used in a positive way to transform individual experiences into collective or shared group experiences, members of an in-group can enhance their cohesion and solidarity by disparaging members of the relevant out-group with aggressive forms of humour.[38] Clearly this can tip over into being maladaptive particularly if members perceive that their in-group is at risk of being judged inferior.[39] There is research examining how humour can be used negatively, for example to humiliate, to create or reinforce hierarchies and restrictions and to discourage members from deviating from group norms[40] (again, you might hear the reply 'can't you take a joke?'). Other group members might be hesitant to step in in case they are humiliated too[41] – enter stage left, the team coach who can shine a light on what's going on.

Group dynamics don't, of course, have to be negative and playfulness can infuse a sense of fun and energy. In this context, Kirsten Barske also reflected on modeling to the group how to support each other during physical challenges. For example, when participants climb and stand on top of a tall pole (with the option to jump off – fully harnessed of course!) and tension or excitement builds, she will never cheer-lead or pressure an individual to push themselves beyond the level of their own choosing, but instead empower them to make their own decisions. For some it might be one step up the pole, for others a backward jump off the top. The point is for the team to recognise their differences and celebrate each person's effort, their starting point and progression, whatever the outcome. If the group starts to get carried away with their encouragement (which might tip into peer pressure or hopefully, less likely, jeer pressure), Kirsten may point out, for example, that a more helpful approach of the group might be to respect the person's autonomy and individual lived-experience by providing support not pressure, however well-intended.

Nankhonde Kasonde-van den Broek made the point that self-management is important if we are being playful in our work so that we don't get carried away in the moment, but stay alert to subtle signs and signals which might give valuable information. She also reflected on the need to develop the skill to bookmark the session, ensuring that there is time for reflection for participants on what they are taking away with them and how they make sense of the experience. Otherwise, they might be left feeling disconnected or separate and that won't support a shift or change.

9.7 Ideas for Addressing Risk

Looking at the coaching relationship, process and outcome, playfulness is not without its risks, particularly when it intertwines with humour. Political polarization, heightened sensitivities, and cancel culture can make this space perhaps feel riskier than ever before. Though of course, we would argue that it is also more needed than ever before (with the appropriate levels of awareness, sensitivity, and ethical awareness of course).

Turning to you and going back to your reflections near the beginning of this chapter, as well as objective risk, there's space for curiosity (there's always space for curiosity) around why you think that there is risk involved in playfulness. Is it to do with the perceived impact on your credibility or not knowing what to expect and so on? If so, reflecting on with whom, in what context, and how you can be authentically playful in your work will be fruitful. There are plenty of ways in which you can be playful at the right risk level for you (remember the Be Playful Onion Model). Staying with you, take the time to reflect on your beliefs and habits around playfulness and develop the capacity to stay grounded in the heat of the moment. Hone your ability to spot if your concern about risk is arising in your interest rather than your clients' and move into the space where playfulness is not something that you're doing to clients, without awareness, flexibility, or spontaneity but where you are co-creating together, contracting, and recontracting as necessary. Can you take risks seriously, hold them with appropriate gravity and with the relevant ethical considerations and yet also a degree of lightness, so that you don't get stuck and misread potential risks as insurmountable barriers?

> Be brave. Take risks. Nothing can substitute experience.
>
> *Paulo Coelho*

Here then are our top tips:

At the contracting stage, discuss the possible use of playfulness and humour. Any clues about humour styles? Possible barriers such as gelotophobia (see

Chapter 11 for more)? What about in group contexts? Get a sense of comfort levels, current group dynamics and norms. Be aware of the possibility of status, diversity, and inclusion (or lack of) and of course psychological safety affecting the openness to and engagement with playfulness.

Keep that awareness going throughout the session, re-contract explicitly where appropriate and implicitly. Do not get carried away for your own benefit (put simply, for you to feel good, or to avoid feeling bad), remember to keep awareness of how playfulness is helping the client and their experience. Keep an eye out whether it's blocking the coaching or creating diversions and defences. Use language which embodies co-creation, exploration, experimentation. Check-in (again, explicitly, or implicitly as appropriate) where participants are at, this has the added benefit of making people feel seen and heard if it is in a positive, inclusive style.

If something has misfired or not landed or you judge that the tone and mood in the session is not right, work with the group or team and/or the individual as appropriate to address it, if necessary by immediately clarifying or facilitating clarification or ensuring an immediate and sincere apology is given. Also remember that everything is data; about the client(s), you and/or the relationship(s). The good news is that research suggests repair is possible by responding nondefensively, attending directly to the alliance and the therapist (we'd add coach) adjusting their behaviour.[42]

Recognise that you and everyone else will have blind spots and trust another's reaction if something hasn't landed with them, work together to repair the rupture. Your modeling of how to do this with empathy and awareness might be great learning for your clients. Remember there's a balance here between the irreverence of playfulness which can act as an ultimately transformative disruptor or facilitator and the need to take your clients on that journey with you (by mutual agreement of course – remember ABC – see more in Part II). Having said that, keep an eye on what's going on at the group level. Are issues coming up for some within the group/team which are not appropriate to address in the group context? If necessary, have a private conversation to scope out the situation or need.

During playful interventions, the shadow side of humour might be amplified as people feel freer or perhaps get carried away. As a coach, we can notice, raise awareness and help build understanding of the impact, though exercise caution not to be the 'rescuer' of the target of the maladaptive humour (or group dynamic issues) lest you contribute to unhelpful dynamics. If you are not already aware of it, take a look at Karpman's Drama Triangle. Aaker and Bagdonas[43] suggest a constellations exercise to explore how a joke has landed which you can play with depending on the context and physically map where participants stand in the range of responses (you can do this online with for example, digital avatars). The rules are to let your body do the thinking (let your instinct lead, don't analyse), be open and honest, be prepared to be an outlier and celebrate shifts. After listening to people's stories and opinions, give them the opportunity to shift position if participants choose. The difficulties of these conversations is what makes them poignant and the goal is to cultivate empathy, awareness and hopefully behavioural change.

Sometimes ruptures can be accelerated. Several of our Storytellers spoke of situations where one of the participants of team coaching (often those in a senior position) refused to engage playfully. What happened in the room – how that person behaved and others reacted – was seen as very useful data about team/leadership dynamics, personal development areas or sometimes served to flag up the incompatibility of the team member who is refusing. This is all potentially useful information to collect and address with the individual and/or the team and/or the ultimate client during the session or afterwards if potentially relevant and appropriate.

Debrief with the client and after that, ask for feedback and learn from each experience.

Our top tips sound rather prescriptive, which sits a little uneasily with us as coaches. We have offered you these ideas, based on our own experiences, conversations with our Storytellers and the literature and research. They are of course intended as ideas, for you to consider, take what you need, disregard what you don't and adapt and build on in your practice. Above all, we hope that you are building an awareness of the complexities of possible risks while at the same time becoming clearer about your relationship with that risk and developing agility in your offer of playfulness accordingly so that you can calibrate your work as you dance with your clients.

Playful Moment

Having spent so long pondering about potential risks, this might be a great time to reconnect with play through a Playful Moment.

Notes

1 Martin, R. & Ford, T. (2018). *The Psychology of Humor: An integrative approach.* Academic Press; Robert, C. (Ed.) (2017). *The Psychology of Humor at Work.* Routledge; Aaker, J. & Bagdonas, N. (2021). *Humor, Seriously.* Currency.

2 Proyer, R. (2012). A Psycho-linguistic Study on Adult Playfulness: Its Hierarchical Structure and Theoretical Considerations. *Journal of Adult Development, 19*(3), 141– 149. Proyer, R. (2013). The well-being of playful adults: Adult playfulness, subjective wellbeing, physical well-being, and the pursuit of enjoyable activities. *European Journal of Humour Research, 1*(1), 84–98.

3 Ruch, W. & Proyer, R. (2009). Extending the study of gelotophobia: On gelotophiles and katagelasticists. *Humor – International Journal of Humor Research, 22*(1–2), 183–212.

4 Proyer, R. & Ruch, W. (2011). The virtuousness of adult playfulness: the relation of playfulness with strengths of character. *Psychology of Well-Being, 1*(1), 1–12.

5 Proyer, R. (2012). Examining playfulness in adults: Testing its correlates with personality, positive psychological functioning, goal aspirations, and multi-methodically assessed ingenuity. *Psychological Test and Assessment Modeling, 54*(2), 103–127.

6 *Ibid,* Proyer & Ruch(2011).

7 Proyer, R. (2013). The well-being of playful adults: Adult playfulness, subjective wellbeing, physical well-being, and the pursuit of enjoyable activities. *European Journal of Humour Research, 1*(1), 84–98.

8 Poynton, R. (2007). *Everything's an offer: How to do more with less.* On Your Feet, p46.

9 Kubie, L. (1970). The destructive potential of humor in psychotherapy. *American Journal of Psychiatry, 127*(7), 866.

10 Kuhlman, T. (1894). *Humor and psychotherapy.* Dow Jones-Irwin Dorsey Professional Books.

11 Pierce, R. (1994). Use and abuse of laughter in psychotherapy. In Strean, H. (Ed.). *The use of humor in psychotherapy.* Jason Aronson, pp105–111.

12 Henry, W. (1998). Science, politics, and the politics of science: The use and misuse of empirically validated treatment research. *Psychotherapy research,* 8(2), 126–140. Grencavage, L. & Norcross, J. (1990). Where are the commonalities among the therapeutic common factors? *Professional psychology: Research and practice, 21*(5), 372. Weinberger, J. (1995). Common factors aren't so common: The common factors dilemma. *Clinical psychology: Science and practice, 2*(1), 45.

13 For example, De Haan, E. (2008). *Relational coaching: journeys towards mastering one-to-one learning.* Wiley. Hall, L. (2013). *Mindful Coaching: How Mindfulness can Transform Coaching Practice.* Kogan Page.

14 Norcross, J. (2014). The Therapeutic Relationship. In Duncan, B. et al (Eds.) *The Heart and Soul of Change: What works in therapy.* (2nd ed.). American Psychological Association, pp 113–141.

15 *Ibid,* Norcross (2014).

16 Bachelor, A. & Horvath, A. (1999). The therapeutic relationship. In Duncan, B. et al (Eds.) *The Heart and Soul of Change: What works in therapy*. (2nd ed.). American Psychological Association, pp133–178.

17 Bordin, E. (1979). The generalizability of the psychoanalytic concept of the working alliance. *Psychotherapy: Theory, research & practice, 16*(3), 252. Horvarth, A. & Greenberg, L. (1994). *The working alliance: Theory, research, and practice*. Wiley and Sons.

18 *Ibid*, Norcross (2014).

19 Brooks (1994) cited in Franzini, L. (2001). Humor in therapy: The case for training therapists in its uses and risks. *The Journal of General Psychology, 128*(2), 170–93.

20 Sultanoff, S. (1994). Choosing to be amusing: Assessing an individual's receptivity to therapeutic humor. *Journal of Nursing Jocularity, 4*(4), 34–35.

21 For example, Jiang, T., Li, H. & Hou, Y. (2019). Cultural differences in humor perception, usage, and implications. *Frontiers in Psychology, 10*, 123.

22 *Ibid*, Martin & Ford (2018, p30).

23 *Ibid*, Proyer & Ruch (2011, p10).

24 Wheeler, S. (2020). An exploration of playfulness in coaching. *International Coaching Psychology Review, 15*(1), 45.

25 *Ibid*, Franzini (2001).

26 De Haan, E. and graduates (2016). *Behind Closed Doors Stories from the Coaching Room*. (2nd edn.). Libri Publishing.

27 For more, see Robert, C. (Ed.). (2017). *The psychology of humor at work*. Routledge.

28 For example, Meyer, J. (2000). Humor as a double-edged sword: Four functions of humor in communication. *Communication Theory, 10*(3), 310–331.

29 *Ibid*, Meyer (2000).

30 Martineau, W. (1972). A model of the social functions of humor. In Goldstein, J. & McGhee, P. (Eds.). *The psychology of humor: Theoretical perspectives and empirical issues*. Academic Press, pp101–125.

31 Bill, B. & Naus, P. (1992). The role of humor in the interpretation of sexist incidents. *Sex Roles. 27*(11–12), 645–664. Johnson, A. (1990). The 'only joking' defense: Attribution bias or impression management? *Psychological Reports, 67*, 1051–1056.

32 *Ibid*, Martin & Ford (2018, p.375).

33 Crandall, C. & Eshleman, A. (2003). A justification-suppression model of the expression and experience of prejudice. *Psychological Bulletin, 129*, 414–446.

34 Robinson, D. & Smith-Lovin, L. (2001). Getting a laugh: Gender, status, and humor in task discussions. *Social Forces, 80*(1), 123–158.

35 Kuipers, G. (2006). *Good humor, bad taste. A sociology of the joke (humor rese)*. Mouton de Gruyter.

36 Janes, L. & Olson, J. (2000). Jeer pressures: The behavioral effects of observing ridicule of others. *Personality & Social Psychology Bulletin, 26*(4), 474–485.

37 Joplin (2007) cited in Spinelli, E. (2008) Coaching and Therapy: Similarities and divergences. *International Coaching Psychologist Review, 3*(3), 241–249.

38 For example, Pogrebin, M. and Poole, E. (1998). Humor in the briefing room: A study of the strategic uses of humor among police. *Journal of Contemporary Ethnography, 17*(2), 183–210.

39 Angelone, D., Hirschman, R., Suniga, S., Armey, M. & Armelie, A. (2005). The influence of peer interactions on sexually oriented joke telling. *Sex Roles, 52*(3–4), 187–199. Hunt, C. & Gonsalkorale, K. (2014). Who cares what she thinks, what does he say? Links between masculinity, in-group bonding and gender harassment. *Sex Roles, 40*(1–2), 14–27. Siebler, F., Sabelus, S. & Bohner, G. (2008). A refined computer harassment paradigm: Validation, and test of hypotheses about target characteristics. *Psychology of Women Quarterly, 32*(1), 22–35.

40 For example, Dwyer, T. (1991). Humor, power, and change in organizations. *Human Relations,.44*(1), 1–19.

41 *Ibid*, Janes & Olson (2000).

42 Safran, J., Muran, J., Samstag, L. & Stevens, C. (2002). Repairing Alliance Ruptures. In Norcross, J. (Ed.), *Psychotherapy relationships that work*. Oxford University Press, pp135–253.

43 Aaker, J. & Bagdonas, N. (2020). *Humor, seriously*. Currency, p197.

Part II

Stepping into Playfulness: From Theory to Practice

DOI: 10.4324/9781003090847-11

Welcome to Part II as we step from theory to practice. Our invitation, particularly for this section of the book, is to engage not just your head, but your heart and body too. We'd be delighted if you would play with this book; read it while walking backwards or standing on your head (no liability accepted) or something even a little different from your normal position/location/approach. Draw in or alongside it, make notes, doodle, be curious and open and play with us in whatever way is right for you. There are lots of reflection pauses; we invite you to experiment with these also, for example, reflecting while moving or using different materials or with music. Tap into your knowledge and experience to build on and change the questions and experiments, see them as prompts rather than rigid instructions. Remember to step outside of your habits and embrace discomfort as a sign of learning.

In other words, experiment with engaging with this book differently, play with it and make it your own.

10
Tending the Seedlings of Playfulness

In this chapter we:

- Invite you to check-in on your level of playfulness
- Consider if anyone can be playful
- Ask how you connect with play
- Help you explore your beliefs and habits around playfulness
- Think about the impact of the stories we tell ourselves
- Consider how Attachment Theory is relevant
- Include a fireside chat with Graham Lee
- Work with the Whole Body to support playfulness
- Explore how you know when you're being playful
- Reflect on what you focus on grows
- Invite you to explore and experiment

Let's take a moment to imagine a doorway opening. It is intriguing; inside lies the promise of new playful adventures. Light is flooding through the doorway, offering many possibilities for playfulness. Notice the details of what you are

DOI: 10.4324/9781003090847-12

imagining: the size of the door, the colours, the surrounding environment. How far is the door open? Beyond, there may be all manner of things: the curious, the new, little, or big experiences, various objects and so on. Instinctively you know the world of playfulness is more than what's visible to the eye; it's also a feeling, a whole range of feelings. Playfulness isn't always joy and fun. It's not always an action or even visible. It's also a stance, an attitude, and a way of being. Using all your senses, notice what you can see, smell, hear, taste, and feel as you come closer. Whatever you can imagine and perceive beyond the doorway makes all the possibilities come to life. Take a peek, dare you step through (more fully)? What is there to gain? What is there to lose? Join us as we wander beyond the door together into further adventures into playfulness.

10.1 Stepping into Playfulness: From Theory to Practice

Welcome to Part II of this book where we start moving ever more from theory to practice. Let's start by recognising and celebrating that the biggest enabler of playfulness is you.

> You can only take people where you are prepared to go yourself.
>
> *Steve Chapman*

The more ease and awareness you have around playfulness, the more equipped you will be to authentically engage playfully in your work and foster playfulness in others. Not least, we came across emotional contagion briefly in Chapter 7 and if you as a coach are comfortable to connect with and share your playfulness, this might help your client to move into that space too. The broader your own personal experience and comfort with play, the wider the variety of ways in which playfulness can be nurtured in your work, giving your clients more freedom to express and experience playfulness in a way which is right for them. You are the main instrument in the coaching space and playfulness is so much more than any tool, object, or material; playfulness is largely about your willingness to play, to be curious, experiment, explore, prepared to not know and improvise, creating the space to enable your clients to do so too.

You will be familiar with this little onion by now. To support our increasing emphasis on practice, you will see that the number of opportunities and prompts for reflection are increasing from this chapter onwards. We'll also be introducing working with your Whole Body so when you pause to reflect, please notice not only what thoughts are arising for you, but also emotions and where you feel them in your body. Be curious. Be specific.

We have written this and the next chapter primarily with you, the practitioner, in mind and how you can find ways to build your capacity for playfulness. Of course, you can use it to work with your clients on increasing their capacity too. You'll also see that we look at some of the ideas from a practice point of view too.

Do you remember Di Gammage's invitation to see play as a moving holo-gram of a jigsaw rather than a binary work/play construct in Chapter 3? Having walked with us through some of the different dimensions and facets of playfulness, we invite you to wear systemic lenses as you read on. In earlier chapters, we've considered the importance and interconnected-ness of our peripheral nervous system and brain, the impact and effect of emotions and how we connect and engage with others as well as how play-fulness affects and engages us on multiple levels simultaneously. We invite you to bear this complexity in mind, to see beyond the linear, not only in terms of what's going on within ourselves and our clients but also in our relational spaces and systems.

10.2 Barometer of Playfulness

'You can't improve what you don't measure' is often attributed to Peter Drucker and a useful place to start. You'll find a longer version of the Barometer of

Playfulness in The Playfulness Scrapbook, but in a moment, we'll introduce you to the shorter version.

First, reflecting on what you've read so far, we invite you to have a Playful Moment then come back to check in with your capacity for playfulness (whether in a given moment or generally) using the Barometer of Playfulness. When answering, notice what comes up for you in your heart, mind, and body. What further questions arise for you and what more do you need?

Barometer of Playfulness

When it comes to playing or being playful, in this moment, what level are you at for each of the following?

Using the scale of 1–5 (from low to high)

1. In this moment, *how* playful are you?
2. Do you *want* more play or to be more playful? How much do you want this?
3. Do you have enough *energy* to play or be playful? What is your current energy level?
4. Are you *able* to play or be playful? At what level is your ability? What would you like it to be?

If you'd like to reflect further, bearing in mind the broad definition of play-fulness of our Be Playful Onion Model, ask yourself:

- *On a scale of 1–5 what is my usual level of playfulness?*
- *Do I have different scores in different situations/areas of life/relationships?*
- *Where in the Be Playful Onion Model do I sit most comfortably, habitually?*
- *Is this different in different contexts?*
- *What usually increases or diminishes my playfulness?*
- *How do I know when I am being playful?*

Now that you have a more nuanced feel of your current state of playfulness, let's begin to explore how you can grow it.

10.3 Can Anyone Be Playful?

> If you hear a voice within you say 'I cannot paint', then by all means paint and that voice will be silenced.
>
> *Vincent van Gogh*

> If you hear a voice within you say 'I cannot play', then by all means play and that voice will be silenced ...or talk with it, draw it, model it and give voice to all other voices, play to move beyond your stuckness, play to gain awareness, play for learning, play for experiencing the novel and different perspectives, play for joy, play for connection and play for life.
>
> *Teresa and Stephanie*

As we've seen in Part I, we are all hardwired to play. In fact, the ability to play is interwoven with lifelong neural plasticity. Even so, it may be that experiences, including but not limited to trauma, have made it harder to access play. The good news is that you are not doomed to a life with little or no playfulness. Even with trauma, some of the effective trauma therapies incorporate play-fulness to overcome trauma and in turn make playfulness in other contexts more accessible: 'trauma cannot be destroyed but it can be dissolved in a sea of resources'[1] including learning how to restore and reconnect with your ability to feel pleasure and joy, to be playful and spontaneous.[2]

> Psychotherapy takes place in the overlap of two areas of playing, that of the patient and that of the therapist. Psychotherapy has to do with two people playing together. The corollary of this is that where playing is not possible then the work done by the therapist is directed towards bringing the patient from a state of not being able to play into a state of being able to play.
>
> *Winnicott*[3]

We've seen in Chapter 6 that to access playfulness, Graham Lee suggests that our body-brain system needs to be in what he describes as the GREEN state for which a key requirement is trust and safety. More broadly, we've found in our own experience that just like a toddler, hunger, lack of sleep or overwhelm, for example, of stimulus or emotion make it much harder to access playfulness or to access playfulness and stay grounded. To use a well-worn metaphor, give a thought to the effectiveness of your oxygen mask; are you in a state, in the broader sense, in which you can be playful? It's also worth considering the state that your clients are in when you're considering extending an invitation to play so that you can either not make it or tailor it accordingly. For instance, have they just rushed to you in the midst of a stressful morning? It may be that you need to help them to 'arrive' and be present first (you might try some light breathing exercises or a mini-meditation or grounding exercise if that's your thing – it is ours when our clients are open to it). On the other hand, they might be experiencing longer term stress, lack of sleep and so on, in which case you'll need to tailor your invitation accordingly. You might apply the same thoughts to yourself as you prepare for a session.

> If all you can do is crawl, start crawling.
>
> *Rumi*

As we've seen, play and playfulness are nuanced and multi-faceted, so a good starting point is to recognise where you habitually sit in the Be Playful Onion Model. Remember, we're not thinking in linear terms, so you will sit at different levels in the three layers, and this will probably be different in different relationships, contexts, and times. To try to arrive at some granularity in your self-awareness, consider Gökhan Güneş' (2021) proposal that we all have a personal play identity which has four components: how you play, your personality, socio-culture/environment and economics/technology.[4] Included in the mix are different aspects of ourselves and our experiences of play as children.

10.4 What Play Habits Did You Take with You into Adulthood?

When you played as a child:

- *Were you the peacemaker or conflict-stirrer?*
- *Were you competitive or co-operative?*
- *Were you a rule setter, follower, or breaker?*
- *Did you feel more comfortable with defined or amorphous play structures?*
- *Did you prefer (or had fewer choices) to play alone, with another or in groups?*
- *What was your experience of playing in groups like?*
- *Did you tend to be one of the quiet or loud ones?*
- *Were there any specific experiences that affected your play habits?*
- *How did you react to losing or winning if the games had a competitive element?*
- *How easily did you switch between all these different possibilities during a game?*

Play helped us to explore these different ways of being and interacting, pruning and strengthening our neural connections as we did so. Eventually, this left us with habits or patterns which shaped how we relate to ourselves, others, and the world during adulthood and not just in the context of play. The work of Dr Allan Shore and the neurobiology of different early attachment experiences is relevant here too. These experiences, together with how we then went on to play during early adolescence impacted how we played and interacted with others as we matured. How we learned to play determined who we became as adults (more on Attachment Theory and playfulness later).

Stephanie relates: *Thanks to Carol Dweck, I noticed how I had adopted a fixed mindset around my own playfulness. In my childhood, I was very happy playing in dyads and smaller groups but some of my larger group experiences were less happy. A memory of being about thirteen stuck with me; an improv game during an English lesson where a few of us were 'volunteered' to stand on the stage and pretend that we were different radio stations with the teacher turning the imaginary dial and tuning into stations. One of the quieter members of the class and one of the 'swots', I was told to be an opera singer. Talk about whizzing straight past the zone of discomfort into overwhelm. At the time, as much as I wanted to join in with the fun, I couldn't get past myself and join in whole-heartedly. It took me until the second year of my MSc in 2017 to truly recognise that deep down, I still carried feelings of lack of safety on some level within groups and found it hard to claim space, find my voice and feel belonging in some group settings, even in nurturing inclusive groups such as our MSc cohort. Without realising it, I had been holding on to an old story I had constructed about myself, groups and my place in them which inhibited my playfulness and was no longer serving me. It was a significant insight for me and since then I have been experimenting with different ways of being in group contexts, feeling increasingly at ease and able to show up more authentically and freely.*

- *What beliefs do you have around your belonging and safety in groups?*
- *Do you behave differently in groups (or certain types of groups)?*
- *What's behind this and how does it impact your playfulness?*

The beliefs which we hold around playfulness can be hugely influential. If you're not careful, enough of these experiences when not balanced out can start forming part of your identity with beliefs such as 'I'm not a playful person', 'I'm an introvert so don't feel comfortable doing this' taking centre stage. The great news is that as coaches, we know that old and unhelpful beliefs can be shifted. Also, through play (by which we mean here exploring different perspectives, ways of doing things and outcomes in low stakes situations) which enables neuroplasticity, we can change who we are and how we show up. We've both found that finding a play buddy to experiment with has been enormously helpful to support and challenge our playfulness development. Writing this book has been extremely challenging due to all the other demands on our time, energy and mental capacity, especially as we started just as Covid-19 made its presence felt. Equally, it has been a joyous experience as it has given us the impetus to explore – to learn, unlearn, relearn, develop and generally be more playful around playfulness. We've reminded each other implicitly or explicitly to come back to playfulness in the face of numerous challenges.

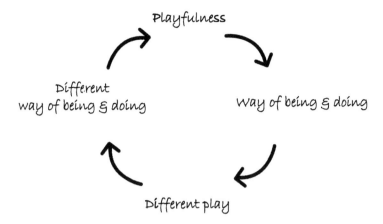

Figure 10.1 The evolution of play

A useful phrase to remember in your practice is: 'It's not about you'. Robert Stephenson told us a story of working with a team who kept talking about having a more playful life. Initially Robert shared lots of what he thought were playful options, but nothing seemed to land. On reflection, he asked 'What does that mean for you?' This unlocked the session as their version of playfulness was serious play. The conversation turned to LEGO® building and the team became brighter, more engaged, and excited. Their idea of playfulness as a structured game with clear instructions was significantly different to Robert's.

Aspects of personality, such as self-perception as a serious person or preference for introversion are likely to influence where in the Be Playful Onion Model is most comfortable. Do we ever invite the playful side of ourselves out and if so, in what way? As the Be Playful Onion Model shows, playfulness can be many things and we can find our own authentic place as well as discovering more possibilities if we are willing to go beyond our comfort zones.

In her story above, Stephanie reflected on how she had changed her self-perception over the years allowing her to be more playful, especially in groups, but of course not everyone wants to increase their capacity for playfulness (or perhaps at least not in the context of, for example, a team coaching session on a serious topic). We hope that the Be Playful Onion Model and reflections have given you some insight into what playfulness means to you. With clients, it is sometimes worth being careful whether and how you use the word 'play' as it might create too much of a barrier. Julie Flower shared an observation with us about working with a team in charge of very serious, analytical processes. With them, she used the term 'play' in terms of intellectual playfulness rather than humour and adjusted how she invited playfulness. Contracting is an opportunity to gain some understanding of the team, its members, and the organisational culture to allow you to frame and flex playfulness accordingly.

10.5 More Stories We Tell Ourselves

> We prohibit play in the strongest terms … The student shall rise at five in the morning summer and winter … The students shall be indulged with nothing which the world calls play. Let this rule be observed with strictest nicety, for those who play when they are young will play when they are old.
> *Methodist boarding school 1780*[5]

Most of us can relate to stories of people (you may even be one) who are convinced that they can't or shouldn't draw, sing, dance, and the like, because at some stage in their lives, usually when they were children or teenagers and still building their picture of who they were, someone (often an influential adult) told them that they couldn't or indeed shouldn't. It still amazes us how some scenes from our past, a comment or experience which others hardly registered can profoundly affect us years later.

In the BBC4 radio programme 'The Confessional' hosted by Stephen Mangan (aired in March 2021), David Tennant, stage and screen actor, tells the story of how for him, being playful/creative and humorous is also intertwined with his first memory of experiencing shame.[6] David explains by sharing the following story: In the run up to his first school nativity play at the age of 5, his class was trying on the costumes for the first time. For some this included wearing tea towels on their heads (the custom at the time). David can't remember why exactly, but he ended up standing at his desk with his class all watching him trying to put the tea towel on his head with a piece of string, failing miserably. Everyone found it very funny and rather than being appalled that he was being laughed at, in that moment he enjoyed the reaction and played with different ways of arranging the tea towel to more gales of laughter from his fellow 5 year olds. At this point it becomes 'a thing' so he carries on, each time being sillier and laughter growing. It's an exciting moment for him as he has his audience in the palm of his hands.

Looking back, he reflects that clearly something in him was responding to the reaction from his fellow 5 year olds and not wanting to let it go so he just kept at it. Back to the point in time in the classroom, even though he's aware he's run out of material (new ways to tie the tea towel), he keeps going and the reaction builds and becomes uproarious. The teacher is sitting at her desk marking books and very dryly and quietly says 'David John MacDonald, sit down and stop showing off'. Silence descends and 'a coldness descended on my soul' at the idea that she cut him down in the flight of his glory. While it made sense for the teacher to tell him to 'behave', at that moment, he received a clear message that taking the spotlight was the wrong thing to do. The implicit message was: 'Who do you think you are? How dare you think you are worthy of attention and how dare you enjoy it?'

Fast-forward to his work as an actor, depending on the roles that he is playing, the fact that you can sense during his performance that he is enjoying himself is part of his charisma. Hearing this reflection from Stephen, David is thrilled but also a little bit ashamed – his teacher's voice is still there in his head. David says that it took a long time for him to process the experience and on reflection, in that moment, she did him quite a lot of damage, inserting a voice fuelling constant self-monitoring. As with many of these internal voices (you might call some of them imposter syndrome if you like to use that term), it does have its moderating benefits from time to time (for example, to pull you back from being insufferable), but even so, it still needs to be listened to with caution. As David says: 'You don't want to leave the stage when the audience is still laughing!'

How many of us are walking around with voices like this which impact our potential playfulness?

- *What messages were you given about being playful?*
- *Do you have one (or more) voices inside you which impact your potential to be playful?*
- *What do they say?*

It might not even have been a direct message which you have absorbed. Andrea Fella, an Insight Meditation teacher talks about recognising that some of our implicit biases and prejudices are the result of 'the soup you were stewing in' during our formative years. In other words, we can look at not just specific positive or negative events which shaped the beliefs which we hold but also the norms and messages which we received from the systems in which we spent our formative years. Andrea Fella speaks of this idea in a different context but we think that it is equally insightful in terms of playfulness. It's a common message in homes, schools, peer groups and so on that playfulness has no role after a certain age.

- *What messages around playfulness were there in your formative systems?*
- *Sitting here now, as an adult, years later, do you still believe these messages?*
- *Can you bring some compassion to the originator(s) of this message(s) knowing what might have sat behind it?*
- *Can you bring some compassion to you as a child hearing these messages?*
- *Are the beliefs which they represent consistent with the beliefs which you hold now?*
- *Are they serving you?*
- *How would you benefit if you held other beliefs which allow space for playfulness?*

For many people the net effect of either specific experiences or the soup in which they stewed is to push playfulness to the margins of what Miller Mair evocatively calls our 'Community of Selves' (for more on this see The Playfulness Scrapbook).

10.6 Attachment Theory

Talking of early experiences, it seems that your attachment style may also impact your playfulness. Attachment Theory[7] is one of the most important conceptual frameworks for understanding the formation of personality and mental health and is based on the quality of the bond between child and caregiver.[8] In essence, there are different attachment styles which describe the particular way in which an individual relates to others. These styles are expectations which we develop about relationships based on our first experience with our initial caregiver. Bartholomew and Horowitz (1991) developed a model with four different attachment styles depending on whether you hold positive or negative thoughts about yourself and positive or negative thoughts about others.[9] We won't go into detail about them here (you can see a brief explanation in the diagram). For our purposes, studies suggest that different levels of self-reported playfulness are associated with specific types of attachment.[10]

Thoughts about others ↑

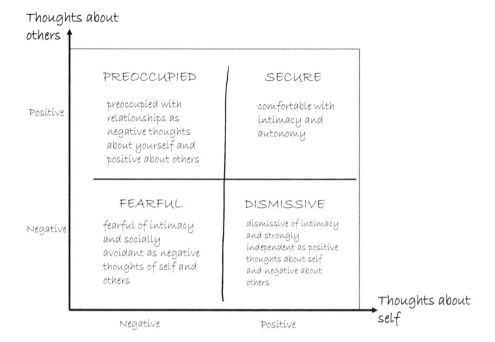

	PREOCCUPIED	SECURE
Positive	preoccupied with relationships as negative thoughts about yourself and positive about others	comfortable with intimacy and autonomy
	FEARFUL	DISMISSIVE
Negative	fearful of intimacy and socially avoidant as negative thoughts of self and others	dismissive of intimacy and strongly independent as positive thoughts about self and negative about others
	Negative	Positive

Thoughts about self →

Figure 10.2 Attachment styles

There is therefore some support for saying that the ease or difficulty with which a person accesses playfulness may depend on their early attachment experiences. Intuitively this makes sense. If we experience enough safety, we are open to exploration, discovery, curiosity. As Graham Lee reflected in our conversation, from this place of safety, you have an 'open system relationship to the wider world'. You can see it in children; to be open to play they need to feel safe enough (we can link this back to the activation of the Parasympathetic Nervous System which we looked at in Chapter 6). While insecure attachment is relatively common,[11] securely attached peers are more curious,[12] their explorations take varied forms including intellectual adventuring,[13] cognitive openness[14] and 'overall approach' behaviour (the movement toward something),[15] all of which are supportive of playfulness and coaching.

Siegel[16] writes of 'feeling felt', in other words, 'being present for others means we resonate with what is going on in their inner worlds, creating the essential way we feel their feelings', which is the basis of secure attachment which we can offer as coaches by offering the experience of being present in a resonant relationship. Secure attachment of the coach might support cooperation and openness to experiencing joy, play and excitement, generally and in their work, while they find it easier to regulate their emotions if things don't go to plan. Equally, a secure attachment experience by a client potentially offered in a coaching relationship might support greater willingness to take risks and experience something new, as in that space the client is better able to regulate their emotions and trust that the coach will hold a safe space.

What's important to appreciate and is also good news in terms of developing play-fulness as adults is that your attachment style is context specific (in other words, it is likely that you show different attachment styles in different relationships) and that it is not set in stone; it is possible for it to change over time.

- *What is your own attachment style in different contexts (personal relationships, individual clients, teams)?*
- *How available is playfulness to you in those contexts?*
- *What is the attachment style of your client(s) in different contexts?*
- *How available is playfulness to them?*

10.7 Beliefs about Playfulness

As we've seen, your ease of accessing playfulness will depend in large part on the beliefs you hold. What of our beliefs around playfulness more generally? Jen Gash works with coaches and non-coaches to tap into and develop their cre-ativity[17] and with her permission, we've adapted some of her questions to help you to reflect on your values and beliefs around playfulness:

- *What does playfulness mean to you?*
- *Where does playfulness come from?*
- *Do you believe you are playful?*
- *What do you feel has helped shape that belief?*
- *When someone says they are playful, what do you immediately think?*
- *What assumptions do you make if people say they would like to be more playful?*
- *What do you believe are the essential components of playfulness?*
- *What are the beliefs that you hold around these?*

10.8 Connecting with Play

We all connect with play in various and sometimes different ways. To increase your capacity for playfulness, work on building your awareness of what connects you with play. By way of example, here's one from us: Teresa relates: *A range of simple things connect me to play, depending on my mood. I love doodling and my notebooks are often strewn with doodles and just the sight of felt tips increases my playfulness. Music and dancing also connect me to a more playful state and short impromptu kitchen discos aren't unusual. While working on this book a long-forgotten memory popped up; as a child I was obsessed with small brightly coloured bouncy balls. As soon as I had pocket money, I'd go to my local toy shop where they had buckets filled with different coloured balls. I loved looking at or playing with them, on my own or with others. Like the pens, seeing them was and is enough to stir up feelings of playfulness. Recently, I noticed a small green smiley ball sitting on my desk. It was given to me at an innovation event many years ago and while I kept it, I hadn't paid it much attention. Having made the connection with my play memory, it now has pride of place on my desk and is an instant reminder of memories, feelings and possibilities of play.*

Each Storyteller has various and unique ways in which play might show up for them and it's about finding the right approach for you (which of course will also evolve over time). There's no correct or one-size-fits-all approach. David Clutterbuck and Neil Mullarky are naturally humorous, mischievous, and witty and this is reflected in how they leverage playfulness in their work. Other Storytellers' playfulness is much more subtle; a warmth, openness, an unspoken implicit quality which overall gives a sense of invitation and permission for playfulness if it might be of service. This openness also makes space for clients to be themselves, self-censoring themselves less, without fear of judgement. In the next chapter, we'll offer you some ideas on how you might expand your playfulness repertoire in a way which is authentic to you.

Some of our Storytellers intentionally plan playful interventions though more generally, playfulness is often not planned, but emerges. Another thread which we also relate to is the resistance to the label of 'playful coach'. In Stephanie's original research, one of the participants summed it up beautifully: 'I would no more call myself a playful coach than I would a serious coach'. What is evident, however, is that authenticity is an important ingredient for allowing playfulness to emerge.

> If you are not playful outside of work, then it will be stiff and forced if you are not authentic in being playful in your work.
>
> *Kirsten Barske*

A quality of playfulness which keeps coming up is that of openness (to different perspectives, ideas, and experiences, for example) and we'll look at this in more detail later. Nurturing your capacity to be open to playfulness outside of work will help you find an authentic way to connect to or amplify your playfulness and you can then conduct authentic mini-experiments in your work or be bolder, it's up to you. When we are speaking of authenticity here, we mean essentially ease with 'being' and 'doing' playfulness and inviting the client to join you. We are also mindful of the broader authenticity which is necessary for playfulness: the coach's availability and capacity to hold internal and external events lightly from a base of self-knowledge, self-acceptance and self-belief. There is some support for this in the literature: spontaneity which is necessary for playfulness,[18] cannot be commanded and the rational cognitive faculties required for self-monitoring obstruct playfulness.[19] Higher self-confidence is associated with playfulness[20] and if you lack confidence as a coach, it will more likely be more difficult to be playful (in service of your client rather than to overcome/hide your insecurity). Again, going back to Stephanie's original research, she found that the potent cocktail of presence and safety/trust within the relationship together with the coach's authenticity are the three cornerstones for playfulness, supporting genuine exploration that is built on and promotes curiosity and novelty. The space created on this foundation then facilitates exploration of different perspectives with lightness while being supportive of vulnerability.

Let's take a solution-focused approach to becoming (even more) playful in thinking about what currently connects you to play:

- *Are you open to playfulness?*
- *What connects you to playfulness?*
- *In what context do you feel at your most playful?*
- *If you had all the time in the world, how would you most like to be playful?*
- *What did you enjoy as a child or have always wanted to try?*
- *What forms of playfulness do you enjoy?*
- *Draw, model, sing or dance (or any other way of expression which you wish) what comes up when you imagine yourself playing or being playful. Reflecting on this afterwards, what does it tell you?*
- *If a magic wand was waved and you were free to be as playful as you wished in your heart to be, what would that look like?*
- *How would you feel, think, act? What would others notice?*
- *Do you invite the play that is in your client?*
- *If not, does your client interpret that as it not being safe to play?*
- *How do you hold the space? Do you have a 'yes, and' approach to work with what emerges from the client and between you?*
- *Can you hold yourself grounded in self-belief, compassion and awareness yet lightly and are you willing to laugh at yourself?*
- *Where is the playfulness in the system that is you and your professional practice?* (Question adapted from one by David Clutterbuck)

With busy lives, playfulness can often be relegated to a luxury which we do without in the face of more pressing and serious priorities. Unless we understand the fundamental importance of playfulness for our well-being, connection to others, learning and development and value-adding capabilities in our different roles at work, home and society, it can be all too easy to neglect making space for playfulness. We're not talking here about the occasional or regular sport which you might play, but engaging in playful exploration, whether in micro-moments or longer periods. Sometimes it's about intentionally opening up to playfulness and turning off the auto-pilot.

When one of Teresa's daughters was three, she took her to their usual play park. Her little one was concerned as they drove past, not realising that she was looking for a place to park. Teresa was preoccupied and on autopilot and explained they were going to the car park. 'Wow, cars have parks too?' came the excited response. Teresa grabbed the moment, thinking of the Herbie films about Disney's sentient anthropomorphic 1963 VW Beetle, she switched to whimsical and fun-seeking mode and they spent the afternoon pretending to be cars playing in the play park. It has stayed a vivid memory for them both and a lovely example of how you can quickly, if you spot and embrace the opportunity, step into a more playful perspective and way of doing and being. In the next chapter, we'll look at some ways to help you access playfulness more readily.

- *When was the last time you experienced play or playfulness?*
- *What things (using all or any of your senses) prompts you to feel (more) playful?*
- *How does it make you feel in your Whole Body?*

Essentially, this is about being open to play and, in our work, allowing playfulness to be a vehicle and not being playful for the sake of being playful. Robert Stephenson conjured a beautiful image to describe how he sees playfulness and how it emerges in practice: imagine our environment as a lake and playfulness as the sky; how often and with ease can you come up out of the water to be into the sky of playfulness?

10.9 Working with the Whole Body

You'll remember from the Be Playful Onion Model that playfulness can take the physical form ('doing') and be more ephemeral ('being'). In other words, it can involve all of you rather than just your body or your mind. This is too simplistic though; as we saw in Chapter 6, our peripheral nervous system and those of others we're in relationship with are also very relevant to our playfulness, as are emotions (Chapter 7). Attempts have long been made to move thinking, particularly in the Western Hemisphere, away from the Descartes' (1596–1650) mind-body dualism. Stephanie remembers having her frames of reference profoundly challenged by reading Fritjof Capra's *The Turning Point*[21] as a teenager (the label 'swot' we came across earlier is perhaps making sense now). In it, Capra, a physicist and systems theorist argued that the Cartesian, Newtonian and reductionist paradigms which underlay much of Western society's thinking was inadequate for modern needs (including ecological needs) and science needed to develop the concepts and insights offered by holism and systems theory to address complex problems. Peter Hawkins and David Clutterbuck have been advocating for a systemic approach to coaching for many years and encourage us to take a more holistic approach to surface what might be going on in the system (we have both completed the Global Team Coaching Institute's Practitioner in Team Coaching course headed by Peter and David). For example, if we notice we are becoming tense, tongue tied, awkward in some way (all distinctly unplayful), the reasons may lie beyond us; it may be that we are picking up on what's happening for the client or within the group or system.

Some coaching approaches such as Gestalt and somatic coaching have always drawn on information beyond the cognitive and there does seem to be an increasing recognition that we're missing a considerable piece of the jigsaw if we're not working with the Whole Body (head, heart, gut, nervous system). You'll remember that we invited you to gather data from your Whole Body in the reflection pauses and will do so also in later experiments. In the Bob and the Daffodils story which you'll come across in The Playfulness Scrapbook, Steve Chapman listened to his own feelings and embodied experience to guide his interventions.

As well as being a rich source of data, working with more than our brains can help fresh insights to emerge. LEGO® Serious Play® facilitators encourage you to 'think with your hands', letting your hands bring to the surface ideas and thoughts which might be out of reach of your conscious mind. The same principle applies in using art or modelling to explore coaching topics. You can then combine this with moving and seeing the result from different perspectives (near/far, high/low, for example) to see if this brings any more insights (checking in with your Whole Body). Whether you are creating something tangible or working with your body in other ways such as mask work or Chairwork, movement can help us to shift into what ACT coaching refers to as our Observing Selves, creating psychological distance and widening our capacity to see different perspectives and possibilities.

Kirsten Barske shared her experience of how encouraging participants to move stimulates their thinking and brings up different emotions for them. With large groups she uses a form of physical mapping, which can help settle a new group and tap into a new source of information. She might, for example, invite participants to stand in places mapping out their current levels of motivation. Bringing self-awareness to how it feels (again, in your Whole Body) to stand in that physical space and look at the physical map overall can bring fresh insights beyond those gained by sitting and talking.

- *Imagine your most playful self. Now notice what you see, feel, hear, smell and taste.*
- *If you were to move playfully, what would that be like? What different sensations arise in your Whole Body?*
- *Bringing your awareness within, if there was a seed of play within you, where might it start to grow?*
- *What do you need right now to be more playful?*
- *Drop your awareness from your head to your heart. Connect with your heart. (To help you may want to put your hands to your heart.) Ask your heart what it would like to share with you about you being playful and what can help you be more playful.*

10.10 How Do You Know When You Are Being Playful?

To help raise your awareness around playfulness, it might be helpful to ask yourself how do you *know* when you are being playful? Let's listen to a few stories to get a flavour of how we might strengthen our playfulness detector.

For us, it's often a feeling in our bodies of connection, a mix of ease and excitement, comfort of the known (reassurance of our coaching skills and experience) and a feeling of groundedness balanced with the discomfort of not knowing where the process is taking us or what the outcome might be. Like a light bulb with a dimmer switch, it can be adjusted up or down. Context and environment dependent (with triggers depending on our own evolving personal play identities, see above), we experience ourselves at a Whole Body level as more open, more curious and at ease with ourselves and others. We notice that we are more flexible, freer in our thinking and ability to shift perspective, stepping in and out of the objective, subjective and embodied experience more fluidly. Creativity, imagination, humour and warmth (compassion, empathy even love) are more accessible, helping to find fresh insight and learnings, playing around with patterns and habits and creating new thoughts and experiences. We are willing to give things a go and experiment, more able to sit it in the unknown, work with uncertainty and varying degrees of discomfort. We are often fully immersed in the process and in the flow state, feeling safe and able to be our authentic selves.

10.10.1 Fireside Chat with Graham Lee

What does 'playfulness in coaching' conjure up for you?

Playfulness in coaching conjures the idea of what Donald Winnicott, the psychoanalyst, called the potential space where creativity occurs. He proposed that the potential space first arises in the 'good enough' relationship between mother and baby, and this space allows the baby to play: to explore, discover and learn, without fear of being abandoned, shamed, or criticised. Winnicott suggested that this intermediate area between self and the other is retained throughout life as the condition for all imaginative living. Our very aliveness depends on our capacity to play. I view good-enough coaching as creating the conditions for clients to play, perhaps most powerfully, with their sense of identity, loosening their self-narratives and fixed mindsets and inventing themselves afresh in more life enhancing ways.

In your most recent book, you describe The Ladder of Capabilities For Facilitating Breakthrough Conversations. At the top of the ladder sits playfulness; of all the capabilities you could have selected, why choose playfulness?

I view playfulness in relationships as the essence of human freedom and creative expression. To be most truly ourselves whilst being truly attuned to others requires us to move fluidly between our self-awareness and our empathy and understanding for others, and an openness to finding new solutions that arise from these interactions. I think playfulness is a good term for capturing such agile movements between self and others.

A common understanding of the term 'playfulness' connects it more to outward play behaviour and an association with fun and amusement. Your approach connects it more to a state and a way of being with a relational element. How do you address this potential mismatch?

I think the only real difference here is between what is external and what is internal. When coaching is playful, we are inviting clients to discover things about themselves and to look at the implications of these discoveries for their impact and fulfilment. We might invite clients to play with their 'internal experiences' – perhaps their self-belief, their shame, their delight, their sadness – or we might invite clients to play with external objects that represent characters or emotions. In either case it is the capacity to stand back and to observe with curiosity these internal and external dynamics that allows for new insights. The sense of fun and amusement often comes from a capacity to observe ourselves and to laugh at how invested we can become in our limiting mindsets.

What would you say to potential clients or coaches sceptical of the role of playfulness in coaching?

I might not necessarily use the term playfulness. I might talk instead in terms of developing mental and emotional agility, or the need to approach new challenges with fresh eyes, and to view coaching as a space that fosters creativity and innovation.

Can anyone access playfulness? What might support this?

I think playfulness is fundamental to all mammals – we can see this in any David Attenborough nature programme – and as coaches it is always useful to wonder what might be getting in the way of playfulness, whether for ourselves or for our clients.

Do you see a need for addressing and developing playfulness in coach training and even perhaps accreditation?

I see 'playfulness' as a metaphor for freedom and creativity, and so if such a focus enhances these aspects of coach training that will be a good thing.

What's your personal favourite expression of playfulness?

One of my favourite manifestations of playfulness is the ordinary, everyday banter between people – couples, colleagues, parents and their children – that celebrates the lighter, more humorous ways of looking at life, even if the things being laughed about are pointing to deeper truths.

Graham Lee is also one of our Storytellers; see Chapter 1 for more about his work.

Some of our Storytellers describe a state or a feeling of warmth, openness (less guarded), being able to engage and be yourself in the act of play and being playful. Emma Skitt, for example, looks within to notice being playful, using the rich metaphor of her inner rag doll – a loose, flexible, at ease, playful feeling. To help us detect it in ourselves, it might be helpful to turn our attention to how we experience playfulness in others. We noticed that as Emma reflected on her inner rag doll, her energy built, and she seemed more alight and even more playful than her 'resting playfulness'. Emma's resting playfulness setting is at an infectiously high level and being in her presence, you can feel your own mood and state shift to brighter and lighter levels. By the end of our conversation, we were all bubbling, buzzing and excitedly interacting as we fizzed with ideas, building and creating insights about playfulness.

> I know I'm being playful when we think of something, and then say let's give it a go, let's try it, let's experiment.
>
> *Robert Stephenson*

There is no correct or better way to experience playfulness. This would be totally at odds with the nature, purpose and spirit of playfulness and it can vary at different times or contexts. You may feel it in a gentle and kind way; a spark, a permission, signalling it is safe to play. Our body might signal play;

just like dogs, cats, and other animals, we too have play postures, which are often reflexive and not calculated. Things to look out for are a tilted head, open, soft eyes, perhaps with briefly raised eyebrows, a smile. We've never met the Dalai Lama or the late Bishop Desmond Tutu, but they seem to us to embody playfulness and we've been fortunate to spend time with others who also have this often quiet, gentle, and grounded spark of playfulness. There is depth of perspective, mixed with curiosity, compassion and openness that is tangible. Alternatively, as Jonathan Passmore reflected, you can notice it on building sites or the armed forces in the form of joshing and bantering, knowing how far to go with it (or sometimes not – thinking back to personal play identities above). We've seen in Chapters 8 and 9 that both humour and playfulness have maladaptive sides and here we are talking about adaptive, positive playfulness.

We'd like to invite you to develop your intentional awareness of playfulness:

- *How do you know when you're being playful?*
- *What do you feel in your Whole Body when you connect to play?*
- *If you could register play or playfulness within your body, where would that be? How would that be – what sensations, shapes, colours, sounds, images arise for you?*
- *What is your capacity to dial this up or down?*

10.11 What You Focus on Grows

The quote 'What you focus on grows' or variations of it has been attributed to a wide range of people. We know the neurobiological truth of that. It is the basis of neuroplasticity and the strengthening of neural connections through repeated practice. Intentionally focusing on something adaptive regularly can have profound effects on our well-being and capacity. This underlies the positive psychology interventions such as '3 good things' or gratitude diaries and has also been shown to apply to playfulness. Whether or not you can increase your playfulness level has yet to be rigorously researched but initial signs are promising. For example, Gander, Proyer & Ruch (2018)[22] found that thinking about using your playfulness in a new way and experiencing positive emotions when doing so may both be useful strategies for increasing playfulness.

Subsequently, Proyer, Gander et al. (2021)[23] conducted the first (to their knowledge) placebo-controlled online study with the aim of increasing levels of playfulness. The interventions required participants to spend 15 minutes at the end of the day journaling, in one of four different ways: (1) three playfulness things that happened during the day, who was involved and what did the participant feel or (2) how the participant used playfulness in a different way during the day, who was involved and what did the participant feel: or (3) reflect on playful experiences during the day either as participant or observer, and record the number of instances; or (4) (as the placebo control) early childhood memories. While the effects were different for different facets of playfulness (remember the OLIW model), all interventions increased expressions in all facets of playfulness. What's more, the interventions had short-term effects of improving the participants' sense of well-being and lowered feelings of depression with the greatest effect coming from documenting how others were playful and from trying to use playfulness in a new way.

> But when you're beginning, you should try to focus on something you love and your own way of doing things.
>
> *Jerry Harrison (Talking Heads)*

There's a lot to be said for being open and curious; finding and connecting with others (whether directly in the same profession or not) who 'do' and 'are' playful for inspiration, reflection, support, and challenge. We have noticed our own capacities for playfulness expand in our lives and work as it has pretty constantly been in our awareness during the writing of this book over the last couple of years. Even during the individual conversations with our Storytellers, it was interesting to notice that in each, we all seemed more playful (somehow brighter, with more energy, warmth, laughter and in the general flow of conversation) by the end. We give so much time and attention to the stressors, imagine the potential effect of giving more attention to playfulness.

Go back for a moment to the Barometer of Playfulness at the beginning of this chapter:

- *What are your answers now?*
- *Are they the same?*
- *Different?*
- *What does this tell you?*

Playful Moment

We invite you to give yourself a Playful Moment and then answer the Barometer of Playfulness questions again – what do you notice?

10.12 Conclusion

We're not suggesting that you'll go from little playfulness to David Clutterbuck or Steve Chapman levels overnight or even any time soon, but by bringing awareness and intention, we believe that you can increase your playfulness levels and (further) develop your own capacity for playfulness. Even if we're wrong, what have you got to lose? Whatever happens, it's likely you'll collect some other experiences, insights, and benefits along the way.

We all have our own authentic ways of accessing playfulness and bringing it to our work and if you want to, you will learn and develop and find what works for you and your clients. For the meditators amongst you, it might mean incorporating playfulness into your practice by dialling up your curiosity, lightness, and compassion. For others it might be experimenting with more playful use of metaphors. More generally, tapping into positive psychology and solution focused coaching, find what you already do playfully (even in a small way) and build on that. How can you experiment by coming out of your comfort zone (but not into overwhelm)? What are you surprised by? How can you experiment with this? Expand it? What happens when you experience times of playfulness by yourself or with others by behaving in a brave, spontaneous, experimental playful way that is outside of the story of who you tell yourself you are or how you should or shouldn't behave (limiting beliefs rather than constructive societal norms)? You cannot un-experience that. Let it sink in though; notice it in your Whole Body; reflect on it. Really experience it in the moment and afterwards to strengthen those neural connections and let a shift in the story you tell yourself around playfulness happen.

Notes

1   Schwarz, R. (2002). *Tools for Transforming Trauma*. Routledge, p67.
2   Schwarz, R. and Braff, E. (2012). *We're No Fun Anymore*. Routledge, p61.
3   Winnicott, D. (1971). *Playing and Reality*. Routledge, p51.
4   Güneş, G. (2021). Personal play identity and the fundamental elements in its development process. *Current Psychology*, 1–11.
5   Robert, C. (2016). *The Psychology of Humor at Work*. Abingdon: Oxford, p122.
6   From a BBC4 radio programme called 'The Confessional' hosted by Stephen Mangan and last aired on 15 March 2021, 11:30.
7   Bowlby, J. (1969). *Attachment and loss*. Basic Books. Winnicott, D. (1972). Basis for Self in Body. *International Journal of Child Psychotherapy*, 1, 7–16.
8   Gordon, G. (2014). Well Played: The Origins and Future of Playfulness. *American Journal of Play*, 6(2), 234–266.
9   Bartholomew, K. & Horowitz, L. (1991). Attachment styles among young adults: a test of a four-category model. *Journal of personality and social psychology*, 61(2), 226.
10 For example, Woll, S. (1989). Personality and relationship correlates of loving styles. *Journal of Research in Personality*, 23, 480–505. Proyer, R. (2014). To love and play: Testing the association of adult playfulness with the relationship personality and relationship satisfaction. *Current Psychology*, 33(4), 50–514.
11 Ainsworth, M., Salter, Blehar, M., Waters, E. & Wall, S. (2015). Classic Edition. *Patterns of Attachment: A Psychological Study of the Strange Situation*. Psychology Press.
12 Mikulincer, M. (1997). Adult Attachment Style and Information Processing: Individual Differences in Curiosity and Cognitive Closure. *Journal of Personality and Social Psychology*, 72, 1217–30. Aspelmeier, J. & Kerns, K. (2003). Love and School: Attachment/Exploration Dynamics in College. *Journal of Social and Personal Relationships*, 20, 5–30.
13 Green, J. & Campbell, W. (2000). Attachment and Exploration in Adults: Chronic and Contextual Accessibility. *Personality and Social Psychology Bulletin*, 26, 452–61.
14 *Ibid*. Mikulincer (1997). Mikulincer, M. & Arad, D. (1999). Attachment Working Models and Cognitive Openness in Close Relationships: A Test of Chronic and Temporary Accessibility Effects. *Journal of Personality and Social Psychology*, 77, 710–25.
15 Elliot, A. & Reis, H. (2003). Attachment and Exploration in Adulthood. *Journal of Personality and Social Psychology*, 85, 317–31. Gordon, G. (2014). Well Played: The Origins and Future of Playfulness. *American Journal of Play*, 6(2), 234–266.

16 Siegel, D. (2013). *Brainstorm: The power and purpose of the teenage brain.* Penguin Putnam, p218.
17 creativityforcoaches.co.uk/
18 Guitard, P., Ferland, F. & Dutil, É. (2005). Toward a Better Understanding of Playfulness in Adults. *OTJR: Occupation, Participation and Health, 25*(1), 9–22.
19 Barnett, referred to in Neyfakh, L. (2014). You can't be serious: New research uncovers the real benefits of playfulness in adults. *Boston Globe*; Boston, Mass., 20 July.
20 For example, Staempfli, M. (2007). Adolescent Playfulness, Stress Perception, Coping and Well Being. *Journal of Leisure Research, 39*(3), 393–412.
21 Capra, F. (1983). *The turning point: Science, society, and the rising culture.* Bantam.
22 Gander, F., Proyer, R. & Ruch, W. (2018). A placebo-controlled online study on potential mediators of a pleasure-based positive psychology intervention: The role of emotional and cognitive components. *Journal of Happiness Studies, 19,* 2035–2048.
23 Proyer, R., Gander, F., Brauer, K. & Chick, G. (2021). Can Playfulness be Stimulated? A Randomised Placebo-Controlled Online Playfulness Intervention Study on Effects on Trait Playfulness, Well-Being, and Depression [published online ahead of print, 2020 Aug 25]. *Appl Psychol Health Well Being, 13*(1), 129–151.

11

Practical Ways to Dial Up (More) Playfulness

In this Chapter we:

- Tap into your environment for play
- Ask you if you have you tried something new lately
- Encourage you to embrace sweet discomfort
- Introduce you to coddiwompling
- Invite you to build on trying something new
- Suggest you having a word with your inner critic and perfectionist
- Address the fear of embarrassment or shame and introduce you (probably) to three new words
- Consider how you can work with your states to support playfulness
- Think about how no one is an island
- Celebrate daydreaming and imagination
- Encourage you to strengthen your humour muscles and laugh more
- Contemplate how presence and mindfulness can support playfulness
- Invite you to create your own Barometer of Playfulness in The Playfulness Scrapbook.

Bring the Be Playful Onion Model to mind and let's use this as a guide to navigate and expand our capacity for playfulness. We'll lightly touch on our external environment and visible ways of playing (or 'doing' playful) – the outer layer of the Onion – and you'll find more play ideas in The Playfulness Scrapbook. We'll focus mostly on our inner world and ways of 'being' playful as an aid to development and practice. Some suggestions will resonate with you, others won't. With a spirit of playfulness though, we invite you to notice what feels a little uncomfortable and be curious whether this is because it represents a learning opportunity, something

DOI: 10.4324/9781003090847-13

outside of your usual perspective or frame of reference and maybe a signal that it's worth exploring. On the other hand, you might decide that it's just not for you; think back to the Sweet Shop at the beginning of Part I .

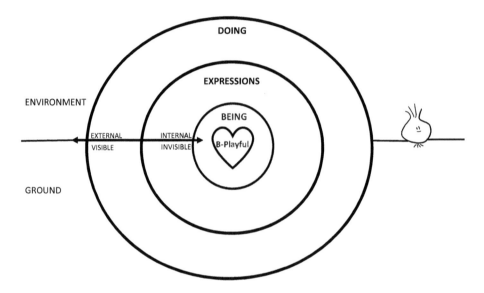

Figure 11.1 Be Playful Onion Model

Remember too, it's not just about you (sorry!); we are seeing playfulness as a relational as well as individual construct and, in the coaching context, in the service of your clients. We believe the more aware and flexible you are in the middle and inner Onion layers, the more you can play with others in a variety of ways which suit them. For example, your coachee loves drawing but maybe it's not your thing. Are you able to embody ease and offer implicit permission as you suggest they experiment with drawing and hold a space for them to do so freely if it might be of service to them?

> You may be a bit afraid that 'you've forgotten how to play'. I promise you, you have not.
>
> *Michael Rosen*[1]

11.1 Tapping into Your Environment for Play

If we want to tap into playfulness, let's use all of our senses. Looking around at our environment, what can we adjust and harness to extend an invitation and permission to be playful? Art and objects can serve as inspiration, anchors and stimulators of our humour, imagination and creativity supporting playfulness. We love seeing photos of artists' studios, particularly the more playful ones such as Matisse, Picasso, and David Shrigley OBE (described by *The New York Times* as the 'master of the incompetent line') full of colourful materials, objects, and paintings. In our modest way, we can think about our own surroundings and whether they stimulate and invite playfulness. Stephanie's office space was intentionally designed to be colourful and playful, through the way books are displayed, choice of pictures and objects, colourful plant pots. As we moved to fully remote working in the early months of the pandemic, her background is often one of the first things which new clients notice and talk about. It radiates warmth and subtly suggests permission and opportunities for playfulness. It also reminds Stephanie to be open to playfulness.

> What you seek is seeking you.
>
> *Rumi*

On a smaller scale, we can do this when we are working in person even when we are in someone else's environment. A funky pencil case, folder, bag, or other accessory can give off playful signals. We can also move some of the furniture around, sit in a different place, tap into what's in the room when we're coaching in premises other than our own. Looking around at our environment, we might adjust things such as closing the blinds if others in the office can see us, and our client is likely to be restricted by that. One of the first things we do when we enter rooms for 1 : 1 sessions is to see if we can at least move the chairs; rather than sitting across the table from clients like in a negotiation. How can we spontaneously work with our environment (even subtly) to signal the possibility of something different? In The Playfulness Scrapbook, we tell how Stephanie suggested her client used sweets in a meeting room to build constellations of his past and present relationships. We might encourage taking a different or multiple perspectives, asking clients what different objects in the room might think or say to the client's thoughts or experience.

Sometimes we can also take a playful approach to where we work with clients. For example, a lot of Steve Chapman's work involves leaving the office, getting outside or to a different location; he told us a wonderful story of an improvised ghost tour of London complete with actors for the backdrop of a coaching session.

In a virtual environment (unless you have access to Virtual Reality or clients have options to adjust their environment or take themselves elsewhere), this can be more challenging. Stephanie remembers one online coaching session where her client was sitting in what looked like the spare room surrounded by heaps of clutter and washing stands with little room to move, another was with a frontline ICU healthcare worker during one of the Covid lockdowns who snatched an hour in one of the empty treatment rooms for the session.

Stephanie found that she needed to pay extra attention to not being distracted through curiosity by the clutter (in another conversation, it might have been helpful to bring the state of the room into the conversation, for example, as a metaphor) or the intensity and stress of the healthcare worker's current reality. We still had playful sessions, though most likely at a different point in the Be Playful Onion Model than if the environments had been different.

Whatever the options, even suggesting a walk while you coach might be playful. We hope this is a nudge to not take the environment as a given but to consider it and its potential to support or obstruct playfulness in your work.

In the previous chapter, we invited you to use your Whole Body for your reflections and we extend the same invitation here.

- *Take a look around your work environment. What could you add/take away/ change to signal invitations to playfulness (to you and your clients)?*
- *How else can you make changes to your environment or the things you bring with you to invite more playfulness?*
- *Do you have options of going to a new environment?*

11.2 Have You Tried Something New Lately?

In his podcast *Huberman Lab*,[2] neuroscientist Prof Andrew Huberman explains that play is essentially an exploration of contingencies. Through play, we can explore new ways of doing things, new ways of being and relationships, including with ourselves. These explorations enable neuroplasticity and increase our capacity (more specifically the capacity of the prefrontal cortex (PFC) region of our brain which is so important in all manner of ways) to develop and find new ways of being and doing. If the PFC is developed, it doesn't just affect play but all the PFC functions.

The prefrontal cortex (PFC) plays a central role in cognitive control functions, and dopamine in the PFC modulates cognitive control, thereby influencing attention, impulse inhibition, prospective memory, and cognitive flexibility.[3]

The willingness to try new things, our 'give-it-a-go-ness', to explore and experiment is key to cultivating playfulness. It can take many forms, from structured classes and instruction to simply experimenting with stepping out of habitual grooves of actions, emotions, and thoughts. You might start with the simple question of how you get out of bed in the morning. What might a different way look like? Can you introduce a playful element either in the way you move (see Primal Play[4] for inspiration if you're scratching your head) or your mindset? How do you start a coaching session? Can you experiment a little, deviating from your habitual way and trying something a little different?

Trying new things just for fun can also allow other parts of us to show up and be nurtured (or addressed if they're maladaptive). David Clutterbuck is a great one for this; every year he sets himself a new challenge, such as learning to perform magic or improv. When we spoke with him, he was disappointed as the pandemic had postponed his plans for airplane wing walking. Yes, you did read that correctly. The idea is to do something for the experience and usually fun (with, as we know by now, sweet discomfort), having-a-go and not with a view to the end product or gaining expertise. Try new things for the experience and for different perspectives. David suggests trying things which are not directly related to coaching such as improv, tuneless choir, laughter yoga or whatever tickles your fancy.

There's a concept in Buddhist psychology in the context of the brahmavihāra (the four noble qualities and associated practices) of near and far enemies. According to this framework, for every desirable habit or state of mind, there is its opposite, the far enemy. As we saw in Chapter 5, Dr Stuart Brown suggests that the opposite of play is 'depression', not 'work' as many might first think. There are also near enemies who are much sneakier as they are hard to spot, seeming at first consideration to be very similar. For example, the near enemy of love might be neediness. In the context of play therapy, often with traumatised children, Di Gammage[5] suggests that the near enemy is 'deadly play' (play is shaped by trauma and which on a closer look bears little resemblance to free, spontaneous, and adaptive play). If we see play as free, spontaneous exploration of different possibilities and perspectives, then we can see how the near enemy of play (though he didn't use these terms) could be as Dr Brown suggested vacillation – the inability to make decisions, you think you might be playing, but you're actually stuck in vacillation. What's important to realise is that the near and far enemies sit on a continuum and almost always have fear at their root, for example, fear of loss of control. We introduce this concept here to nudge you to reflect what your near enemy of playfulness might be and how it might be getting in the way of your playfulness.

- *How often do you try something new or a new way of doing things or being?*
- *Does your openness to experimentation and exploration need some retuning, or fine tuning?*
- *Where can you practice expanding your 'give-it-a-go-ness' (with sweet discomfort but not overwhelm) in different spheres of life?*
- *What have you always (or just now!) fancied having a go at?*
- *If you can't think of anything, what did you or would you have loved to try when you were a child but didn't have the chance?*
- *What did you love to do but had to stop?*
- *Why are you not giving yourself the permission to have a go?*
- *What do you need in order to give yourself permission?*

Although we, Teresa and Stephanie, don't often give ourselves the gift of time (it's all too easy to prioritise other people and things especially when squeezing in writing a book during a pandemic), we love experiencing something different, separately and together. Our scanners are always on the lookout for opportunities, even if we can't fit them in straight away. We've had so much fun and wonderful experiences together which helped us see ourselves, others, and the world from different perspectives. Particularly memorable ones were a mask workshop facilitated by Steve Chapman in 2022 and the Playing Human Conference in 2018 where we were at times well out of our comfort zones and played with many wonderful humans including Patch Adams.

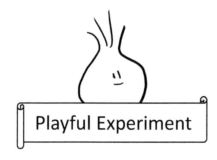

Playful Experiment

If you want to consider this further and start to envision your playful self even more please check out the Playful Experiments section in The Playfulness Scrapbook. This section has been specifically created to help you reconnect with and enliven your playfulness.

11.2.1 Embracing Sweet Discomfort

We have mentioned the concept of varying levels of comfort several times so far and thought it was time to look at this idea a bit more closely. You are most probably familiar with the idea of 'comfort zone' in learning theory. The phrase was popularised by management thinker, Judith Bardwick, in her book *Danger in the Comfort Zone* (1991) though the idea of a Goldilocks zone of learning was identified by behavioural psychologists Robert Yerkes and John Dodson back in 1907. Essentially, for learning, we need to be outside our comfort zone but not in overwhelm or distress; the learning occurs in the middle zone. Miki Kashdan, co-founder of Bay Area Nonviolent Communication and founder and Lead Collaboration Consultant at the Center for Efficient Collaboration, sometimes uses the term 'sweet discomfort' for where we find ourselves in this middle zone. This term really resonates with us; it's not a comfortable place to be but, knowing you're there is encouraging, exciting even, as you know learning is taking place. It is a balance: stay too comfortable and you don't learn, and your comfort zone shrinks over time; venture too far and you go into overwhelm or distress, where, as we've seen, our nervous system will be triggered into flight/flight/freeze and our Whole Body has much fewer options available to it. The upshot is, if you want to develop your capacity for playfulness, you will need to be prepared to step out of your comfort zone and be mindful of your level of discomfort. Of course, this applies not only to expanding your capacity for playfulness but also when you are being/doing playfulness in the service of other learning.

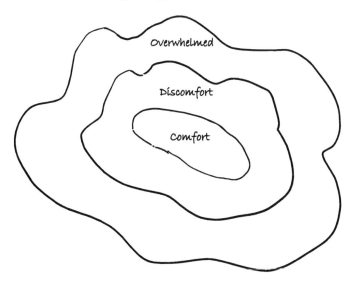

To help you along the way, Steve Chapman has an inspirational attitude to discomfort and uncertainty. He shared with us that he prefers to frame it as becoming increasingly familiar with discomfort rather than comfortable. After all, how can you become comfortable with things that are putting you out of your comfort zone? Instead, when those familiar feelings of discomfort arise, he suggests that you acknowledge them in the spirit of 'Ah there you are my old friend, I know you, we have met you many times before'. In response to that internal voice complaining at the twanging of the elastic of the comfort zone, for example, 'Why have I agreed to do this?', 'Why on earth am I putting myself in this position – yet again?!', in that moment, we can recognise our reaction for what it is: a natural desire to avoid risk and return to the warmth of the known, the certain, the comfortable. However, if we follow the call of this desire without awareness, we may well operate in increasingly smaller comfort zones and miss the opportunity to bring awareness to our reaction and stretch ourselves, including in our capacity for playfulness. Kelly McGonigal invites us to see stress as 'what happens in your brain and your body when something you care about is at stake' and if we learn to embrace it, it can actually make us happier, healthier, and smarter (and we'd add more playful). Some counsellors help reframe fear of uncertainty or risk by using the metaphor of the circle of concern and circle of influence, emphasising which lens you are seeing the world through can change your perspective and subsequent response.

Reminder: neuroplasticity requires enough challenge to need a degree of effort and focus (releasing some adrenaline, dopamine, and opioids) – that sweet spot of discomfort for learning – but not so much that we go into overwhelm (too much adrenaline and our fight/flight/freeze response kicks in and play circuits shut down).

A superpower for when it comes to moving to embracing the sweet spot of discomfort rather than pulling away from it is developing your capacity for curiosity. It's a multi-purpose superpower; it's pretty self-evident that curiosity and playfulness are close supportive friends and curiosity is a rich coaching quality. Todd Kashdan's book *Curious?*[6] and his more recent *The Art of Insubordination*[7] gives you many tools (and reasons why you'd want to) strengthen your curiosity.

'What if I fail?'
'Oh, but my darling, what if you fly?'

Alice in Wonderland, C. S. Lewis

Beyond the need to experience discomfort to extend our own capacity for play-fulness, playfulness by its very nature twangs the elastic of our comfort zone, as it takes us into the domain of exploration and experimentation (and dis-covery, learning and development). When we are playing, experimenting, cre-ating, and engaging our imagination in our work, we can't predict or overly predefine the exact outcomes as we are focused on the process rather than any predetermined outcome. As coaches, we are helping clients find their own answers, but it can be hard to let go of being the expert. Yet if we are to be playful as coaches, we need to let go of being the expert, quieten down our egos and be fully present and flexible in the moment. In our conversation with Graham Lee, he reflected:

> You know, I think we as coaches can get overly caught up in what the solution should be rather than thinking: 'Why is this a challenge? What's stopping this person from being playful enough to solve their own problems?'

With this approach, we can then be curious about how to create conditions for our clients to find their own playful capacity; if they find their own playful capacity, then as Graham went on to say:

> They're meeting life with a sense of flexibility and fluidity and vitality and our job is done. They don't need you to tell them how to live their life. They just need to be freed up.

When we to get comfortable and embrace the value of not knowing, our egos feel much lighter and this is reflected in the constant contracting and re-contracting that playfulness often requires: 'Shall we try something?', 'Shall we see if this changes things?'. Remembering to offer playfulness lightly without attachment, so if the invitation isn't accepted, that's fine, it's not about you, it's about what is of service to the client in that moment (though remembering too that sometimes clients need a bit of a nudge or encouragement to find their own sweet discomfort). Co-creating the sessions is true collaboration, when we and our clients are playing and seeing where the session will take us. The principles of improv and learning to relax that part of our brain which is censoring us in case we are judged or rejected are very useful here. You'll know by now that this is a world away from arriving with a bag of 'toys' and saying, 'Right, we are going to play now and it's this game with these rules'. That's not to say that such an approach isn't play or is wrong (during that game, you might still play by experimenting with different perspectives and so on), but playfulness is much richer than you might have initially thought, so the possible discomfort is worth it.

> Playfulness is an intent is to be of service to the client, not for your own needs – because you are bored, need to show off or being harsh to someone. Playfulness is a vehicle to free thinking/imagineering.
>
> *David Clutterbuck*

You will know yourself whether you like to gradually increase your comfort zone or whether you're a 'launcher' like us. Don't get us wrong, our inner critics are still very much vocal, but we've got a more friendly relationship with them now and we've come to realise that launching ourselves into learning situations energises us and pushes us forward in our development. That way, our comfort zones grow, and we have fun laughing at experiences afterwards (once we've recovered and while gleaning the learning). We should add that we stay out of the overwhelm zone. We've realised that this is what improvisors call the 'yes, and' approach to life. Failing or the prospect of it doesn't fill us with joy and of course we care, but equally, we've worked on taking a light-hearted perspective in the moment on the possibility of failing before we jump into our next challenge – in the scheme of things, it's not a big thing and who knows what exciting possibilities or connections will open as a result. Our time here is short, there's much to learn, explore and friendships to be made, laughter and joy to be found. This willingness to try something new is, we think, one of the characteristics of our playfulness, more so than for example, 'doing' extroverted play in front of a large group (though we're hopefully constantly evolving and expanding our zones of comfort).

While some of us are launchers, it would be a mistake to make the assumption that this is how we all prefer to experiment, learn and develop in other words, to play. Particularly in groups or teams, depending on their level of psychological safety, there is much to be said for building playfulness gradually, all the time assessing the room (fully embodied, not just intellectually) and whether it is ready for more. Many of our Storytellers told of the need to build up to more risky playfulness, facilitating experiences that try to move the participants to be more comfortable with not being experts, not knowing and moving past thinking that they might get something wrong to where there is no right or wrong. Julie Flower's experience is that you can still do this quite quickly, though it does need to be gradual; like stepping stones up a mountain rather than a big leap and falling flat or leaving some of the room behind you. Also, as coaches, we all know the power of reframing, and this can be particularly useful where fear or uncertainty is holding clients (and us of course) back. Julie emphasised the power of framing questions when asking teams/groups to come up with ideas (something which can give rise to fear of judgment, embarrassment, failure and so on). Asking for ideas in a playful way; 'What is your *wild* idea about … ?' can elicit quite different responses from merely asking for ideas. Asking for 'wild' ideas gives implicit permission that it is OK to be expansive, experimental, creative, in fact, it is welcomed. This allows ideas to flow and build, creating an environment for divergent thinking; the convergent thinking can come later.

- *What is your relationship to your zone of discomfort? (Remember we are playing in a zone of sweet discomfort but not overwhelm.)*
- *How often do you take steps out of your comfort zone?*
- *How do you hold your discomfort?*
- How are you with varying degrees of uncertainty?
- *What little experiments could you conduct to expand your comfort zone?*
- *How can you expand your capacity for spontaneity and flexibility?*
- *Do you approach things with a mindset of scarcity or abundance?*
- *How curious are you?*
- *What can you do to increase your capacity for curiosity?*
- *What do you need to make you feel safe enough to play? (Question from conversation with Graham Lee.) In your work, that might include training, structure, supervision, and so forth.*

11.3 Building on Trying Something New

Intrinsically linked with being open to trying something new (whether through action, thought or emotion), is an attitude of give-it-a-go-ness, spontaneity, adapting, experimenting, and improvising. When you think about the times when you are most playful or playing, it is likely that you were in flow, fully present and engaged with your Whole Body. In this state, it's also likely that you were spontaneous and adaptive in the moment, building on ideas, using the improvisor's 'yes, and' approach (see The Playfulness Scrapbook for more). Spontaneity is a key component of playfulness. Moreno (1964)[8] pioneer of group psychotherapy and founder of psychodrama believed that spontaneity and creativity are necessities for change and psychodrama's theories of change include action theory and spontaneity-creativity theory which are core to every psychodrama enactment.[9] Moreno defined spontaneity as the ability to:

> respond with some degree of adequacy to a new situation or with some degree of novelty to an old situation.[10]

With these thoughts in mind, we offer you a few questions for reflection:

- *Generally, in life and in your work, how spontaneous or adaptive are you?*
- *In which zone does the thought of freewheeling in the moment place you (comfort/discomfort/overwhelm)?*
- *In which zone does the thought of not knowing what to do next place you?*
- *Do you need to control things and have certainty in the moment in all or some situations? Which ones?*
- *How can you free up more to allow yourself to be more playful? (Reflective question from our conversation with Graham Lee)*
- *As you're reflecting on these questions, what's happening in your Whole Body?*
- *What insights can you find which relate to your playfulness?*

If you are realising that this is an area of development for you, one approach is to incorporate little experiments with this frame of mind or even playfulness into our daily lives. In this way, we can be authentically more playful in our work. If, for example, you'd like to experiment with art in your work, then dabble yourself in your free time; you get the picture (sorry, couldn't resist). Remember, you are not trying to become an expert in whatever you're experimenting with; that would undermine the playfulness. You will, however, have a level of comfort (and perhaps an appreciation of the client's potential discomfort) when offering a little experiment to your client for the first time.

We've spoken about the superpower of curiosity in this and the previous chapter (aka playfulness' best friend) for navigating the unknown and being in your learning zone. Developing your capacity for curiosity can strengthen your attitude of give-it-a-go-ness, spontaneity, adapting, experimenting, and improvising. In turn, playfulness in coaching in particular requires ABC (Always Be Contracting) and doing so in the frame of an invitation to explore together can help not only ease your own discomfort with uncertainties of experimenting (for example, 'will I get it right?') as well as your client's and but is also honest and authentic – you are modelling these behaviours by allowing yourself to co-create in the messiness rather than sitting more removed role of expert. These (re-)contracting offers might include: 'We are in the unknown, would it be helpful to explore this a bit more?', 'Shall we play with this a bit more, or try it out a bit, experiment and see what arises?'. Your comfort with experimentation, not-knowing and spontaneity is important as it creates a space for your client to try this, possibly different, way of approaching things. We frequently share our favourite word with our clients 'coddiwomple' as it contains an explicit permission to play in the moment and see what emerges.

Coddiwompling

To travel in a purposeful manner towards a vague destination.

(One of our favourite words and maybe even our life philosophy)

Those working with a Gestalt approach use the terms 'what if-ness' and 'shall we give it go-ness' as a way of gently inviting the stepping into and exploring the new, unknown territories through playing with ideas to more full ranging experiments. Beyond this, we may want to cultivate our personal capability of being in the moment and being able to pivot, adapt and improvise. Taking part in improv classes is a great avenue for developing this capacity and a number of our Storytellers are very accomplished in this skill, not least Neil Mullarkey, Julie Flower, Steve Chapman, and Heather Simpkin. Like David Clutterbuck. Stephanie took part in improv classes just for fun and yet found that perhaps inevitably that it impacted her coaching too.

- *How at ease are you currently to invite someone to play with ideas?*
- *How willing are you to step into a playful experiment?*
- *Do you have a 'yes, and' approach?*

11.4 Having a Word with The Inner Critic and Perfectionism

One of the things that can get in the way of this is the inner critic. We spoke with Steve Chapman about his inner critic workshops with Simon Cavicchia; their approach is to encourage participants to hold any experience of judgment of self and others whether negative or positive as the territory of the inner critic which is more about us and our idealised sense of self and society, rooted in childhood, than anything else. The inner critic can be a useful moderator but it's unhelpful if it's diminishing or inflating us or others and we can't control other people's inner critics. It may be that another's inner critic is preventing them from joining in with playfulness and filling the room with judgment making it difficult for others to join in. In a satisfyingly circular way, it seems that playfulness might help calm down the inner critic and help in overcoming imposter syndrome.[11]

Letting go of certainty and control can be particularly challenging for perfectionists, though, to be fair, it can be challenging for non-perfectionists too. Perfectionism is a topic which many coaches will have come across whether during their own development or with clients[12] and the effect of playfulness on increasing resilience to maladaptive perfectionism would be an interesting area for future research.

11.5 Addressing Fear of Embarrassment or Shame

> Fear of embarrassment, making mistakes, looking silly or stupid are some of the great killers of creativity of all kinds.
>
> *von Oech*[13]

Fear of shame is linked to maladaptive perfectionism.[14] More generally, loosening the grip of fear of shame or embarrassment can really support playfulness as the fear of shame, embarrassment, or of re-experiencing slightly traumatising experiences of shame blocks the path of curiosity and shuts down play. In coaching, the experience of shame and its milder form, embarrassment, contributes to a contraction of the space for inquiry, dialogue, and thinking which would, when present, allow spontaneity and improvisation[15] which are important for playfulness. These fears might be linked to past experiences of shame or embarrassment or limiting assumptions such as lack of confidence or (get ready for possibly a new word for your vocabulary) gelotophobia. This is the fear of being laughed at and appearing ridiculous to others.[16] Gelotophobes experience laughter independently of its intention and perceive it as ridicule which is aimed at them.[17] Particularly relevant to our context, Platt (2008) concluded that 'humor/laughter are not relaxing and joyful social experiences' for gelotophobes.[18] While Proyer (2012)[19] concluded that there is no negative correlation with gelotophobia and playfulness, this predates the OLIW model and Proyer's (2017)[20] definition of playfulness (see Chapter 5). To give you another word, gelotophilia is the joy of being laughed at, although Brauer & Proyer (2020)[21] suggest that gelotophobia and gelotophilia are more than simply opposites of the same dimension.

For some people, a fear of being laughed at can present a very real barrier to some expressions of playfulness. In a laughter yoga session that Stephanie ran some years ago, one of the first-time participants found it a very uncomfortable experience and left. Laughter yoga is all about laughing for no reason and the ethos is very much grounded in laughing with, not at each other. Stephanie was surprised as she knew the participant and thought that she would enjoy the session. She has no idea whether this person was experiencing a form of gelotophobia (Stephanie wasn't aware of the concept then) but it was a stark reminder to be sensitive to other people's experience even in what we and the rest of the group might perceive as a joyful experience and in team coaching, even more so if someone is, or perceives they are, not included. It may of course be necessary to look a little behind the behaviour to spot the fear. It might for example manifest as anger. This might potentially sound a little intimidating, but if we remember to hold our offer of playfulness lightly and without attachment and see everything as data (see Chapter 9), whatever emerges can support the work which we are doing with our clients.

Proyer & Ruch (2020)[22] have conducted research into the overlap between gelotophobia, gelotophilia and katagelasticism (the joy of laughing at others; another new word; you're welcome!) and attributional styles (how you explain the causes of events in your life). It could well be that gelotophobes underestimate their strengths and feel like intellectual frauds (for example, Brauer & Proyer, 2019;[23] Proyer et al., 2009,[24] 2014),[25] hallmarks of imposter syndrome. The word 'overlap' between gelotophobia and attributional styles is used as more research is needed to tease out whether the effect is bi-directional or causal and the impact of internal and external experiences. Experiencing resistance to playfulness in coaching situations which seem to come from a fear or discomfort of being laughed at (particularly where it does not seem that the laughter or playfulness is directed at that person), might open up interesting conversations about that person's attributional styles (which seem to be open to change)[26] and the (specific and more general) impact of holding the associated beliefs.

11.6 Working with Your States to Support Playfulness

Have you ever noticed how quickly your state can change when you're around playfulness? What this might look like for individuals will vary. For us, a reliable source is watching and engaging with our dogs when they are playful. We're not talking about the avoidant retreat into cat videos (of value in its own right from time to time) but how being open and present with playfulness can cause a shift in your state. What do we mean by state in this context? The sense of what state your Whole Body is in and which is the result of physical factors (for example, exercise, diet, posture, oxygenation, even how you're dressed), mental processes (for example, memories, beliefs, inner dialogue, filters) and biochemistry (for example, hormones, nervous system, medication, or drugs). We've seen how in Chapter 6, with awareness, we can identify what our peripheral nervous system is up to and as Graham Lee describes bring awareness to whether our body-brain is in the GREEN, AMBER, or RED state.[27] Graham shared with us in our conversation that in the RED state, there is no opportunity for play as we are in survival mode. In an AMBER state, our playfulness will be driven by our habitual systems. We see this when people use their humour in familiar ways. It's still possibly funny but lacks the freshness of invention or discovery. In a GREEN state there is optimal ease and mental agility and so the playfulness can be most fluid, transformative, and potentially creative.

We can experiment with moving into a more playful state for example, by moving our bodies and dancing, by listening to happy music (even better if we associate playful memories with it) or by imagining or remembering in detail a time when we felt playful. Nobantu Mpotulo shared with us that she sometimes invites her coachees to play music which will get them into a helpful state for the session. Prof Amy Cuddy's research into power stances show how your physical posture can influence both our internal state and how we are perceived by others. Inspired by this idea, we've experimented to find our own playful stance (just like the power stance, usually done in private in case you're getting concerned and involving some form of movement). At the moment, for Teresa, it's jumping up and down, usually playing air guitar for a few seconds with or without music, whereas, for Stephanie it's a quick dance to a favourite song or messing with our dog and adopting a puppy's play stance (our kids will be mortified or resigned to read this, if they ever do). We ran an online workshop on playfulness for coaches recently and, just beforehand, our nerves were kicking in. Our inner voices were doubting whether we'd make the technology work, remember all the information and so on. Teresa was in the kitchen with her husband who provocatively asked, 'How playful are you feeling?'. Grateful for the prompt, Teresa did a few seconds of a silly dance with her husband. A few minutes later, she was ready to start, feeling energised and playful. She shared the story with Stephanie in the moments before the session started, they had a good laugh about it and Stephanie too moved into a more playful state. All in a matter of minutes. We've found that even visualising doing these (when embarrassment would prevent us from actually doing them) has a noticeable effect. Brain imaging research shows that imagining a threat lights up similar regions as experiencing it does, suggesting that perhaps imagination can be a powerful tool in overcoming phobias or post-traumatic stress.[28] Maybe it works for playfulness too and we can tap into our imagination to help us be and feel more playful. Your own ways of stepping into a more playful state might be small, subtle, and graceful, don't worry!

For many of us, our working hours are spent sitting down so taking any opportunity to move around the room or outside can help shift states (yours and your clients) and support more expansive thinking and playfulness. Coaching in nature provides a multitude of ways in which your state can change including through experiencing awe, perspective, and savouring. Kirsten Barske whose systemic team coaching is experiential and mostly in nature described the first thing she does is to get participants moving in small warm-up tasks to understand what they have in common and get them in a more playful state. Soldiers are trained to manage their states in challenging circumstances. Why then, wouldn't we build more capacity for awareness and flexibility in moving our states towards playfulness?

- *How easily can you bring awareness to what state you're in?*
- *Do you do this regularly?*
- *What external things (sounds/sights/smells/taste/textures) shift you into a more playful stance?*
- *What pose or movement helps you shift to a more playful stance? (Find your own personal playfulness pose!)*
- *How can you tap into physical factors, mental processes, and your biochemistry, to move into a (more) playful state?*
- *What playfulness prompts can you collect for yourself (memories, music, and objects for example)?*

With greater awareness, we can check our readiness for playfulness (as well as other things of course) before a session. If other emotions and sensations are present which are not helpful for the coaching space, we can learn to put these to one side for the session and get into a state which includes a readiness for playfulness. We might imagine a favourite uplifting colour, adding in some sparkles for extra energy or putting down the rucksack of worries or things which might get in the way of our coaching presence. As we'll see next, changes in our state can't help but have an impact on the states of others.

11.7 No One is an Island

John Donne's (1572–1631) famous line 'No man is an island'[29] spoke of our interconnectedness, a concept at the heart of Buddhism. If you want to explore this concept more from a scientific frame, *The Self Delusion*[30] by Tom Oliver argues that on a physical, psychological, and cultural level, we are all much more intertwined than we realise. We looked at our nervous systems and neuroception in Chapter 6. Consider this with the concept of emotional contagion which Panksepp (who, you'll remember was the rat tickler who identified the mammalian PLAY circuitry) and Lahvis[31] described as a phenomenon where the observed behaviour of one individual leads to the reflexive production of the same behaviour by others. These 'copiers' then feel the same emotions of the person who made the original behaviour change. Graham Lee[32] considers the impact we have on each other in terms of the radial effect of our emotions and nervous system signals on others and the impact on our clients and us as coaches. We can tap into this if we want to expand our capacity for playfulness by spending time in the company of those who are playful, particularly by being present and aware in the moment and fostering those other qualities such as curiosity and experimentation which we discussed above.

Equally, if we want to foster playfulness in our work, we need to be aware of our own emotions and nervous system states as they will be affecting our clients. Can we remain in a GREEN state and help our clients to be there too, so that we create a space for playfulness, spontaneity and all those other rich states of mind? If you would like to explore practical ways of working with our clients' nervous systems, the work of Deb Dana[33] explains how to incorporate the Polyvagal Theory into therapeutic practice and much of her work is interesting for coaches too. Developing awareness (of self and others), emotional agility, emotional and social intelligence are useful for creating conditions for playful practice. Being intentional and authentic in your playfulness when priming yourself and your environment for a coaching session while maintaining an awareness of what the impact might be on your clients.

- *Do you spend time with others who are playful?*
- *How could you do more of this (should you want to)?*
- *Next time you do, bring your attention to your Whole Body, and check in with how you feel.*
- *How aware are you of the state in which you are in?*
- *How could you take steps to increase this awareness?*
- *How could this impact your work?*
- *What explorations are you drawn to?*

One of the ways of developing that awareness is through mindfulness and more specifically Relational Mindfulness which we'll look at in more detail below.

11.8 Making Space for Your Imagination and Daydreaming

How often do you allow yourself to daydream? It seems that for many of us, the time which we might have spent daydreaming is too easily absorbed through checking our phones for the hundredth time that day or being distracted by the many other things which pull at our attention. We wonder what this is doing for our capacity to daydream and engage our imagination (in a good way rather down the rabbit hole of rumination or tussles with our inner critic). We are of course not alone in our wonderings and the impact of spending so much of our time with our Task Focused Network activated over the course of many years isn't yet known (and a potential concern and research topic particularly in relation to children and teenagers). As a reminder, we explored the benefit and indeed, the need to access the Default Mode Network for creativity and effective coaching in Chapter 6.

> Go to Chapter 7 for explanation of Task Focused Network (TFN), Default Mode Network (DMN) and Parasympathetic Nervous System (PNS)

Why does it matter? Some evidence has accumulated during the past 30 years that implicates the DMN being activated when we 'daydream, our mind wanders, our thoughts flit from one thing to another, or we seem to be mentally "idling"'.[34] In those moments when we are not focusing on a task that needs deliberate processing, we free our minds from our immediate surroundings and allow them to wander and 'engage in abstract thought and imaginative ramblings, picturing the future, and contemplating 'what if' scenarios without constraints' as Bateson & Martin consider in Play, Playfulness, Creativity, and Innovation.[35] They argue that in a sense daydreaming is analogous to play as it might also be seen as non-serious and a waste of time. And yet, like play, it is a valuable resource for creativity; in this mode, functional magnetic resonance imaging (fMRI) shows that when we daydream, different regions of our brains which normally aren't active simultaneously and which are not normally strongly connected are active at the same time.[36] It's argued that this allows us to understand and express new associations and connections or 'novel orderly relationships'[37] as well as accessing memories, random pieces of stored knowledge and memories. This then is why, when we're stuck on something, taking a break (for us ideally by letting our dogs take us for a walk in the nearby countryside) often then leads to possibilities popping into our head seemingly out of nowhere.

On Daydreaming:

> As in play, different ideas or ways of doing things may be brought together creatively.
>
> Bateson and Martin[38]

'What?', you might ask, 'You want me to practise doing nothing? Daydreaming? I'm too busy!!'. We hear you and also often feel like we're paddling on the surface of a never-ending, always-growing to-do-list. Yet, like meditation, it is precisely when we are so busy that clearing some time from tasks and attention sponges is so valuable.

The Buddha meets a wealthy businessman.
'What must I do to reach enlightenment?' asks the man.
'Meditate for an hour a day' comes the reply.
'What?? I'm far too busy!'.
'In that case, you must meditate for two hours a day'.

It's often on those dog walks (which usually feel like a luxury in terms of time) that a chapter structure or workshop idea will fall into place on something that had us chasing our tails (so, actually a very valuable use of our time). To daydream, then, our PNS needs to be activated and we need to not be overly focused on a current situation or task but letting our minds wander. Even engaging in simple external tasks that allow the mind to wander may facilitate creative problem solving.[39]

Let's move onto imagination, which unlike daydreaming is voluntary and can be deliberately accessed. In Chapters 6 and 7, we looked at Intentional Change Theory and the importance it places on the Positive Emotional Attractor (PEA) which, it suggests, allows us to be more open to new ideas, emotions, people and consider possibilities for the future. We also saw ways to activate the PEA include eliciting compassion, mindfulness, and hope (supported by your imagination, for example by imagining your future ideal self) and playfulness. Winnicott makes the distinction between fantasy and imagination and describes a case study where a woman was often lost in fantasy because she was in a state of dissociation, so much so that the disappearance into fantasy was symptomatic of her illness and inability to be fully present and active in her real life and external world.[40] You'll remember from the same chapter that dissociation is linked to the freeze state of our nervous system; we mention this here as a reminder of the systemic complexity of playfulness.

Stuart Brown[41] makes the point that our imaginations are continually active, predicting the future and examining the consequences of our actions before they take place: 'Just like in children, adult streams of consciousness [internal narratives] are enriched through the simulations of childlike imaginative play'. By imagining possibilities, we can mentally simulate what might be and test it against the reality of our experience (ideally through play, which is a low-stakes environment). This ability to pre-experience the future in our minds is called 'prospection'[42] and it allows us to represent and evaluate possible futures.[43] Prospection can lead to sense-making[44] as well as fantasizing[45] and has been linked to the activation of parts of the DMN[46] (again, more on this in Chapter 6) which is believed to be associated with thinking about possibilities, daydreaming, immersing yourself in imagination. We mentioned brain imaging research (in the context of fear and trauma) a little while ago which suggests that imagining an experience and really experiencing it fires up similar areas in the brain. Let's build on this and if we want to increase our capacity for playfulness, try using our imagination for example by imagining and playing out different scenarios of what that might look like. It's worth a try surely.

All said, we're inviting you to develop your awareness and deliberativeness around daydreaming and imagination. How often do you let yourself daydream and tap into your imagination whether sitting in your favourite chair or out walking for instance? You might also try meditations which invite you to visualise, or playing with LEGO®, doodling or other simple tasks which allow your mind to wander and explore. Here are some more ideas:

- *'Can I imagine…?' Ask yourself this from time to time, adding in extra layers to develop what is being imagined: engaging the senses, what can I see, hear, taste, smell, feel. Build out the picture.*
- *The well-known Disney technique evoking the dreamer, the realist, and the critic to consider different perspectives, draws heavily on the imagination. You can use the technique to increase your capacity for playfulness.*
- *Walk the Be Playful Onion Model (see The Playfulness Scrapbook).*
- *On Imagineering, see* One Little Spark: Mickey's Ten Commandments and the Road to Imagineering *by Martin Sklar.*[47]

11.9 Strengthen Your Humour Muscles and Laugh More

While playfulness is so much more than fun and laughter, developing your capacity for humour and bringing more laughter into your life can help foster your playfulness. We looked at humour and laughter in a bit more detail in Part I and here, we want to remind you that you can strengthen your humour muscle (see the work of McGhee[48]) and seek out opportunities for laughter whether in joyful laughter yoga classes which have the added bonus of rich moments of connection with others or more impromptu ones. Just as we encourage you to wear your curiosity glasses (more on these in The Playfulness Scrapbook), you can also don your laughter lenses and play with seeing the lighter side of life and bask in all the other benefits that laughter has to offer. You can then take this levity and compassionate perspective into your work giving you greater capacity to hold the seriousness and at times heaviness both in the moment with your client and for yourself (to nurture yourself in what can be intensive and, if not balanced with self-care, depleting work). We are adding compassion to the mix, not least as without it, there's a possibility that the humour might tip into the unhelpful for example, mocking. (We should add that we try to stay out of the overwhelm zone; being in that zone can seriously impede humour.).

Auriel Majumdar shared with us that Gestalt and existentialism form the foundations of her philosophy which enables her to compassionately laugh at the absurdity of the human experience. We can develop our capacity to step outside of our direct experience and have a giggle; the Observing Self, as it's referred to in ACT coaching, with a keen sense of humour. Rather than being hijacked by emotions, we can then reflect on our experience of those emotions ('I am feeling anger – what is that like?' and so on, rather than 'I am angry') and inject some gentle humour. This creates a lighter perspective and space for being open to change or moving your position rather than being in the grip of the current experience; it's very effective for working with group dynamics as those who laugh (genuinely) together experience connection, greater warmth, and trust.

- *Where/how present is laughter in your life?*
- *Where/how can you find more opportunities for laughter?*
- *How open are you to opportunities for laughter?*
- *Where is the laughter in the system that is you, your life, and your professional practice? (Adapted from a question by David Clutterbuck)*

11.10 Presence, Mindfulness and Playfulness

We heartedly agree with Kestly[49] who argues, in the context of play therapy, that there is an inter-relationship with playfulness, mindfulness and compassion, as these support relational flow by facilitating awareness of our inner selves without judging, allowing a state of calm in the therapist (we'd add coach), and genuinely feeling compassion for self and client. Mindfulness cultivates courage and resilience to accept ambiguity and complexity[50] and we have seen that a preference for complexity is a component of one of the definitions of playfulness.[51] Moreover, mindfulness has been shown to encourage authenticity through aligning actions with values[52] and we have seen how authenticity is an important consideration in relation to playfulness. Examining the literature on playfulness, improvisation, and mindfulness in the context of creativity, Hassan[53] argues that research literature supports that there are strong links among the three (though the review utilised a narrower definition of playfulness which centres predominantly on positive emotions). When you think about it, for many forms of play, we are in flow which requires us to be present here in the moment.

What do we mean by 'presence' and 'mindfulness'? Silsbee[54] defines presence as 'the state that allows us to be the most resourceful, resilient and self-generative person we can be, and this is in fact, the promise of coaching', while for Reynolds[55] coaching mastery is the deepening of presence. Siegel writes that presence for adults is often a conscious choice supported by mindfulness.[56] Mindfulness practice is defined by Kabat-Zinn as 'the intentional focus of attention on moment-to-moment experience without being swept up by judgments or preconceived ideas and expectations'.[57]

> Action, spontaneity and creativity are only accessible in the here-and-now.
> *Moreno[58]*

The good news is that mindfulness and therefore presence can be learned and developed (naturally, given neuroplasticity coupled with a growth mindset). It stands to reason that the more aware, attuned and present we are in the moment, the more we can be spontaneous, flexible, improvise and engage in those other attitudes and behaviours which we discussed in the context of uncertainty and discomfort above. As we've seen, at the heart of playfulness is the exploration of different possibilities and mindfulness too can build our capacity for this. Through practice, we can learn to step into the shoes of (again, as referred to in ACT) the Observing Self, creating some psychological distance, allowing more space and detachment from emotions and thoughts which is what playfulness can also facilitate. We give you some ideas in The Playfulness Scrapbook of what this might look like in practice. We encouraged you earlier to bring your Whole Body into playfulness and mindfulness can also help you build your awareness in this context. What's more, the Observing Self also enables us as coaches to check in and reflect-in-action (and of course afterwards, on-action) that we are 'using' playfulness in the service of the client rather than for any of our own motivations as we looked at in the context of risks in Part I.

Insight Dialogue, founded by Gregory Kramer, is an interpersonal (or relational) meditation practice based on the teachings of the Buddha; in effect, it takes meditation off the cushion (an introspective, personal practice) and into relationships. Kramer suggests that *'thinking we know costs us all we don't know – which is nearly everything'*[59] and the practice supports developing a beginner's mind about our experience and the experience of others, developing an awareness of our somatic experience, and has some overlaps with the aspects of playfulness which we've discussed above. In a completely unscientifically backed observation, we've noticed that as a group, a large proportion of Buddhist monastics (our experience is limited to those following the teachings of Thich Nhat Hanh) have that playful twinkle in the eye, presence, mindfulness and playfulness and some aspects of monastic life are infused with playfulness. Perhaps developing our capacity for presence and mindfulness (and compassion) through Relational Mindfulness training or otherwise strengthens our ability, willingness, and comfort in entering the unknown with our coaching clients and truly letting go of tools, pre-planned processes and so on to scaffold the sessions, which will also allow us to be more playful. At the time of writing, Stephanie is embarking on her second year of Relational Mindfulness training with a small group of wonderful coaches instructed by Dr Emma Donaldson-Feilder and our lived experience is that it has much to offer our coaching practice (and life generally) and, Stephanie has found, creating the space and conditions for playfulness.

Whether or not you practise meditation regularly, guided meditation can be a fun area to explore increasing your capacity for playfulness. Similar to story-telling, a meditation guide if they are playful and insightful, might take you on an adventure. Your more meditative and relaxed state may facilitate deeper immersion, awareness, and insight, for example, helping you to nurture your imagination, creating vivid images, envisioning stories that feel like dreaming while you're awake, allowing your brain to wander freely and play.

- *How aware, attuned and present are you in the moment?*
- *How do you know?*
- *In those moments, what do you notice about opportunities for playfulness?*
- *In what ways can you cultivate your awareness?*
- *What benefit would developing this capacity further bring to you and your practice?*

11.11 Conclusion

The intention of this chapter is to give you lots of practical ideas to build your capacity for playfulness as well as the resources for interesting theoretical paths to follow down if your curiosity is ignited. If you'd like to experiment with incorporating more playfulness in your practice, in order to do so authentically, we'd suggest that you gain a greater understanding of your current level of playfulness (remembering the multi-faceted Be Playful Onion Model) and explore ways of strengthening your various playfulness muscles and finding your own version of being and becoming more playful. From this place then, you can also work with your clients, should they wish, to think about and grow their capacity for playfulness or find playful means of working on different topics with your clients. Conveniently, the next two chapters will support you in doing just that. Before this, if you haven't already, check out the Barometer of Playfulness in the The Playfulness Scrapbook, to gauge your current level of playfulness and take the time to consider the implications more deeply for you personally, and for your practice.

Notes

1 Rosen, M. (2020). *Book of Play! Why play really matters and 101 ways to get more if it in your life.* Wellcome Collection, p17.
2 podcastnotes.org/huberman-lab/power-of-play-huberman-lab-podcast-58
3 Pizzorno, J. & Murray, M. (Eds). (2020). *Textbook of Natural Medicine* (5th ed.). Churchill Livingstone.
4 primalplay.com
5 Gammage, D. (2017). *Playful Awakening: Releasing the Gift of Play in Your Life.* Jessica Kingsley Publishers, p138.
6 Kashdan, T. (2009). *Curious? Discover the missing ingredient to a fulfilling life.* William Morrow & Co
7 Kashdan, T. (2022). *The Art of Insubordination: How to dissent and defy effectively.* Avery.
8 Moreno, J. (1964). *Psychodrama, first volume* (3rd ed.). Beacon House Press, pxii.
9 Giacomucci, S. (2021). *Social Work, Sociometry, and Psychodrama, Experiential Approaches for Group Therapists, Community Leaders, and Social Workers.* (Vol. 1) Springer Nature. *Open Access.*
10 *Ibid,* Moreno (1964, p.xii).
11 Brauer, K. & Proyer, R. (2017). Are Impostors playful? Testing the association of adult playfulness with the Impostor Phenomenon. *Personality and Individual Differences,* 116, 57–62.

12 For example, Watts, G. & Morgan, K. (2015). *The Coach's Casebook: Mastering the Twelve Traits That Trap Us*. Inspect & Adapt.

13 Van Oech, R. (2010). *A Whack On The Side Of The Head: How You Can be More Creative*. (Special ed.). Creative Think.

14 Schalwijk, F. (2019). A clinical interpretation of shame regulation in maladaptive perfectionism. *Personality and Individual Differences, 138*, 19–23.

15 Cavicchia, S. (2010). Shame in the coaching relationship: reflections on organisational vulnerability. *Journal of Management Development, 29*(10), 877–890.

16 Ruch, W. & Proyer, R. (2009). Extending the study of gelotophobia: On gelotophiles and katagelasticists. *Humor - International Journal of Humor Research, 22*(1–2), 183–212.

17 Ruch, W. & Proyer, R. (2008). The fear of being laughed at: Individual and group differences in gelotophobia. *Humor: International Journal of Humor Research, 21*, 47–67.

18 Platt T. (2008). Emotional responses to ridicule and teasing: Should gelotophobes react differently? *Humor: International Journal of Humor Research. 21*(2),105–128

19 Proyer, R. (2012). Examining playfulness in adults: Testing its correlates with personality, positive psychological functioning, goal aspirations, and multimethodically assessed ingenuity. *Psychological Test and Assessment Modeling, 54*(2), 103–127.

20 Proyer, R. (2017). A new structural model for the study of adult playfulness: Assessment and exploration of an understudied individual differences variable. *Personality and Individual Differences, 108*, 103–122.

21 Brauer, K. & Proyer, R. (2020). Is it me or the circumstances? Examining the relationships between individual differences in causal attributions and dispositions toward ridicule and being laughed at. *Personality and Individual Differences, 165*, 110135.

22 *Ibid*, Brauer & Proyer (2020).

23 Brauer, K., & Proyer, R. (2019). The ridiculed Impostor: Testing the associations between dispositions toward ridicule and being laughed at and the Impostor Phenomenon. *Current Psychology*, 1–10.

24 Proyer, R. & Ruch, W. (2009). Intelligence and gelotophobia: The relations of selfestimated and psychometrically measured intelligence to the fear of being laughed at. *Humor: International Journal of Humor Research, 22*, 165–181.

25 Proyer, R., Wellenzohn, S. & Ruch, W. (2014). Character and dealing with laughter: The relation of self- and peer-reported strengths of character with gelotophobia, gelotophilia, and katagelasticism. *Journal of Psychology: Interdisciplinary and Applied, 148*, 113–132.

26 *Ibid*, Proyer and Ruch (2020).

27 Lee, G. (2021). *Breakthrough Conversations for Coaches, Consultants and Leaders*. Routledge.

28 Reddan, M., Wager, T. & Schiller, D. (2018). Attenuating Neural Threat Expression with Imagination. *Neuron, 100*(4), 994.

29 Donne, J. (1839). Devotions Upon Emergent Occasions MEDITATION XVII. *The Works of John Donne*. Vol III. Henry Alford (Ed.). John W. Parker, p574–5.

30 Oliver, T. (2020). *The Self Delusion: The surprising science of how we are connected and why it matters.* Weidenfeld & Nicolson.

31 Panksepp, J. & Lahvis, G. (2011). Rodent empathy and affective neuroscience. *Neuroscience & Biobehavioral Reviews, 35*(9), 1864–1875. Hess, U., & Blairy, S. (2001). Facial mimicry and emotional contagion to dynamic emotional facial expressions and their influence on decoding accuracy. *International journal of psychophysiology, 40*(2), 129–141. Lundqvist, L. & Dimberg, U. (1995). Facial expressions are contagious. *Journal of psychophysiology, 9*, 203–203.

32 *Ibid*, Lee (2021).

33 www.rhythmofregulation.com

34 Schott, G. (2011). Doodling and the default network of the brain. *The Lancet, 378*(9797), 1133–1134.

35 Bateson, P. & Martin, P. (2013). *Play, Playfulness, Creativity and Innovation.* Cambridge University Press.

36 Mason, M., Norton, M., Van Horn, J., Wegner, D., Grafton, S. & Macrae, C. (2007). Wandering Minds: the default network and stimulus-independent thought. *Science, 315*, 393–5.

37 Heilman, N.K., Nadeau, S.E. & Beversdorf, D.O. (2003), Creative innovation: possible brain mechanisms. *Neurocase, 9*, 369–79.

38 *Ibid*, Bateson & Martin (2013, p115).

39 Baird, B., Smallwood, J., Mrazek, M., Kam, J., Franklin, M. & Schooler, J. (2012). Inspired by Distraction: Mind Wandering Facilitates Creative Incubation. *Psychological Science, 23*(10), 1117–1122.

40 Winnicott, D. (1971), *Playing and Reality.* Routledge Classics, p35–50.

41 Brown, S. (2009). *Play How it Shapes the Brain, Open the Imagination, and Invigorates the Soul.* Penguin Books Ltd, p37.

42 Gilbert, D. & Wilson, T. (2007). Prospection: experiencing the future, *Science, 317*(5843), 1351–1354.

43 Bulley, A. & Schacter, D. (2020). Deliberating trade-offs with the future. *Nature Human Behaviour, 4*(3), 238–247.

44 Vazeou-Nieuwenhuis, A., Orehek, E. & Scheier, M. (2017). The meaning of action: do selfregulatory processes contribute to a purposeful life? *Personality and Individual Differences, 116*, 115–122.

45 Oettingen, G. & Mayer, D. (2002). The motivating function of thinking about the future: expectations versus fantasies. *Journal of Personality and Social Psychology, 83*(5), 1198.

46 Seligman, M., Railton, P., Baumeister, R. & Sripada, C. (2013). Navigating into the future or driven by the past. *Perspectives on Psychological Science, 8*(2), 119–141.

47 (2015). Disney Editions: California

48 McGhee, P. (2010). *Humor as survival training for a stressed-out world: The 7 Humor Habits Program.* Author House.

49 Kestly, T. (2016). Presence and Play: Why Mindfulness Matters. *Journal of Play Therapy, 25*(1), 14–23.

50 Schootstra, E., Deichmann, D. & Dolgova, E. (2017). Can 10 minutes of meditation make you more creative? *Harvard Business Review*. https://hbr.org/2017/08/can-10-minutes-of-meditation-make-you-more-creative [Accessed on 23 May 2022]

51 *Ibid*, Proyer (2017).

52 Christie, A., Atkins, P. & Donald, J. (2016). The Meaning and Doing of Mindfulness: The Role of Values in the Link Between Mindfulness and Well-Being. *Mindfulness*, August.

53 Hassan, D. (2019). Creativity trilateral dynamics: playfulness, mindfulness, and improvisation. *Creativity Studies*, *12*(1), 1–14.

54 Silsbee, D. (2010). *The Mindful Coach 7 Roles for Facilitating Leader Development* (2nd edn.). Jossey-Bass.

55 Reynolds, M. (2017). Presence, Coaching Culture and Cross-roads. linkedin.com/pulse/dr-marcia-reynolds-presence-coaching-culturemichael-bungay-stanier [Accessed on 23 May 2022]

56 Siegel, D. (2007). *The mindful brain: Reflection and attunement in the cultivation of wellbeing*. Guildford Press.

57 Kabat-Zinn, J. (2005). *Coming to our senses*. New York: Hyperion. Kabat-Zinn, J. (2012). *Mindfulness for Beginners: Reclaiming the Present Moment – and Your Life*. Sounds True, pxlix.

58 *Ibid*, Giacomucci. (2021, p61.)

59 Kramer, G. (2007). Insight Dialogue: The Interpersonal Path to Freedom. Shambhala, p144.

12
Things to Consider in Practice

In this chapter, we:

- Encourage you to see resistance as information rather a barrier
- Consider things that might get in your way
- Invite you to think about things that might get in your clients' way
- Remind you of the value of reflection as you go forward (playfully)

The previous chapters in Part II have focused on nurturing your playfulness, including by being aware of and addressing potential barriers that you may come across. In the context of your work with clients, there may be additional considerations to take into account, and we're highlighting a few here. Also, as we pointed out in Chapter 9, sometimes it's less than clear where barriers end and risks begin and vice versa, so some of the ideas explored in that chapter pop up again here and we'd suggest that you read both chapters if you're dipping in and out of the book. Our intention, of course, is not to discourage you, but to support you in bringing increased awareness and discernment to playfulness in your practice.

Throughout, we've been emphasising the wide range of ways in which playfulness can be present and there is of course a judgment to be made both in terms of how open you want to be to playfulness and your willingness to experiment as well as the degree to which you are playful in the context of your relationships (work or otherwise). We talked about this a little in Chapter 9; again, it's not about you (sorry!) but what is of service to the relationship and the client. Reading the room and cultivating the conditions to support the client is, of course, of paramount importance; we are not talking about playfulness for its own sake, nor is it necessarily appropriate in every context with every client. When we say 'it', keep in mind the Be Playful Onion Model and remember that there is a huge range, from a gentle compassionate playfully provocative question to whole teams playing energetic games and beyond.

DOI: 10.4324/9781003090847-14

It's important to acknowledge that our focus isn't solely on overcoming barriers. If we treat everything as useful information, in the spirit of Gestalt, then noticing barriers within self, others or systems might be an important flag that there are some other things which need to be addressed before we can engage in playfulness, or that we need to consider where in the Be Playful Onion Model our playfulness would appropriately sit in the current circumstances. Sometimes, the barriers just mean that we have to rethink how we incorporate playfulness in a particular context, rather than turning away from it completely, or that they are telling us important information about us, our rapport, our clients, or their systems. Remembering again that playfulness in our work is in the service of our clients not for its own sake or ours (sorry if we are labouring the point, but it is important to acknowledge and remember).

We invite you to take a multi-dimensional approach. We introduced Andrea Fella's metaphor of soup in which we stew in Chapter 10; let's also look at barriers as a whole in a similar way, as ingredients for a stew. Bear with us! The individual barriers might be there and in different quantities, and they sit alongside other ingredients such as what playfulness means to you (for example, do you consider playfulness in coaching as a tablespoon of humour with a pinch of visually creative metaphors or a cup of experiential somatic playful experiences with a teaspoon of whimsical playfulness?), what it means to your client, your relationship, the context in which you are working and so on.

12.1 Things That Might Get in Your Way

Perhaps there might still be some things that feel as if they are getting in the way of your fluidity and flexibility in accessing playfulness in your work. Schwarz & Braff (2001) observe that 'professionals often unconsciously justify and rationalise their personal issues by relying on professional narratives that support their own psychological defences'.[1] We think that this is an interesting point to bear in mind as you reflect on your own barriers to playfulness. An obvious example for our context is avoiding playfulness for fear that it will dent professional credibility. Some of the reluctance here is we'd suggest also to do with how we define playfulness and you've seen our Be Playful Onion Model encourages playfulness to be seen as far more than potentially childish play behaviour. As we go through other potential barriers below, it's worth bearing Schwarz & Braff's observation in mind and checking in from time to time if it applies to you.

12.1.1 Capacity

We mentioned in Chapter 10 that some basic needs have to be met before you can fully engage in playfulness; hunger, lack of sleep or overwhelm, for example, of stimulus or emotion make it much harder to access playfulness or to access playfulness and stay grounded. Sometimes you (and your clients of course) simply don't have the capacity for playfulness at a point in time. Not only relevant for you, think also of your clients who might be facing a demanding and unrelenting workload. Teresa shares a story of when she signed up to a new course while writing this book and was already juggling too many other things. As she joined her new learning group, the other participants were saying that they would like to learn and be together in a playful way.

Teresa relates:

> PLAY?!! We don't have time for play!!

> 'PLAY?!!' I could hear my inner voice scream in exasperation and frustration, not unlike Thomas Shelby, the character in Peaky Blinders (TV show) when he's astonished and angry at someone's ridiculous suggestion. My inner voice was incredulous, repeating the question: '"Play?!! You want me to play?!" I am seriously up against it, the clock is ticking and the pressure couldn't be greater. I am overwhelmed, tired and running on empty. I don't want to do any of the things which I need to get done. I really want to be on a beach, chilling. No scrub that, I am too tired for the beach and fun times. I really just want to go to sleep and switch off from the rest of the world. How on earth is play going to be of any use in the current situation?'.

> In that single moment, I experienced a flash of intense feelings and racing thoughts in response to the suggestion of play by this lovely lighthearted and joyful group. At the same time, the irony of my reaction wasn't lost on me. More than that, it was mildly amusing. Isn't it funny how we can be in the grip of intense emotions and thoughts and at the same time realise how faintly ironic they are? I took a breath and asked myself: 'What an odd response. What is going on with me? I know the power of play, so what is this reaction telling me?' As the group conversation continued, I made a note to reflect further on my reaction later.

> When the session was over, I used the Barometer of Playfulness (in The Playfulness Scrapbook) to reflect on what it was that I needed. I knew the answer straight away: I was tired and so my capacity for playfulness was low. I had very little energy, just enough to do the bare minimum – playfulness, creativity, or anything new seemed too much effort. Also, at that time, the learning group wasn't my top priority, I had pressing challenges which needed every ounce of my creativity and new thinking. I felt guilty about joining the group in this state of mind and signing up to the course knowing it would be a struggle alongside my other competing and higher priorities. Once I acknowledged my tiredness and guilt, my inner voice calmed. I realised that I was going to have to accept my depleted capacity for playfulness in that forum for the time being while I addressed how to get my energy to a good enough level to be able to join in more playfully in the future.

On reflection, Teresa saw her lack of capacity for playfulness as information which was telling her that she was tired, overwhelmed with competing demands and needed to attend to her energy levels. The Barometer of Playfulness is designed to help you to reflect on your capacity for playfulness and identify any needs which you might need to address. Other barriers to playfulness might be time or intent; many parents can relate to being half-present when an insistent child wants to play, either because they are too tired or distracted by other thoughts or things. Sometimes, realising this, you can pull yourself back in the moment and reconnect with an intent to play (Teresa's story of playing with her daughter in Chapter 10 for example), other times one or more of your needs might require addressing first.

12.1.2 Confidence

In Stephanie's MSc research dissertation on playfulness in coaching,[2] one of the barriers encountered by coaches, especially reflecting back on the earlier stages of their coaching career, was a lack of confidence which, in turn, pulled them back from saying something that might land as slightly ridiculous or playful. Of course, if your coach training embraced the concepts inherent to playfulness or were closely linked to play, such as coaching with art, movement or even play, you will presumably have gone through your own developmental journey in relation to playfulness and feel much more comfortable to build your competence while being open to playfulness in your practice. A beginner's stance, taking nothing as given can be fuel for creative playful thinking and questions which embody this approach can be very helpful to disrupt thought patterns and shift perspectives. This stance can be difficult to take if the coach isn't feeling confident and worried about seemingly asking a silly or obvious question, especially with senior clients or with teams.

Wobbly confidence might also lead us to over-relying on tools or, in terms of Transactional Analysis, the adult or even parent ego-state, focusing on structured or evidence-led interventions which leave less space for spontaneity, creativity, intuition or improvisation associated with the child state. Going back to Stephanie's research, she found that those coaches who saw playfulness closer to humour and whimsical playfulness than intellectual or serious playfulness (according to the OLIW model, see Chapter 5), and/or positioned themselves more on the consultant/directive spectrum of coaching, experienced greater barriers both in terms of number and perceived insurmountability. On balance, we need to be heedful of what is appropriate and of service to the client but not let our own internal barriers and stories get in the way.

We think the approach which Heather Simpkin shared with us is very helpful in this context: remember it's not about you as a coach, but about the experience of participants whom you are in service to. To realise that as a coach, I have the confidence to share what I'm offering – an opportunity to experience play which may help you learn and develop, individually and collectively, but if you don't want that, that's ok. I'm not taking it as a reflection on me personally or my professional ability (though of course engaging in reflection and supervision to uncover my blind spots and examine various perspectives; there is always room for learning and growth).

We found James Flaherty's observation that in coaching, there are always two (in the context of 1 : 1, presumably more in the context of groups/teams) scared people in the room very reassuring.[3] This might be even more so with play-fulness as there are no guarantees. As we've seen, playfulness involves finding comfort with the not-knowing, spontaneity, being adaptive and curious rather than following a predetermined process or expecting a certain outcome (the extent of which will of course depend on the position in the Be Playful Onion Model). To stay playful, you need to be happy with potential 'failure', authen-ticity, vulnerability, to learn and stretch and hold the space for your clients to do the same. It may be that you experience a degree of fear every time you step into that space (and develop an awareness, appreciation, and adaptive relationship to this fear), or over time that you have so much faith in the pro-cess that such fear no longer arises. Normalise nerves beforehand. If you stop having them, are you still being truly playful, or falling into routine (perhaps this is different for different types of playfulness, for example, serious play and creativity/creative playfulness). It's important to go back to the idea of the sweet discomfort and to realise that being in the learning zone brings with it potential discomfort and anxiety and fear without going into overwhelm or distress (see also Chapter 11). Can you reframe those nerves as excitement, curiosity, or the start of an adventure (see also Chapter 6)? Can you hold that lightly with a sense of self-awareness, self-compassion and humour?

- *How can I be more expansive within what's appropriate and of service to my client?*
- *Can I reframe my fear as excitement, curiosity, the start of an adventure? (See the work of Kelly McGonigal).*
- *Can I hold any fear lightly with a sense of self-compassion and humour?*
- *What is this fear telling me that I need to pay attention to?*

12.1.3 Complacency

If you are thinking, 'Nah, I'm good thanks' to our previous reflections on confidence, walk with us to the other side of that coin. It's possible for more experienced coaches to get used to working in a certain way and to fall into habits both in coaching relationships or in their approach to coaching more generally and these might not support playfulness. We've seen in Chapter 10 how the stories that we tell ourselves can impact our playfulness and of course we also tell ourselves stories about coaching and our approach and effectiveness. Some of these might obviously or inadvertently get in the way of playfulness that might have been of service to our clients (and support us in our work, see for example Chapter 4). We're assuming that reflection and supervision is an important part of your practice, and you might like to shine the spotlight on your approach and beliefs around playfulness from time to time.

- *What were the messages (implicit and explicit) around playfulness in my training?*
- *What habits have I fallen into in my work?*
- *What am I taking for granted?*
- *Have I shown curiosity towards my philosophy recently (see Chapter 5)?*
- *What are my fears around being more expansive?*
- *What can I let go of?*
- *How can I keep learning?*
- *Where is the playfulness in the system that is me and my work? (A question offered by David Clutterbuck).*

12.1.4 Competence and Capability

Competence and capability might be worth considering in the context of offering or engaging in playfulness in your coaching. Competence usually relates to training or a skill, whereas capability relates more to experience and 'inner' work. In this respect, do you feel you are competent and capable enough and if not, what do you need? Many of the ideas in Chapters 10 and 11 will help in considering these questions.

12.1.5 Credibility

We mentioned earlier the potential fear of damaging our credibility if we or our methods are perceived as playful, let's look at this a little closer. This fear might come up particularly early in the relationship with a client who has a particular view of playfulness, who or might find it challenging and/or is constructing their perception of our expertise. Of course, playfulness isn't always a good fit or appropriate and it might well damage our credibility if we don't recognise this. As we've said, sometimes it is appropriate to shimmy around the Be Playful Onion Model to exercise discernment and at other times it's just not the time or place for playfulness. It's worth considering though that sometimes, we have an idea of what professional behaviour should look like, probably heavily influenced by ideas formed in childhood, and we might constrain ourselves by that, letting our own seriousness create a barrier to playfulness. Going back to Transactional Analysis; are you as coach behaving as a controlling parent? Does your child ever get an outing?

- *What is your idea of professional behaviour?*
- *What is your seriousness facilitating? What is it obstructing?*
- *How can you find more balance (should you or your clients want it)?*
- *Are you behaving as the controlling parent or adult or does your creative, curious child (all in terms of Transactional Analysis) get the opportunity to show up in your work?*
- *What would you lose and gain if it did?*
- *Where is the humility in your credibility?*
- *Where is the curiosity?*

12.2 Things Affecting Your Client Which Might Get in the Way

Clients and coaches alike are subject to the same personal, social, and cultural limitations to playfulness which we have already discussed. It's worth considering a few other things which might get in the way of playfulness for our clients. Needless to say, these are not always discrete and unconnected, so they are worth thinking about in the round.

12.2.1 Don't Want to Be There or Don't Want to Change

A number of our Storytellers shared stories with us (and we've had similar experiences) of clients who feel to some extent that the coaching is being imposed on them by their organisation and do not want to take part in the process or they are not really interested in doing the work demanded of them by engaging in coaching. It may be completely unrelated to playfulness. On the other hand, playfulness might not resonate at all with the client. If we don't have an agenda to push or sell playfulness (see Chapter 9), then we can hold this compassionately and with perspective.

Kirsten Barske whose work with teams is nature-based and very experiential, does from time to time come across resistance. Sometimes this shows up as quiet withdrawal and sometimes vocal push-back. She reflected in our conversation that for some, who are not used to being playful at work, or even in life generally, the invitation to play may bring with it the potential for embarrassment or feeling awkward and to address or assuage this fear (which might not be verbalised), they might need more time, space, encouragement, and the creation of a feeling of safety and/or acceptance. Kirsten's response is to stay calm (remember the effect of neuroception) and empathise: 'You don't like this, I can see that'. She'll ask if she can speak individually with them during the next break, not to persuade them, but to speak with them about what is behind the team activity they are engaged in. Depending on the circumstances, she might then explain that they are not playing for fun but to gain awareness of how the group functions collectively, how they engage with each other and experience each other. She'll make it clear that they are free to leave if they wish, but if they stay, they must stay as participant and not spectator (which would upset the dynamic particularly if the person in question is the team leader). Kirsten's experience is that when the person sees that their objections are being taken seriously and they have the choice of whether to engage or leave and Kirsten is fine with either, they relax. In all her years of experience, she has never had someone leave. When they rejoin the session, Kirsten will keep an eye on them (discreetly!) and if they become more engaged, she doesn't make a big thing about it, but takes it easy, observing without attachment.

12.2.2 Individual Considerations

As we've seen, research into both adult playfulness and humour is at a relatively early stage, and particularly for playfulness for the most part has looked
at the construct in the context of the general population. An understanding
of the barriers to playfulness, which facets might be easier to access and
evidence-led ways of reducing any barriers, has yet to be developed for special
population groups such as those with depression, anxiety, gelotophobia and
some neurodiverse members of the population. In the meantime, there is not
much in the literature, for example, Berger et al., 2018[4] suggest that clients
with undiagnosed or unshared depression or anxiety may have a decreased
ability to think playfully. Recent evidence points towards reduced playfulness in adults with anxiety disorders (Versluys, 2017[5]). Sometimes the way
playfulness has landed might be a flag that counselling or therapy may be
appropriate.

12.2.3 Psychological Safety and Group Dynamics

We looked at addressing fears of embarrassment and shame to open up to
playfulness in the previous chapter and this is also relevant in the context of
psychological safety. Let's now move our focus to the experience within teams/
groups and more specifically whether the system(s) in which the client(s)
are working, are psychologically safe enough for playfulness. Exploration
and experimentation in a relatively low risk space is essential for playfulness and, of course, considerations such as diversity and inclusion, status and
group dynamics are important. Some of the group might feel safe to be playful
whereas others might not.

To some extent it's a chicken and egg situation. Playfulness can help build
psychological safety if done with awareness and sensitivity, so low levels of psychological safety don't rule out playfulness and psychological safety supports
playfulness. However, done badly, it can damage psychological safety. Low
levels require the coach to be aware, alert and prepared to be playful themselves
by improvising, being flexible, working with what's in the room rather than
imposing a prepared playfulness agenda on the group. Remember the myriad
of ways in which playfulness can be present. We'll look in The Playfulness
Scrapbook at stories and ideas of what this might look like in practice. Heather
Simpkin has a theatre background and her work with teams or groups can
involve very playful activities. She spoke with us about the need to carefully
structure activities (and model behaviour) which encourage participants to be
prepared to let go, at least a bit, of the fear of 'looking stupid' and where she

judges it's safe and appropriate, she might offer whimsical activities (think back to the OLIW model), to create sufficient safety within the group to venture into intellectual playfulness subsequently.

There may be other factors in the group dynamics which pose a barrier for playfulness. Resentment or anger, for example, makes playfulness difficult if not impossible, so there may be other work which needs to be done first to open a space for playfulness.

- *How has your contracting and research/fact finding influenced your invitation for playfulness?*
- *How will you ensure that you show flexibility and sensitivity in the moment of playfulness to take into account, and to respond to what might be going on in the room?*
- *How flexible are you prepared to be if other matters become evident which need attending to before playfulness is welcomed or possible?*

12.2.4 Gender

Gender can be a barrier to playfulness in different ways, such as in the risk of being misconstrued or misfiring (see Chapter 9 for more on this). It might also be that the gender balance of the group and the opposite/same gender of the coach might make it difficult for some forms of playfulness to emerge. Heather Simpkin gave us an example of coaching a team of men in a male-dominated organisation and sector which was very challenging given the group norm and the individual beliefs around playfulness. Applying our Be Playful Onion Model, the team were sitting in a very different part of the model than the space into which Heather had initially intended to take them. We don't know what additional impact on playfulness there might have been if the coach had also been male – perhaps none – but we're putting it in the mix as something to ponder in individual circumstances. Given Heather's skill, she navigated them all to a playful space through experimentation and exploration, it was just different from what her initial expectations (held lightly) might have been. Knowing that there are many ways of being playful allows the coach to experiment with what feels like a helpful way to introduce playfulness and then gradually build it (or, of course, decide it's not helpful at a particular time).

Nankhonde Kasonde-van den Broek, reflected how in some contexts, she has experienced very different dynamics between men and women; sometimes with the men in that space showing up as very masculine and hierarchical. On occasion, her response included evening-out the playing field by bringing it to an adult-to-adult level (in Transactional Analysis terms) by encouraging reflection and listening. It wasn't the specific goal, but by facilitating a more collaborative dynamic, more space for playfulness emerged.

12.2.5 Culture: Organisational and More Generally

We are thinking here of organisational culture as well as the culture(s) of the coach and client and the culture of the wider context of the coaching relationship.

> When we are at work, we ought to be at work. When we are at play, we ought to be at play
>
> *Henry Ford*[6]

The simple team activity based on improv, called 'Morph Ball' is described in The Playfulness Scrapbook. It's possible to play it in person or online and can help people to connect and be present. In her reflections with us, Julie Flower was struck how sometimes this simple team activity can fall flat. It's an insight to recognise that some of us are more risk averse than others and throwing an imaginary ball around is more of a stretch for some than others, particularly in certain contexts. How 'risky' a playful activity will feel to the individual participants will of course also depend on the context of their team, organisation, and other relevant systems. It's worth considering whether the barriers are in fact coming from the systems or from stories which our clients (and we) are telling ourselves and how these are perhaps tied in with our values and our perceptions of ourselves and others.

Darryl Edwards, a former banking technologist and founder of Primal Play Method (integrating health, physical activity, and play) tells how one of the reasons why he left his job was because sharing a joke at the water cooler and even just smiling was frowned upon. Working with clients in such organisational cultures, particularly teams with 'serious' group norms and in their office environment, may well pose significant barriers to playfulness. Sensitivity and judgement as to the level/kind of playfulness will be needed, but perhaps it is not necessary to rule it out completely. Remember that playfulness can be a disruptor as well as a facilitator and sometimes barriers might be a sign that disruption would be of service to the client. An adjustment or change to the physical environment might be helpful (whether it's closing the blinds or finding a location away from the office, for example) and more generally, contracting and recontracting are clearly especially important in this situation.

- *Am I going into this situation telling myself that playfulness would not be appropriate/acceptable?*
- *How is playfulness seen in the system in which I will be working?*
- *How dependent is my story around playfulness on my understanding of me, or the team, or the organisation or other systems (whichever are relevant)?*
- *What assumptions underlie my stories?*
- *Is this story worth further exploration both in terms of my thinking and experimenting to move out of my comfort zone?*
- *Are the same questions relevant to my client(s)?*

Moving our focus to culture more generally, much of the published research into adult playfulness has been Western-centric with the main geographic sources of research being predominantly Europe and also China and the Far East. We don't really yet understand the cultural impact of playfulness; there may be greater variations among regions in some countries than across countries and research tends to focus on playfulness as an individual difference variable, often still associated with fun (see Chapter 5) rather than a relational construct. Sometimes though, there can be insurmountable barriers to playfulness of culture. In Stephanie's original research, for example, one of the male participants reflected that your scope for playfulness is diminished significantly with female clients based in the Middle East.

It might also be that there are specific cultural considerations which need to be borne in mind. For instance, Nankhonde Kasonde-van den Broek shared with us that Zambia is quite a religious, spiritual society (whether Muslim, Christian or Hindu for example). This is reflected in the Constitution and religious metaphors are commonly used and awareness and sensitivity to this is required in the coaching space.

As coaches, we need to be culturally sensitive with self-awareness of our own assumptions, beliefs, and frames of reference, keeping a beginner's mind and flexibility, so that we can investigate and inquire where there might be cultural boundaries and negotiate what's appropriate and helpful (within ethical boundaries of course). This is no different in the context of playfulness.

12.3 Reflection

As a starting point, the Barometer of Playfulness (short version in Chapter 10 and longer version in The Playfulness Scrapbook) has been created for you to check in with your playfulness and understand whether any unfulfilled needs might be getting in the way.

More generally, as there are such a multitude of ways in which playfulness can be present in coaching, you might never come across any of the potential barriers which we've considered in this and earlier chapters. Our intention is certainly not to put you off! We've included reflection questions along the way, so if you do come across barriers, you will be equipped to address them with awareness and see them as providing useful information and learning both for you and your clients. We've suggested throughout that invitations for playfulness are offered with lightness and without attachment. If they misfire, it's all information and if you are framing your invitation as an exploration and experiment, saying to your client 'well, that didn't work!' might lead the session to a fruitful area of inquiry and reflection. We'd suggest that you take care that your ego doesn't get in the way if you encounter barriers as there's a danger that if you let it, you take it personally or that your client is left with the feeling that they did something wrong or that they are somehow at fault. As a reminder if you've skipped past it, we looked at risk in Chapter 9 and shared our top tips of what you might do if you come across a bump in the road.

It's worth remembering that certain barriers particularly with particular clients at particular times or contexts may be more than the discomfort of learning and may be insurmountable and depending on the situation may even be a signal that the coach is not the right person for the client. It's also worth noting that the same barriers may be accepted as insurmountable by some coaches but as capable of being overcome by others through additional layers of conversation(s) which might not be necessary with different clients or circumstances.

Whatever barriers you might encounter, it's food for thought whether the coach's role and perhaps the nature of playfulness is sometimes irreverence; treating both the coach's and client's and even the system's resistance with sensitivity and respect, of course, but also a degree of levity and irreverence – the twinkle in the eye which is found in the heart of the Be Playful Onion Model.

Notes

1 Schwarz, R. & Braff, E. (2011). *We're No Fun Anymore: Helping Couples Cultivate Joyful Marriages Through the Power of Play*. Routledge, p164.
2 Subsequently developed into Wheeler, S. (2020). An exploration of playfulness in coaching. *International Coaching Psychology Review*, 15(1), 45.
3 Flaherty, J. (2022). *Coaching: Evoking Excellence in Others*. (4th ed.). Routledge.
4 Berger, P., Bitsch, F., Bröhl, H. & Falkenberg, I. (2018). Play and playfulness in psychiatry: a selective review. *International Journal of Play*, 7(2), 210–225.
5 Versluys, B. (2017). Adults with an anxiety disorder or with an obsessive-compulsive disorder are less playful: A matched control comparison. *The Arts in Psychotherapy*, 56, 117–128.
6 Benyon, H. (1980). *Working for Ford*. Penguin.

13
The Playfulness Scrapbook: A Collection of Stories, Ideas, and Tools

In this chapter we

- Remind you of a few key points for practice
- Offer you a mix and match scrapbook of ideas for you to explore, experiment with, layer, and combine in creative and playful ways in co-creation with your clients

Including:

- Contracting and re-contracting
- Tone and climate
- The Invitation
- Smaller experiments
- Bigger experiments

Welcome to your very own Playfulness Scrapbook. A rich collection of practical ideas, stories, and experiments to bring playfulness into coaching practice from our own and our Storytellers' experience. Our hope is that it is easy for you to use, integrate into your current way of working and a source to dip into for inspiration. Our intent is for you to adapt and develop the ideas as you and your clients think useful in the moment and your context. This is why it is a scrapbook after all; it is unfinished and ever-growing as you play with it and develop it further in your unique way as your capacity and the world of playful practice evolves.

As you know, we feel strongly that we would be doing playfulness a disservice by giving you a tick-box list of 'playfulness tools'; it's possible to offer an inherently playful tool or engage in a potentially playful activity but to offer it, hold the space or engage in it unplayfully.

DOI: 10.4324/9781003090847-15

To give some structure to The Playfulness Scrapbook, if only to make it easier to navigate, we've loosely grouped what follows into different categories, ranging from ideas for conversations such as questions, metaphors and storytelling which you can sprinkle into your coaching conversations to more immersive and experiential experiments such as art, modelling, music, movement. The ideas build to increasing levels of experimentation and experiences like Chairwork, improvisation, role playing, or real playing. The ideas can be layered and combined, so play and be creative.

You will find that there are a number of repetitions of stories and ideas from earlier in the book. This is intentional as The Playfulness Scrapbook is a resource you might dip into long after you've read the book or before you've read it. Earlier chapters of Part II were more focused on how you increase your own capacity for playfulness and The Playfulness Scrapbook is more focused on your work with clients though of course, much of the information in the previous chapters are relevant here too.

A few reminders and thoughts before you dive in:

- Remember the Be Playful Onion Model and the multi-faceted fluid nature of playfulness. The Onion's core represents playfulness as a way of being and some of this is about the questions you ask and how you ask them; your tone, energy, body language, state, your willingness to experiment and play with not knowing and the space you hold with opportunities and invitations for playfulness and experimentation.
- As Steve Chapman said, 'You can only take people where you are prepared to go yourself' (Chapter 10), so the more at ease you are and capacity you have to create the conditions for playfulness and hold that space, the more freedom your clients have to travel wherever they wish or need to in the experimental and playful space which you create together.
- In the context of co-created sessions, rather than pre-designed workshops, we and many of our Storytellers don't set out with an intention to be playful but are open to the opportunities for play and aware of the benefits it can bring to the coachee(s) as well as the barriers and risks. The key question is: '*Is it in service of the client?*'; we are not being playful for playfulness' sake. If what is leading is our intention to be playful, we risk misfiring or getting carried away and losing focus on what really matters in the moment.
- There are many, many ways for you to access playfulness and imbue your work with it. Experiment and find what feels authentic to you and remember to challenge yourself about your assumptions and beliefs too and step into the sweet discomfort (but not overwhelm) so that your

own capacity develops. Remember too that how your clients prefer to access playfulness may well be different from you, and where their zones of comfort/discomfort/overwhelm are is almost certainly different from yours.

- Your openness and authenticity in offering playfulness lets your clients know that together you are creating a space where you both have permission to be playful (and stop whenever they want). It creates the space for you to experiment, to be a bit wacky, to be creative, to fail, to be vulnerable, to show up fully and unconditionally as yourself all in service of your clients and holding the space for them to do the same.

In The Playfulness Scrapbook, we include some ideas which specifically relate to groups or teams and many of the ideas can be adapted for team and group work. Remember though that particularly in teams and groups, trust and safety is important for playfulness. We (mostly) talk in jest of the emotional scars we bear from awful team building sessions early in our professional lives where undercurrents of conflict and lack of safety present in the group were brought to the surface without adequate facilitation. Our Storytellers who run more overtly playful sessions for teams and groups emphasised that they deliberately and carefully ensure that the required trust and safety is present as they incrementally increase the level of experiential playfulness and calibrate it according to what's present.

Play is to … try something different, think something different, do something different, feel something different, be something different, consider different possibilities and perspectives in a relatively low-risk space, often with joy in connection …

With all of this in mind, let's start at the beginning.

The Playfulness Scrapbook

13.1 Getting Started: Contracting and The First Invitation to Play

We (Stephanie and Teresa) know that whatever level of the Be Playful Onion Model we'll tap into with a particular client at a particular moment during the course of a coaching engagement, it is likely that some form of playfulness will emerge in our sessions. We don't go in with an intention or expectation of playfulness, but we are open to the possibilities of inviting it in. As a result, we explain in both our chemistry and contracting conversations that we might, if the moment feels right, offer opportunities for experiments which might or might not work as expected but will usually provide learning and increased awareness. Like many of our Storytellers, we may or may not use the word 'playful' depending on the context. We make sure to emphasise that we will always offer the possibility without attachment and with flexibility, intending to co-create with the client in the moment. It holds a promise of possibility of experimentation and perhaps fun and more often than not, helps in establishing rapport.

The key here is the word 'offer'. As playfulness often takes us into exploration and experimentation territory where neither we or the clients know exactly what is going to happen or how they are going to feel, it is important that play is offered, that it is always open to anyone involved to either decline to take part or stop at any point. That is reflected not just in the initial contracting, but also in the way playful interventions are offered and the in-the-moment re-contracting which takes place regularly (the ABC rule 'always be contracting', is so important to co-creation). Not least, this keeps the focus in the moment on the fact that the purpose of the playful intervention is purely in service of the client and not for example, the need of the coach.

By re-contracting in the moment, we have the opportunity to explore where our clients' sweet discomfort is (see Chapter 11), supporting learning beyond the comfort zone but not into overwhelm or distress. It is an exploration we make in partnership with our clients. It's worth noting though that sometimes moving out of their comfort zone can trigger an initial reaction of pulling away, not wishing to engage. Always with care and following ethical coaching guidelines, perhaps sometimes the role of playfulness of the coach is to hold that resistance lightly and with perspective and irreverence; sometimes a nudge is warranted for the client to experience a certain amount of discomfort. Kirsten Barske sets expectations using gentle humour and warmth, explaining that their work together will be experience-based and will sometimes lead to discomfort. She might say: 'If you think parts of today are going to be awkward or embarrassing, don't worry, they probably will'. Steve Chapman will sometimes agree on a 'safe word' when he feels it will add an extra level of control for the client on big set-pieces that he has set up. Doing so helps to form an agreement that there will be a certain amount of movement outside the comfort zone with the safety of knowing that it is always available to the client to draw the line and decide what is too much.

When we were novice coaches, we were very concerned about inadvertently crossing the coaching/therapy boundary. While we are, of course, still mindful of the ethics of staying within the coaching boundary, we've come to see this as a fuzzy space[1] rather than a barbed wire fence. In this fuzzy space, we no longer fear that we might 'do something' to the client to push them over the boundary, but have come to realise that we are in partnership within the fuzzy space. By re-contracting as appropriate (also informally with gentle questions) we agree with the client in the moment where the boundary lies, assuming there are no underlying issues which would cause us to be more cautious. And, if we come to a place where there is resistance to engage in something, following the spirit of Gestalt: everything is data. If we notice that the client is averse to playfulness and our offer is leading to a particular reaction, that information is also something which we as coaches can work with (and it might tell us something about ourselves rather than the client!). Of course, sometimes it's appropriate to take it at face value and accept that our invitation is being declined as it just doesn't connect with our client.

The language which we use to make such invitations to try something which is often novel and might make clients feel initially vulnerable ('I'll look silly', 'I can't do this' etc.) is important. We might use phrases such as the following as an invitation to work in a playful way in service of the bigger goal; to find out, raise self-awareness, interrupt patterns and so on:

- *What if…?*
- *Shall we try…?*
- *What if we try…?*
- *Shall we improvise that a bit…?*
- *Shall we experiment with this?*

13.2 Being Playful with What a Coaching Session 'Should' Look Like

It helps to hold the questions above in our own head, even about the basic 'givens' of our work with our clients. You will see in the Bob and the Daffodils story later on, that Steve Chapman brought this approach to the assumption that the coaching session would take place in Bob's office. Suggesting a change of environment led to opportunities for Bob to experience something new, to disrupt his usual patterns in service of his coaching goals. Robert Stephenson told us how he has worked with clients in the Royal Festival Hall (a large con-cert venue in London) to dance spontaneously to stretch their comfort zones or to shout their presentations from the theatre balcony to help them not to speak so quietly and timidly. They are games that they enter into and play together. Kirsten Barske specialises in working with teams in nature including in the awe-inspiring Austrian and German mountains and sometimes in challenging weather conditions. Working together in these environments frees them from the norms and roles they inhabit in their place of work which can help raise awareness of self, others, and group dynamics. If we want to classify these examples, we could put them in the middle layer of the Be Playful Onion Model; us as coaches expressing playfulness through how/where we approach the coaching session.

The exhausted executive and time to reflect

In a similar vein, Christian van Nieuwerburgh told us of a session with a client (let's call him Javier) who was going through a lot of challenges at work and was exhausted. Rather than the 'heavy lifting' of a coaching session, they both agreed that more than anything, in that moment, Javier needed time to gather his thoughts. Often at times like this, outside of coaching sessions, Javier would pray. Christian asked him whether he'd like to use the session to do just that. To give Javier time and space, Christian would leave him alone in the room for a while, go and have a coffee giving Javier time on his own to pray, reflect and write down his thoughts. Javier glanced at Christian seeking permission and Christian could see in his unspoken response that Javier wasn't sure if that was 'allowed' especially as his company was paying for the sessions. Christian asked, 'Why not? This seems to be what is most needed right now'. In this way the session felt a bit playful. While still very much in service of Javier's needs, the usual norms had been broken. Javier fed back later that it had been a very beneficial use of his time. He had been 'given' much needed time to be alone, reflect and write to really focus on his thoughts and needs, boosted by the unorthodox, slightly naughty/special vibe. When Christian returned a while later, Javier was beaming, he had really needed that time and space to focus on his needs and thoughts. The remaining time of the session was very productive. Christian reflected that the overall effect of being playful with the expectations of the structure of the session was empowering for Javier and strengthened their coaching relationship. Christian's stance in the moment was spontaneous: this seems to be the right thing, right now, there are no 'rules' (apart from of course coaching ethics and contracting). They decided how to use the available time most productively and brought their authentic selves rather than a bag of 'shoulds'. It served Javier's needs, supported their work together and Christian enjoyed the coffee!

It's this playful holding of our own assumptions of what coaching *should* be which opens up the door for us to be more flexible and creative in holding the space in a way which may be of greater service to our clients. We've heard of a similar story from another coach who saw the exhaustion and stress cloaking his senior client when she arrived for her session. Without a long explanation, the coach suggested that instead of staying in the usual office, they would take a taxi to the nearby park. They travelled and then sat in silence, looking at the trees and the park scene for some considerable time until the client was ready and then proceeded to have a very deep and meaningful session.

Much of our work has at least for now moved online. At first glance, the restrictions of client and coach sitting at their screens for their sessions might make it more difficult to bring a playful approach. Though perhaps, it merely presents us with a challenge of being open to possibilities and not settling for the norm or routine. When working with clients 1:1, we often explore and experiment with them to discover what they would find most useful in the moment. For example, we might work with the camera off during all or some of a session, or where it is not necessary for us to see what is unfolding, we might invite them to go to a different part of the room out of camera shot (where they can still hear us) for a while or to move away from their work space for a change in perspective.

One client Stephanie worked with a few years ago was a business owner and a keen amateur artist. Let's call her Claire. She had a studio space in her garden. During a telephone coaching session, Claire was getting stuck in a cycle of thinking and Stephanie noticed that she too was being sucked into the whirl-pool. Stephanie invited Claire to move to her art space and express what was swirling around in her head on paper. There was silence on the line for a good while as Claire put the phone aside and got to work. Though Stephanie never saw the finished picture, it formed the basis for the rest of the conversation rich with metaphor and storytelling which brought about the much sought for break-through. Fast forward during Covid times, Stephanie was working with a senior leader, let's call him John. After the initial online sessions, when rapport had been built Stephanie wondered whether having these sessions in the same chair/room/layout as all of her client's virtual meetings was impacting his thinking. Stephanie encouraged him to sit at the window, away from his work desk to be able to look out over the garden and later sessions were conducted on the phone with John walking in the countryside. As well as the increasingly documented benefits of coaching in nature (and the well-being effects of moving and being outside when most of the day was spent sitting in the home office), this also allowed John and Stephanie to playfully incorporate elements of his environ-ment into the conversation to enable him to take different perspectives.

The prison governor and the rose garden

Using external spaces in creative ways can provide new insights and be liber-ating for clients, allowing them for example, to release their work personas and be more themselves, to connect in a different way and engage in a different kind of conversation. Jonathan Passmore shared a story of when he was working with a prison governor, let's call him Paul. Often in their work together, they would meet for coaching sessions at the prison or in an office. Paul would always attend in work mode: suit, tie, bunch of keys, very regimented, very focused. He was always very prepared and always did his 'homework'. Jonathan wondered (silently) whether the prison walls were metaphors for the psychological prison Paul had created for his thinking. As an experiment, their next session took place in a National Trust rose garden nearby. Jonathan hoped that this would create the space for Paul to think about different topics and bring these into the coaching session: why he had come into the job, what his motives had been and are now, his values, what he wanted to bring to the job. The rose garden setting allowed him to imagine different ways of being that might in some ways begin to enable change, taking into account the wider context, including cultural changes within his institution and how he might influence the wider system with more creativity and flexibility. Being in this environment helped Paul to liberate his thinking and widen his perspective, leading to more options and ways to move forwards.

Many of our Storytellers aren't Gestalt coaches and it's not a prerequisite for playfulness but we can see elements of Gestalt in many of the stories. As Auriel Majumdar reflected, Gestalt gives you permission and a framework to experiment and try; it's light and loose, investigative without the burden and constraints of predetermined outcome/achievement. If you are not already, becoming aware of Gestalt principles might help you to experiment and work with what arises in the moment.

The type of questions you might ask yourself before a session include:

• *What am I assuming about where and how this session should take place?*
• *Are these assumptions supporting open, expansive thinking or constricting possibilities?*
• *What opportunities for exploration and experimentation might I miss by holding these assumptions?*
• *How can I create the space for exploring and co-creating alternatives with my clients?*

On a practical note, it's also more fun and energising for us as coaches to switch off our automatic pilot and be open to different ways of doing things (especially if we're sitting in front of our computers for long stretches of time).

Jot down a few ideas about if and where there is more space for playfulness in your approach to your work (or use the space to doodle – it's yours after all)

13.3 Being Playful: Tone and Climate

Let's explore what we mean by tone and climate by reflecting on our conversation with one of our Storytellers. It was clear from our conversation with Nobantu Mpotulo that she relishes bringing playfulness into her work and her enthusiasm is infectious. Her tone, body language and energy helped create the climate for a playful conversation about playfulness. When we met for the first time (sadly, virtually, as she was in South Africa and we were in the UK), her warmth and ease meant that within moments we were all smiling, speaking freely, emergently. Nobantu's opening invitation was that she wasn't sure what she could bring to the conversation but invited us to start and see where we would go. In fact, all our conversations with our Storytellers started in a similar open way. Our conversations had little pre-planned structure and started with an invitation to talk about playfulness and how it shows up in their work without prior prompts or preparation. Holding these conversations without expectations as to structure or content created a space of warmth, openness and flow, allowing the creation of new thinking, fresh insights, and perspectives. Our conversations ended with the observation by the Storytellers that it was not only fun to talk about playfulness, but insightful, as for many, it was the first time they focused specifically on playfulness in their work. Overall, the climate and open structure allowed for playful, purposeful, and rich conversations.

We've considered at length the impact of our peripheral nervous system on our and those around us ability to access playfulness and how we can move into different states including that of playfulness (Chapters 6, 7, 10 and 11 in particular). These considerations will of course impact the tone and climate which we're creating.

Let's turn back a moment to the very beginning of conversations with our clients. Christian van Nieuwerburgh shared with us that often at the start of a session, he will ask 'where do you want to go with this?'. It conveys that the session about to unfold is very much in the service of the client and driven by their needs and in this respect, it feels to us, somewhat playful. It's a small detail, but as we know, language matters and can suggest a sense of the space which is being created and the possibilities which might be generated.

Thoughts for practice:

- The coach conveys subtly or expressly that there are opportunities for playfulness. It is primarily the coach who creates the climate and tone for those opportunities to arise and holds the space with generosity, compassion, non-judgment, and non-attachment.
- The loose structure of a session allows space for emergent conversations and insights; freewheeling and playful, yet purposeful.

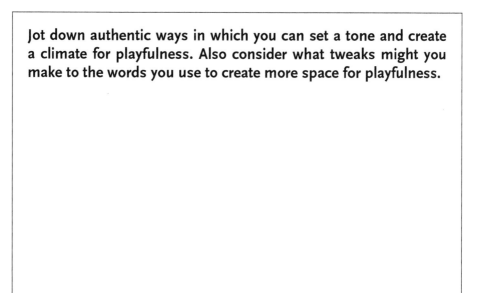

Jot down authentic ways in which you can set a tone and create a climate for playfulness. Also consider what tweaks might you make to the words you use to create more space for playfulness.

13.4 The Invitation

Assuming you are primed and open to opportunities for playfulness, there are quite a few straightforward things that you can do to start to incorporate elements of play, some of which you might well already do. A question phrased and said in a playful way, an invitation to experiment, to explore, to look at things in another way, can all be considered playful when held more lightly, tapping into curiosity and openness. The easiest way to get started, at an opportune time, is with a simple and open question along the lines of:

> Shall we play (or experiment) with this a bit to explore more?

This simple question, or something similar, invites us to step into a different space, a space of play, experimentation, and exploration. What we do in this space will vary but the climate and expectation is already implied, particularly when it is accompanied with an open, warm tone inviting curiosity. As Robert Stephenson told us: 'I know I'm being playful when I think "Let's give it a go, let's experiment"'. There is an implied lightness, unattachment, free from the expectation of perfection and getting it right, space for spontaneity; it's just play, after all, just an experiment, let's just see what it may give us or not, whatever happens, it's information we can use. This is of course, in the context of the need to ABC ('Always Be Contracting'). In all our years in practice we haven't encountered a client yet, when invited, who will not give our suggestion a go, though often we end up doing something different that we had initially expected or offered, as co-creation followed the original invitation.

Here are some more examples to invite playfulness, experimentation, and creativity:

- *Can you imagine … ?*
- *What if we explore … ?*
- *What are the different ways that we can explore or experiment with this some more?*
- *Shall we play a bit/experiment with this?*
- *Tell me what is the most ridiculous thing that has happened to you this month? (David Clutterbuck shared this as a playful icebreaker early into a session which can result in a visible easing of tension and state change in those present).*
- *Let's assume for a minute that none of this matters; what does that free you up to do? (David Clutterbuck shared this as a question which can help free up the focus from the current situation to future possibilities).*
- *What is the wildest thing you can imagine in regard to … ?*
- *If we had complete freedom, what would we do?*
- *(Christian van Nieuwerburgh suggested this question in one of our conversations)*
- *What about that gets you really excited and curious?*
- *Where is the playfulness in the system that is you and your role?*

Jot down other questions that invite playfulness and experimentation …

Where you go from these invitations will depend on factors including your client(s) and your context. You might stay in conversation or move to an experimental or embodied approach. You might invite the use of playful activities, using materials such as art, LEGO®, music or poetry. You may suggest a well-known model, tool or technique and play with it, co-creating together something which suits and supports your client in your work together.

13.5 Word Play

We have mentioned above that the words which we use are of course very important. Words have meaning, not only in the direct sense but also in the additional meanings that we associate with them. Depending on what we understand them to mean, our experiences and perspectives, maybe we love or just don't like the sound of a word. A single word might pack enough meaning for a person which can move them towards or away, to engage or disengage. During a recent workshop which we ran on incorporating play into practice, one of the participants, an experienced coach, shared her hesitancy and resistance. She told us that while she felt she *could* be playful, she wasn't *brave enough* to play. The word 'play' for her was clearly a loaded word which carried negative connotations and represented being or behaving in a way which was childish and not professionally credible. As a reminder, we have made this distinction between childlike and childish frequently. When we asked her which word could replace 'play', she responded 'experiment' without hesitation. Her demeanour changed, you could see the change in energy and possibility. By changing a single word, she was able to have a different relationship to the things getting in her way and engage more positively with playfulness. Choosing and noticing our words with care and, if we think it might be helpful, playing with words, might be just the ticket to move things forward.

We'll share a story with you to explore the possibilities of playing with words a bit further. Teresa worked with a student recently who was struggling to do the revision which she needed to do for her studies, let's call her Anne. After years of study, Anne was sick and tired of revising and she felt resistance and defeat at the mere mention of the word '*revising*'. Yet, if she was to succeed in her studies, it was crucial. As Anne shared her feelings, Teresa sensed an opportunity, she wondered whether exploration around the word 'revise' could be helpful. So she invited Anne to play with this word a little, holding the space with light curiosity and a touch of amusement. Anne accepted the invitation immediately and as they both reflected on the word, it seemed that it was very loaded, disengaging and creating all sorts of stuckness within Anne. Teresa invited her to imagine the word 'revising' objectively and separately from the act of revising and to imagine the word appearing in front of her. Teresa then invited Anne to imagine spinning the word around, seeing it in different fonts, sizes and colours and viewing it from all angles, objectively, and with the curiosity due to a new object which has just dropped down from another planet. Having done this, they then together explored the real purpose of the act of revision, the benefits it brings and its necessity. The natural progression was for Teresa to ask 'OK, how else could you describe this?'. Anne blinked, slightly tilted her head and paused for a long time. Teresa wasn't sure if Anne was thinking of alternatives or thinking that this was all a bit odd, but she held the silent space. When she was ready, Anne looked at Teresa and said in a very clear and direct voice 'Oh, I'm absorbing information' followed by a sigh of relief and a chuckle. In that moment, her whole being changed with an overall sense of relief and in what followed, she was more direct, assured and engaged. With enthusiasm and curiosity, Teresa then asked her, 'What does the term 'absorbing information' give you that 'revising' doesn't?'. Immediately, Anne replied 'I don't know' followed quickly by 'It seems easier and fresher somehow, like plants and osmosis, they absorb light effortlessly and I will do the same'. A change of word gave Anne a fresh, unburdened way to engage in the work that she needed to do. All of this took no more than 10 minutes and Anne now had a perspective which worked better for her and moved her forward.

We can infuse our sessions with playfulness by thinking about how we word our questions, how we introduce concepts, give invitations, or encourage perspective taking. In our Be Playful Onion Model, we can position this in the middle layer (expressions of playfulness). Julie Flower gives the example in the context of team coaching, of rather than asking the team what would be an idea for improvement, changing the language and asking for members to give their 'wild ideas'. She noticed that this lifted the energy and rallied the team members: *oh, if it's a wild idea, well then … .* With language, we can introduce a playful tone, even in the context of complex or challenging topics, we can encourage a childlike curiosity and search different perspectives.

Matthew Pugh told us of a session which he had with his coach where the topic was a problematic relationship at work. Matthew specialises in Chairwork (more on which below) and he was working with his coach in this way to access the part of himself who was able to give good advice on the issue. Matthew's coach played with the wording of his question and asked: 'Who is as cool as a cucumber who can manage this situation really well and engage with this guy?'. You can think of more serious ways in which he could have asked this question. However, framing it in this playful way prompted Matthew to respond with a smile 'Ryan Gosling!'. His coach invited Matthew to move to a chair to channel his inner Ryan Gosling. The rest of the session was playful and felt like mucking about and (rather than 'but'!) was hugely engaging and helpful. Thereafter, Matthew had his inner Ryan Gosling he could summon up as a quick anchor in moments of need. Matthew's experience of engaging in Chairwork himself and working in this way as a practitioner, is that the shifts which happen are completely different from rationally, cognitively discussing an issue.

Thoughts for practice:

On a general note:

- *Engaging your Whole Body, are there some words which your client loves or finds motivating? Any that they have a dislike for or find demotivating or disengaging?*
- *What assumptions are you making about the words you like/dislike?*
- *How wide is your repertoire of playful words?*

More specifically:

- *Are you/your client using words that are not useful? Do they disengage or demotivate?*
- *What is the purpose of these words?*
- *Consider exploring a word that is unhelpful objectively, create a sense of detachment (for example you can imagine, draw, model or even express the word through music or posture or dance!) so that the client can get some psychological distance from it and view it from different perspectives.*
- *What alternative words can your client come up with (they can be anything, even gibberish) that can help reframe and support engagement / empowerment/motivation?*
- *Do you notice your client or you lighting up when certain words are used? Are there any that are more engaging, empowering or have a positive effect?*

Jot down or doodle some observations here ...

13.6 Playful Anchors and Playing with Identities

The idea of having a quick reference/anchor of desired behaviour came up several times in our conversations. Neil Mullarkey shared how in the Comedy Store in London, in group workshops, Neil will invite people to come up on stage and say, 'Hello', as themselves. Often, they find it really difficult and stand on stage nervously and quietly. Neil then explains that actors find it difficult coming on as themselves too unless they embody a character. If he says '*Come on be yourself!*', it's really hard. However, inviting people to play by coming on as someone else makes it easier somehow. So, instead he will invite them to come on by saying, '*Just be Billy Connolly*', with extra reassurances of, '*just give it a go…it's a laboratory … there's no right or wrong*', and the like. Participants come on stage differently, more capable and with increased access to inner resources. Not just in the words and tone they use but notably their body language. It shows them their body can do more, they can do more than they expect once unshackled from their own persona and the limiting stories they tell themselves. Heather Simpkin shared a similar story of using the anchor of a real or imagined person to effect change. For example, if someone is wishing to feel more confident, they might bring to mind Angelina Jolie. Heather with her theatre director background will encourage the person to think about the details like an actor: how would Angelina hold herself, in terms of posture, movement, body language and so on? Trying out this way of physically embodying a more confident way of entering and being in a room for example and somatically experiencing confidence can be very effective (again, rather than discussing it intellectually).

This idea of using a different persona can be a way of injecting some levity and playfulness. During coaching sessions, asking clients, '*What would Michelle*

Obama/Barack Obama/your best friend, and so forth, say?' is a useful and quick way of seeing things from a different perspective. We can use the body for this too and invite clients to embody and/or use the voice of whomever they are helpfully bringing to mind:

- *What does that stance/posture/movement, and so forth, feel like?*
- *What does using that tone of voice/speed/pause feel like?*
- *What impact does that have on your emotions?*
- *Your thinking?*

To access a different perspective, it is sometimes helpful to include in the repertoire of alternatives sources well-known people relevant to the context at hand for example, Richard Branson and ask what they might do. Or, more playfully, what would Marge Simpson (or other cartoon character) do? Even in a 'heavy' or serious coaching conversation, this often brings a smile. You can try it with any film or historical character. Neil Mullarkey shared with us one that often provokes laughter is asking what Genghis Khan would do. (Answer: Probably kill everyone!). Using exaggerated or humorous anchors can help clients engage in a playful way to help them make sense of the world and their situation, find new perspective and a degree of lightness, all helpful for identifying options. Powerful too is to ask your client to come up with the anchor: What resonates most with them as a helpful anchor?

13.7 Metaphors

Playful and/or humorous metaphors are one of the easiest ways of incorporating more playfulness into your coaching. Metaphors are also useful gateways to shifting perspectives and the relationships to our thoughts as well as making sense of our emotions and developing more value-led behaviour. The ACT (Acceptance and Commitment Therapy) coaching approach has many inherently playful elements, and we heartily recommend ACT resources if you are looking for ways to infuse your coaching with (more) playfulness. ACT coaching draws heavily on metaphors. Well-known metaphors include working on cognitive diffusion by imagining your thoughts as leaves on a stream, passengers on a bus, or sushi on a conveyor belt. *The Big Book of ACT Metaphors*[2] is a valuable source for many metaphors and stories to use with your clients. We've got first-hand experience of how these deceptively simple metaphors or stories can have lasting impact on disrupting clients' habitual thinking/emotion/behaviour patterns and can be a real help in establishing new, value-led behaviours. The metaphors can be used for different elements of ACT, one of which is stepping into the Observing Self which we've come across several times in previous chapters. A word of caution though, make sure to check in with your client whether or not a metaphor is resonating with them (rather than you with your own lens on the world) or invite them to find a metaphor which resonates even more and together you can play with it in service of your work together.

13.8 Game of Thrones

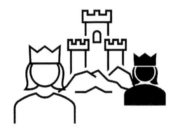

Graham Lee's client, Sally, had just been promoted to head of marketing in a large subsidiary as a result of her boss being promoted to head up sales and marketing of the parent company. New in her role, Sally felt undermined by the degree to which her former boss was going straight to other executives in the subsidiary and cutting her out of key conversations. On the day they spoke, she had hardly slept the night before with worry. She said to Graham that she was in 'a bit of a panic'. Graham saw the first priority was to attend to her triggered emotional system and to support her to find her capacity for groundedness and resourcefulness. She managed to do this readily by being invited to bring a gentle, 'playful' curiosity to her embodied experiences, to breathe with them without rushing to change them. The conversation took on a more relaxed tone, with a playful observation of what Sally's former boss could be like, especially if her boss was also feeling uncertain about her new role.

The conversation then moved a little deeper, acknowledging that Sally is female, from an ethnic minority, and younger than many of her colleagues on the executive team. Graham recognised that there was some frustration and grief about how hard she had to work to be respected as an executive. They started to explore the soreness of this and finding space for a little bit of compassion around that, while also giving space to that part of her which had a real desire to make an impact, to achieve and be successful. They had moved past the earlier jokiness but she was still playing in so far as she was moving fluidly between the tender parts of her emotional experience and how that was playing through into her current state of mind and emotion.

They started to find metaphors for what she was describing; alighting on Cersei from the Game of Thrones and playing with the idea of what would the situation be like if it was the Game of Thrones? In the series, Arya is the daughter of the Stark family, arch rivals to Cersei's family, the Lannister's. Arya, initially a naïve tomboy, small and childlike, through the story becomes an accomplished assassin. She learns to have as much impact as Cersei, despite her apparent initial inferiority. Sally was using this metaphor to playfully connect with her strength and potency – not that she was intending to assassinate her former boss!

The conversation moved to what she was going to do next. Her first response was that she needed to be very tough with her former boss. Graham asked whether this was akin to declaring war and asked whether she had the allegiance of the executive team and of the CEO. Moving to a different metaphor, was she NATO in relation to Putin? If NATO isn't strong, Putin will pick people off …

The conversation continued a little longer, Graham's client coming up with a strategy she was happy to go forward with.

Graham's story of his relatively short conversation of about 25 minutes was a wonderful example of many of the elements of playfulness in coaching which we've considered earlier in this book; sensitivity to the client's state (profoundly safe v sufficiently safe to play), a fluid, compassionate, sensitive playful conversation with laughter and tears.

Another use of metaphors is to listen for those that are used by clients during our conversations and to build on these to construct stories which they can then use to stimulate their thinking. Julie Flower told us of a session where her client, let's say Anna, who kept referring to the issues at hand and the people involved as being 'like a game of snakes and ladders' (a board game popular in the UK and Ireland where you advance when you land on a ladder and slide back down when you land on a snake head). Playfully, Julie asked what Anna's current situation would look like if it *was* actually a game of snake of ladders? Where on the board would she be? What could she see? Where on the board would the other people be? Playing with her metaphor in this way helped Anna to step back and see her situation with a degree of levity, curiosity, and humour. Suddenly a light bulb turned on, Anna took hold of the idea and started to play with it. She developed a metaphoric game which helped her explore how she could navigate the situation, climb the corporate ladder, what the impact on others of her possible actions might be and so on.

13.9 Storytelling

Throughout history, stories have been a universal way of sharing information, values, feelings, memories and so on, in a memorable and engaging way, passed down through generations to learn, understand, and connect with one another in various ways, including play. For example, seanchaí (pronounced shan-key) were traditional Irish storytellers who were for centuries, in effect, the custodians of Irish history. They travelled throughout Ireland and could recite ancient lore, long lyric poems and tales of wisdom and were in a way the search engines of fadó fadó (pronounced f'doe which means 'long, long ago' in Irish and equivalent to 'once upon a time'). The act of storytelling can be very powerful either in 1 : 1 or team coaching contexts to help clients make sense of the world either based on their direct experience or the experience of others. For example, asking members of a team or group to share stories of when they felt isolated (or very included) in a group can be a powerful way of seeing not just the professionals but the humans in the room, getting closer to a compassionate understanding of others' lived experiences. Storytelling can help move you away from the 'should' perspective to sharing information and experiences which normalise, offer insights to solutions, and build inclusion and cohesion and psychological safety. Stories can be playful ways of breaking the format of what is traditionally seen as the way in which serious conversations should be conducted. You can also be playful with how stories are shared – whether sitting down and talking, incorporating them into constellations or physical mapping exercises, using different materials, or poetry or music to give just a few examples.

Ubuntu is part of African Indigenous Wisdom which means 'I Am Because We Are'. It requires coaches to embody the following mantra: See More, Hear More, Love More, Illuminate More, Be More for the clients to Become more and Do Less. This is done with compassion, co-creation, care, curiosity, connectedness, courage and commitment to action and is aligned to the ICF Updated Core Competencies.

Nobantu Mpotulo, who has done much to spread awareness of Ubuntu Coaching, is from South Africa and told us that stories such as folklore and the Bible are an important part of her culture. She often draws on these stories by asking her coachee how a character in a particular story might relate to the coachee's situation or, she might ask what lessons the coachee can draw from a particular story. Such stories might not only provide information, but importantly, they might help the coachee relate to their situation from a different perspective.

A little while ago, Stephanie was working with a client who was thinking about how he could encourage his team to be less focused purely on specific tasks and take more ownership of the team's projects. It didn't seem directly on point, but Stephanie had a story which she'd read about that might throw some light from a different perspective and asked whether he would like to hear it, adding that it might be useful or not. Her client accepted the offer and Stephanie told the story of a research study of porters in NHS Hospitals who regarded their role in listening and talking to patients as central to the NHS's commitment to patient safety and patient care more generally. They were disrupting the restrictive prescriptions of their job description in response to their own occupational values as shaped by the dynamic context of their work.[3] Even though it was not part of their job description, many saw listening and talking to patients as part of their role. The story helped him realise that the team's context was that the system in which they were operating (the department as a whole) had also fallen into a pattern of focusing on specific projects rather than seeing its part in the wider system of the organisation and stakeholders. He realised that to affect change, he needed to have conversations not just with the individual team members, but also with various stakeholders to try to shift how the department, as a whole, approached projects.

The nature and detail of the story shared can of course vary depending on your client, culture and context and it may be true or fictional and for example, from research, books, films, songs or personal experience. Remember that you are not offering stories as the expert passing on a lesson or 'the answer' like Aesop's fables; playfulness would demand that you offer it lightly, as something which might help bring another perspective. Asking your client if any stories they know might have relevance to their situation might also prove to be a rich resource to gain fresh insights and generate new awareness.

As well as stories, individual characters, or their relationships or dynamics within a story, might also be a useful resource. Matthew Pugh shared with us that he sometimes refers to fictional characters and asks his client what that character would have to say about the topic at hand. Neil Mullarky told us how sometimes going to an extreme in a light and playful way can be useful to release tension and get things out which can then support a more level-headed and realistic approach. For example, 'I hear that you're struggling with your colleagues; what advice would Genghis Khan give you?'. The laughter which follows might give some relief from the tension surrounding the issue. You might then move onto asking what Mother Teresa might advise. The coachee's conclusions about their own potential actions might then lie somewhere in between the two extremes (or at least closer to Mother Teresa than Genghis Khan hopefully!). You might also ask your client who they can think of that can provide them with advice (again, real or fictional) and what that might be (again, a common question is to ask what your client's best friend would tell them if they were in that situation).

13.9.1 Thoughts for Practice

Questions for you:

* *Do you take the time to listen to/read/watch stories?*
* *How rich is your story library?*

Questions for your clients:

* *What story (or film, metaphor, parable, and so forth) best describes your current situation?*
* *What lessons can you draw from the story which might be useful to your current situation?*
* *What advice do you think Character X would give you about this?*
* *What do you think Character X would have to say or do about this?*
* *In this story, who do you most relate to and why?*
* *In this story, who can you think of that could provide you with the advice you require? What would they share with you?*

> **Jot down which stories have resonated with you and well-known characters (fictional or real) who might be useful to draw upon ...**

13.10 Writing

Writing, for those drawn to it, can be useful in coaching not only for reflective practice but also for engaging the imagination and creating a fruitful space for exploration and playful creativity. Teresa will sometimes invite her coachee, during a session, to take some time to write down their reflections on what has emerged for them during the session rather than inviting them to speak about it. This invitation gives the coachee time to go within and reflect in a different way than they would if they were speaking. We both often invite coachees to write about or draw (or both) the topic at hand either during a session or after. We shared Christian van Nieuwerburgh's story above when he invited his client to take time to reflect through writing. Connecting or reconnecting with writing in playful and creative ways can also be a rich resource (and fun!). Auriel Majumdar told us how she rekindled her early love of writing poetry and how resourceful and uplifted it made her feel. She was curious whether some of her coachees might also benefit from introducing poetry into their work together; they did and now Auriel runs experimental workshops to ignite your dormant inner poet.

13.10.1 Ideas for Practice

- *Let your pen flow. Invite your coachee, either in or between sessions depending on what works with the time available, to write for a period of time (10–20 mins) uninterrupted and in freestyle, allowing their pen to flow and write whatever comes to mind without stopping to think and plan. The intention is to facilitate a stream of consciousness. Explain that it doesn't need to make sense and any grammar or punctuation mistakes are irrelevant as focusing on these can block flow. What's important is to allow whatever wants to arise to do so. (This method is described in detail in Julia Cameron's The Artist's Way[4]).*
- *Write a haiku. This can be very effective to gain insight and integrate what is important.*
- *Welcome limericks, songs, poems and so on into your work, either sourcing or creating them to gain insight and reflect.*

> **Jot down forms of writing and ideas which inspire you or you want to investigate further ...**

13.11 Music

Music has the potential to be a fun, engaging and useful resource in your work. Nobantu Mpotulo told us how she sometimes invites her clients to select music to listen or dance to during their work together, to help shift states, re-energise or liberate their thinking. Music can affect the state of our nervous system, our general state (see more below), evoke memories and different perspectives, facilitate a flow state and creative thinking. Music can also help us reconnect to our hearing sense as we can sometimes become overly focused on one or two of our senses. When doing the *Five Senses Walk* exercise below for the first time, Teresa remembers she realised she had tuned out her hearing sense; during the exercise she heard the birds singing for the first time in quite a while. For working with teams or groups, there has been research into the effect on empathy[5] and the helpfulness[6] of moving together in synchrony to music (not necessarily dancing) and the results look promising. Finding ways in which groups can experience this (for example, keeping a beat, clapping or swaying if dancing is a stretch too far) might have a positive effect on empathy, helpfulness and therefore group dynamics.

13.11.1 Ideas for practice

- *Play music before and at the start of the session as your client(s) arrives and settles down, to set the tone and mood and signal the transition to a different type of space.*
- *Play music during a session to help change state, energise, calm, and so on. Remember ABC ('Always Be Contracting', not the 1980s pop band); 'Would you like some music?', 'Shall we listen to some music that seems relevant here?'. As Nobantu does, you can invite your client to get up and dance (away from the camera/with camera off if the client prefers in virtual sessions). Dancing creates a more embodied experience and can amplify some of the effects of music. It may also feel liberating to move and dance in a safe and playful space. One way to invite this is to ask, 'What does your body want to do right now?'.*
- *Tap into music to aid reflection (see Writing above) or relaxation or meditation, for example to move to a calmer state or recharge.*
- *If you know your client is musical or has a love of music, you could ask them how they would express an emotion in music or which song, or piece of music resonates with what they are saying or feeling. Or, similar to Stories above, ask what the perspective from various songs or artists/composers might be to the topic at hand.*
- *Music and particularly dancing can help support somatic coaching and dancing with your eyes closed or for virtual sessions with the camera off can help remove inhibition, strengthen mind/body awareness, and bring awareness to and release emotions.*

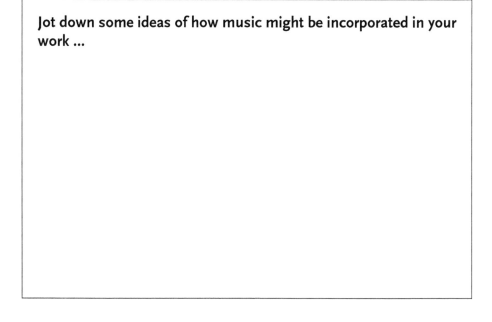

Jot down some ideas of how music might be incorporated in your work …

13.12 Movement

Let's stay with movement for a moment. We've seen above how physically moving to a different environment or moving your body can help shift patterns and habits and encourage clients to engage in a different experience and see things from different perspectives.

Remembering that we are more than our brains, engaging with the Whole Body can be a useful resource. It doesn't even have to be deliberate, related movements like the ones we've seen above. As we've seen in Chapter 11, ideas and creativity often emerge more fluidly when we allow our brains to wander as the body is moving rather than when the body is rooted to a chair. Observing this in herself led Teresa to often wonder at the start of her coaching career why so much coaching was taking place sitting down and in a conversational style. Embracing movement within coaching sessions seems to be increasingly evident and it can be incorporated in all sorts of ways. One way is to get up to draw or create a model to represent something, moving around during its creation, letting your hands do the thinking and, afterwards the client and you can both take a step back and look at the creation from a variety of angles. This allows the client to obtain more data from the different perspectives as well as having the benefit of being able to step out into different more objective observing positions.

Teresa sometimes invites clients to move either to music or enact whatever it is that they want to describe, enabling them to change their energy and states. She will often offer layered experiments which include different forms of movement to help coachees connect with different perspectives or parts of themselves in order to observe and collect more information from their Whole Body (see Chapter 10). This might look like simply placing several cards on the floor, coloured, written Post-it® notes labelled with whatever terms might be relevant, for example, levels of motivation/engagement or type of roles. Then she might invite her client to go and stand on the spot that most relates to them now and describe what's coming up for them at the Whole Body level. She might then invite them to move to another space, which might be a desired space and again explore what is emerging for them. Often her client will notice the difference from moving from one spot to another which can create data, insights and sometimes shifts or a-ha moments.

Kirsten Barske's work with teams heavily features movement. For example, at the beginning of a team coaching session, she often invites participants to move to different parts of the room to help group or connect people, starting with non-work-related categories (for example, all cat owners stand on that square) which can then be developed to include work-related categories. She uses this physical mapping to help people move, describe, and share where they are and see the dynamics with everyone else both in their little group and the group as a whole. If she's checking in on the team's motivation, for example, she might also do this with physical mapping.

In the world of constellations coaching, physical maps can be created with objects or the participants themselves to represent situations, relationships and whole systems and their internal and external connections within to name but a few and questions/exercises layered to help create more awareness and experiment.

13.12.1 Beyond Conversations Towards Bigger Experiments

There are rich and resourceful parts of us which cannot easily be accessed or conveyed by words alone, so why limit ourselves? There are many playful ways to facilitate moving beyond words which can be informative and illuminating in powerful ways to access and express the known and, as yet, unknown.

13.13 Playing with imagery, visual mapping and modelling

A picture can paint a thousand words.

Our systems, adaptive and changing, hold so much complexity. Representing parts of our inner and outer world through imagery, visual mapping, and modelling can help us make sense of complexity, communicate our perspective to others, arrive at shared understandings, see different perspectives and play with possibilities. Sometimes it is difficult to articulate something such as a situation, relationship dynamics or emotion. No matter what our creative or artistic ability, it can be easier to think, feel and express something through making a representation which can be used to explain the subjective and also see it as something objective and more psychologically distant. The act of creation might also reveal what is under the level of consciousness, making the unconscious conscious. By then stepping back and looking at the representation from different perspectives, more meaning and insights may be revealed.

> To know what you're going to draw, you have to begin drawing.
>
> *Picasso*

As we invited you to do at the beginning, you can, of course, layer different approaches in your work and not only in your work with clients but also in supervision; for example, McManus & Giraldez Hayes (2021)[7] have explored the experience of using music and creative mark-making as a reflective tool during coaching supervision.

Imagery, drawing, visual mapping, and modelling can help access thoughts, memories and connections that are not available to us through rational logical deduction alone. In LEGO® Serious Play®, we invite participants to 'think with their hands' which we looked at in Chapters 4 and 10 (and we suggest this approach is used for all methods we're considering here), in other words, like with the free-writing above, to get into flow, park your inner critic and allow your hands to do the thinking.

You can use art, pebbles, buttons, wooden pegs, LEGO® and so on, the list is endless. Nobantu Mpotulo often brings a box of trinkets to her coaching sessions that contains an assortment of little things which can be utilised for representations (of for example, feelings, people, work issues and so on). They can be used by her clients to create insight, support expression and deepen reflection. For in person work, Stephanie often brings a (surprisingly small!) bag with coloured pens, some wooden shapes (simple, organic shapes, lovely to look at and touch and useful for impromptu constellations work), paper, playdough. She brings these without expectation that any of them will be used but they are available should if required.

It is worth giving some thought as to how these are presented. Auriel Majumdar for example, remembers the first time she was invited to draw her reality in a coaching session (as client) and was offered large children's crayons which took her back to her childhood. She recalls how fabulous it was to be invited into that space and to be given permission. She experienced joy whilst working on something complex and challenging and remembers being immersed and in flow. So, if you are bringing materials, consider what type (serious, professional graphic drawing pens v brush pens for example), as we don't want to wake up our client's inner critic by feeling under pressure to create something artistic. Instead, we want to tap into the childlike joy of giving something a go and experimenting. In her earlier research, one of Stephanie's participants shared how she brought coloured pens in a Mickey Mouse pencil case to her coaching sessions. It sometimes felt a bit risky in the corporate environments of her clients but served well to help her clients feel freer in their doodling and thinking.

13.13.1 Ideas for Practice

13.13.1.1 LEGO® Serious Play®

Stephanie is a LEGO® Serious Play® (LSP) facilitator trained by the Association of Master Trainers and is a contributing editor of The LSP Magazine[8] including writing for and developing its coaching section. There are exciting possibilities of using LEGO® in 1:1 sessions and running shorter and longer workshops with groups and teams, looking at everything from supporting value-creating teams to taking a complex adaptive systemic approach to issues facing organisations. Over a longer (2 day) session with a team, you could, for example, facilitate the building of complex systems and the relationships between the team or organisation and its stakeholders, enabling facilitated role play, to respond and adapt to real or imagined challenges. One of the underlying principles of LSP is that everyone is equally listened to; in a playful way often disrupting existing group dynamics and drawing on the wisdom of the whole group rather than primarily the habitually more dominant members.

As well as learning the LSP methodology, you can of course use LEGO® bricks in many different ways with individuals and teams such as building constellations and current and future realities. The underlying premise is that by letting your hands do the thinking, you are bypassing your inner filter to go beyond the restrictions of rational, logical thinking. Working in this way and opening channels of curiosity and exploration you can gain access to and represent thoughts, ideas and insights which might otherwise have stayed uncovered (and in teams, communicate these in an effective, relatable and memorable way).

13.13.1.2 Drawing and Art

There are many ways to incorporate art into your coaching (for inspiration, see, for example, Jen Gash's book, *Coaching Creativity*[9] and her online course, or Anna Sheather's book, *Coaching Beyond Words*[10]).

A fun group/team exercise to get going is to divide the group into pairs and spend a few minutes drawing a 'rubbish portrait' (call it what feels appropriate) by drawing with the non-dominant hand. Another is to ask pairs to take turns talking and listening; the listener closes their eyes and draws what they hear and afterwards they share their picture. The aim is to let go of trying to get it right, not to be concerned about how you or others might judge you/your art and to have fun in the process.

Here is a longer exercise:

- At the outset, it's important to emphasise to your client that this isn't about artistic or creative ability; we are working in the abstract and if you can make a mark on the page (or whatever you're using), you have all the ability you need for this.
- *TIP*: If there is resistance or fear of judgement, draw some images yourself: a stickman, a simple flower, or similar (be playful and not 'perfect'!) and ask what it might represent. It's a quick way of showing that we can all represent things, no artistic merit is required but what matters is getting stuck in and putting the images/representations on paper.
- Invite your client to draw their reality as a garden. Ask them to draw what they are seeing/feeling/doing, and so on. Invite them to describe the elements of the drawing (some insights might come from this alone) and when finished, ask them to look at the drawing from different perspectives (near/far, and the like) to notice any patterns, relationships or meaning (for example, in relation to the use of colours, symbols, sizes, positions, and so forth) from these perspectives.
- In teams, you might ask them to reflect on their drawings in pairs or as a team. Remember to be aware of potential discomfort, fear of being judged, psychological safety in the room; if all the drawings are laid out, you might invite the team to reflect on the similarities or common threads (to avoid individuals feeling different or singled out – unless of course you are celebrating outliers and diversity of what's emerging, it'll be a judgment call given the group dynamics and context).
- If it's relevant, you can then ask them to put that aside and start anew representing what might be; for example, their ideal self or a realistic positive future at meaningful milestones. After they have reflected on this (in the same way as the first drawing), ask them to compare the two.
- What small steps could they take to bridge the current to the future/ideal?

13.13.1.3 The Roundabout of B*ll*cks

Emma Skitt shared a very relatable story with a punchy phrase which emerged during team coaching when she invited participants to draw their reality as a garden. This exercise is helpful for uncovering and representing things in a different way from conventional conversation and may yield new insights and information. The insight and phrase which emerged from Emma's session is a great example.

As in our exercise above, once the teams' drawings are complete, the main aim is to step back and reflect on what has been represented both by the individuals and collectively in order to gain insights. It's important to emphasise that the participants need to be clear that this isn't an exercise in judging artistic merit (particularly in a group setting, participants can feel self-conscious about being judged or judge themselves on this). Once the pictures are ready, the coach encourages observation of noticeable elements, such as use of colours, symbols, size, proximity and so on. We saw above how stepping back and looking at the pictures from different perspectives can also give new information and meaning.

Before we share more, we hope the title of this story doesn't offend. We did try to play with the words, but the feedback we received was that deviating from the original had the effect of diluting the overall impact and meaning.

Back to Emma's story then. She was working with a team in a manufacturing firm. One of the team included a roundabout in his drawing. When asked by his colleagues what this represented, he replied, pointing to parts of the drawing: 'This is us and that is the roundabout of b*ll*cks we are always on when trying to make decisions!' On hearing this, the team, including their leader roared with laughter and there was a deep appreciation of the insight and honesty. The visual image and its meaning cut through and got to the heart of the matter in a relatively short and memorably clear way. It helped articulate some of the challenges this team had.

Emma noticed the unifying effect it had on the team and the atmosphere in the room. There's a well-known saying: 'You name it, you tame it' and his drawing clearly had hit the nail on the head. Emma also noticed the physical difference she observed in the creator of the roundabout image after he had shared his drawing as the lack of team decisiveness had been a real source of frustration. When she returned a year later, the term, 'roundabout of b*ll*cks', had made its way into the team's culture and was helpful for the team to use to call out and address old habits of indecisiveness if they reappeared.

You're not limited to drawing of course, we invite you to explore different ways of mark-making or for example, collage. During one session, a client with whom Teresa worked, noticed that there were lots of doors and doorknobs in the collage she had made which led to the insight that a transition was underway with new doors opening and others closing.

13.13.1.4 Draw Your Team as a Character

During an initial session with a team, Teresa asked each of them to draw a character representing their team in order to get them to think about: the team as a whole and how it saw itself and importantly, how it was seen by others and how this impacted how other teams related to and connected with it. Everyone embraced the invitation to play and to show and explain their image to the rest of the team. As each character was explained, the team noticed a pattern emerging. The team leader went last and addressed the elephant in the room, pulling all the themes together. Teresa then invited them to individually come up with a character which might represent the team after it had addressed some of the issues which had been surfaced by the discussions. The team gained new insights and left feeling energised and ready for change. One of the team members later merged all the new images into a collage and it became their team logo which they put on the office wall and their online space.

13.13.1.5 Post-it® Notes

Using Post-it® notes with a group or team is also very effective. Invite one person to describe their topic. The rest of the group listens silently and then draws images inspired by what they heard on the notes, taking turns to describe them. The aim is not to provide answers but to gather representations of what was coming up for others in the group when the person was speaking. The speaker then reflects on all the images and uninterrupted shares any new insights and thoughts.

13.13.1.6 Collections of Art Cards and Images

In a workshop for coaches, we invited them to select an image card which best represented their practice and why. One chose a beautiful oriental bridge as it represented how her practice was like a bridge, facilitating her clients crossing from one side to the other. She hadn't thought about her work in that way before and this insight gave her more clarity around a core part of her work and what was meaningful to her.

13.13.1.7 Playing with Image Cards Visual Mapping

There are many types of image cards available, and you can of course be playful in your choice or make your own. Here is an idea of one way of using them:

- Lay out the cards. Invite your client to select the image(s) that is most relevant to the area of focus and to place somewhere.
- Invite them to pick out other relevant cards, taking their time to reflect why each image resonates and then place them near or far in relation to the original card (like a constellation).
- Ask them to reflect on the visual map in front of them; the whole, where individual cards are and their relationship to others (near/far, clusters, and so forth), any patterns in colours, symbols, inferred meanings, and the like.
- What insights might be found in relation to the topic at hand?
- Next ask them to step back and change position and from this new position(s), ask if there is anything new now emerging.
- Then ask your client to select images which would be helpful to move them in relation to the topic and repeat until they have finished.
- You could ask them to create a visual map from these new cards and then repeat the earlier steps.
- Finally, you could then ask them to compare both visual maps and explore whether anything helpful might emerge.

13.13.1.8 Modelling and Using Objects

Objects or 3-D representations offer an alternative way of aiding reflection, communication, understanding and insight. Nobantu Mpotulo carries a little box of things with her to draw on her in work and Christian van Nieuwerbergh told us that when he started as a coach, he used to bring a box of small random objects with him (for example, ball, LEGO®, little characters, playdough, string) to help his clients with reflection and seeing different perspectives. It's effective online too in 1:1 sessions or with groups or teams; we have run (virtual) workshops inviting participants to use objects at hand to build representations which then form the basis for reflection and discussion.

The executive and the Russian dolls

Auriel Majumdar has inherited a set of Russian dolls which she uses in some of her coaching sessions. She's found that they have opened a new way of talking with clients and to uncover new information. She shared with us a story of working with, let's say, 'Jo' who came to the session with a concern about a situation at work. Auriel offered that Jo might use the Russian dolls to illustrate herself and the other players in the scenario, to show Auriel what it was like to be in this tricky situation. Jo accepted and Auriel asked her to arrange them without explaining each step to Auriel and using her hands to do the thinking. Jo was sitting on the floor and Auriel on a low sofa. After Jo arranged the Russian dolls, Auriel and Jo turned and chatted. Jo shared how exposed she felt in this work situation, as if she was on stage. When they turned, they saw the dolls, and both jokingly asked whether the dolls had moved since the way in which they were arranged precisely captured Jo's situation. Exploding with laughter, they ridiculed the notion that the dolls could have moved but also were astonished by how they captured what Jo had shared. The moment was full of joy and silliness. It gave them a new way, a door into new data and allowed their work to continue with deeper insight.

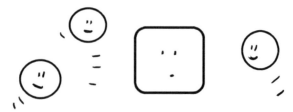

I'm a square surrounded by a team of bouncy balls

Christian shared a story with us about a session in which his client gained insight into himself and team dynamics through the use of playdough. He came to the session to find better ways of working with and connecting with his team. Most of them were extroverts and formed connections by involving each other in their social lives, attending each other's weddings, birthdays, and parties. The client felt uncomfortable with this, wanting to keep his private and work lives separate, staying true to himself but also wanting to build better work relationships. He wasn't an obviously playful person, but Christian remembered he had previously mentioned that he used to like playing with playdough when he was a child. He accepted Christian's invitation to experiment with playdough to see what he might create while thinking about this team dynamic. As he talked, he created a neat, perfectly formed cube. Christian asked what insights emerge from looking at the playdough model. A clear metaphor emerged: 'I'm a square surrounded by a team of bouncy balls'. This led to a number of realisations around the benefits of pushing yourself a bit out of your comfort zone (what would it be like to round the corners of the cube a little?) but also accepting and respecting differences (the world needs both cubes and bouncy balls). The client asked to take the little playdough cube home with him and the session marked a turning point in their work together; both in terms of insights during the session but also when they spoke some months later, the client had softened some of his edges.

While we can bring materials with us, it's also possible (and fun!) to work spontaneously with what's available in the environment. Stephanie sat with a client (let's say, 'Richard') in a trendy but small and windowless office. The conversation felt quite transactional and superficial. As Richard spoke about the issues which he wanted to address, Stephanie spotted a jar of sweets nearby. She invited Richard to build a constellation of the current relevant relationships using the sweets. She then invited him to build a constellation of prominent relationships in his university years and also in his family of origin. Looking at the three constellation systems he had built with the sweets, Richard sat back and for the first time saw that he was finding himself in repeated patterns of relationships and that his current concern mirrored this repeated pattern. It gave him the insight to start thinking about how changes in his own thoughts and behaviours might influence his situation.

13.14 Stepping into Playfulness

What do you picture when you think of children at play? They are in flow, fully engaged in the moment with their heart, mind and body. When we move beyond conversation to experiencing playfulness, we cannot help but engage our emotions. As coaches, we can then see these emotions as sources of information and insight. Inspired by Gestalt and somatic coaching, we can also include the body (ours and our clients') as a further rich resource.

13.14.1 Ideas for Practice

13.14.1.1 *Put on the 'Curiosity Glasses' Experiment*

'Curiouser and curiouser!' Cried Alice (she was so much surprised, that for the moment she quite forgot how to speak good English).

Lewis Carroll

You can use a pair of prop glasses (if you want to have fun, in different shapes and colours to represent 'curiouser' or rose-tinted glasses) or imaginary glasses. If using more than one, different glasses can have different lenses through which to see the world. Explain to your client that as soon as they put on the curiosity glasses, they will become curious – as if they are seeing and thinking about things for the first time – about everything which they see, feel, and hear which is relevant to the topic at hand. The glasses let you connect fully to the superpower of curiosity and overcome assumptions and find hidden beliefs. Invite your client to put the glasses on and have a play with them at first, testing them out on an example, whether tangible or intangible. Then go back to the topic at hand and invite them to reconsider it through the curiosity glasses prompting such questions as *'What might really be going on here?'* and

'*What do I have to believe to assume that?*'. The client can then wear (real or imaginary) different glasses to see what different perspectives are generated and insights emerge.

> If you can change the way you look at things, the things you look at change.
> *Dr Wayne Dyer*

13.14.1.2 *Five Senses Walk*

> When you walk, arrive with every step. That is walking meditation. There's nothing else to it.
> *Thích Nhất Hạnh*

Take a short walk (or invite your client to do this with or without you) outdoors, in a safe place where you can wander freely without distraction. As you are walking, bring your attention lightly to your body (feel your feet touch the ground, the pressure, the movement as you shift your weight, your breath, and so on). Give yourself a moment to get used to this. Pretend that you are a child in this environment for the first time or a video camera capturing what you see and hear and make a detailed note of what you feel, smell and taste. Pretending in this way will help you focus on the present experience and not get caught up in your thoughts. You might notice a beautiful yellow rose bush, you look properly at the bush, the different leaves, colours and shapes and maybe smell the sweet fragrance. Looking more deeply, you notice the details of the flowers or the light reflecting on the leaves, you might hear a slight rustling as the wind passes through and feel the soft touch of the petals. If any thoughts or inner narrative arise, gently observe them, like clouds passing overhead, and go back to what your senses are picking up in this moment. After 5 minutes (or more – whatever is right for you), reflect on what you noticed and check in with your Whole Body and notice how you are feeling.

13.14.1.3 *Body Talk*

A simple way to access more than our thinking is to invite exploration and curiosity of how thoughts are linked to emotions which then show up in our bodies: '*Where can you feel this in your body right now?*' and, '*what does that tell you? Do you want to sit with this for a while?*'. These invitations and questions can be offered playfully and depending on how you work, you might like to invite your client to describe the feeling (density, shape, colour, and so on; once again, this can be done playfully) and breathe around the feeling and if appropriate, gradually through it. You can tap into metaphor, imagination and breathing and body connection. We both worked with clients (predominantly women) who after some coaching sessions realise that they don't feel like they have a voice, and their underlying need is to be heard. We have worked with them to recognise where they feel this and to release the feeling, allowing them to move on and consider what behaviours might help them to do what they can to find their voice. It can also be helpful to change perspective by asking: '*What does your heart (or gut) think/have to say about this?*' Taking time to consider this question can lead to a surprising amount of new information from different perspectives. We felt it important to highlight the possibility of incorporating the Whole Body as generally when you are fully engaged in playfulness and in flow, you tend to be absorbed and fully engaged in the experience – heart, mind and body. Recognising this and tapping into the information which can be collected from the Whole Body can be a rich resource.

13.14.1.4 *Playing with States*

Our dogs' abilities to switch between a state of rest into bounding play inspires us. We only have to say, 'let's go for a walk' and their lethargy is replaced with high energy. Our states too can change quickly with the right stimulus (see Chapters 6, 10 and 11). One such stimulus is people around us; when others (especially babies or children) laugh it's hard to suppress a smile or giggle and children's distress is contagious too. We looked at emotional contagion briefly in Chapter 6 and 7 and with awareness, you can notice the mood of a room and how it affects us. We can apply logic and reasoning to understand why we're in a particular state and what could move us to another, or we could find other ways. Going for a walk in nature, shinrin-yoku ('forest bathing'), dancing, exercising are all ways in which we can change states. We can incorporate playfulness with dancing, fun music, activities resonant of childhood play, take part in laughter yoga or on the other end of the spectrum, meditate or do some restorative yoga.

The executive creating 'Calmly Joy'

Teresa relates: *I was working with a client, let's call her Anne. Some sessions into our work together, Anne revealed that she had developed social anxiety after working from home and was now finding it difficult to work in groups. I asked her if she would like to try a small experiment to experience state changes and to explore if this might be useful for her. Before we began, I spent a little time explaining the concept of states. There was little room for movement where we were, so I asked Anne to imagine an orb in front of her and Anne started to build the orb with light guidance from me. Once Anne visualised this orb, I asked her what state she would most like to experience, and Anne replied 'calm'. I asked which colour represents calm for her while I cultivated a calm state and tone of voice. Anne replied 'yellowy orange, like a warm sun but one you can look at and makes you feel joy'. We spent a short time building this up, how it feels and what it looks like. Once the orb was sufficiently tangible for Anne, I asked if she would like to make it bigger and grow it more, with even more calmness, warmth, and joy. By now we were both feeling calm and glowing with a quiet joy. Finally, I asked her if she wanted to immerse herself in the orb. Anne imagined herself completely immersed and sat 'bathing' like this for some time, in silence. The room and atmosphere were filled with this calm warmth. She shed a few gentle tears as a feeling of relief washed over her. This spontaneous, playful, experiment showed her it was possible to change states through imagination in a relatively short time (20 minutes); nothing else had changed in the outside world but how she felt had changed. As we brought the experiment to a close, I asked her if she would like to name it, so we could refer to it in future. She paused for a second before responding 'it's my calmly joy'. We were able to use this in later sessions to move her more swiftly into that state. She shared the relief of knowing that she could access this state and how this experiment helped address something which she had been struggling with for many years. I have since used this with others with similar effect.*

Other practical ideas for the coaching space include:

- *Stepping into safety and connection.* As in the calmly joy story above, experimenting with clients to access and experience different states.
- *What is your playfulness power move?* Amy Cuddy PhD is perhaps the best known of the three researchers who started a wave of interest in the impact of postures on our emotions and behaviours. The original research[11] concluded that by assuming two simple one-minute poses, you can embody power and instantly feel more powerful and this has real-world, actionable implications. There has been a flurry of research in the intermitting years and the current consensus is that posture does matter when it comes to subjectively experienced feelings of power.[12] Building on this, we invite you to create your signature playfulness move. We've experimented with this and have found short moves/poses (and even imagining adopting them) can help us feel more playful.

13.14.1.5 *Playing with Time*

> I will live in the Past, the Present, and the Future. The Spirits of all Three shall strive within me. I will not shut out the lessons that they teach.
>
> *Ebenezer Scrooge (Charles Dickens)*

Imagine having a key to your very own time machine. The essence of play is looking at situations from different perspectives and possible imagined outcomes. Time travel lends itself beautifully to this. To be fair, we need to make do with imagined time travel, but when facilitated in a light, playful and experimental way, it can nevertheless give us an ability to witness, explore, experiment with different perspectives, and help find clarity and insight. Ideas for work with clients include:

- Building on the 'miracle question': If you had a time machine, how would this help you? What time would you travel to and why? How would you know the issue had been resolved? What would you feel, do, think differently? What would other people notice?
- Think back to yourself as a child (you might need to imagine a happier, more playful child, in which case, we send you compassion), what would this child say to you about the issue at hand? Nobantu Mpotulo sometimes asks her clients for stories from their childhood which might have relevance to the issue at hand, helping them to tap into their inner resources, insights, and creativity. Or alternatively, tapping into another child's perspective can also give them that playful insight. She told us a story when working with one senior client who was very serious, non-emotional and wishing to be creative. She knew his young son was very playful and full of life and she asked in a playful way 'What can you learn from your son?'. This simple playful question had a transformative effect as he tried to have a more playful perspective and get in touch with his heart, as he knew his son would. This different way of approaching things stayed with him and was noticed by his staff.
- This playful experiment is inspired by Scott Giacomucci's book *Social Work, Sociometry, and Psychodrama*.[13] Here, we are focusing on your future playful self but you could replace this with another future version of yourself. We invite you to imagine a point in the future where you are your playful self. Take a moment to imagine this. Now write a letter from your future playful self to your present self. In the letter include what it is like, what it has given you and some lessons you have learned. At the end of the letter include one thing that your present self can do to embark upon a more playful way of being.

- A more advanced technique would be to invite the client to walk their timeline or different versions of their timeline towards a more playful future. This does require skill and experience on the part of the coach as it may bring up difficult issues for the client.

13.14.1.6 Playing with Perspective: The External World

Just as we can play with increasing our curiosity, we can find playful ways of stepping out of our goldfish bowl and see the world from various angles and different perspectives with the potential for new information, lightness, perspective, new understanding, awareness and insight. We have touched on this in *Playful anchors and playing with identities* above. Other experiments include:

- *Trying on someone else's shoes:* Use these techniques to tap into different external personalities to gain a fresh perspective, shift energy, bring some levity and perhaps gain new information and insight. You can be playful with your clients as to who you choose: Christian van Nieuwerburgh showed us a little toy Yoda with a quizzical, wise, open face, which he sometimes shows to clients as he asks, 'What would Yoda ask/think/do?'. Stephanie has a Finnish figure of a wizard with a long white beard and a button nose, a handy prop for 'What would your inner wizard think/do/ask?'. Teresa likes to use Deadpool as a different perspective sometimes (he doesn't take himself too seriously). Clearly these work best if your client understands the childlike character you're referring to and asking your client who they might suggest, as a great resource for them to tap into might be even more powerful.
- *Connecting with a childlike approach:* We shared Nobantu's story above about the power of tapping into a childlike perspective.
- *Tapping into ridiculous or extreme personalities:* David Clutterbuck and Neil Mullarkey both shared stories with us of helping clients to access ridiculous or extreme perspectives in a playful and lightly provocative way to help bring levity or perspective, for example, what would Genghis Khan's advice be about leading your challenging team members?
- *Using the environment:* Looking around your environment for inspiration of different perspectives can be very powerful. Stephanie: I sometimes encourage clients to play with how we work together; for example, a client who spent most of his days in virtual meetings began by finding a different spot in his house to sit during sessions, next to a window overlooking the garden (so that there was a break from the work/meeting mindset). After a few sessions, we switched to telephone coaching so that he could use our

time together to walk in the surrounding countryside to help his thinking and reflection by broadening his perspective and moving. During one session, he felt stuck about what to do about an issue and was looking for advice and insight (I dodged the request for advice and focused on helping *him* find insight). I asked him where he was now. He had walked to the top of a hill and described a beautiful oak tree nearby. It felt a bit risky given his professional role and title, but Stephanie asked in a light way, what would the tree think? The tree had the triple advantage of lon-gevity, being tall so having an overview as well as standing on a hill so having an even more expansive perspective of the surrounding landscape. It was an invitation to step into a different perspective, offered lightly and without attachment. We had worked with metaphors previously and he thought for a while in silence (I held the silence though wondered whether the question had landed). Then the floodgates of his thoughts opened. We reflected afterwards on the impact of taking the tree's per-spective. I asked whether he could name the tree so that he had access to this perspective at other times. In a later session, he shared how he had been wrestling with a work challenge and had asked himself what the tree would think, and this had proved very useful to him. I think one of the reasons why it was so impactful was that it came after we had built rapport and an understanding of how he liked to learn/think. Also, the tree's per-spective was offered lightly and he was given plenty of time to think and develop how this might be a helpful alternative perspective for him and his habitual ways of thinking.

13.14.1.7 *Playing with Perspectives: The Internal World*

Here are a few different ideas and approaches to playing with perspectives in your clients' internal world:

- We considered Intentional Change Theory in Chapter 7 in which the ideal self is the driver for intentional change[14] (a recent paper looks at this as a dynamic rather than static concept).[15] With help from questions form the coach, the client is able to build a strong picture of their ideal self – an imaginative and creative holistic dream not a forecast, including passion, purpose, values, and identity.[16]
- Ethan Kross, in his book *Chatter*,[17] writes of his research and practical ways in which you can use playful approaches, for example, speaking to yourself in the third person or asking what your superhero/alter-ego would

do in a situation, to create psychological distance from unhelpful internal dialogue. Our clients whom we've shared these ideas with have found them very helpful.

- Working with multiple selves in the present context, the Disney Creativity Strategy (details are readily available including online) allows the coachee to access their inner dreamer, critic, and realist, often untangling these different perspectives and helping to generate clarity of thought and insight.

Many coaches are familiar with Chairwork (sometimes referred to as Meta-Mirror technique): physically sitting in different chairs and engaging in imaginary dialogue with others. This involves literally sitting in the different perspectives including the observer's, opening up the possibility of playing with extremes or saying what needs to be said, and finding a range of possibilities or letting different aspects of yourself speak and listen to each other. Chairwork has roots in psychodrama, and its founder, Jacob Moreno, came up with the idea while watching children being playful and role playing in the gardens of Vienna in the first half of the twentieth century. He realised that it may be helpful not simply to talk about problems but to bring problems to life through action, spontaneity, and role-playing.

Through attending some of Dr Matthew Pugh's training and speaking with him for this book, we've come to realise that Chairwork techniques are in fact seen by many clinicians as amongst the most powerful therapeutic tools and has been incorporated in a range of approaches including cognitive-behavioural therapy. Matthew trains clinicians and coaches, has published numerous articles and his book *Cognitive Behavioural Chairwork: Distinctive Features*[18] is a practical and very informative resource. Moving beyond imaginary dialogues with others, we have a rich resource of alternative perspective within us; Miller Mair's[19] rich evocation of the 'Community of Selves' reminds us that all too often we can give one part of ourselves the bulk of the airtime (often unquestioned) without letting the more marginalised parts be heard and understood too (this brings to mind as well the psychotherapeutic approach of Internal Family Systems). It was eye-opening for us how Chairwork can be used for internal dialogues, for example, with your inner critic and as the dialogue unfolds, powerful changes in your feelings, thoughts and perception of others can take place. A nod to the coaching/therapy boundary here and the need to work within your capability as a coach. How is this relevant to playfulness? We come back again to our point that the spirit in which something is facilitated or held, and the tone and nature of the questions can infuse a technique with playfulness.

'Hello Niggle'

Teresa relates: *A client I worked with, let's call her Sam, was plagued by a recurring 'niggle' – self-doubt and second-guessing which opened up rabbit holes of rumination. An issue from work which had been resolved might pop into her head months later bringing with it anxious emotions. It was taking away from her ability to be present in the moment, making it hard to appreciate moments such as her son's birthday party or concentrate at work. I offered that we try a playful experiment to get a different perspective. I wasn't sure what exactly we'd end up doing but we'd be playfully curious, and we contracted for this. You could already see a slight shift and relief in Sam's voice. We were working online, and Sam's space was limited. I asked Sam if she could name her experience and she replied 'Niggle'. I asked her to point to where Niggle was in the room and to visualise and describe it. Sam said it was a jelly-like character, green with a cartoon face. I facilitated a conversation between Sam and Niggle and asked what Niggle needed to share that we didn't already know. Sam came to understand Niggle's intention to protect her and they agreed on a few action points for Sam at work. Afterwards, Sam reflected that knowing that Niggle's primary aim was to protect her, she changed her relationship to it, realising that its voice had gotten increasingly loud as it hadn't been given attention. Sam changed her relationship to Niggle and therefore to a part of herself. She felt lighter and relieved and subsequently Niggle didn't show up again.*

Stephanie has also used Chairwork for 'outer' as well as 'inner' dialogues; holding the space in a respectful, compassionate and playful way. It is invariably a powerful experience with feedback from clients that the playful approach enabled them to try something which felt silly and uncomfortable for them at the time or at the beginning but caused a real shift for them. Playfulness can also help us keep within the coaching/therapy boundary where relevant.

Time for another story …

13.14.2 Ambassador and Gremlins

Emma Skitt shared a playful activity which she uses to great effect with individuals, teams, and large groups to access the ambassador and gremlin we all hold within us, acknowledge the roles they play and work with them. The feedback she gets is enthusiastic with serious learning and transformation occurring in a short period of time and the experience staying with individuals and teams long afterwards. Emma developed the 'angels and demons' type activity by combining the concepts of the Gremlin (Carson, 1983[20]) and the Future Ambassador (Smith, 1997[21]). The Gremlin is our self-limiting inner narrative and the Ambassador the advocate for a successful future. She has seen that if the activity is offered in a playful and practical way, clients are able to engage with it even more to more powerful effect.

With individuals: Invite your coachee to imagine or draw their Ambassador and Gremlin. Invite them to be specific in their descriptions, adding as much detail as possible to make it sufficiently tangible to be able to connect with it (for example, what it looks like, its characteristics, its posture and gait, the noises it makes, its voice, even the kind of food it eats). It can work well and embed more strongly when you give them ridiculous or exaggerated features, use non-corporate language, and even make it physical by, for example, enacting both. They can then be drawn upon in whatever ways are useful in the session. For example, when considering the topic at hand, invite the Ambassador to comment and encourage from a successful future/advocate point of view and the Gremlin from a perceived current reality/critical point of view.

In teams and groups: Divide into pairs asking them to draw or imagine their Ambassadors and Gremlins as above. You can also ask them to form two lines facing each other, one line the Ambassadors, the other the Gremlins. Give them the same task/dilemma and ask them to take turns (all Ambassadors at the same time and then all the Gremlins or vice versa) in speaking from that perspective. You can encourage voice and physical engagement as above. The different energies and noises different aspects of this creates is interesting and can be useful to reflect on with the group.

Emma emphasises it is important to build up the feeling of safety sufficiently before this activity, so that participants feel relaxed enough to engage in front of others. Usually, Emma builds up to this activity towards the end of a two or three day programme so that there is sufficient psychological safety for participants.

Virtual version: Emma has adapted this for an online group/team activity. To support sufficient psychological safety, there is clear contracting, and it is offered as an experiment. Emma might ask if participants are up for a game to experiment with our inner gremlins and ambassadors for seven minutes and she will be guided by the group chat response. If it is agreed to go ahead, she explains the role of the Gremlin. One person volunteers to be the Gremlin and the rest of the group type in the chat what the Gremlin should say about the topic at hand. The volunteer may put on a funny voice or embody the Gremlin, using their own initiative and guided by the group. The same is done for the Ambassador. The group/team is then guided in its reflections of the experience; it is a great way to give voice to different perspectives in an engaging, playful, and memorable way.

13.15 Improv and Other, Bigger Experiments

13.15.1 Improv

Improv demonstrates many of the qualities of playfulness which we've repeatedly come back to in this book, including experimentation, exploration, working with what's in the space at that moment in a flexible, spontaneous, and authentic way. There are a number of books on improv in the contexts of organisations and *Training to imagine: Practical improvisational theatre techniques to enhance creativity, leadership, teamwork and learning*[22] contains a collection of ideas for improv exercises for applied work.

An easy exercise which we've referred to earlier in the book is the Morph Ball which works in groups, online or in person. It can help people to 'arrive' and connect. In essence, you take it in turn to throw an imaginary ball to a selected member of the group and miming its characteristics (size, weight, consistency, and shape) as you hold and throw it. You can also ask participants to add an imaginary sound which the ball makes as it's thrown. The person catching it receives it with the same characteristics (and sound). The receiver then gives the ball other imagined characteristics and throws it to someone else (with a new sound). The idea is for the morph ball to be passed fluidly and at a pace which is comfortable for the group (they might need a little support to keep the pace going). This works online if participants have their names visible on their screens and the person throwing calls out the name of the recipient as they throw. If you want to add reflection afterwards, you could, for example, ask the group to think about what the game felt like, what was hard and easy and what surprised them.

13.15.2 The Character Compass with Playfulness Experiment

Here is an experiment inspired by Graham Lee's Character Compass (see Chapter 5) to give you an embodied experience of connecting more with playfulness, particularly with the view to preparing for playful practice:

- In a safe and comfortable space, turn your attention within, to your breath and to the present moment, as we prepare to focus on you and playfulness within you.
- Firstly, bring your awareness to your feet. Feel connected to the earth, grounded and stable with every breath you take. Like the roots of a tree, soak up all the stability, security and respect you need. From the ground, you remember your playful practice will be respectful, grounded, and in service of your client(s) and any goal they might bring to your session.
- Now with every breath in, like a tree expanding its branches, you open your arms and invite in spaciousness, openness, and warmth. Allowing any personal distractions to move aside as you become more centred, open, curious, even more secure, and present.
- Lastly, bring your attention to your head and look upwards and outwards. Connect fully within yourself and ready yourself to be present for another. Turn on your ability to be even more focused, present, warm, spacious, open, outward, seeking, exploring and overall playful. You are ready to explore and walk fully with your client(s).
- Stay in this space for a moment and explore what is needed within you to be grounded, spacious, warm and exploring and playful.
- Finally, bring your awareness back to the room and reflect on what you experienced.

13.15.3 Bigger Experiments

Using materials such as those we've mentioned can help structure larger workshops for groups and teams. The movement, experience, and new insights gained by such formats can lead to sustained change and improvements in psychological safety. Once you have experienced something especially with others, you can't 'un-experience' it and it can alter the group norms for the better, especially if we as coaches create the space for reflecting on and integrating the learnings from the experience.

13.15.4 Bob and the Daffodils

Bob, a financial director in a London City firm, sought coaching to improve his public speaking. At first glance, Bob lived up to the stereotype of a no-nonsense suited and booted corporate director. Restrained by the idea of how a corporate director should behave, Bob was getting feedback that his public speaking didn't engage his colleagues or wider audiences, who often switched off when he spoke, finding his manner stiff and boring. As Bob spent most of his day in his office, Steve Chapman, his coach, suggested that some of their coaching sessions would take place outdoors, to leave Bob's normal environment and create opportunities for something different.

A few sessions in, Bob and Steve go for a walk in a nearby park and Bob talks about how he might improve his overall delivery. Steve notices that he is getting bored and disinterested with Bob's use of very jargony corporate language and focus on talking purely about business and Steve's empathy with Bob's audience members grows. Steve continues to listen and rather than dismiss his boredom and disengagement, uses his internal felt experience as information (or 'self as instrument' as it's known in Gestalt), turning his attention towards it. As his boredom grows, so in parallel, does his curiosity and excitement; now we have something to work with! Steve feels the beginnings of an experiment bubbling up. But will Bob play?

Next to the path they are walking along, Steve notices a host of golden daffodils stretching out into the distance. Not yet quite sure of what is going to emerge, Steve asks Bob whether he might try an experiment. This is not totally unexpected; during their chemistry meeting, they had agreed that Steve might suggest ad hoc experiments throughout their coaching sessions. Bob agrees. To Bob's surprise, Steve lies on his front amongst the daffodils inviting Bob to see the daffodils as his audience and speak to them as he might his corporate teams. Bob, a bit unsure of what he's to make of this turn of events, plays along and starts giving a speech to the daffodils. Meanwhile, Steve starts moving the daffodils (gently of course*) and giving them different voices as they talk amongst themselves: 'What's he saying, I don't understand?', 'This is boring', 'How is this relevant to me?', 'Shall we sneak out to lunch', and the like. Steve was using playful humour in a live and authentic way, not acting, or trying, but channelling a possibly repressed part of himself in that moment.

Bob hears the chatter of the daffodils as he's giving his presentation. He starts to change the way he's saying things, there's a change in his demeanour and body language, his hands are getting more animated. He's trying to engage the daffodils, to stop their side-chat and is starting to get annoyed. Although he's engaging in the experiment and taking steps to adapt his way of communicating, he's still holding on to his stiff corporate persona. The daffodils remain unimpressed and continue their unrest. Finally, one daffodil says in an exasperated tone, 'I don't understand, I'm a daffodil!'

Bob's frustration and the absurdity of the situation gets the better of him and he breaks into laughter. There's a twinkle in his eyes. In that moment, Steve witnesses Bob dropping what Bob thinks is the corporate mask he is expected to wear. The daffodils might have cheered or said, 'Ahh now we understand'. Suddenly the real Bob, Bob the human rather than Bob the corporate suit is standing there. They stopped there as nothing else was needed. Steve had witnessed Bob and he had experienced himself in a more unguarded way. The micro-moment of Bob's mask 'cracking' was enough to allow him to experience a more authentic version of himself.

Once the experiment finishes, with the daffodils duly thanked, Bob and Steve go for a coffee to reflect on what just happened and discuss what insights and awareness they can gather from the experience. They agree that Bob will carry out his own little practical experiments to embed his learning and to practise. When he feels himself slipping into the corporate mask during presentations, Bob plans to pretend that some of his audience members have been replaced by daffodils.

*No daffodils were hurt during this experiment.

13.15.5 Groups/teams

13.15.5.1 *The Rapping Nurse*

Julie Flower recalls a group session in a research organisation. At the end of a day of structured activities, she took the temperature of the room and suggested a free-form session; participants divided into little groups to imagine what great research looked and felt like in whatever way they wished. The playfulness in the room was quite distinctive, there was a feeling of curiosity, openness and warmth which led to all sorts of things being created on this important topic in various ways. One group did a respectful but comedic version. The most memorable was a senior nurse rapping in front of 80 of her colleagues why she loved research. It was the highlight of the day and was referred to across the organisation several years later.

Julie shares that it was one of those moments you couldn't script or plan and a great example of improv and spontaneity which came from playfulness and the underlying conditions of warmth and safety within the group. Even though it was a serious matter, the expression of the answer in rap form was impactful and memorable and resulted in a shared visceral experience. It is also a great example of how we can create the conditions and opportunities for play and playfulness and creative expression, but ultimately, it's about co-creation rather than imposition.

Julie's experience was reflected in the research paper which Stephanie co-authored with Jonathan Passmore and Richard Gold in 2020 looking at LEGO® Serious Play® and more specifically Real Time Strategy for the Team workshops and their effect on team cohesion, collaboration, and psychological safety.[23] One of the findings was that the experience helped to create a novel, common and shared language which served to affect the team in a positive way after the workshop.

A powerful way of tapping into playfulness to see different perspectives and increase awareness is through role playing. In the safety of the coaching space, this can enable clients to connect or reconnect with parts of themselves that may not usually show up due to the (real or perceived) expectations of their roles and/or the stories we hold about ourselves based on our circumstances or experiences. It can be surprisingly transformative and is a powerful way to understand more deeply our own feelings and thoughts as well as the perspectives of others and to play out various possibilities and contingencies in a low risk environment. As Di Gammage observes, 'whatever our medium of play, what lies at the heart is the motivation, … to express, externalize, and realize what is within. To make the unconscious conscious'.[24]

> Man is least himself when he talks in his own person.
> Give him a mask and he'll tell you the truth.
>
> *Oscar Wilde*

Heather Simpkin shared a story of working with a group, one of whom wanted to address a challenge which he had with his boss. Heather facilitated role plays of how he might address the challenge, playing with different possibilities. Some of the group were involved, the others observed. She heard from him a little while later and he said that he didn't actually need to have the conversation with his boss; the experience had the effect of evaporating the feelings and tensions he had been holding. What's more, because he allowed himself to be honest and vulnerable in the group session, the other members of the group experienced a shift as well as they engaged with and reflected on a collective experience which had the added impact of strengthening their connection with each other. Many of our Storytellers reflected that playing in this way can be far more impactful in terms of collective engagement and learning than purely rational cognitive-based conversations.

13.15.5.2 *Forum Theatre*

Part of Neil Mullarkey's work includes running workshops based on improv ethos which has much in common with provocative therapy and Gestalt, where in general terms, you take a small idea, listen to what others are saying, use that and bounce it back. One such format is 'forum theatre' which Neil uses with groups and teams. A possible version might look as follows:

Having worked with a group to develop improv skills throughout the morning, in a Playful Moment Neil will invite someone, let's say David, to tell the story of a particular situation. David will start by being the director and various members of the group play different characters including David. Neil might play a role of the antagonist, and often will over-exaggerate, stretch, or stylise the characteristics until, with feedback from David, he gets the nuances right. During the experiment, Neil may ask David as director about details such as how and where everyone is sitting, pondering whether this or that is right and helpful, throwing in other suggestions ad hoc. Neil can then moderate the tone as if he was the director and playfully provoke once sufficient safety is established (for example, '*Of course he'd say that, he hates you!*'). Such provocation can be similar to the intention and effect of provocative coaching (see Chapter 8 and, for example, the work of Jaap Hollander).

Overall, David gets to see the situation, relationships, and so on from the detached position of the director to create insight, also into his role in the system. David is then invited to sit in different positions including lastly as himself.

In the safe environment, which is created, the shifts in perspectives including through provocative prompts and the experience of acting out their own realities as well as acting as other people moves beyond rationalising and can bring thoughts into the open and give members the chance to try out different personas, perspectives, and ways of approaching things.

The feedback Neil receives for these sessions is extremely positive. Participants share their insights, solutions or just empathy; the problem is shared and therefore halved, and participants come away with options if not solutions. Clearly these sessions are facilitated with skill and care and Neil reflected that you can see physical changes in the participants with lasting change months after the workshop. A vivid example of how playfulness can be profound and provide lasting and change-facilitating insights.

As an aside, we have taken part in one of Steve Chapman's Mask Workshops which we highly recommend as an experience and for personal development. Facilitating this and other 'bigger experiments' takes training and skill which is why we haven't included what might be mistaken as 'how-to' descriptions which might also be taken too literally. As your capacity and experience of working playfully evolves, we have no doubt you will find (as a place along the journey rather than a final destination) ways to incorporate playfulness into your practice in a way which is authentic and unique to you and your work.

13.16 Working Remotely

Many of us are doing at least a substantial proportion of our work remotely and most of the ideas above can be adapted with a little creativity, imagination and planning to create a playful climate and experience. As we described above, it is worth giving thought to your actual and/or virtual backdrop as this helps create the space you are sharing with your clients. It might be colourful pictures and objects, as in Stephanie's real life screen background, or Teresa's choice of virtual backgrounds, often taking her clients to where they would like to be to work together most effectively (for example, at the ocean or in a forest). Also notice your client's space; is it conducive? If not, is there flexibility in slightly rearranging the space or relocating or for example switching to telephone or off-camera to give more flexibility?

One of the benefits of working remotely is that clients are in their own safe spaces; they may be working from home, so might be more relaxed, able to be themselves and express themselves in ways that they might find more difficult in the office or if you are working together in real life. We don't have to see what they are doing, whether, for example, it's dancing, moving in other ways, drawing or modelling; it's up to them how much they'd like to share directly or limit to description or reflection. Of course, in particular if you are working flexibly like this, it is important to keep coaching ethics in mind and work within the range of your capability and be alert for signs of potential issues which might need addressing.

13.16.1 Further Ideas for Practice

13.16.1.1 Fishbowl Online

Creating a virtual fishbowl can be very effective when working in teams/groups; with active participants (in the fishbowl) and the others acting as observers (muted and off-camera). You can play (and contract to of course) with the roles/perspectives of the active participants, as for example, in the virtual Ambassador and Gremlin activity above. At points within the session, participants and observers can swap. This can work really well and for some, this is a more accessible way of actively participating than if they were observed or distracted by the presence of a physical group. You can be creative and playful in how observations are shared, for example using on-line tools (see below) or the chat function.

13.16.1.2 Online Tools

There are a number of online tools which you can experiment with to support or create a more playful approach. Examples include MURAL, Miro, Lucidspark.

13.16.1.3 Virtual Reality Coaching

Increasingly, therapies such as CBT are using virtual reality for therapeutic purposes. It allows the creation of safe spaces for clients to experiment with challenging topics in a playful way, for example, with public speaking or anxiety in public spaces. David Clutterbuck shared with us that he has started to experiment with coaching in virtual reality, finding amusing and novel environments as his and client's avatars meet for example on a cloud or the edge of a birthday cake, engaging in an insightful and purposeful and playful session.

13.17 Bringing It All Together

As we stated at the outset, our intention with this chapter is to give you some ideas and inspiration to experiment and explore your own version of playfulness in your work. Many of the ideas can be layered, interwoven, and re-jigged in a myriad of ways depending on you, your client, the context and purpose of your work together. Remember too that a tool or approach can be inherently playful but delivered in an unplayful way, similarly, many non-playful tools/approaches can be adapted; this is one of the main reasons why we felt strongly we didn't want to give you a tick-box list of tools.[25] From powerful questions and coaching conversations that invite the client to play with an idea, to more immersive experiences and experiments opening up different perspectives, to the possibility of embodying different possibilities (whether real or virtual) and connecting with different resources in various ways with the Whole Body, there are infinite ways and degrees of bringing (more) playfulness into your serious work together.

Barometer of Playfulness

We introduced you to a short Barometer of Playfulness in Chapter 10 and now it's time to introduce you to the longer version. We hope that you will find it useful to come back to from time to time. You can either do a quick check-in by answering the four questions below or explore your playfulness more fully with the reflective questions which follow. The purpose of the Barometer of Playfulness is to give you a quick gauge of where you are in terms of your capacity for play (whether in a given moment or generally), whether you'd like to increase this and what needs you might need to address to do so. It serves to shine a light on some of the factors that influence your playfulness and equip you to dial it up in ways that are right for you. For both the shorter and longer versions, before answering, notice what comes up for you in your heart, mind, and body. What further questions arise for you and what more do you need?

13.18 When It Comes to Playing or Being Playful, What Level Are You for Each of the Below?

Using the scale of 1–5 (from low to high)

1. *In this moment, how playful are you?*
2. *Do you want more play or to be more playful? How much do you want this?*
3. *Do you have enough energy to play or be playful? What is your current energy level?*
4. *Are you able to play or be playful? At what level is your ability? What would you like it to be?*

For deeper exploration, reflect on the questions above first in the context of you as a whole and then your work. Go beyond your head and also notice what you feel, both emotionally and where and how in your body. Be curious. Be specific. Reflect in any way that suits your mood – silently, sing, write a poem, doodle, build a LEGO® model, be still, move, stay where you are, change your environment; whatever grabs and supports you to explore further. For extra input, you might want to think about the different layers of the Be Playful Onion Model. You might also find it helpful to look at the Playfulness Mixing Desk (also in The Playfulness Scrapbook) for inspiration.

Questions to explore include:

- *What information is this giving you about you and your playfulness?*
- *Are the levels that you've identified for questions 1–4 above where you would like them to be? If not, what are the levels that you'd like for yourself? Why? What difference would you notice in how you think, feel, and behave? What would others notice?*
- *As you think of the various measurements (questions 1–4 above), what do you need more of, less of, the same amount of?*
- *What is the relational/situational/environment impact on your playfulness? How can you take steps to influence this in the direction which you desire?*
- *What else can you do to influence the levels?*
- *What other questions would you find helpful?*

If you would like to dial up your playfulness:

- *How do you know when you are being playful?*
- *Now think of some times when you are playful (if you can't think of any, you can imagine yourself or even someone else being playful).*
- *Notice what was playful about those moments. Again, bring in your heart, mind, and body.*
- *Notice where in your body, mind and heart playfulness resides. Does it have a colour? Shape? Sound?*
- *Can you tap into these in moments when you wish to connect more to play?*
- *What are your values? How do these relate to playfulness? If they support playfulness, how can you find ways of more values-led ways of being and behaving which also support playfulness?*
- *What do you stand to lose by not being more playful? What would more playfulness bring you?*

As you move through this book and your journey into playfulness, and reflect and experiment, come back to the Barometer of Playfulness again and see if anything has shifted. During these further reflections, questions to ask yourself might include:

- *What do I need to pay attention to?*
- *What assumptions about myself and my playfulness have I not challenged for a while?*
- *What barriers are there to my playfulness? What resources and support can I call on to address these?*

- *How can I grow and tap into my network of support to access more playfulness?*
- *What conversations could I usefully have with my idealised, playful self?*

We have sprinkled the Barometer of Playfulness icon throughout this book to remind you to either do a quick check-in on your levels of playfulness – which is asking yourself the four questions, or to do a fuller check-in and reflection from time to time.

Playfulness Mixing Deck

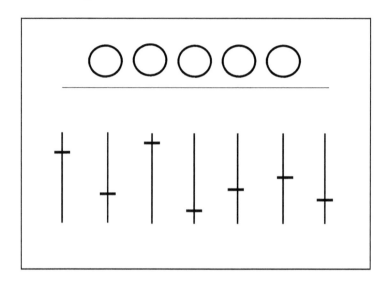

Welcome to your very own Playfulness Mixing Deck. You'll have seen by now how playfulness in coaching is multi-faceted, fluid, and relational. We offer you the mixing desk to help you raise your awareness around playfulness, consider the influences, the levels which they are currently at and what you would like to dial up or down as you experiment and explore with playfulness in your practice (and life).

Consider all the different influences on your playfulness. Notice that some are internal, some external, some relational, and some situational.

- *Which settings are you most drawn to?*
- *Which represents the most challenge?*
- *What would be your ideal settings in life generally, in different relationships, in your work?*

Perhaps draw your own mixing desk or take a copy of this one. Add in your own factors which impact your playfulness. For each, write a number from 1–10 for where you are now and for where you'd like to be.

Thinking about where you'd like to be:

- *How would what you feel, do and think be different and what would others notice about you?*
- *What do you need to see change?*
- *What small steps can you take?*

Consider creating a mixing desk for coaching practice as you prepare for a session.

- As a coach, when it comes to practice what do you need to dial up or down before the session? *As an example, dial up focus, presence, listening, curiosity, security. Dialling down personal distractors.*

Take a Playful Moment

Welcome to Playful Moments. An invitation to put this book down and engage beyond reading to experiment with reconnecting with and incorporating more play into your day. A Playful Moment is a chance to get up, get moving and do something for the sole purpose of playing and fun. We invite you to bring a beginner's mindset with a healthy dose of give-it-a-go-ness. It can last a moment or longer, it's your choice.

Photo of Poppy, Steph's dog, taken by Laura Poole 2022.

As an example of a Playful Moment, sometimes in our own homes, when we are feeling a 'mah', a bit tired, or in need of a boost, we'll turn on music and dance with abandon for a few minutes. Moving and jumping about in ways we mostly wouldn't in front of others, fully uninhibited which often makes us smile, sometimes giggle, or laugh and change state. For us, these are Playful Moments and you will find ones which resonate with you. We're sharing some ideas for inspiration and wholeheartedly encourage you to create Playful Moments in whatever way is right for you. Come, build some more Playful Moments into your daily life, and notice the change.

If you like, after a Playful Moment, take a moment to ask yourself what you notice in your heart, mind, and body and what has changed. How did you know you were being playful? Do a quick check-in with the Barometer of Playfulness. Below are some ideas for inspiration but really this is about taking a moment to be playful however you desire.

13.19 A Moment for Play

- Giving yourself the permission to play for this moment, when you think about playing, or being playful, what comes up for you? Can you experience this now or plan it in? Alternatively, what is the simplest and easiest thing you can imagine that is playful?[26]
- Extra challenge:
    - What would you love to experience that is your most playful?
    - Act as the most playful person or animal you know.

13.20 Playlist of Playful Moments to Randomly Select

Use the list below or create your own. Choose a Playful Moment that you would like to do or randomly pick one (or your own adapted version). To randomly pick: just think of a number between one and ten without looking at the list or writing numbers on pieces of paper and pick a number:

1. Drawing and colouring.
2. Modelling with whatever objects are to hand.
3. Skipping.
4. Playing with a ball.
5. Play a game.

6. Be goofy (not the dog from Disney but you could impersonate him!) or silly for a few moments in whatever way you are inspired.
7. Watch a playful video clip or something that inspires you.
8. Any arts or crafts (as long as you're doing it for fun and keeping your inner critic out of it).
9. Get moving and dancing.
10. Pick a Playful Moment from below or create your own.

13.20.1 Meeting Your Playful Self Through Art, Modelling or Imagination

- Draw or model your playful self, use whatever materials you have to hand. Or, if you prefer, imagine your most playful self. Whatever your medium, add colour, all the senses, symbols – whatever you are inspired to do, let yourself have freedom of expression.
- *Playful extra challenge*: Draw or model your non-playful self. Looking at these two representations side-by-side, what do you notice? Step back and look at them from different perspectives – what else do you notice?
- Try all three (art, modelling and imagination) and notice what is different in your expressions. Take photos and repeat this experiment in a few months. Notice what has changed.

13.20.2 Let's Get Jiggly

- Dance like no one's watching. Put on a song you love to dance to and get dancing. Bust out the most random, silly moves. Let go and get your body moving playfully with heart, mind, and body connection. Find some moves that get you into a playful, fun state. If mobility is an issue, do it in a way which is possible and comfortable for you (you can also try imagining yourself busting these moves).

13.20.3 Playful Extra Challenge

- Dance even more wildly. Exahggerate the moves. Sing at the top of your voice … loudly or in a funny voice! Tap into your inner child and dance as a child. Invite others to join in. Do what is right for you to reduce your inhibitions and freely express yourself. Again, if mobility is an issue, do it in a way which is possible and comfortable for you.

- Create your playful playlist of songs – get up and dance or where it's not possible, imagine yourself dancing.

13.20.4 Explore The Treasure Map of Playfulness

- Go to the Treasure Map of Playfulness in the Welcome chapter and see what you notice.
- Seek the different parts of this book which relate to elements on the map that interest you.
- Colour in the elements of that map that you recognise.
- Create your own Playfulness Treasure Map including symbols and images that are meaningful to you. Alternatively, doodle on our version.

13.20.5 Be the Playful Human and Build Fun into Your Day

Moving around the house (or anywhere), can you do this in a playful way? What other ways can you incorporate these micro-fun moments? Primal Play[27] has resources for incorporating fun and playful ways of moving aimed at increasing your fitness.

13.20.6 Create Your Playful Hat

- Create your own playful hat including elements that represent play or help you become playful. These may be different objects, colours or materials.
- You may wish to draw it or model it or actually create a hat to wear.

13.20.7 Create Your Playful Vision Board

- Create your own playful vision board including all the elements that represent and connect you to play, playfulness, and being playful. There are no limits or constraints on what can be included, just anything that has meaning for you – images, symbols, quotes, movie references, people, songs, jokes, colours, scents, pieces of material…
- Alternatively, create a model or picture version. Or, you could create an electronic version incorporating images, sounds, video clips and so on.
- Place your playful vision board somewhere so you can connect and reflect.
- *Playful extra challenge*: Step back and reflect what you have created. Look for any deeper meaning or patterns emerging that you might not have intended. Step back further again or into a different observing position and see if you notice anything else.

Whatever your Playful Moments look like, we hope that you enjoy them and will incorporate them more intentionally and spontaneously into your life. As you progress through the book, you might want to revisit some of these moments (or your own) and notice if anything has changed (if you like, using the Barometer of Playfulness). The Playful Experiments which you might want to try are designed to be more intentional to connect you with play with the view of priming yourself as a coach for practice or experimenting with your clients.

To encourage and remind you to take a Playful Moment from time to time, we've scattered this symbol by way of invitation throughout the book:

Playful Experiments for Life and Work

The purpose of these experiments is to explore and play with a variety of ways to connect with your playfulness beyond the cerebral and conversational. Unlike the Playful Moments, these experiments are more intentional and reflective, designed with the view to priming yourself as a coach or incorporating playfulness into your work with clients.

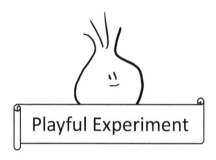

Playful Experiment

As you engage with these experiments, you might find that you have a different perspective if you are doing so in your capacity of coach. You may find no difference at all, though perhaps you might have different insights or areas of focus. For example, you might be perceived as a serious coach with gravitas but in your non-work life you consider yourself playful. How does holding these contradictions feel like for you? What assumptions are you making and are they serving you and your clients? You might want to do the experiments more than once and from different perspectives.

For all of the experiments, do remember the multi-faceted construct represented by the Be Playful Onion Model and it might be helpful to expand your reflections and questions below to the different layers of the model.

13.21 Envisioning Your Playful Self

The next few experiments are designed to help you envision and connect with your playful self and state. We invite you to check in with the Barometer of Playfulness before and after.

- Bring your attention within. Take a moment to focus on the term 'playful' and how it relates to you. Imagine a simple and easy moment when you are playful. What comes up for you? What are you doing and being like?
- *Playful extra challenge*: Drop your focus from your head to your body. Start to move your body in a playful way. Try out different moves. For a moment,

exaggerate those that are more playful. Now notice within you, heart, mind, and body the different sensations that arise. Allow and notice as an observer what is coming in without rationalising or solutioning.

- Ask where in my body does play reside right now? Is there a sensation, colour(s) or other signals? If you were to give this a symbol/name/character, what would it be?

13.22 Stepping into Your Playful Self

Here is another way of visualising and connecting with your playful self:

- Using your imagination, visualise a circle on the floor in front of you.
- In the circle, imagine an image of yourself; a hologram.
- Now build your playful hologram from the outside in. See your playful self. Notice external characteristics: your hair, clothes, expression. Now ask these questions *about your playful hologram*: How are you standing or moving? How are you feeling? How do you know you are being playful? How does this show up in your Whole Body (see Chapter 10)? Notice your level of playfulness on a scale of 1–5. Now dial this up more.
- Also consider your playful hologram and ask: What don't you have that you would like? What don't you want? What are your boundaries?
- When you have built this hologram out enough and are happy with it and the level of playfulness, step into the circle and your playful hologram. Like trying on a new set of clothes, made especially with you in mind, step into your playful self.
- Notice with your Whole Body what this feels like.
- When you're done, take some time to reflect.
- *Playful extra challenge:* You could separately imagine your non-playful self. Notice the difference. However afterwards, do intentionally refresh and move yourself back into a good state.

13.23 Draw or Model Your Playful Self

Draw or model your playful self, using whatever materials are to hand (pens, felt tips, playdough, LEGO®, and so on). This is a version of the experiment above. This might be a helpful way to help you envision your hologram and to see yourself more objectively. You may wish to experiment with both and see what arises.

13.24 Playful Extra Challenge

- Draw or model your non-playful self.
- Now, reflect on what differences you notice between the two.
    - Step back and look from different perspectives – further back, low, and close, from above. Notice what you see, feel, any patterns, insights, new ideas.
    - Reflect on what this gave you. You can use the Barometer of Playfulness as an aid to reflection.

13.25 Connecting with Your Playful Side Using Chairwork

Using Chairwork facilitated by another coach, meet some of your Community of Selves (see The Playfulness Scrapbook for more on this) and explore some of your underlying beliefs around playfulness from different perspectives. If your playful self has been pushed to the outer margins of your Community of Selves, you might wish to welcome her/him/them back into the fold. See also The Playfulness Scrapbook for what this might look like facilitated in a playful way.

13.26 Playful Relationships

In this experiment we invite you to reflect on the qualities of your playfulness when you are by yourself, with others and in different contexts/environments. We hope that this increases your self-awareness around your playfulness and what you can build on, develop, and dial up or down and what factors might support or hinder your playfulness. We have noticed in ourselves and others that playfulness can be individual but also relational and situational; we may be more or less playful with certain people and in certain contexts and environments.

Using the image above as inspiration:

- Take a moment to think about a person or group you are more playful with.
- You may like to draw an image or construct a model to represent this person or group (at the end, we'll invite you to step back and look at it from different angles).
- Draw an image or make a model representing yourself.
- How are you different when you are with them and how do you perceive them?
- Draw (or use Post-it® notes, for example) to represent the relationship arc, filling it in using words or symbols representing the qualities that are present and supportive or unsupportive. You might want to use '+' to represent supportive and '–' as unsupportive.
- Now thinking about the context and environment. What is present? Again, distinguish between that which is supportive or not to your playfulness.

- Once you have sufficiently completed the picture/model, step back. View it from different positions (for example, far and near, from up higher and lower) and notice if anything else emerges.
- You might like to take a photo of the model for yourself or to share with others.

13.27 Playful Extra Challenge

- Do another drawing/model as above, with a different relationship/context/environment. See if there are any common themes or differences and any insights to be found.
- You might also do the same experiment with someone/environment/context you aren't so playful with.
- When you've finished, consider the qualities of those you are more playful with and the qualities of your relationship and what this tells you. Notice those you are less playful with and consider what might you authentically feel, think, or do to cultivate more playfulness within this relationship if that's what you'd like. You may find this experiment helpful in the context of your work if you are finding it harder to access playfulness in some sessions than others.

Notes

1 Joplin, A. (2007) cited in Spinelli, E. (2008) Coaching and Therapy: Similarities and divergences. *International Coaching Psychologist Review*, 3(3), 241–249. Jopling, A. (2007). *The fuzzy space: Exploring the experience of space between psychotherapy and executive coaching*. London: Unpublished MSc dissertation, New School of Psychotherapy and Counselling.
2 Stoddard, J. and Afari, N. (2014). *The Big Book of ACT Metaphors: A Practitioner's Guide to Experiential Exercises and Metaphors in Acceptance and Commitment Therapy*. Oakland, CA: New Harbinger Publications, Inc.
3 Fuller, A. and Unwin, L. (2017). Job Crafting and Identity in Low-Grade Work: How Hospital Porters Redefine the Value of their Work and Expertise. *Vocations and Learning*, 10, 307–324.
4 Cameron, J. (2020). *The Artist's Way: A Spiritual Path to Higher Creativity*. Souvenir Press: London.
5 Silverstein, J. & Whitfield Davidson, J. (2017). Trait Empathy associated with Agreeableness and rhythmic entrainment in a spontaneous movement to music task: Preliminary exploratory investigations, *Musicae Scientiae*, 23(1), 5–24.
6 Cirelli, L., Wan, S. & Trainor, L. (2014). Fourteen-month-old infants use interpersonal synchrony as a cue to direct helpfulness. *Philosophical transactions of the Royal Society of London. Series B, Biological sciences*, 369(1658), 20130400.

7 McManus, B. & Giraldez Hayes, A. (2021). Exploring the experience of using music and creative mark-making as a reflective tool during coaching supervision: An Interpretative Phenomenological Analysis. *Philosophy of Coaching: An International Journal*, 6(2), 22–46.

8 lspmagazine.com

9 Gash, J. (2016). *Coaching creativity: Transforming your practice*. Routledge.

10 Sheather, A. (2019). *Coaching Beyond Words: Using Art to Deepen and Enrich Our Conversations*. Routledge.

11 Carney, D., Cuddy, A. & Yap, A. (2010). Power posing: Brief nonverbal displays affect neuroendocrine levels and risk tolerance. *Psychological science*, 21(10), 1363–1368.

12 Carney, D., Cuddy, A. & Yap, A. (2015). Review and summary of research on the embodied effects of expansive (vs. contractive) nonverbal displays. *Psychological science*, 26(5), 657–663.

13 Giacomucci, S. (2021). *Social work, sociometry, and psychodrama: Experiential approaches for group therapists, community leaders, and social workers* (Vol. 1). Springer Nature.

14 Boyatzis, R. & Akrivou, K. (2006). The ideal self as the driver of intentional change. *Journal of management development*, 25(7), 624–642.

15 Boyatzis, R., & Dhar, U. (2021). Dynamics of the ideal self. *Journal of Management Development*, 41(1), 1–9.

16 For more on what this might look like in practice: Boyatzis, R., Smith, M. & Van Oosten, E. (2019). *Helping people change: Coaching with compassion for lifelong learning and growth*. Harvard Business Press.

17 Kross, E. (2021). *Chatter: The Voice in Our Head, why it Matters, and how to Harness it*. Crown.

18 Pugh, M. (2019). *Cognitive Behavioural Chairwork: Distinctive Features*. Routledge.

19 Mair, M. (2014). In Winter, D. & Reed, N. (Eds.) *Towards a Radical Redefinition of Psychology: The selected works of Miller Mair* (1st ed.). Routledge.

20 Carson, R. (1983). *Taming Your Gremlin: A Surprisingly Simple Method for Getting Out of Your Own Way*. (Revised in 2003). Quill.

21 Smith, C. (1997). *The Merlin factor : keys to the complete corporate kingdom*. Gower.

22 Koppett, K. (2001). *Training to imagine: Practical improvisational theatre techniques to enhance creativity, leadership, teamwork and learning*. Stylus Publishing.

23 Wheeler, S., Passmore, J. & Gold, R. (2020). All to play for: LEGO® SERIOUS PLAY® and its impact on team cohesion, collaboration and psychological safety in organisational settings using a coaching approach. *Journal of Work-Applied Management*, 12(2), 141–157.

24 Gammage, D. (2017). *Playful Awakening: Releasing the Gift of Play in Your Life*. Jessica Kingsley Publishers, p186.

25 If you are looking for a tools resource, here's one: Passmore, J., Day, C., Flower, J., Grieve, M. & Jovanovic Moon, J. (Eds). (2021). *Coaching Tools: 101 coaching tools and techniques for executive coaches, team coaches, mentors and supervisors: WeCoach!* Libri Publishing.

26 If you need inspiration, have a look at Rosen, M. (2020). *Book of Play! Why play really matters and 101 ways to get more if it in your life*. Wellcome Collection.

27 primalplay.com/

14
The Next Chapter

Perhaps you're starting on this page, in which case welcome! We hope you find fun, challenge, deeper understanding, and an appreciation of playfulness in coaching and inspiration as you get to know the other pages. If you've read from page 1 or are dipping in and out, perhaps you have already experienced some changes. We hope to have challenged some of your preconceptions and assumptions around playfulness and got you curious or even excited about inviting your clients to explore and experiment. If you're already seeing playfulness in your coaching, we hope we've given you more food for thought and particularly that you found that The Playfulness Scrapbook is a useful resource to spark your creativity and imagination further.

We've shared a small selection of our own and our Storytellers' experiences in the hope of helping you imagine how you might bring more playfulness to your work with your clients, adapted to who you and your clients are, your relationship, the environment in which you're in and how you work together at your best. How playfulness can manifest in coaching is perhaps best seen as a beautiful kaleidoscope. There really are limitless possibilities. By thinking about where you sit most comfortably in the Be Playful Onion Model (for now and in different relationships), drawing on the theory, research, stories, and ideas for practice that we've explored in this book, you can start to experiment with introducing more playfulness into your life and work in a way which feels authentic (and perhaps sweetly uncomfortable). As playfulness is so beautifully multi-faceted, how do you know if it's been a playful session? It's a question that we've asked ourselves and our Storytellers. A theme emerged that perhaps it's when, on foundations of trust and curiosity, something unexpected happens which leads to change, sometimes of mood, the coaching relationship, or insight, or all three, or more.

Recognising that playfulness in coaching is many things, at its heart, the qualities required include a willingness to let go of knowing, to step into different perspectives, listen to others with a 'yes, and' approach to what you

DOI: 10.4324/9781003090847-16

hear, to hold a degree of irreverence to the givens of how things are done and perceived, allowing for spontaneity and creativity. Through playfulness, we can help our clients to access more than their cognitive power and move into somatic, physical, experiential coaching realms which might well challenge some assumptions about themselves, others, and the topic at hand. Once you've experienced something, perhaps particularly in a group context, you can't un-experience it and the effect can be transformative. Playfulness has more to offer than initial assumptions and preconceptions might suggest, and it can show up in unexpected ways. It can cater for the serious, the emotional, complex, and difficult challenges as well as being a valuable resource for well-being, creativity, innovation, learning and development, relationships and collaboration and let's not forget fun.

Through playfulness, we can come back to simplicity while recognising both complexity and paradox and trying to make sense of the systemic nature of everything (multiple interdependent and possibly changing causative factors and interrelatedness). At its best, playfulness deepens relationships and is supported by a capacity for attention, groundedness with expansiveness as well as empathy and care for ourselves, and others. All of these seem very much needed not just by individuals (us and our clients) but if we take a systemic view, in our relationships, the teams and organisations within which we work, stakeholders and the wider systemic context. Playfulness can help us change the narrative and give us imaginative, creative ways to act and respond rather than reacting to 'givens' and can be the difference between surviving and thriving. Why would you not be open to playfulness? We venture as far as saying that the future needs us and our clients to take playfulness more seriously as a rich resource and for it to become a normal part of our range in exploring potential, and meeting challenges.

Whether you are tentatively dipping your toes into playfulness in coaching, diving right in, or already comfortably bobbing and ready to stretch yourself further, we hope that you now have at your fingertips ways of increasing your and your clients' capacities for playfulness and an appreciation of its potential power. This book is intended as your companion during further exploration and experiments and for you to supplement with your own ideas, reminders, notes and doodles. Think of us as your trusty play companions as your (and our) playfulness changes and develops over time and you and your clients find authentic ways of tapping into playfulness in service of your work together.

Just as we welcomed you in the first page of this book, we now invite you to join us as we continue to experiment and learn as we all do our small bit in developing this area of coaching. We'd love to hear from you; how you're getting on, what resonated with you, where you're feeling stuck and what you are looking for and for you to share your experience, wisdom, and insights (our contact details are in Chapter 1). As coaches, we are all walking alongside our clients as we work with them to overcome challenges and reach their potential and that's the spirit in which we're embracing our exploration with you.

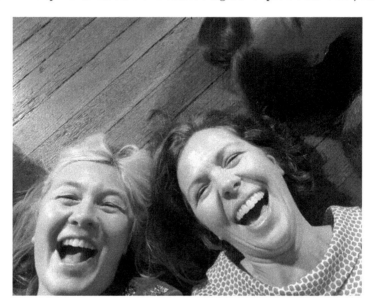

About the Authors

Stephanie and Teresa both hold an MSc in Coaching for Behavioural Change, from Henley Business School. They are accredited individual and systemic team coaches passionate about supporting the development and flourishing of individuals, teams and organisations.

Stephanie is a LEGO® Serious Play® facilitator, writes for The LSP Magazine and has written peer-reviewed research articles. Teresa is an agile coach and supervisor with experience of leading hi-tech, complex change.

Teresa and Stephanie are both interested in the possibilities offered by playful thinking in complex environments, supporting individual development and team maturation as well as the co-creation of new ideas and solutions across teams and organisations. They also work with coaches to support them in finding authentic ways to connect with more playfulness.

Photo taken by Rosie Parsons Photography 2022.

Index

Note: Page numbers in *italics* indicate figures on the corresponding pages.

Aaker, J. 161, 187
ABC (Always Be Contracting) 173, 187, 237, 271, 279
Acceptance and Commitment Therapy (ACT) 62, 156, 216, 247, 285–286
ACT coaching 13, 139, 156, 216, 247
adrenaline 8, 94, 95, 110, 232
alliance, therapeutic 155, 176, 187; repair of rupture of 177
Ambassadors and Gremlins exercise 313–314
American Psychological- Association (APA) 30, 31
anxiety 57, 106, 119, 130, 135, 147, 153, 258, 262
Apter, Michael 73
art and drawing 297–298, 330, 335
art cards and images 301
Art of Insubordination, The- 232
Association for Applied and Therapeutic Humor 150
Attachment Theory 17, 197, 203, 208–210, *209*
Attenborough, David 219
Autonomic Nervous System (ANS) 94–95, 103, 106

Bachkirova, Tatiana 31, 81
Bagdonas, N. 161, 187
balance, finding 61
Bardwick, Judith 231
Barnett, L. 40, 65

Barometer of Playfulness 23, *24*, 199–201, 323
barriers, hitting too hard 179
Barske, Kirsten 15, 50, 110; on authenticity 212; on group dynamics 184–185, 273; movement used by 294–295; on physical mapping 216; on resistance in clients 261; on setting expectations 271–272; on warm-up tasks 241
Bartholomew, K. 208
Bateson, P. 244
behavioural change and positive emotions 55, 63–64, 134–136
behavioural change and humour 11, 30, 34, 156–157
Be Here Now 61
beliefs about playfulness 210–211
benefits of playfulness in coaching 55–56, 65–66; accessing the state in which we can learn, connect, co-create and expand 58; capacity to deal with change 61; capacity to deal with the 'hard stuff' 61–62; creating space for exploration 57–58; creativity 59–60; deepening connection to heart and body 62–63; deepening relationships and positive emotions 63–64; finding balance 61; flow 58–59; imagination 60; opening up different possibilities through accessing different perspectives 56–57; well-being 64–65
Be Playful Onion Model 21, 70, 144, 164, 186, 201, 215, 226, 269, 339; conclusions on 84–87, *85*, *86*; heart of the

Onion-playful way of being 79–82; middle layer-expressions of playfulness 73–79, 74; the Onion in 70–71, 71; outer layer-'doing' play in 71–73; reflections on 82–83; self-perception and 205

Berger, P. 262

Bettelheim, Bruno 41

Biddulph, Steve 139

Big Book of ACT Metaphors, The 285

Bion, W. 138

B-love 80

Bob and the Daffodils, The 83, 316–317

body-brain states 108, 202, 240, 243

body talk 305–306

Box, George E. P. 70

Boyatzis, Richard 64, 98, 104, 128–131

B-playfulness 80

Braff, E. 255

brain *See* neurobiology

Brauer, K. 118, 239

Breakthrough Conversations 17, 86, 104, 108

Brewer, Jud 135

broaden-and-build theory 64, 127, 131–133

Brown, Casey 135

Brown, Stuart 36, 44, 57, 81, 229, 245

Caesar, Sid 146

capability 12, 109, 136, 237; competence and 259–260

capacity: to deal with change 61; playfulness 255–257

Capra, Fritjof 215

Carroll, Lewis 304

Cartesian Dualism 30, 215

Cavicchia, Simon 238

Chairwork 63, 311–312, 335–336

challenges for playfulness in coaching 254–255; capacity 255–257; clients who don't want to be there or don't want to change 261; competence and capability 259–260; complacency 259; confidence 257–258; credibility 260; culture 264–266; gender 263–264; individual 262; psychological safety and group dynamics 262–263; reflection on 266–267; things affecting your client which might get in the way 261–266; things that might get in the way 255–260

change, capacity to deal with 61

Chaplin, Charlie 29

Chapman, Steve 16, 48–50, 198, 215, 222, 230, 237, 273; on capacity for playfulness 269; on discomfort and uncertainty 181, 232; humour used by 159; on inner critic 238; on location of work 227; Mask Workshops 320; on safe words 272

Character Compass Model 85, 86, 86–87, 315

Chatter 310–311

childish v childlike approaches 27, 30, 33, 37, 42–43, 51, 255, 281

climate and tone 47, 48, 278–279

Clutterbuck, David 13, 16, 44, 222, 237, 280, 309; on conversations 144; fireside chat with 45–47; on new challenges 229; on playfulness 234; on systemic approach to coaching 84, 215; use of humour by 159, 211; on virtual reality coaching 321–322

coddiwompling 237

Coelho, Paulo 186

Cognitive Behavioural Chairwork: Distinctive Features 311

Cognitive Behavioural Therapy (CBT) 321

cohesion 9, 64, 133, 176, 288, 318; group 176, 184–185

Cohn, M. 121

Community of Selves 208, 311

compassion 11, 14, 46, 52, 148, 154, 177; curiosity and 50, 116; doing 79; nervous system and 95, 98–90, 103; playfulness as vehicle for 64, 66; self- 51, 61, 116, 121, 138

competence 137, 169–170, 259–260

complacency 259

complex adaptive systems 13, 62, 63, 104, 297

complexity 57, 59, 60, 66, 74, 76, 87, 118, 132, 149, 245, 340; honouring 92, 159; mindfulness and 247–248; uncertainty and 105–106

confidence 6, 30, 82, 83, 257–258

congruence 176

connecting with play 211–214

containing 85, 109, 138

contracting and the first invitation to play 271–272

Conway, Horton 29

Conway, M. 62

cooperation theory of brain networks 99

countertransference 177

Covey, Stephen 12
Covid-19 pandemic 21, 35, 65, 204
creativity 29, 32, 34, 35, 59–60, 97, 99, 135,
    217; as element of playfulness 109, 145,
    180, 218; flow and 58; humour and 145,
    148, 156, 163; pleasant emotions and 121,
    132; self and 42–43
credibility 9, 83, 172, 176, 255, 260
Crowe, J. 149, 156
Csikszentmihalyi, Mihalyi 58
Cuddy, Amy 307
culture 6, 12, 41, 177; cancel 186; emotions
    and 117; organisational 264–266, 300; play
    as necessary for 42; views on love and 123
curiosity 33–34, 57–58, 116, 124, 232, 236
curiosity glasses 246
curiosity glasses experiment 304–305
Curious 232

Dalai Lama 76, 79
damaging rapport 175–177
Dana, Deb 243
dancing 211, 240, 292–293, 306, 330–331
Danger in the Comfort Zone 231
daydreaming 243–246
Default Mode network (DMN) 97, 98–99,
    244; emotions and 115; positive and
    negative emotional attractors and 128
depression 80, 152–153, 221, 229, 262
Descartes, René 215
Dickens, Charles 308
Disney Creativity Strategy 311
D-love 80
Dodson, John 231
Donaldson-Feilder, Emma 13, 249
Donne, John 242
Drama Triangle 187
drawing and art 297–298, 330, 335
draw your team as a character 300
Drucker, Peter 199
Dube, L. 62
Dweck, Carol 203
Dyer, Wayne 305

Edwards, Darryl 264
Einstein, Albert 30, 59, 70
Ellis, Albert 155
embarrassment, fear of 47, 238–239, 261, 262
embracing sweet discomfort 231–235

emotional contagion 103, 129, 198, 242, 306
emotional intelligence 42, 64, 129
emotions 114–115, 139–140; broaden-
    and-build theory and 127, 131–133; in
    coaching 116–118; and how we think, feel
    and behave 126–133; humour and 148,
    152–153; Intentional Change Theory
    (ICT) and 128–131; of joy 121–122;
    kaleidoscope of positive 124–126; love
    and 123; neurobiology and 115–116;
    playfulness, behavioural change, and
    positive 134–136; playfulness and positive
    118–120, 126–128; playfulness in coaching
    and negative 136–139
empathy 64, 176, 177
environment for play 226–228
envisioning your playful self 333–334
Ernstheiterkeit 75, 139
eros 123
existentialism 80, 247
external world experiments 309–310

Farrelly, Frank 155
feedback 133, 149, 177, 178, 188, 312, 313,
    316, 319, 320
Feldman-Barrett, Lisa 101, 117–118
Fella, Andrea 207, 255
Fierce Compassion 138
fight and flight responses 93, 94–96
fishbowl, virtual 321
five senses walk 305
Flaherty, James 258
Flourish 8
flow 39, 58–59, 83–84, 86–87, 247–248, 296
Flower, Julie 16, 47, 182, 205, 234, 237, 264,
    282, 318
Flow Genome Project 58
Fogg, B. J. 134
Ford, Henry 264
Ford, Thomas 73, 145–147, 151, 154, 165,
    178
Forum Theatre 319–320
Franzini, Louis 150
Fredrickson, Barbara 35, 121, 123–124, 131,
    135
freeze response 96, 115
Fry, William 158
Fully Human 139
fuzzy space 43, 84, 185, 272

Game of Thrones 286–287
gamification 134
Gammage, D. 44, 59, 80, 199, 229, 318–319
Gander, F. 220–221
Gash, Jen 210, 297
gelotophilia 239
gelotophobia 238–239, 262
gender barriers to playfulness 263–264
genuineness 49, 149, 176, 212, 247
Germer, Chris 138
Gestalt approach 13, 48, 125, 145, 215, 237, 247, 255, 277
Giacomucci, Scott 308
Giraldez Hayes, A. 296
goal consensus and collaboration 176
Groos, K. 40
groups/team 181–186; damage to psychological safety or cohesion of 184–185; dynamics of 185–186, 262–263; *Forum Theatre* 319–320; humour in 156, 182–183; met where they're at 182; *The Rapping Nurse* 318–319
GROW model 31
Güneş, Gökhan 202

Hadfield, Chris 137
Hanh, Thich Nhat 249, 305
Hardingham, Alison 73
'hard' stuff, capacity to deal with 61–62
hard to read invitations 178–179
Harrison, Jerry 221
Hawkins, Peter 32, 215
Hawkins and Smith 32
Haydon, Benjamin 43
heart and body connection 62–63
Heart and Soul of Change, Delivering What Works in Therapy 176
Hoagland, Edward 140
Hofstadter, Richard 28
holding environment 14, 138
Holmes, Oliver Wendell Jr. 92
Holmes, Oliver Wendell Sr. 92
homo ludens 41–42, 75–76, 78
hope 35–37, 64, 91, 98, 99, 108, 124, 129
Horowitz, L. 208
How to Change 134
Huberman, Andrew 57, 228
Huberman Lab 228
Huizinga, J. 41–42, 75

Humor Styles Questionnaire 160, *160*
humour 143–145, 164–165; in coaching 150–152; defined 145–146; emotional and interpersonal benefits of 148; facilitating new ways of thinking 154–156; functions of laughter, play and 146–149; in groups 156, 182–183; as personal and complex 157–160; playfulness and 145–146; in psychotherapy 175; regulation of emotions with 152–153; shadow side of 149–157; social functions of 148–149; strengthening 246–247; styles of 160, 160–162, *161*; supporting behavioural change 156–157; tension relief and coping through 147–148
Humour, Seriously 161, 163
Humour Styles Matrix 161, *161*

Ibarra, H. 57
ideal self 60, 98, 245, 298, 310
identities, playing with 284–285
image cards 301
imagery 26, 156, 295–303
imagination 60, 243–246, 330
improv 314–315
inner critic 27, 234, 238, 244, 296, 311, 330
Intellectual playfulness 47, 75–78, 109, 120, 125, 144, 205, 263
Intentional Change Theory (ICT) 98, 99, 128–131, 310
internal world experiments 310–312
International Coaching Psychology Review 9, 82
interoception 117–118
Introduction to Coaching Skills, An 81
Isen, Alice 131–132

Jack, Tony 98
jeer pressure 184
joy 32, 42, 65, 71, 75, 119–122, 124, 138–139, 201–202, 234, 239

Kabat-Zinn, J. 248
Kashdan, Miki 124, 231, 265
Kashdan, Todd 57, 232
Kasonde-van den Broek, Nankhonde 16, 50, 51, 148, 186, 264
Kasthan, Inbal 124
katagelasticism 239
Kaufman, Scott Barry 80
Keats, John 43–44, 84

Keltner, Dacher 95
Kestly, T. 247
Kets de Vries, Manfred F.R. 42, 43, 63, 64
Kline, Nancy 13
Kotler, Steven 58
Kramer, Gregory 248–249
Kross, Ethan 62, 310–311
Kubie, L. 175
Kuhlman, Thomas 175

Lamia 43–44
laughter yoga 239
learning through play 42
Lee, Graham 17, 104, 108–109, 139, 154, 178, 242; Be Playful Onion and Character Compass Models 86–87; on body-brain states 108, 202, 240; on coaches' own playful capacities 233; fireside chat with 217–220; Game of Thrones metaphors used by 286–287; on trust and safety required for play 22, 209
LEGO® 20, 63, 72, 127, 138, 205, 246, 281, 296, 323, 335
LEGO® Serious Play® 62–63, 122, 127, 149, 205, 281, 297, 318; imagination in 72, 137–139; thinking with hands in 296
Lenker, Adrianne 139
Leyman, Teresa 10–13, 20–21, 201, 211, 214, 256–257, 281–282
Lieberman, J. 40
Lighthearted playfulness 75, 78, 84
lightness 50, 65–66, 80, 103, 105–108, 122, 135–136, 144, 154, 186, 222, 279, 285, 309
Logical Levels 73
love 36, 64, 80, 121–124, 152, 229
Love 2.0 123
Lucidspark 321

Magnuson, C. 65
Mair, Miller 208, 311
Majumdar, Auriel 17, 147, 247, 291, 296, 302
Martin, P. 244
Martin, Rod 73, 145–147, 151, 154, 160, 165, 178
Martineau, William 183
masculinity 62
Mask Workshops 320
Maslow, Abraham 79–80
McGhee, P. 158, 246

McGonigal, Kelly 103, 232
McKee, A. 64
McManus, B. 296
Megginson, David 44, 84, 144
metaphors 3, 28, 48, 60, 63, 83, 127, 156, 159, 170, 222, 228, 269, 275, 276, 285–286, 303, 305, 310; circle of concern and influence 232; dropping the anchor 102; Game of Thrones 286–287; Mama Bear 138; oxygen mask 202; playfulness as 219; sword and shield 172; tapestry 45
Metz, Christian 39
Meyer, J. 182–183
Milkman, K. 134
mind and body connection 62–63
mindful coaching 98
Mindful Leadership Coaching 42
mindfulness 135, 247–249
Miro 321
misfiring 177–178
misreading 178
modelling 295–303, 330, 335
modernism 30–31
Moreno, Jacob 235–236, 311
movement 294–295, 330–331
Mpotulo, Nobantu 17, 240, 278, 289, 292, 296, 301–302
Mullarkey, Neil 17–18, 156, 211, 237, 284, 285, 309, 319–320
multiculturalism 11, 16, 118
MURAL 321
music 139, 211, 240, 292–293, 296, 306

Nachmanovitch, Stephen 44
National Institute for Play 44
Neff, Kirsten 138
Negative Emotional Attractors (NEA) 127–128
neoteny 42
neural networks 96–97, 244
neurobiology 90–92, 110–112; accessing playfulness in coaching and 104–106; Autonomic Nervous System (ANS) 94–95, 103, 106; body-brain states and 108, 202, 240, 243; brain imaging and 97; brain states and 93–96; complexity of 92; creating safety through play and 107–108; different perceptions of safety and 106–107; emotions and 115–116; fight and flight responses and 93, 94–96;

freeze response and 96; implications for playfulness 100–101; mind and body connection and 62–63; neural networks and 96–97, 115, 128, 244; Parasympathetic Nervous System (PNS) 58, 62, 95–96, 98, 104, 106, 108, 128, 244; Polyvagal Theory and 94–95, 100, 109, 243; prefrontal cortex (PFC) 228; relationship between playfulness and 92–93; relevance to playfulness coaching 98–100; safety as base for play and 108–110; Sympathetic Nervous System (SNS) 94–96, 103–104, 107–110, 128
neuroception 117
neuroplasticity 42, 56, 204, 220, 228, 232, 248
neurosis 61
Nonviolent Communication 13, 124, 138
Norcross, John 176, 177

objects, using 301–303
Observing Self 62, 139, 247, 248, 285–286
Office, The 32
Oliver, Tom 242
OLIW model of playfulness *74*, 74–75, 83–85, 145, 239
Olson, H. 154
open-loop brain functioning 100
organisational culture 264–266
Other-directed playfulness 75, 84

Panksepp, Jaak 64, 119, 131, 146
Parasympathetic Nervous System (PNS) 58, 62, 95–96, 98, 104, 106, 108; daydreaming and 244–245; emotions and 115; positive and negative emotional attractors and 128
Passmore, Jonathan 18, 47, 276, 318
peer pressure 185
Pellegrini, Anthony 40
perceptions of safety 106–107
perfectionism 238
Peterson, C. 146
Petriglieri, J. 57
Picasso, Pablo 296
Pierce, R. 175
Plato 62
Platt, T. 238–239
Play, Playfulness, Creativity, and Innovation 244
Play and Playfulness For Public Health and Wellbeing 135

playful anchors 284–285
Playful Awakening 44
Playful Experiments 23, 24–26, 333–337
playful hats 331
Playful Moment 23, 24, 81–82, 107, 328–332
playfulness: in anyone 201–202; assuming different identities during 57; Attachment Theory and 208–210, *209*; Barometer of 23, 24, 199–201, 323; beliefs about 210–211; benefits of 28–30; connecting with 211–214; creating safety through 107–108, 111; curiosity in 57–58, 124, 232; defining 43–45, 73, 74; expressions of 73–79, *74*; humour and 145–146; intellectual 75, 76; leading to deep work 180–181; learning and creativity in 42, 59–60; levels of 323–325; manifestation in coaching 47–52; OLIW model of *74*, 74–75, 83–85, 145, 239; play habits taken from childhood into adulthood and 203–206, *205*; positive emotions and 118–120, 126–128, 134–136; reasons for human 40–43; recognition of 216–220; safety as base for 108–110; serious 76, 83–84; shadow side of 171; stories about lack of 206–208; strategies for increasing (*See* strategies for increasing playfulness); tending the seedlings of 197–223; from theory to practice 198–199; as universal 55–56; as verb 73; working with the whole body 215–216
playfulness in coaching 27–28, 339–341; authors' approach to 13–14, 33–34; benefits of (*See* benefits of playfulness in coaching); characteristics of 47–52; defining 45–47; getting started with 23–26; hope in 35–37; humour and 150–152; introduction to 5–7; neurobiology and (*See* neurobiology); neurobiology and accessing 104–106; practice considerations with (*see* challenges for playfulness in coaching); qualities underpinning 50–52; reasons for 30–31; research into 39–40; seeds and writing of book on 19–22; Stephanie Wheeler's history with 8–10; storytellers in 14–19; Teresa Leyman's history with 10–13; what can go wrong with 32–33
Playfulness Mixing Deck 326–327
Playfulness Scrapbook tools 23, 24, 83, 155, 268–270; Ambassadors and Gremlins

313–314; being playful with what a coaching session 'should' look like 273–277; bigger experiments 315–316; body talk 305–306; bringing it all together 322–323; Character Compass 315; collections of art cards and images 301; contracting and the first invitation to play 271–272; curiosity glasses experiment 304–305; drawing and art 297–298; draw your team as a character 300; external world experiments 309–310; fishbowl online 321; five senses walk 305; groups/teams 318–320; improv 314–315; internal world experiments 310–312; invitation 279–281; LEGO® Serious Play® 297; levels of playing or being playful and 323–325; metaphors 285–287; modelling and using objects 301–303; movement 294–295; music 292–293; online tools 321; playful anchors and playing with identities 284–285; Playful Experiments 333–337; Playful Moments 328–332; Playfulness Mixing Deck 326–327; playing with image cards visual mapping 301; playing with imagery, visual mapping and modelling 295–303; playing with senses 306–307; playing with time 308–309; Post-it® notes 300–301; roundabout of b*ll*cks 299–300; stepping into playfulness 303–314; storytelling 288–290; tone and climate 278–279; virtual reality coaching 321–322; word play 281–283; working remotely 320–322; writing 291–292
playful relationships 336–337
playful vision boards 331–332
playful way of being 79–82
playing with identities 284–285
Polanyi, M. 63
Polyvagal Theory 94–95, 100, 109, 243
Porges, Stephen 64, 94, 95, 109, 117
Positive Emotional Attractors (PEA) 127–128, 245
positive regard 176
positivism 31
Post-it® notes 300–301
postmodernism 30–32, 36, 81
Power of Fun, The 83
prefrontal cortex (PFC) 228
presence 79, 80, 82, 212, 247–249
Price, Catherine 83

Primal Play Method 264, 331
provocative therapy and coaching 154, 155–156, 319–320
Proyer, René: OLIW Model 74, 74–75, 83–85, 145, 239; on facets of playfulness 73–74, 118; fireside chat with 77–79; on gelotophobia 239; on increasing playfulness 220–221; on levels of playfulness 76; on playfulness and character strengths 179; on serious playfulness 49, 83–84, 118
psychological safety 184–185, 187, 262–263
Psychology of Humor at Work, The 149, 163
Psychology of Humour, An Integrative Approach 73, 146, 163
psychosclerosis 42, 120
Pugh, Matthew 18, 282–283, 289, 311
Pythagoras 83

quality of relational interpretations 177

Rahner, Hugo 75, 139
Ram Dass 61
Rapping Nurse, The 318–319
rapport 64; damaging 175–177
rational emotive behaviour therapy (REBT) 155
Real Time Strategy for the Organisation workshop 62
recognition of playfulness 216–220
Reflection Questions 6, 23, 111–112, 122, 157, 162–163, 164, 174, 180, 199, 201, 203, 207, 208, 210, 211, 213, 214, 216, 220, 222, 228, 230, 235, 236, 237, 241, 243, 247, 249, 258, 259, 260, 263, 265
Relational Mindfulness 13, 249
relationships: deepening of positive emotions and 63–64; playful 336–337
remote work 320–322
repair of alliance rupture 177
resilience 65, 103, 132, 138, 147, 159, 238, 247
resistance in clients 261
Reynolds, M. 248
risks 169–170; and additional considerations at group level 181–186; attitude to 171–174; authors' approach to 170–171; for the coach, not the client(s) 179–180; damaging rapport 175–177; general things to look out for with 174–175; hard to read 178–179; hitting barriers too hard 179; ideas for addressing 186–188; individual

level 174–180; misfiring 177–178;
  misreading 178; playfulness leading to
  deep work and 180–181; shadow side of
  playfulness and 171
Rodden, F. 76
Rogers, Carl 123
role playing 62, 104–105, 122, 269, 297, 311,
  318–319
Rosen, Michael 61, 226
roundabout of b*ll*cks 299–300
Ruch, W. 159, 179, 220–221, 239
Rumi 137, 202, 227

safety: as base for play 108–110; created
  through play 107–108, 111; perceptions of
  106–107; psychological 184–185, 262–263;
  safe words and 272
Schiller, Friedrich 41
Schwarz, R. 255
Scott, Sophie 149
seedlings of playfulness 197–198, 222–223;
  in anyone 201–202; attachment theory
  208–210, 209; barometer of playfulness
  and 199–201; beliefs and 210 211; child
  play habits taken into adulthood as
  203–206, 205; connecting with play and
  211–214; focusing on 220–222; recognition
  of playfulness and 216–220; stepping
  into playfulness from theory to practice
  and 198–199; stories of lack of play and
  206–208; working with the Whole Body
  215–216
self-actualization 80
Self Delusion, The 242
self-disclosure 151, 177
Seligman, Martin 8, 58, 146
senses, playing with 306–307
serious playfulness 76, 83–84
serious play 22, 49, 63, 74, 76, 83, 84, 145,
  184, 205, 257, 258
Seven Humor Habits Program 158
Seven Steps to Improve Your People Skills 18
shadow side of playfulness 171
shame 42, 206, 238–239
Shaw, George Bernard 42
Shore, Allan 203
Siegel, D. 209, 248
Silsbee, D. 248
Simpkin, Heather 18, 237, 257–258, 262,
  263, 284, 319

Skitt, Emma 18, 48, 159, 299–300, 313–314
Smith, N. 32
Social Work, Sociometry, and Psychodrama 308
Sofer, Oren Jay 61
space for exploration 57–58
spontaneity 235–236
Stephenson, Robert 19, 48, 219
stepping into your playful self 334
Storytellers 14–19, 50–52, 269–270; Auriel
  Majumdar 17; Christian van Nieuwerburgh
  19; David Clutterbuck 45–47; Emma
  Skitt 18; Graham Lee 17, 22; Heather
  Simpkin 18; Jonathan Passmore 18; Julie
  Flower 16; Kirsten Barske 15; Matthew
  Pugh 18; Nankhonde Kasonde-van den
  Broek 16; Neil Mullarkey 17–18; Nobantu
  Mpotulo 17; Robert Stephenson 19; Steve
  Chapman 16
storytelling 288–290
strategies for increasing playfulness 220–222,
  225–226, 226, 250; addressing fear of
  embarrassment or shame 238–239; building
  on trying something new 235–237;
  embracing sweet discomfort 231–235;
  having a word with the inner critic and
  perfectionism 238; making space for
  imagination and daydreaming 243–246;
  no one is an island 242–243; presence,
  mindfulness and 247–249; strengthening
  your humour muscles and laughing more
  246–247; tapping into your environment
  226–228; trying something new 228–235;
  working with your states to support
  playfulness 240–242
stress 58, 147–148
Sultanoff, S. 177
Sutton-Smith, Brian 57, 80–81, 148
sweet discomfort 14, 33, 229, 230, 231–235,
  258, 269, 271
Sympathetic Nervous System (SNS) 94–96,
  105, 107–108; activating the 103–104;
  emotions and 115; play blending the
  social engagement system and 109–110;
  positive and negative emotional attractors
  and 128

Task Focused Network (TFN) 244
Task Positive Network (TPN) 97, 98–99;
  emotions and 115; positive and negative
  emotional attractors and 128

Tennant, David 206–207
Ten Percent meditation app 61
time, playing with 308–309
Time to Think 13
Tiny Habits 134
toddler's rules of possession- 56, 57
Tomkins, Sylvan 124
tone and climate 278–279
Toward a Psychology of Being 80
Transactional Analysis 257, 264
Transcend 80
transcendence 79–80, 146
trauma 46, 94, 101, 180–181, 201–202, 229, 238, 241, 245
Treasure Map of Playfulness 25, 26, 331
true self 42
Turning Point, The 215
turtles 94, 96
Tutu, Desmond 76, 79

Ubuntu Coaching 288–290
unconditional positive regard 64, 123

vagal tone 95, 103
vagus nerve 95, 103
van Gogh, Vincent 201

van Nieuwerburgh, Christian 19, 81, 274, 278, 291, 301–303
van Oech, R. 238
virtual reality coaching 321–322
visual mapping 295–303
Volatile, Uncertain, Complex, Ambiguous (VUCA) environments 28–29, 35, 43

Waititi, Taika 59
Warren, Jeff 150
well-being 61, 64–65
Wheeler, Stephanie 8–10, 20–21, 50–51, 82, 171–172, 201, 240–241
Whimsical playfulness 75, 78, 84
Whole Body 139, 179, 215–216, 217, 231, 235
Wilde, Oscar 319
Winnicott, Donald 14, 42, 55–56, 138, 202, 218
Wood, A. 155
word play 281–283
Wordsworth, William 43
writing 291–292

Yerkes, Robert 231

Zen philosophy 48

Ingram Content Group UK Ltd.
Milton Keynes UK
UKHW020628090723
424768UK00010B/40